ETHNOGRAPHIC CHICAGO

Considering College Students and Ethiopian & Tamilian Immigrants Missiologically

Edited by
Cody C. Lorance

Chicago Metropolitan
Baptist Association
www.chicagobaptist.com

IBSN – 978-0-615-21862-5

Copyright © 2008 by Chicago Metropolitan Baptist Association. All rights reserved. No portion of this book may be reproduced in any form, except for brief excerpts in reviews, without prior written permission of the publisher.

Published by Chicago Metropolitan Baptist Association (SBC), 2237 West 120th Street, Blue Island, IL 60406, U.S.A. in partnership with Trinity International Baptist Mission (SBC), 112 Horizon Circle, Carol Stream, IL 60188 and Illinois Baptist State Association (SBC), 3085 Stevenson Drive, Springfield, IL 62703.

Printed in the United States of America. General Editor: Cody C. Lorance. Assistant editor: Katherine Lorance. Cover design: Vincent Lee.

All Scripture quotations, unless otherwise indicated are from *The Holy Bible, English Standard Version*, copyright 2001 by Crossway Bibles, a division of Good News Publishers. Used by permission. All rights reserved.

To Katherine

TABLE OF CONTENTS

1	An Introduction to Christ-Oriented Ethnographic Field Research Cody C. Lorance	5
2	An Executive Summary of *Ethnographic Chicago* Cody C. Lorance	14

PART I: CROSS-CULTURAL RESEARCH IN CHICAGOLAND

3	Tamilians in Chicagoland: *Worship Perspectives of Hindus and Hindu-Background Christians with Missiological Applications* Cody C. Lorance	30
4	Tamilians in Mission History: *Considering the Example of Roberto de Nobili and his Contextualization Efforts in 17th Century Tamil Nadu* Cody C. Lorance	84
5	Tamilians in Spiritual Context: *Considering the Folk Hindu Spirit World and its Implications for Mission* Cody C. Lorance	100
6	A Case Study of Tamilian Hindus Seeking Jesus through Contextualized Spiritual Festival: *The Passover Healing Ceremony* Cody C. Lorance	119
7	Ethiopians in Chicagoland: *Ethnographic Insights for Mission Advance* Jeffrey Davis & Donna Herron	136
8	Raw Data on Ethiopians in Chicagoland Jeffrey Davis & Donna Herron	171
9	Ethiopian Immigrants in Social Context: *The Impact of Immigration to the United States on Gender Roles in Marriage* Talargie Y. Tafesse	226

PART II: NEXT GENERATION RESEARCH IN CHICAGOLAND

10   Art Students at Chicago Loop-Area Colleges: *A Compilation of Field Work*   264
       Luke Burton & Michelle Yu

11   Observing Art Students: *Reflections on Participant Observations of Two Art Student Events in the Chicago Loop*   320
       Tony Romero

12   Law Students at Chicago Loop-Area Colleges: *A Compilation of Field Work*   324
       Felicia Schwake & Sean Watson

13   Connecting with Law Students in the Chicago Loop: *Considering the Missiological Implications of Student-led Organizations*   381
       Cody C. Lorance

14   Building God's Church in Postmodern and Cross-Cultural Contexts: *Discipleship Rituals in the Book of Ezra*   395
       Cody C. Lorance

Chapter 1:
An Introduction to Christ-Oriented Ethnographic Field Research

Cody C. Lorance
Church Planting Leader / Pastor
Trinity International Baptist Mission
Carol Stream, IL

What is Research?

Research – "to search again, to examine anew," the "laborious or continued search after truth" – is a rather core concept for this entire book (Webster, 1828). It has been defined as "careful or diligent search," "studious inquiry or examination," and "investigation . . . aimed at the discovery and interpretation of facts, revision of accepted theories or laws in the light of new facts, or practical application of such new or revised theories or laws" (Merriam-Webster, Inc.). Field research is simply taking this investigative process out into "the field." That is, field research is focused on gathering information through direct engagement with and observation of the research subjects. Field research becomes "ethnographic" in nature when it has a fundamental aim of understanding people or groups.

Ethnographic field research (EFR) includes both quantitative and qualitative research methods. Quantitative methods focus on gathering measurable data. It asks what, where, when, and how many and employs tools such as automated counting and surveys. Qualitative research, on the other hand, looks to deepen understanding by asking how and why. It chiefly employs interviews, observations, and document examination. In short, quantitative research enumerates and qualitative research explains.

You still there?

I know this stuff seems a bit dry and academic. Contained in this book are hundreds of pages of information resulting from countless hours of ethnographic field research. It often sounds theoretical, heady, and meaningless. And you may be asking, "Would somebody please explain to me why this is important?" Missionary practitioners and their supervisors aren't often interested in burning a lot of time on aimless theorizing and pointless intellectual gymnastics. They are men and women of the frontline not the ivory tower. Perhaps you see the faces of lostness and experience the brokenness of sin and Satan every day in your mission field. What you need is spiritual breakthrough. You don't need the latest models, theories, surveys, and focus-group tested evangelism strategies. You need the mind of Christ. You need the face of God.

Am I getting warm? Don't worry. If I just described you, then we have something in common. I too am a missionary on the field and I have little interest in research or academia for its own sake. But I do believe that included in Christ's command to love God with all our mind is a call for missionary practitioners to be great thinkers for the glory of God and to use our brains as much as our hearts and bodies to participate in the advancement of His Kingdom. In this introductory chapter, I intend to lay out four theological foundations for EFR that help us not only to see how critically important it is for missionaries to engage in this kind of research but also how we can do so in a way that truly magnifies the Lord Jesus Christ.

Christ-Oriented EFR

As followers of Jesus deeply concerned with loving Him and making disciples for His glory among all peoples, it is not enough for us to simply understand and employ secular research methods to Christian interests. We desire to seek, please, and magnify the Lord in everything we do, including research. In order to bring a true Christ-orientation to EFR, we must found our work upon sound, Biblical, and theological principles. I believe that means that we should have a Christ-inspired focus, a Christ-determined goal, and a Christ-pleasing approach.

Christ-Inspired Focus

This has to do with the problem on which your research focuses. All field research is inspired by the identification of some kind of problem. A food manufacturer knows that the latest diet craze is hurting business. A relief organization knows that refugees from Somalia are struggling in the cold climate of Minneapolis. A church planter has learned that many people in his community identify themselves as Christian but do not attend any church. Research projects sponsored by secular organizations sometimes address issues close to God's heart but often times do not. In our case, we stand in faith believing that Jesus Christ, our Lord, wants us to care about what He cares about. This gives us our first theological foundation.

> **1st Theological Foundation for EFR:** *Jesus Christ wants us to care about what He cares about.*

Biblical support for this idea is not difficult to find. The stories of Jesus feeding the multitudes are great examples of Christ teaching His disciples that they should care about whom and what He cares about. In the Sermon on the Mount, Jesus challenged His listeners by saying that instead of being preoccupied with material things, they should "seek first the kingdom of God" (Matt. 6:33).

This being true, in Christ-oriented EFR, we make God's concerns, rather than our own, primary. What does God care about? How is God directing our focus in this research project? What problem is God putting on our hearts?

Christ-Determined Goal

Next, we move on to the core motivation of our research. Most secular research is pragmatically oriented. How can we best solve the problem? The food manufacturer wants to know how to improve business. The non-profit organization wants to help Somalis get through the winter. If we are not careful, we can easily slip into this trap as well. After all, we do want to solve the problems that we identify in our mission fields and ministries. Even after feeling convinced that we have a truly Christ-inspired focus, we can be too quick to formulate our own goals for the research. So the church planter I mentioned before may set out to research how to get unchurched Christians to come to his church without taking the time to hear from God. In Christ-oriented EFR, however, we must shift our focus higher. We stand on the truth that Jesus Christ wants us to know and do His will.

> **2nd Theological Foundation for EFR:** *Jesus Christ wants us to know and do His will.*

Again, we have no difficulty here in finding Scriptural support for this principle. Jesus once said to His disciples, "No longer do I call you servants, for the servant does not know what his master is doing; but I have called you friends, for all that I have heard from the Father I have made known to you" (John 15:15). Christ made it clear how important doing the will of God was to Him when He said to a crowd, "Whoever does the will of God, he is my brother and sister and mother" (Mark 3:35). In his letter to the church at Ephesus, the Apostle Paul exhorted believers to "not be foolish, but understand what the will of the Lord is" (Eph. 5:17).

We must always keep in mind that we are Christ-followers and not mere spiritual problem-solvers. The fact is there may often be lots of decent and sensible ways of dealing with a problem but the Bible says that doing the will of God has sure, eternal significance (1 John 2:17).

Ultimately, in our research we must continually and prayerfully ask, "What is God's will?"

Christ-Pleasing Approach

Again, it is not sufficient to simply throw secular research methods at Christian problems with Christian goals. Unfortunately, it is here that Christian researchers are probably most prone to lose sight of God. It is as if once the "real work" begins, God is asked to kindly get out of the way. This will not do for us. Instead we confess that Jesus Christ wants us to trust Him in all things and to continually seek to be transformed into His likeness.

> **3rd Theological Foundation for EFR:** *Jesus Christ wants us to trust Him in all things and to continually seek to be transformed into His likeness.*

So many passages come to mind at this point. I'll mention here just a few. Consider how walking in obedience to these Scriptures would radically impact the way we conduct EFR.

> *Trust in the LORD with all your heart, and do not lean on your own understanding. In all your ways acknowledge him, and he will make straight your paths.* (Prov. 3:5-6)

> *Not by might, nor by power, but by my Spirit, says the LORD.* (Zech. 4:6)

> *Pray without ceasing* (1 Thess. 5:17)

> *And we all, with unveiled face, beholding the glory of the Lord, are being transformed into the same image from one degree of glory to another. For this comes from the Lord who is the Spirit.* (2 Cor. 3:18)

It is critical that we deliberately ask the Lord to be actively working in and through us and the whole research process. First, since God's work ultimately depends upon God, we want to intentionally integrate prayer into every facet of the work. We pray for wisdom and guidance in decisions, for strength, self-discipline, and skill, and for His blessing on the research as a whole. We also pray on-site for the people we meet considering that as God reveals problems to us about which He cares deeply He also calls us to intercede in those situations.

Furthermore, we want to seek to be like Jesus. That means that maintaining godly ethics and integrity in our research is non-negotiable. We want to honor Christ and represent well His love to the people we interact with and in the places we go. What will our lifelong pursuit of Christ-likeness mean for our work ethic and personal discipline, our honesty in recording and reporting, our behavior towards fellow researchers and research subjects, and all the other areas of our research work?

Once we've prayerfully discerned God's focus and goal for our research and committed to following Jesus faithfully in every aspect of the process, we are well on our way to conducting EFR in a way that truly brings glory to God. I believe that God is pleased to work through Christ-oriented EFR to bring tremendous spiritual breakthroughs to our mission fields.

Biblical Precedents and Mandates for EFR

Before we leave this introductory chapter, a final element is needed to round out our theological foundation for EFR. After all, research often seems very heady, time-consuming, and just not very spiritual. The preceding foundations are solid enough, but is there really a Scriptural basis for performing hardcore research? The answer, I think, is yes.

> **4th Theological Foundation for EFR:** *There are both Biblical precedents and mandates for engaging in research in order to better understand the will of God.*

Biblical Precedents

First, let's consider some of the Scriptural precedents for EFR. Are there examples of this kind of research in Scripture? Let me mention just a few.

It seems clear from our reading of the gospels that Luke's approach to writing about Jesus and the early church was significantly different than that of the other gospel writers. Luke, after all, didn't know Jesus personally. And he tells his readers clearly that in preparation for writing, he carefully examined all the extant information (Luke 1:1-4). It seems clear not only from his preface statement but also from the content of his writings themselves that Luke spoke to eyewitnesses, read other biographical accounts of Jesus, and personally investigated sites relevant to the life and history of the early Christian movement. From a research perspective, we can say that Luke conducted interviews, literature review, and site observations in preparation for writing his account.

A second example can be found as the early church tries to sort through the controversial subject of how to treat Gentiles who come to faith in Christ. This incendiary issue prompted a variety of investigatory activities including hearing eyewitness accounts (Acts 11:1-18) and considering case studies (Acts 15:3-4, 12) as well as making first-hand field observations (Acts 11:22).

Finally, we can consider how Paul's own missionary methodology was shaped by his personal engagement in EFR. It seems clear that while in Athens Paul spent time in research prior to commencing evangelistic work. He studied and explored the religion and religious symbolism of the city (Acts 17:16, 23), he engaged in discussion and observation in the city centers (Acts 17:17), and he examined the indigenous literature (Acts 17:28). Ultimately, the form and content of the sermon Paul preached at the Areopagus was greatly influenced by what he learned.

Biblical Mandates

Precedents are one thing, but can we really say that God has called and directed us to engage in this kind of research? Let's consider Paul once again.

In his letter to the church at Ephesus, Paul, under the inspiration of the Holy Spirit, gives an interesting command. He says, "Walk as children of light . . . and *try to discern* [italics added] what is pleasing to the Lord" (Eph. 5:8, 10). The question one must ask is, "How am I to obey this command?" The word translated here as "discern" is in the Greek δοκιμαζοντες which means to test or examine. It's actually not much different from the definition we gave for "research" earlier. A few verses later, Paul gives a related command, "Do not be *foolish, but understand* [italics added] what the will of the Lord is" (Eph. 5:17). Here the word "foolish" is the Greek αφρονες which means senseless, stupid, and without reflection. Paul contrasts that with the word συνιετε ("understand"), meaning to put together mentally. The idea Paul seems to be trying to get across is that we shouldn't be ignorant, non-reflective people. Rather, as followers of Jesus, we should test, examine, and otherwise use our intellects in an effort to discover what God's will is in a given situation.

Paul has the same idea in his letter to the Roman believers when he commands them to "not be conformed to this world, but be transformed by the renewal of your mind, *that by testing you may discern* [italics added] what is the will of God, what is good and acceptable and perfect" (Rom. 12:2).

By looking at only these few passages from the New Testament, we can clearly see that God does not want us to just wait around idly for someone to tell us what His will is. Rather, we are to diligently search it out. This search will involve continual prayer, much time in God's word, and active, loving communion with His body. But often, as was the case for Luke, Peter, Barnabas, and Paul, it will also involve hardcore research.

I'm convinced that missionary work inevitably involves much frustration and confusion. However, I'm also convinced that many missionaries are right now "banging their heads up against a wall" for no good reason. God has made a way for us to discover His will and break down those walls. We can test and examine, investigate and explore—we can research the problems of our mission field. And we can learn to do it well. As we do, I believe we will discover a God who is ready to lift the veil and shine His light upon these challenges.

In the chapters that follow, you will find the results of Chicago Metropolitan Baptist Association's first serious attempt to utilize Christ-oriented EFR to understand some of the challenges in our mission field. What we intend to offer here is not a model for how it should be done but rather an example of a rookie effort to "try to discern" God's will for us as missionaries in a few different areas. We readily admit that our efforts are quite flawed and that there is much we have to learn. However we also believe that God has blessed our research efforts with some truly valuable insights. In fact, as I write these lines, some of these insights have already been translated into missional action that has directly resulted in wonderful Kingdom advance. Our hope is that many of these insights as well as the concept of Christ-oriented EFR itself will prove invaluable to you as you continue to faithfully engage your mission field for the glory of God.

References

Research. Merriam-Webster Online Dictionary. Merriam-Webster, Inc. Retrieved February 18, 2008, from http://www.merriam-webster.com/dictionary/research

Research. In N. Webster, American Dictionary of the English Language. (1828). Foundation for American Christian Education.

Chapter 2:
An Executive Summary of *Ethnographic Chicago*

Cody C. Lorance
Church Planting Leader / Pastor
Trinity International Baptist Mission
Carol Stream, IL

Overview of *Ethnographic Chicago*

In order to more faithfully and effectively carry out the Great Commission among the least-reached and least-engaged people groups and population segments of the Chicagoland area, the Church must take the time to more thoroughly understand the various cultures, subcultures, families, and individuals that make up this great city. To facilitate this learning, Chicago Metro Baptist Association (CMBA) decided to conduct an ethnographic research project during the summer of 2007 focusing on a few key people groups and population segments. The work for this project began in early June and continued to the end of the year. Our prayer has been that God would guide, empower, and shape us throughout the process and that through it He would graciously grant us wisdom and insight that we might more faithfully and more clearly manifest to the peoples of His heart the love, hope, wholeness, and Good News of Jesus Christ.

The project itself, it was determined, would focus on utilizing a combination of qualitative and quantitative research methods, guided by a Christ-centered orientation, in the study of four people groups / population segments in the Chicago area. The specific groups studied were discerned and decided upon by the researchers through prayer and prayerwalking experiences. The name, *Ethnographic Chicago 2007*, was selected as a title for the project. Along with CMBA, the Illinois Baptist State Association (IBSA), Chicagoland Community Church, and Trinity International Baptist Mission all participated at some level as strategic partners.

The Chronology of Ethnographic Chicago

May – June 2007

Preliminary preparations for the project began very early in the summer. Dates were scheduled, budgeting decisions were made and agreed upon, field researchers were interviewed and hired, and decisions about the nature of the project were made. Initially, it was decided that the project would consist of research focusing on at least three people groups / population segments. It was also determined that some of the research would concentrate on college students in the Chicago Loop and some would have a more cross-cultural focus.

June 6-7, 2007

The new team of researchers, consisting of undergraduate college students serving as summer missionaries, assembled for a two-day training workshop hosted by CMBA at its Des Plaines, IL offices. I (Cody Lorance) led this training time which focused on providing a basic orientation to the project, instruction in the principles and methods of Christ-oriented ethnographic field research, and time for prayer and reflection.

During this training time, the team worked prayerfully to narrow down the project's research foci. The result was the identification of three primary areas of focus:

- Art students in the Chicago Loop
- Law students in the Chicago Loop
- First-generation Ethiopian immigrants

Each of these areas would be assigned to a pair of researchers. In addition, if time permitted, I would include my own research among first-generation Tamilian (India) immigrants.

June – July 2007

Over the next several weeks (most of the researchers couldn't work beyond July 21), the team engaged in Christ-oriented EFR which included:

- Reviewing extant literature relevant to the subject being researched
- Conducting interviews
- Conducting participant observations
- Conducting surveys
- Analyzing data
- Prayer ministry

On a weekly basis, the entire research team gathered at my house for further training in relevant research principles and methods, fellowship, prayer, and encouragement. Additionally, the two groups that performed research among college students in the Loop met each week in Chicago with Jon Pennington, pastor of Chicagoland Community Church and New Work Development Team member for CMBA.

August – September 2007

By the second week of August, the last of the summer missionaries that were a part of the research team came to the end of their terms of service and returned home. None of the three pairs had successfully completed all of the essential components of the research project and only one group had actually written up a report of their work. I began to develop and carry out a strategy of completion for the project in hopes of producing a valuable final product. For several weeks in August and September, I engaged in field work, data analysis, and other work with a view towards completing the original goals of the research project. Tony Romero, then serving with CMBA as a semester missionary, helped to provide some additional field work during this time.

November – December 2007

Due to complications and delays in the project, I revised my completion strategy and began writing and editing the *Ethnographic Chicago* report. The chapters attributed to Tony Romero and Talargie Tafesse were submitted at this time.

December 2007

The final written report on *Ethnographic Chicago* was completed and submitted to CMBA.

Statistical Overview of the Project

This written report of *Ethnographic Chicago* represents hundreds of hours of labor by a number of individuals who performed research, provided supervision, trained researchers, and analyzed data. In the following table, I have attempted only a partial accounting of this work (see table 1).

Table 1: *Statistical Overview of the Project*

Type of Work	Amount
Pieces of literature reviewed / consulted	186
Artifacts gathered and reviewed	45
Loop-area law schools identified	6
Loop-area art schools identified	5
Chicago-area Ethiopian evangelical / Protestant churches identified	3
Chicago-area Ethiopian Orthodox churches identified	1
Chicago-area Tamil-language evangelical churches identified	2
Field work time	236 hrs 45 min
Interview transcription time	81 hrs 30 min
Subjects interviewed	36
Participant observations conducted	20
Completed surveys collected	95
Training workshops held	1 two-day workshop
Weekly training sessions	7

Summary of Research by People Group / Population Segment

Tamilian Immigrants in the Chicago Area

Overview of the Research

Tamilians are just one of a dozen or so people group clusters in the Chicago area that are, by majority, Hindu. In all, there are well over a hundred thousand Asian Indians in Chicagoland, making them the largest Asian American group in the metro area (Indo-American Center, 2003, p. 10). Tamilians therefore represent one of the most important parts of the multicultural mission field that is Chicagoland—the tens of thousands of Hindus that now call this city home.

Globally, there are more than 66 million Tamil speakers scattered throughout countries like Sri Lanka, Singapore, Fiji, Malaysia, Germany and the U.S. (Gordon, 2005). Most, of course, live in India where the Tamilian population is near 60 million (Gordon, 2005). The vast majority of Tamilians are Hindus and more than 60% belong to the category of "Unreached Peoples." (The U.S. Center for World Mission, 2008).

My research into Tamilians for this project consisted of four major parts that are here represented by four chapters. In Chapter 3, "Tamilians in Chicagoland: Worship Perspectives of Hindus and Hindu-Background Christians with Missiological Applications," I present missiological insights based on ethnographic field work among Tamilians in the Chicago area. Chapter 4 puts the issue of contextualization among Tamilian Hindus in historic perspective through a consideration of the missionary efforts of Roberto de Nobili. In "Tamilians in Spiritual Context: Considering the Folk Hindu Spirit World and its Implications for Mission," I consider popular Hindu conceptions of spirituality and present a model of holistic spiritual conflict as a primary method of disciple-making among them. Finally, I round out the Tamilian section of this book with chapter 6 which presents a case study from an actual attempt at contextualized Christian outreach among Tamilian Hindus in the Chicago area.

Major Missiological Insights and Conclusions

So what do we as missionaries do with all this information? Are there actionable insights that can actually shape our work among Tamilians and other Hindu-majority people groups? While I have included extensive conclusion sections in each of the previously mentioned chapters, I will take a moment here to provide a brief summary of two major missiological insights.

First, almost leaping off the pages, is the importance of contextualization in our missionary efforts. Dean Gilliland has said that contextualization is about enabling "an understanding of what it means that Jesus Christ, the Word, is authentically experienced in each and every human situation" (2000, p. 225). Alluding to the first chapter of John, he goes on to explain that the "Word must dwell among all families of humankind today as truly as Jesus lived among his own kin." Contextualization, far more than a trendy new missionary method, is grounded in Biblical themes as foundational as the incarnation and was utilized frequently by the Church's earliest missionaries who strove to "become all things to all people, that by all means" they might reach some (1 Cor. 9:22). Nevertheless, missiological literature regarding India and Indians often suggests that Western missionaries by and large have failed in this area. It seems that the Church's long-standing failure to consistently and effectively contextualize the gospel message and Christian spirituality to Hindus is largely to blame for our inability to significantly impact them for Christ. In 1980, The Mini-Consultation on

Reaching Hindus which met as part of the Lausanne Consultation on World Evangelism cited "the Christian way of worship which is predominately non-Indian" as one of the key hindrances to the effective spread of the gospel among Hindus (1980, p. 11).

Certainly, the case of Roberto de Nobili and his missionary efforts among Tamilians in the 17th century goes far to illustrate the power of contextualization to connect Hindus to Biblical truth. While holding firmly to orthodox Christian theology, de Nobili strove to distinguish gospel from culture and to present Jesus Christ incarnationally to the south Indian Hindu context. His experiment worked and thousands of caste Hindus, including many from the highest castes, embraced the Savior. Less than a century after his death, the number of de Nobili's disciples had surpassed 100,000 (Rajamanickam, 1987, p. 130).

The scene in Chicagoland however is much different. As is evident from the interviews and participant observations I conducted, Christian and Hindu spirituality among Tamilians living here could not be more disparate. In particular, Tamilian Hindu spirituality emphasizes interpersonal connections and sacred time and space through the use of rituals, ceremonies, festivals, and symbols. This stands in great contrast to the more individualistic and low-context worship services typical in Chicago area Tamilian churches. Therefore, contextualization efforts among Tamilian Hindus should, among other things, seek to employ spiritual festivals in the communication of Biblical truth. When done well, spiritual festivals allow missionaries to minister incarnationally to Tamilian Hindus who are thus enabled to connect more profoundly to both the message and the messengers of the gospel.

A second important missiological insight for ministering among Tamilians is related to the idea of holistic ministry. American Christians have a tendency to separate, at least subconsciously, their life experiences, their questions, and the world around them into distinctive spiritual and secular categories. While serving as a missionary in India, American Paul Hiebert was able to identify this dualism in his own worldview and reflect on how it differed radically from the worldview of his Indian friends:

> *I had excluded the middle level of supernatural but this-worldly beings and forces from my own world view. As a scientist, I had been trained to deal with the empirical world in naturalistic terms. As a theologian, I was taught to answer ultimate questions in theistic terms. For me the middle zone did not really exist. Unlike Indian villagers, I had given little thought to spirits of this world, to local*

> ancestors and ghosts, or to the souls of animals. For me
> these belonged to the realm of fairies, trolls, and other
> mythical beings. Consequently, I had no answers for the
> questions they raised (Hiebert, 1985, p. 9).

Hiebert has referred to this as the "flaw of the excluded middle," in which Westerners typically understand everything in either transcendent religious or naturalistic scientific terms. On one end of the experience spectrum are the ultimate questions of life. Why am I here? Where did we all come from? What is my purpose? What is God like? How can I get to heaven when I die? At the opposite end is the natural world where questions are dealt with in a purely naturalistic and mechanistic way. What's wrong with my car? How can I get over this cough? What's the formula for a good marriage? In this typically Western perspective, if a question doesn't fit into either of these categories, it usually remains unanswered.

The problem with this dualistic perspective is that many people in the world, including many Tamilians, are constantly seeking answers to questions that don't fit well in either the transcendent or naturalistic realms. Hiebert is worth quoting at length here:

> What are the questions of the middle level? Here one
> finds the questions of the uncertainty of the future, the
> crises of present life, and the unknowns of the past . . . .
> How can one prevent accidents or guarantee success in
> the future? How can one make sure that a marriage will
> be fruitful and happy, and endure? How can one avoid
> getting on a plane that will crash? In the West, these
> questions are left unanswered. They are "accidents,"
> "luck," or "unforeseeable events," hence unexplainable.
> But many people are not content to leave so important a
> set of questions unanswered, and the answers they give
> are often in terms of ancestors, demons, witches and local
> gods, or in terms of magic and astrology. (1985, p. 10)

Hiebert goes on to speak about middle level questions about the present and past. Why is my business doing poorly? Why is my son sick? Why did my wife die last year? Western missionaries often have no satisfying answer to questions like these. When we say something like, "Your son is sick because he contracted a disease," our answer falls short in the eye of the parent who is really asking what spirits or forces are behind this misfortune. Hiebert stresses the importance of Christian missionaries giving the right kind of answers:

> *What is a Christian theology of ancestors, of animals and plants, of local spirits and spirit possession, and of 'principalities, powers and rulers of the darkness of this world'? What does one say when new tribal converts want to know how the Christian God tells them where and when to hunt, whether they should marry this daughter to that young man, or where they can find the lost money? Given no answer, they return to the diviner who gave them definite answers, for these are the problems that loom large in their everyday lives.* (1985, p. 11)

Tamilian Hindus have a lot of middle-level questions and experiences. It isn't uncommon for our neighbors to ask for our prayers for sick children, a new job, or success in school. I've heard from them of their experiences with demons, ghosts, curses, and black magic as well as of their belief in the power of astrologers and shamanistic holy men. These people will never follow a Christ who doesn't show His relevance and power in earthly, everyday affairs. Therefore, it is imperative that missionaries seek to present the good news of Jesus Christ holistically. We should not stop teaching English, helping people find jobs and get good medical care, preaching the message of Jesus and teaching the Bible. But the work of an evangelist, a bearer of good news, doesn't end there. We must adopt the Biblical practices of healing the sick and casting out demons as well. Our call is an apostolic one—we must go to the nations presenting the gospel as good news where it is needed most.

Ethiopian Immigrants in the Chicago Area

Overview of the Research

Ethiopia is a multiethnic East African country of over 76 million people. Evangelical Protestantism began growing rapidly in the country's southern states in the 1970s and today, Ethiopia is home to a strong evangelical church which makes up more than 14% of the nation's population (Bush, 1998). Still, the vast majority of Ethiopians identify themselves as either Ethiopian Orthodox or Muslim.

In 1974, there was a military coup in Ethiopia which left the country in the hands of a repressive Soviet-backed Marxist regime known as the

Derg. Subsequent years brought more hardships in the form of drought, famine, and military conflict. The first Ethiopians seeking asylum in the U.S. arrived in 1980 with tens of thousands following them. Today, as many as 250,000 now live in cities throughout North America with the most significant populations in and around cities like Washington D.C., Atlanta, Dallas, and Houston (Kemp). Ethiopians living in Chicagoland estimate that some 10,000 live in the metro area.

The research into Ethiopians for this project consisted of two major parts that are here represented by three chapters. In Chapter 7, "Ethiopians in Chicagoland: Ethnographic Insights for Mission Advance," Jeffrey Davis and Donna Herron present thoughts from their field work among Ethiopian immigrants living in the Chicago area. Their major goal was to discover bridges and barriers for the gospel among members of the Ethiopian Orthodox Church living in the metro area. This being Jeffrey and Donna's first experience with ethnographic field research, I've taken the liberty of including as a supplement Chapter 8, "Raw Data on Ethiopians in Chicagoland" for further information. Talargie Tafesse, an Ethiopian church leader in the Chicago area, contributes Chapter 9, "Ethiopian Immigrants in Social Context: The Impact of Immigration to the U.S. on Gender Roles in Marriage."

Major Missiological Insights and Conclusions

A few thoughts come to mind as I reflect upon the work Jeffrey, Donna, and Talargie have contributed to *Ethnographic Chicago*. First, it seems clear that much more work is needed in order to arrive at more solid missiological conclusions. The research here is a start but more interviews, observations, and demographic work would be very helpful. In particular, a thorough participant observation of a worship service at the Ethiopian Orthodox church should be conducted in order to better understand the differences between the two traditions.

What cannot be missed however, even with the little research we've conducted, is the amazing opportunity we now have to advance the gospel among Ethiopians in Chicago. Like perhaps nowhere else, Chicagoland is home to a significant number of Ethiopians who are without an Ethiopian Orthodox church that truly meets their needs. The simple fact that the one Ethiopian Orthodox church building in Chicago is located far on the south side of the city, miles away from where most Ethiopians actually live, means that there are needs traditionally met by the Ethiopian Orthodox Church that are now being neglected. For Ethiopians, the Ethiopian Orthodox Church commonly serves much more than a religious role in

Ethiopia. It is more or less the center of society and culture. In Ethiopia, you go to church not just to meet with God but to meet with your family, your village, your culture, and your self. In Chicagoland, the Ethiopian Orthodox Church cannot play that role and so Ethiopians must look to fill that vacuum by hanging out at Ethiopian restaurants and grocery stores or by getting involved with a community center. There is a gap. Ethiopian immigrants may love living in the U.S. but they also long to connect to their own culture. They may not feel their souls' hunger for God because of the tremendous hunger of their hearts for connecting with what it means to them to be Ethiopian.

So what is the opportunity? Ethiopian evangelicals have always been criticized by members of the Ethiopian Orthodox Church as being anti-Ethiopian—as somehow betraying their culture and national identity by leaving the Ethiopian Orthodox Church. Now, the evangelicals have an opportunity to come alongside Ethiopians in Chicago in order to provide an answer to their need to connect with Ethiopian culture. In particular, the formation of a church / community center for Ethiopians located in the Edgewater community, a central area for the Ethiopian population of Chicago, could lead to huge breakthroughs. This "Ethiopian Friendship Center" could be a place for community events, need-meeting services, strategic witness, and church activities. I believe that such a place would prove immensely popular to Ethiopians who don't yet know Christ but who hunger to connect with other Ethiopians and with their native culture. Such connections could lead to hundreds of opportunities to develop redemptive relationships and share Christ. Similar breakthroughs could result from mission-minded Ethiopian believers who open Ethiopian restaurants or shops. The main idea is for Ethiopian followers of Jesus to take the lead in preserving and sharing Ethiopian culture in Chicagoland. Such leadership will undoubtedly win the respect and appreciation of many Ethiopian immigrants who will in turn offer friendship and become softened to the gospel.

College Students in the Chicago Loop

Overview of the Research

By all accounts, the Chicago Loop is now the biggest college town in Illinois with more than 50,000 students attending schools there (Fuechtmann, McLaughlin, Kelly, Hewings, & Morgenthaler, 2005). Unfortunately, little has been accomplished for the cause of Christ among these students. The *Ethnographic Chicago* project conducted field research among two different groups of college students in the Loop—Art students and Law students. Our research is here represented by four chapters which present the work of Luke Burton and Michelle Yu, Tony Romero, Felicia Schwake and Sean Watson, and myself.

Major Missiological Insights and Conclusions

Our research among Loop-area college students is perhaps the most incomplete of the whole project. There is much need for further interviews, surveys, observations and more. Nevertheless, the work that has been completed has not been without its important insights. I mention here only two of the more significant ones.

In their field work among art students, Luke and Michelle conducted nearly a hundred surveys with questions that focused on spiritual issues. The results of the survey indicated that art students had a very high opinion of Jesus Christ and of Christians in general but a very low opinion of organized religion or "church." This finding, combined with the seeming popularity of attending art showings and galleries by art students, may be instructive for missionaries seeking to penetrate this community with the gospel. Perhaps instead of "church" planting, we should consider planting in the Loop an art gallery which emphasizes the person of Jesus. Discussion groups, worship services, and other forms of social interaction and expression emphasizing the pursuit of Jesus in the context of rewarding relationships could be developed around the gallery. As in the case of the Ethiopian community, it seems that believers have an opportunity to engage art students as a true friend of the community.

Among law students, perhaps the most interesting insights came from an examination of the student-led organizations in which many of these students are involved. The information gleaned from this part of our research points to the longing of law students to make connections during their years of studies that will help their careers and their senses of purpose. Numerous opportunities for effective Christian witness exist for missionaries who will consider this longing for connectedness and seek to engage students at the point of their needs.

Considering the Strengths and Weaknesses of this Project: A Final Report

Before I leave this chapter, I want to share a few brief thoughts on the *Ethnographic Chicago* project as a whole. Obviously, this was CMBA's rookie effort to utilize ethnographic field research in our mission context and the process has not been without its shortcomings. Experienced ethnographers will not have to spend much time reviewing this work before these many failings start to show up. Nevertheless, the process has been a helpful one for me as a missionary practitioner. As one personally engaged in mission among Ethiopians, Tamilians, and college students in Chicagoland, I can testify to the immense value of the insights I have gleaned from this research. I thank God for the work of summer and semester missionaries and the partnership of many career missionaries who have been involved in a variety of ways. As for my future as an ethnographer, I am taking away three important lessons.

First, good and useful research just takes time. This project relied heavily upon the work of summer missionaries who had only about two months in which to conduct all of their research. Considering the fact that none of them knew anything about ethnographic research at the beginning of the summer, they did quite well. However, at the end of the day, it was clear that they simply didn't have enough time. In retrospect, a team of semester missionaries with 4 to 5 months of time to devote to this project would be better suited to produce successful work. More time also needs to be allotted for all the editing and writing that follows the initial field work. A project of this nature should not be expected to be completed in less than one year.

Secondly, I learned that good training is a key to successful research. Again, the summer missionaries did a remarkable job of learning the basics of prayerwalking, literature review, interviewing, observing, and more in a very short amount of time. They essentially had to learn everything in the two day workshop and during weekly follow-up meetings. Perhaps if they had been experienced writers or library-based researchers this would have been enough; however they were not. The end results testify to the fact that much more training was needed. The initial workshop could easily be expanded to about five days and some pre-project reading and writing assignments could be given. The follow-up meetings could be expanded as well. In general, the supervision structure would need to be much more direct in order for the project to be successful.

Finally, it is of tremendous importance that a group seeking to undertake a project such as this be clear and unanimously passionate about its purpose. From the beginning of *Ethnographic Chicago* it seems that different parties were interested in seeing different outcomes from the research and that some people were altogether unconvinced of the value of such work for mission. This fact continued to create difficulties for the work throughout its duration. A clearer vision for the utilization of ethnography in mission should be communicated in the future and I suspect this book itself will go far in helping to do that.

References

Bush, L. (1998, May 7). *The Move of God in Ethiopia*. Retrieved from AD 2000 and Beyond Movement: http://www.ad2000.org/index.htm

Consultation on World Evangelism: Mini-Consultation on Reaching Hindus. (1980). *Christian Witness to Hindus*. Wheaton, IL: Lausanne Committee for World Evangelization.

Fuechtmann, T. G., McLaughlin, G. W., Kelly, J. S., Hewings, G., & Morgenthaler, S. (2005). *Higher Education in the Loop and South Loop: An Impact Study*. Chicago: Greater State Street Council and Central Michigan Avenue Association.

Gilliland, D. (2000). Contextualization. In A. S. Moreau (Ed.), *The Evangelical Dictionary of World Missions* (p. 225). Grand Rapids: Baker Books.

Gordon, R. G. (Ed.). (2005). *Ethnologue: Languages of the World*, Fifteenth edition. (SIL International) Retrieved January 11, 2007, from http://www.ethnologue.com/show_language.asp?code=tam

Hiebert, P. (1985). *Anthropological Insights for Missionaries*. Grand Rapids: Baker Book House.

Indo-American Center. (2003). *Images of America: Asian Indians of Chicago*. (L. Menon, P. Rangaswamy, & D. Shah, Eds.) Chicago: Arcadia Publishing.

Kemp, C. (n.d.). *Ethiopian Refugees*. Retrieved Februrary 26, 2008, from Refugee Health-- Immigrant Health: http://www3.baylor.edu/~Charles_Kemp/ethiopian_refugees.htm

Rajamanickam, S. (1987). The Old Madura Mission: A Chronological Table. *Indian Church History Review*, 21, 130-135.

The U.S. Center for World Mission. (2008, January 11). *Great Commission Status of the Tamil People Cluster*. Retrieved January 11, 2008, from Joshua Project: Bringing Definition to the Unfinished Task: http://www.joshuaproject.net/people-clusters.php?rop2=C0213

PART I: CROSS-CULTURAL RESEARCH IN CHICAGOLAND

Chapter 3:
Tamilians in Chicagoland: *Worship Perspectives of Hindus and Hindu-Background Christians with Missiological Applications*

Cody C. Lorance
Pastor / Church Planting Leader
Trinity International Baptist Mission
Carol Stream, IL

Abstract

This study examines worship among immigrant Tamilian Hindus and compares it to that of Christians who are also of Tamil origins. A literature review, interviews, and observations of Christian and Hindu worship events were utilized to discover how and to what extent Tamilians living in Chicago worship and how this was different from their experiences in India. Considerations for the development of indigenous Christian worship are provided, including: contextualizing the traditional Christian perspective of sacred space, diversifying worship, generating more sensory appeal, elevating the role of festivals, and integrating social dimensions into Christian worship. It is suggested that the Tamilian church is faced with both obstacles to and great opportunities for penetrating Hinduism with the gospel.

Part 1: Introduction

Within about a generation from the time of Francis Xavier's 16th century mission amongst the poor Tamilian fishermen of south India's Pearl Fishery Coast, Christianity had already become known as a religion of outcastes. This negative reputation proved impossible to shake over the next several centuries and, as a result, Christianity never gained a significant following among the Hindus of caste. To typical Tamilian Hindu immigrants of the 21st century—mostly well-educated professionals—caste distinctions have lost some of their importance. Nevertheless, Christianity is still viewed as essentially non-Indian and thus a non-option for the Tamilian Hindu who wishes to retain some sense of cultural identity.

My wife and I began working as missionaries amongst the Tamilian Hindu immigrants of suburban Chicago in 2004. Very quickly we learned that their perception of the Christian faith as a foreign religion presented one of the most significant barriers to the effective spread of the gospel. As I sat with him in his living room, one Tamilian man described his impression of Protestant Christians in India as unfriendly and "always shouting." He added that they tended to dress differently, did not go to the cinema like everyone else, and refused to accept food that Hindus offered them during festivals. In his mind, the Indian Christians seemed less than Indian.

Indeed, Christendom has rightfully earned the reputation of being foreign to Tamilians through a consistent practice of missionary methods that neglect or reject the Tamil cultural context. Over the years, practically everything about Tamilian culture has been labeled idolatrous and summarily discarded by one missionary or another. The resulting expression of Tamilian Christianity is one that has a distinctly Western flavor and is consequently unattractive to the many Hindus that encounter it.

If we were going to have success in our efforts to reach immigrant Tamilian Hindus with the love of Jesus Christ, my wife and I knew that developing an authentically Tamilian expression of Christian worship would be essential. We also knew that such a goal would not be easy to accomplish. We had no idea what it meant to be a Tamilian Hindu in the United States either from a practical or a spiritual standpoint. Neither did we know what expressions of worship were meaningful to them or what their hearts yearned for now that they were immigrants in a foreign country. We knew only that we had been charged by God with the task of presenting Christ and a way of worshipping Him that was relevant and meaningful to Tamilians and that He was deeply interested in the splendor, glory, and honor of *their* nation being brought into His eternal kingdom (Rev. 21:24-26). And so, with these motivations driving me, I came to this research project. My main research questions were:

- How and to what extent do immigrant Tamilian Hindus worship in Chicago?
- How do the worship experiences of immigrant Tamilian Hindus in Chicago compare to their previous experiences of worship in India?
- How do the worship experiences of immigrant Tamilian Hindus in Chicago compare with those of their Christian counterparts?

A number of operational questions guided my research including:

- What worship expressions are most meaningful to immigrant Tamilian Hindus?
- What roles do prayer, music, and festivals play in the worship experiences of immigrant Tamilian Hindus?
- What impact did immigrating to the United States have on the worship lives of Tamilian Hindus?
- Do immigrant Tamilian Hindus feel satisfied by their experiences as worshippers or is there a conscious sense of spiritual hunger? Why do they feel this way?

Definition of Terms

Listed below are a number of words and phrases that appear in this chapter and are of particular importance to this study. Since readers may not be familiar with one or more of these terms, they have been defined here for easy reference.

Missiological Terms

- Worship: responses or overtures to God or gods that are motivated by need, devotion, gratitude, love, reverence, awe, or a sense of duty
- Expression(s): the specific forms or compilation of forms that worship takes (e.g. music, feasting, offerings, festivals, prayer, etc.)

- Indigenous: the degree to which a given worship expression is relevant and meaningful to historically specified and determined people(s)
- Contextualization: the active process of developing indigenous forms of Christian expression
- Gospel: refers to the good news of Jesus Christ's advent, life, death, resurrection and ascension and the offer of forgiveness, cleansing, freedom, eternal life and reconciliation with God that is available through faith in Him

Demographic Terms

- Tamil: a south Indian language and cultural group
- Tamilian: related to Tamil culture; a Tamilian is one who identifies with the Tamil language and culture
- Tamil Nadu: a south Indian state whose people are largely Tamilian
- Pondicherry: a south Indian union territory whose people are largely Tamilian
- Immigrant: refers to a native of Tamil Nadu or Pondicherry who has established permanent residency in the United States

Interviewee Expressions

- "used to": this phrase was used imprecisely by interview subjects. Often the phrase was employed to describe activities that the subjects continued to participate in (i.e. "I used to pray" = "I currently have a practice of regular prayer").
- "worship" and "pray": these two words were at times used interchangeably by the Hindu interview subjects
- "auspicious day": refers to a day that is of special religious significance for Hindus

Hindu Terms

- Hinduism: religious system characterized by practical polytheism and the use of idols and images in worship; it is known as *Sanātana Dharma* by many of its adherents
- Hindu: one who practices or adheres to the religion of Hinduism
- Hindu-background Christian: a Christian who formerly adhered to Hinduism

- Caste: a fixed and hereditary social class in Hindu society
- Outcaste: refers to an individual or group that is considered "untouchable" and is thus expelled from a Hindu caste; this may be by birth or by violating the rules of caste
- Hindu of caste: refers to a Hindu who maintains caste rules and distinctions
- Brahmin: a member of the highest Hindu caste; sometimes considered to be the "priestly" caste
- Vishnu: one of the three Hindu gods that make up what is sometimes referred to as the "Hindu Trinity" (Brahman, Siva, and Vishnu); known as the Preserver; Vishnu-followers are known as Vaisnavas
- Siva: another member of the Hindu Trinity—known as the Destroyer; Siva-followers are known as Saivites
- Murugan: a Hindu god, particularly popular among Tamilians
- Devotee: one who follows a particular Hindu god as a primary (though not usually exclusive) object of worship
- Festival: a sacred time regularly (usually annually) observed by worshipping communities
- Pongal: a 3-day Tamilian Hindu harvest festival
- Deepavali: important pan-Indian Hindu festival
- Pooja: Hindu worship ritual usually involving prayers and offerings
- Pooja room: a room designated by Hindu families for worship, usually housing a shrine with various pratikas
- Aarti: the presentation of elements such as fire to a god; Tamilians often refer to this as "showing fire"
- Pratika: an image or idol used by Hindus in worship
- Sari: a traditional garment worn by Indian women consisting of a long rectangle of fabric reaching the feet, wrapped and pleated around the waist over an underskirt and fitted top, and draped over the shoulder
- Ghunghat: a head covering worn by Hindu women
- Veshti: ceremonial, skirt-like garment worn by Hindu men
- Sandalwood paste: usually a white or yellow paste that is applied to the forehead
- Carnatic/Hindustani: forms of music indigenous to India
- Tabla: a set of two hand drums indigenous to south India

Christian Terms

- Baptistery: a tank used for baptisms by immersion
- Pew: a typically wooden bench with a straight back used by worshippers in a church
- Pulpit: a lectern or podium in a church from which a pastor preaches or leads a service
- Offering plate: a plate or bowl used to collect monetary offerings in a church
- Sanctuary: an area in a Christian church that is set aside primarily for worship events

Part 2: Literature Review

In examining the topic of indigenous worship for Tamilian Hindus, it is necessary to consider scholarship that relates not only to Tamilians in particular but also to Hindu peoples in general. Beyond that, Christian missiologists and missionary practitioners who have in mind issues regarding contextualization among the Tamil Hindus can also glean valuable insights from scholars who have researched indigenous worship either from a more general perspective or with regards to an entirely different cultural group. In my survey of this scholarly literature I identified eight categories of thought: the need for indigenous worship for Hindu-background Christians, the danger of syncretism, the use of Western worship forms in the Indian church, indigenous Indian worship forms, the creation of new worship forms, the process of developing indigenous worship expressions, case studies that relate to indigenous worship for Christians, and India's ability to make significant contributions to the Church universal with regards to worship.

The Need for Indigenous Worship for Hindu-background Christians

The issue of indigenous worship was one that I found was always approached out of some type of deep concern. Most writers felt that in spite of its long history, the Indian church is "still perceived as less than Indian" (Hedlund, 1998, p. 162). The Mini-Consultation on Reaching Hindus which met in Thailand as part of the 1980 Lausanne Consultation on World Evangelization cited "the Christian way of worship which is predominately non-Indian" as a key hindrance to the effective spread of the gospel among Hindus (p. 11). The consultation's report went on to explain that this decontextualized form of worship has the effect of alienating those outside the Church (1980, p.11).

The Danger of Syncretism

Certain scholars were more concerned about the dangers of syncretism than they were with developing indigenous worship among Indian Christians. S.P. Adinarayan, himself an Indian Christian, wrote, "Personally I think that the significance of the foreignness of Indian Christian worship has been considerably exaggerated" (1956, p. 28). For Adinarayan, the greater threat was "that indigenization may eventually lead to absorption" into Hinduism (1956, p. 27).

The Use of Western Worship Forms in the Indian Church

Invariably, the foreign nature of Indian Christian worship was attributed to the use of Western forms of worship in the Indian church. Attitudes on the use of these forms varied. Adinarayan, for example, boldly declared, "The great hymns of the Church have thrilled everyone irrespective of one's capacity to appreciate or participate in Western music" (1956, p. 28). T.S. Garrett was another advocate of the "universal fellowship" (Garrett, 1958, p. 112) that he believed was the result of at least a limited use of Western worship forms in Indian churches. On the other side of the debate were prohibitionists like Vide Chenoweth who believed that any introduction of Western forms to a non-Western culture was a mistake. According to Chenoweth "each culture should produce its own songs, pray its own prayers, and thus worship with true understanding" (1984, p. 32). The particular Western worship forms cited by scholars in their writings on this subject included such elements as musical styles and songs, preaching styles, styles of prayer, architecture, furnishings, sculpture, and painting.

Indigenous Indian Worship Forms

Much of the available scholarship related to this subject was devoted to an examination of indigenous Indian—usually Hindu—forms of worship. Padma Rangaswamy discussed the heightened role of temples for immigrant Hindus living in Chicago when compared to the role of temples in India. "Here in the United States," explained Rangaswamy, "the Indians feel impelled to enforce their religious identity in structured ways, for example, by visiting the temple every Sunday to pray" (1995, p. 449). V. Francis Vineeth provided a wealth of insights into the function of festivals in Hindu worship. He explained that festivals like Pongal and Deepavali were comprised of three major components—a mythical story, dramatic reenactment, and a celebration—which together function to bring about unity with God, unity with other people, unity with nature, and unity with self (1987). Swami Bhajanananda described not only various elements of Hindu worship but traced the historical development of those elements as well. In particular, he discussed *pooja*, temple worship, *pratikas*, the "divinization of man," and *aarti* (1980). Noel Sheth discussed the subjective dimension of worship noting a variety of themes in Hindu spirituality including mystery, presence, experience, non-attachment, devotion, and freedom (1973.)

A number of scholars went a step further and discussed how indigenous forms could be used in worship for Christians. For example, Gerald L. Carner promoted the use of *kirthans*, a form of preaching or storytelling that is sung with musical accompaniment, by Christians in evangelism, discipleship, and worship (1998). Bede Griffiths advocated the use of yoga and other meditative or devotional practices for Christians and considered the Christian ashram rather than the church to be ideal (1973b). Finally, Garrett suggested the use of chant by setting "the whole Eucharistic service to Carnatic *ragas*, the celebrant chanting the prayers, the readers chanting the lessons, the deacon the litany" (1958, p. 131).

The Creation of New Worship Forms

Some scholars saw the need for a more dynamic perspective of indigenous worship that called for the continual creation of new worship forms in order to be relevant to "historically specified and determined men and women" (Scott, 1986, p. 83). David Scott believed that worship that was truly indigenous would not be lodged either in the West's or in India's past; "hence the words used to proclaim, and the signs performed to interpret, must be such that those who celebrate can experience the meaning of the death and resurrection [of Jesus Christ] as something that takes place in their lives and in their life-situations" (1986, p. 83). In this vein, Matthew Lederle suggested the development of Indian Christian painting as just one avenue towards the creation of new forms of worship for Hindu-background Christians (1973).

The Process of Developing Indigenous Worship Expressions

Much has been written regarding how indigenous worship expressions can be developed within Christian communities. Garrett wrote about the goal which should motivate the development of indigenous worship expressions: "The new convert, when he comes to church for the first time, will inevitably find some things strange and new to him; but in the main he ought to feel that the service in which he is taking part is something which could soon belong to him and to which he could soon belong" (1958, p. 130). The most common suggestion given by scholars for fostering this developmental process was to empower indigenous worship leaders and creators. Chenoweth asserted that a missionary has the responsibility to encourage and legitimize the act of "creating music in the local idiom" (1984, p. 32). M. Amaladoss suggested that "the young" be trained to be sensitive to Indian modes of expression and then be encouraged to experiment (1973, p. 37, 40). Carner recommended a step-by-step process for training young Indian seminary students to use *kirthans* effectively (1998, p. 186). Lederle stressed, "We have to encourage our artists, we have to give them tasks to be done" (1973, p. 139). Perhaps this sentiment was summed up best by Sheth who believed that the key to developing a truly indigenous Indian Christian worship was to "surround the young with all the resources, Indian and Christian, at our disposal, create an Indian atmosphere of life, remove whatever might be an obstacle, and then . . . let them grow and experience God as they are and with all that they are" (1973, p. 121).

Case Studies Related to Indigenous Worship for Indian Christians

A variety of case studies regarding indigenous worship provided powerful insights. Carner detailed the historical use of *kirthans* showing their power to attract large crowds and to influence hearers especially in the accounts of Narayan Vaman Tilak and Pandurang Shastri Athavale (1998). Roger Hedlund also took a historical approach in presenting the stories of various contextualization efforts throughout the history of the Indian church (1998). Paul Younger presented three cases of Christian worship settings in south India that have successfully attracted large numbers of Hindus through what he called a "sharing" of worship forms (1993, p. 197). Finally, Cindy Perry offered two enlightening case studies on Christian participation in Hindu festivals in Nepal (1990).

Indian Contributions to Global Christianity

The final area of thought explored by scholars regarding indigenous worship for Indian Christians had to do with the notion of the Indian church contributing to the Church universal in the area of worship. A number of authors believed that the Indian culture has been largely underestimated and overlooked by Christians in the West who could benefit greatly from Indians in the area of worship. Griffiths, for example, said that "the basic principles of Yoga need to be adopted in all our Christian prayer" (1973a, p. 113). According to Hedlund, "India has much to teach the world from her perception of Christ" (1998, p. 173). Scott agreed, "Indian-Christians will contribute to the correction and completion of other realizations of the Gospel" (1986, p. 84).

Part 3: Methods

This study utilized a combination of qualitative research methods. I interviewed 5 Tamilian immigrants—3 Hindus, 1 Hindu-background Christian, and 1 Christian who was born into a Christian family—in 3 interview sessions. I made use of interview guides prepared for each session and recorded the interviews using a video camera. Participant observations were conducted of 2 Hindu worship experiences and 2 Christian worship experiences. In each of these cases, my observations were recorded in a notebook.

*Description of Research Subjects**

My research focused on Tamilian immigrants in Chicago and put me in close contact with 3 Tamil families—2 Hindu and 1 Christian—who had immigrated in the late 1990s to Chicago from India. In addition, I had the opportunity to observe 2 Christian worship services at Tamilian churches in the Chicago area.

The Rams and Rajans

Much of my time was spent with 2 Hindu families, the Rams and the Rajans. The men in these families, Kārttikeya (Kart) Ram and Arum Rajan, were both computer scientists in their early thirties. Their wives, Suganthi and Neela respectively, each had college educations yet neither of the women worked outside the home. Much of Suganthi's time was spent caring for their 18-month-old son, Kumaran. The Rajans, on the other hand, did not have any children. Each couple had been married for just over 2 years. They were all friends.

In terms of their educational background, career choices, economic situations, immigration experiences, family values, and religious practices, the Rams and Rajans were typical Tamilian Hindu immigrants. According to Padma Rangaswamy's research, a 1992 survey showed that 94% of

---

* Names have been changed to preserve the anonymity of the subjects.

Indian immigrants in Chicago had college educations, 69% had incomes greater than $50,000 per year, and 53% were employed as professionals in their fields (1995, p. 444-445). Both the Rams and the Rajans were among the majority in each of these categories.

I conducted personal interviews with Kart, Arum, and Neela. The latter 2 were interviewed together with Kart observing and adding an occasional comment. In addition to the two interviews, I conducted participant observations of 2 Hindu festivals that the Rams celebrated in their home with the Rajans in attendance as well.

The Joshua Family

Raj and Kali Joshua were a Tamil couple that had been married just over fifteen years. They had two children. Economically and occupationally, they had much in common with the Rams and the Rajans. The Joshua family, however, was Christian. In particular, Raj grew up in a Lutheran home in Tamil Nadu while his wife Kali converted to Christianity from Hinduism during her high school years. They were active members of Chicago Tamil Church. I conducted a personal interview with Raj and Kali in their home.

Tamil United Church of Christ and Chicago Tamil Church

At the time of my research, there were three Tamil churches in the Chicago area that drew members from a small Tamilian Christian population that was scattered throughout various communities. Tamil United Church of Christ (Tamil UCC) in Westchester and Chicago Tamil Church (CTC) in Hickory Hills were two of these churches. Tamil UCC was started in 1997. A few years later, some of its members formed CTC. Although Tamil UCC was affiliated with the United Church of Christ, both churches' pastors described their churches as non-denominational. Both churches also met in rented church buildings that were used primarily by larger, English-speaking congregations. I conducted a participant observation of a worship service at each of these churches.

The Research Sample in Perspective

The 3 families studied offer a good representation of Tamilian immigrants in Chicago; however, it is impossible to make sweeping generalizations based on such a sample due to its various demographic limitations. A study of Tamilian immigrants who are elderly, poor, or who have lived in the United States for significantly longer periods of time would likely yield somewhat different findings. Nevertheless, these families adhered to strong religious currents that are common among Tamilians globally and thus have provided a wealth of valuable insights into the realm of Tamilian worship life.

Limitations

The most glaring shortcoming of this research relates to the size of the research sample. It would be wise to at least double this sample in order to strengthen the research.

The research was affected by several other limitations as well. My observations at the Tamil churches happened to fall on weeks when, according to the pastor of each church, attendance was significantly lower than usual. It also seems clear to me that my presence at the services affected how the services were carried out. Both pastors took the time to introduce me and the pastor of CTC even stated that he used more English than usual for my benefit.

Despite these and undoubtedly other limitations, my research still managed to successfully probe into the worship experiences of Tamilians in a significant enough way as to provide important insights on the subject.

Part 4: Findings

As has been mentioned already, my research brought me in contact with 2 Tamilian Hindu families and 1 Tamilian Christian family. I had the opportunity to conduct in-depth interviews with these 3 families as well as to observe them in worship.

Kārttikeya Ram

By the time Kart and I sat down in his living room on November 1, 2004, to discuss his experiences and feelings about worship, more than a year had passed since our first meeting and we had become good friends. He was a 31-year-old computer programmer with a wife of less than 3 years and a toddler son. I was in my late twenties, married almost 3 years with a son who had recently turned 2-years-old. On most occasions when our two families got together, Kart and I had to struggle through piecemeal conversations that were broken up by the incessant babbling, crying, and yelling of our kids, but on that particular evening Kart's wife and son were out of town visiting family and I had come alone. Thus, I was eager to hear Kart tell his story in what was for us an unusually serene environment.

Kart's Life History

Kārttikeya (Kart) Ram was born in south India's union territory of Pondicherry in 1972. His parents sacrificed much to raise their nine children and to provide them with opportunities to get a good education, a fact that was not forgotten by Kart. During our interview, I asked Kart if he had ever felt overwhelmed with thankfulness. He quickly responded, "You know the first person that I obviously think about is my mom and dad. They used to sacrifice a lot. I always think about . . . what they sacrificed and withstood. I used to tell my brothers and sisters how they sacrificed their life to raise their kids. . . . I always think about them." Indeed he had good reason to be thankful. Kart was able to earn both a master's degree in mathematics as well as a master's diploma in computer science.

Kart began his professional career as a teacher but then quickly entered the field of computer programming. After 3 years of programming work in India the opportunity arose for him to take a job in the United States. Kart described the series of events that led to his leaving India for the U.S. as one that left him feeling amazed by the gods:

> One of my friends, he was working in the United States, he referenced me to his employer and he interviewed me and so I got a job in the United States . . . . It's not happening to everyone. Like it's kind of happened to me. There are— I know for sure—there are more geniuses and there are more people that they wanted to come. But I never thought about coming to the United States to work. It all happened just like that. Like in 2 hours . . . I go to as many temples as I can before I come to the United States. So I did offer prayers to a lot of gods.

Kart had been in the United States for about 5 years when I interviewed him. Four of those years were spent in the Chicago area. In 2002, his parents arranged for him to marry another well-educated Tamilian, Suganthi, who had also earned a master's degree in computer science. They were wed in India and then returned to the Chicago area together. Less than a year after their wedding, Kart and Suganthi welcomed their son, Kumaran, into the world. Soon thereafter, the Rams bought and moved into a duplex in the western Chicago suburb of Carol Stream in August 2003. I first met them a few weeks later when I moved my own young family into the duplex next door.

Kart's Experiences as a Worshipper

Kart described himself as a Hindu and a devotee of the god Siva. He explained,

> Hindu . . . the major groups would be Vaisnavas and Saivas. Most of the people who believe in Siva, they treat Siva as the primary god. And the other group would treat Vishnu as their primary god. I think mine is Siva. I think so. But we used to, you know, believe in all the gods, but my background would go with Siva I guess.

Celebrating festivals.

Our discussion of worship began with the topic of traditional Hindu festivals. Kart started by telling me about one of his two favorites, *Thamizar Thirnuan*, which is more popularly known as *Pongal*.

Kart explained that *Pongal* was basically a "farmers' festival," but it was celebrated by all Tamilian Hindus. He called it a "major festival," lasting 3 days. Kart described some of the activities that went on during those days:

> *The first day is called* Pongal. *The second day is called* Mauda-pongal. *Maud means cow. It's the second day is for the cow. Which is, you know, in India the farmers are using the cows and buffaloes for their needs—to cultivate their lands and for milk and stuff. So the second day is mainly for cows and buffaloes. They used to decorate the carts. They decorate the cows . . . . They would put some kind of bells, and they would paint the . . . top of the head . . . . They would put some leaves around the neck and also some threads, and some colorful dress.*

Kart said that the third day of the festival was called *Karna Pongal*.

> *On the second day . . . the elders will give money to the youngers, like parents and family members will give money to their kids and nieces and nephew and that kind of stuff. And the third day people would really enjoy spending the money and going to the movies. Basically, that day is for the kids—get more money and spend it.*

The *Pongal* celebrations that Kart experienced in India also always featured receiving gifts of new clothing, ritual cooking of *pongal* rice, and worshipping the sun.

Kart's other favorite festival is *Deepavali*. He said that there was a story behind the festival that Hindus try to remember through their celebration. He described:

> Deepavali *is after a person really . . . . who is doing all kinds of illegal things—very arrogant . . . . was called* Arkan. Arkan *. . . will do all kinds of illegal activities, and he will mess up with the people, spanking them and that kind of stuff. And one day, one of the gods, called* Murugan, *he killed him. And before that bad guy dies he requested to the god that since he did all the bad things people wanted to enjoy his death and celebrating the day with sweets and new dress, crackers and that kind of stuff.*

So celebrate they did. Kart fondly recounted his experiences of sharing sweet foods with family and friends, receiving gifts of new clothing, and offering prayers early in the morning, before sunrise.

When I asked Kart why *Pongal* and *Deepavali* were more important to him than the others, I expected that he would tell me that it was because they were the biggest of all Hindu festivals. I was wrong. Instead he emphasized that at those festivals,

> *You would meet like your friends and friends' relatives, but the rest of the festivals are not kind of really . . . . You would get money and new dresses for* Deepawali *and* Pongal, *but not for the rest of the festivals. So that's the difference.*

The role of prayer.

I wanted to probe deeper into Kart's experiences with worship so I began asking about specific forms of worship that were familiar to me as a Christian in the West. In particular, I asked about prayer and music.

Kart said that he typically prayed by himself early in the morning after bathing. He would offer his prayers first to the god Ganesh and on occasion would also pray to some of the other gods. Suganthi and Kumaran would usually pray later in the morning, after Kart went to work. "But during the festivals," Kart added, "we will do the prayers together."

He went on to explain that the content of his prayers focused on petitioning the gods to meet the felt needs of himself and his family: "I used to say thanks to whatever I got and I used to ask whatever I need. And nowadays, most of the prayers will be related to my son—like, for his health."

The role of music.

When I asked about the role that music played in his culture, Kart said that it was closely connected with religious expression. He explained that each god had particular devotional songs that were associated with it and that "whenever you offer prayer back in home . . . people will be singing." Music played a role in his daily life as a worshipper; he said, "I used to always pray with Ganesh with a song—with a prayer song . . . every morning." He told me that he even enjoyed listening to devotional music in the car on his way to work and that doing so was something of a "spiritual experience" for him.

The experience of worship in temples.

Kart also spoke of the role that Hindu temples played in his life as a worshipper. I had asked him to tell me about times when he had experienced a deep sense of peace. He replied:

> *I used to get those kind of time when I go to temples. When I go to temples . . . I used to feel that my mind is very light and I have sometimes a kind of peace. . . . I used to get kind of excitation of the god, like when I talk. I think that god is directly talking to me . . . god is listening to me. So that's the most peaceful time for me, and also, internally, the most enjoyable time I ever had. You know, like when I pray to the god I would . . . feel that I got a response from the god. . . . so that's really, really the great enjoyment for me.*

The Impact of Living in the United States on Kart's Spiritual Life

One theme that recurred throughout my conversation with Kart was how living in the United States had significantly impacted his spiritual life. At one point, I asked him plainly how he felt his spiritual life had changed since moving to the U.S. He responded,

> Yeah, it's been changed quite a lot I guess. Back in India, I used to go to the temples more often, but not in the United States. You know, but I still think about god for each and every thing, but I think my spiritual thing is reduced.

He confessed that the festivals seemed to lose their meaning for him when he left India:

> You know, I would really enjoy if I were in India, but after coming here I wasn't really enjoying the festivals. It's kind of a, honestly, I had to do. My parents would ask, "Did you do this?" So . . . I'm really not enjoying the celebrations, because if it's in India that's different. We would have holidays and we would meet the friends and family members and that kind of stuff. Here it is different . . . . Honestly, after I came to the United States, I have no meaning to the festivals. I just, you know, I'm doing because I had to.

In general, Kart felt closer to the gods when he was in India but he did mention that because life for him in Chicago was focused only on work and his immediate family, he felt he had the opportunity to think more about spiritual things. He also mentioned that the birth of their son had motivated him to celebrate the festivals more consistently because, "We are trying to teach our culture and festivals and everything to our son."

I brought our interview to a close by asking Kart to reflect upon his life as a Hindu and to evaluate what his experiences had meant to him. I wanted to know how he felt about the quality of his spiritual life. He responded,

> I'm not really like a hundred percentage worship person in the sense that there are more people that they do more prayers, they go to temples always—like regularly, weekly, or daily. I'm trying to catch up—to go with the god more close—but I can't.

When I asked if he had ever had what he would describe as a "life changing experience" through his interaction with the gods, Kart responded, "Not really, but I want it. I did not have that kind of experience. . . . I never felt that way, that my life was really changed or that kind of stuff."

Arum and Neela Rajan

Kart's long time friend Arum Rajan and his wife Neela had moved to the Chicago area in the spring of 2003. During the several months that we had known them, my wife and I had also been able to develop a friendship with them, but before my interview with the couple on November 9, 2004, we had never visited their home. So when I asked Arum if he would be willing to let me interview him, the 32-year-old computer programmer not only readily agreed but insisted that we have dinner together in their home as well.

My wife Katherine, son Christopher, and I arrived at the Rajans' apartment in the northwest Chicago suburb of Schaumburg at about 7:00 pm and were greeted outside by Arum. He led us into their one-bedroom apartment, which was sparingly furnished with only a small entertainment center in the living room and a bed and computer desk in the bedroom. The Rams, who had also been invited for dinner, arrived shortly after we did. After eating as much as we all could of the huge meal that Neela probably spent most of the day preparing, the Rajans invited me to join them in the bedroom to start the interview.

Arum's Life History

Like Kart, Arum was also a native of Pondicherry. Growing up, he attended a Seventh Day Adventist school from kindergarten to tenth grade where he was first exposed to the Bible. He later earned a graduate degree in computer science from Tagore Arts College where he also became friends with Kart, who was a fellow student there. Arum pointed out that the college was named after Nobel laureate Rabindranath Tagore "but," he said with a chuckle, speaking of Kart and himself, "we guys spoil his name."

Arum worked for about 5 years in Pondicherry after college as a computer programmer before a friend recommended him for a job in the United States. In December 1999, he left India to begin his life in the U.S. He then spent about 4 years in California before making the move to the Chicago area.

Neela's Life History

In 2002, Arum's parents arranged for him to marry Neela. She had been born in the south Indian state of Tamil Nadu in the early 1980s and was schooled as a youth in an "Anglo-Indian school" in her hometown of Villupuram. Neela described what happened next:

> *We moved from Villupuram to Pondicherry. Main reason was my father wanted me to do medicine. Okay, so you need at least 5 years of education in Pondicherry state to take up medicine—or you should be a citizen. You are not a citizen. Okay, so let's do 5 years of education. If I start from 8th to 12th it would be 5 years of education. So we came to Pondicherry, and gradually I lost interest in medicine. So I thought of doing engineering. I didn't get into any engineering colleges in Pondicherry. I got back in Tamil Nadu again. Tiruvannamalai was in Tamil Nadu. So I went there. I thought my life is engineering, just engineering. Just get a degree, then do a work, get a job. And if I'm lucky, grad school, go to U.S. I just finished—I didn't even finish my first year, I got engaged.*

Neela and Arum were wed in India and a month later, Neela joined her new husband in the United States. When I met with them, Arum had a job as a consultant working in downtown Chicago.

The Rajans' Experiences as Worshippers

Both Arum and Neela described themselves as Hindus who were "very much traditional about religion and worship." Arum explained that he grew up in a family that was "somewhat strict" about it. Neela's parents, on the other hand, were more "liberal" about such matters. Like Kart, they were eager to talk about their experience of celebrating the Hindu festivals and *Deepavali*, which they were preparing to celebrate just 2 days after our interview, was first on their list.

Celebrating festivals.

They described *Deepavali* as being a "big celebration" with decorations, colorful lights, firecrackers, sweet foods that were exchanged between neighbors and family, and gifts of new clothes. Arum said he liked the celebration mainly because he enjoyed watching children have so much fun but Neela did not hesitate to call *Deepavali* her personal favorite. Smiling broadly she said,

> Deepavali *is always fun—bursting crackers, sweets, and— it's always fun . . . . I love crackers. You know my friends*

> *say I'm a grown up, I don't burst crackers, yeah. No, I'm still a kid! I* like *bursting crackers.*

The Rajans also talked about *Pongal*, which Arum described as a traditional Tamilian festival, saying,

> *They have like 3 days of celebration for that. First day is for farmers ... so they make sweet rice and worship the sun. So second day is like, in olden days they used a bullock to plow the land.... it's not exactly to worship but thanks—thanking the animal too.*

They went on to describe a traditional contest that Arum called "a manly game," which they said only happened in the smaller villages. Arum continued, "On that day is like bullfighting. It is with bare hands. They don't use spears or whatever, sword or anything. They'll have something on the head—those horns—and they have to remove it." Neela added,

> *They'll have money or gold—something tied to the horns. So whoever is capable to get the ox down, they can take it. It's like a prize.... And the horns will be sharp. They are sharpened during that time. If the ox hits you, that's it. Whatever is inside will come out. Whatever you had in the morning, it will come out.*

On the third day of *Pongal*, they said, people would celebrate near a lake or river. The day would involve receiving gifts of money from elders, distributing sweet foods to one another, and flying kites.

The Rajans briefly mentioned several other festivals including *Chadookti*, Tamil New Year, *Karthigai Deepam*, and *Ayutha Pooja*. The latter they said was an important time to worship tools of trade. Neela explained that when she was still a student she would use that time to "keep books, pens, and all that and do pooja. I mean, we were studying so we want the year to be fruitful—to score good marks and all that."

The role of prayer.

The Rajans said that they generally prayed together on Fridays addressing specific gods like Ganesh but Arum also pointed out that he sometimes prayed while taking the train to work. When I asked what they prayed about, he responded, "We pray what we want, what we are in need of, and if someone is sick." Arum went on to describe an experience in which he felt his prayers had been answered,

> *If I worship, yeah it definitely happens—whatever I wish, I get it. If my mom was sick or something, if I just don't worship and she doesn't get cured at all. I went to India recently. She was supposed to be discharged [from the hospital] before I go there, but she was there for ten days. Till then, I didn't worship for her. But when I worshipped [for] her, immediately in 2 days she was discharged—she was alright and she was discharged. There are instances like that.*

Neela was less confident about her prayer life, confessing, "I have not taken so much deep prayers like that. When I was in school, I pray, 'Okay, I should get more marks. God please help me.' Nothing more than that." However, she added that being far away from friends and family has added depth to her prayers:

> *When I am here, if my sister is sick or my dad had a mild stroke, that time I will pray, "Okay, I am here. I cannot be there to take care of. So just look—look for me as I would look. Look for them."*

The role of music.

When I asked about the role that music played in their culture, they explained that it was very important at life cycle events like baby showers, births, weddings, and funerals. They also mentioned that there was specific music for working and specific music for worship. Arum said that basically there was music "for everything . . . . It's part of our life."

For Neela, music was particularly important because she found it helped her not to feel so alone when Arum was at work: "I don't like being silent—all alone—so I need someone talking to. I can't just talk to myself . . . so I just keep the music around me. So that fills the house." Arum enjoyed listening to music at night to help him sleep. In the mornings or during *poojas*, they would listen to worship songs.

The experience of worship in temples.

The role of temples in worship seemed to be an important one to the Rajans. They explained that going to temples and taking the time to "just sit there" gave them a very peaceful feeling. They found that the older temples were more peaceful than the newer ones because, as Arum said, "the vibrations there are still good."

The Impact of Living in the United States on the Rajans' Spiritual Lives

I wanted to know how they felt coming to the United States had impacted their spiritual life. They responded by saying that the impact had been largely a negative one for two basic reasons. For one, they said that in the United States, life was "more practical" and that there was "not much time." However, they noted that a more important factor was the fact that being separated from friends and family had significantly affected their desire to worship, follow Hindu customs and observe the festivals. Neela stressed this last point,

> See Deepavali, *it's a big festival. We want to be with our parents. We cannot be there. We wanted to be with relatives. Actually, true enjoyment is when you are around everyone enjoying it, and if you are not there—just sitting over here celebrating* Deepavali—*it is not* Deepavali.

They also said that celebrating *Deepavali* in the United States meant "no crackers" and not many friends to whom they could give sweet foods. Arum said, "We make sweets and stuff and we eat ourselves. We don't have much friends. I can give to Kart and Kart can give to me and that's it." He added, "I mean, it's almost nothing here." Neela continued,

> *You don't feel that it is actually, "Okay, today is a big celebration." You don't feel that at all when you are here. When you are in India, you feel, "Oh, okay, this is* Deepavali!*" You can see that actually. Here you can't see nothing. It's just an ordinary day passing by.*

The Rajans indicated that their family members had played something of an accountability role in their spiritual lives before moving to the United States. "In India," Neela explained, "they keep on saying, 'Do this,' 'This is the auspicious day,' 'The festival is coming—you have to do fasting,' and all that." She added, "Over here, there is no one to tell all that. Maybe you don't get into it." They said that in the U.S., "Nobody's there to control us. Nobody's there to look over."

Neela went on to explain that they were not following the Hindu custom of not eating non-vegetarian foods on auspicious days.

> *We go at least an egg or something on Friday . . . . After coming here, we don't see what day it is, we just take. It's like getting pure. In the sense of being pure when going to temple—not taking non-vegetarian—being pure. We are not following that after coming here. There would at least be someone to tell us in India. Even though we know, we just don't care about it. I wouldn't say we don't care about it. Just—okay, who's there to look after? Who's going to know about it?*

I brought our interview to a close by asking the Rajans to reflect upon their lives as Hindus and to evaluate what their experiences had meant to them. I wanted to know how they felt about the quality of their spiritual life. Arum responded first by saying that he did not "get too much into spiritual life" at this point in his life but he planned to concentrate more on it when he got older. Neela recounted how her life had been full of constant relocation and change from one place to the next. She told how she had thought she was going to become an engineer until marriage changed those plans, "So I thought, 'Okay, I'm not going to decide anything hereafter.' Nothing is there in my hands. Everything gets twisted . . . . I'm looking for what's the next change going to be."

As with my interview with Kart, I asked if they had ever experienced God in a personal or life-changing way. After a long pause, Arum answered simply, "I mean, I'm thinking. I think I'm not lucky enough to go through what you explained."

The Rams and Rajans at Worship

My family and I were able to join the Rams and the Rajans for celebrations of 2 Hindu festivals that Kart and Suganthi hosted in their home. Both celebrations were held in the evenings and attended only by our three families. On neither occasion did my wife and I realize that a festival was being celebrated until some time after we had arrived.

Celebrating Thalial

On October 16, 2004, Kart called us in the afternoon to invite us over for dinner. Since our families had something of a history of inviting each other to do things at the last minute, we were glad to oblige. We arrived at their home at 6:00 pm—about 15 minutes after the time Kart had suggested—and were greeted at the front door by Arum and Neela. As we entered the house and removed our shoes, the aroma of deep-fried cakes filled our nostrils. Kart then appeared from the kitchen, greeted us with a smile, and took our shoes to put them in a nearby closet.

The front door opened into a living room area where the Rams' 18-month old son Kumaran was playing with his million-or-so toys. I had been carrying my 2-year old son Christopher and at that point decided to put him down so that he and Kumaran could play together. My wife, Katherine, then disappeared into the kitchen looking for Suganthi who was busily preparing the meal. I followed Kart and Arum into a room adjacent to the kitchen where Arum and I took a seat on a sofa and began watching a Tamil-language film on television.

After about twenty minutes, during which time Arum and I had been chatting about the movie, Kart announced, "Okay, let's eat." We all hesitated for a moment until he encouraged us a bit more. Finally, because Kart was looking at me, I got up from the couch and slowly approached the kitchen table. I observed that about a dozen dishes, mostly rice-based, covered the table. Katherine asked if they were celebrating a special occasion since the meal seemed to be unusually large. The 4 Tamilians explained, "Today we celebrate Lord Vishnu." Arum commented, "It is just an excuse to eat good food." I found out later from Kart that the festival was called *Thalial* and that it was a relatively small celebration among the Tamilian Hindus.

Since so many dishes made it impossible for us to eat at the table, we mostly ate seated on the floor or on the couch, in front of the television. We enjoyed conversation and after dinner began watching wedding videos—first of Kart's sister's and then of his own. Aside from some explanatory comments regarding what we were seeing in the videos, nothing further was said about the god Vishnu, the celebration of *Thalial*, or religion in general.

The wedding videos.

I felt that the wedding videos themselves provided an interesting contrast between the kind of celebrations that occurred in India and the one I had been observing that night in the United States. The first video Kart showed us was from a celebration dinner that was held the night before his sister's wedding. Hundreds of family and friends had filled a large banquet hall to share a meal. Guests sat at long tables eating food with their hands and conversing freely with each other.

Much of the video footage was of the bride and groom posing with various assortments of friends and relatives. The groom wore a grey Western-style suit and tie and stood next to his bride who was adorned in a blue, silken sari with many jewels and flowers completing her extravagant ensemble.

A final scene from the eve of the wedding featured live musical performances by friends and family. Many of the guests sat in chairs watching the performances while others danced energetically in the middle of the room.

Since Kart had not yet received the video of his sister's actual wedding day, he let us watch the video from his and Suganthi's wedding. Like his sister's wedding eve celebration, the Rams' wedding eve featured a banquet with hundreds of friends and family, music, food, and elaborate dress. The wedding day involved a number of ritual activities including presentations of traditional Tamil wedding garments by the future in-laws; ceremonial baths for the bride, groom, and their parents; the presentation of gifts to the bride and groom by family and friends; and various sacrifices and Sanskrit prayers offered by a Brahmin priest on behalf of the couple. At one point in the wedding ceremony, a drama was acted out. The groom received an umbrella and began to walk away from his bride. The bride's family followed him and began washing his feet in order to "convince" him to stay and go through with the marriage. The assuaged groom then returned to his bride to complete the ceremony. None of the Tamilians were sure why they performed the drama except that it was customary to do so.

By the time we had finished watching the videos, three-and-a-half hours had passed and it was time for Kumaran and Christopher to go to bed. So we said our goodbyes and went home.

Celebrating Karthigai Deepam

Arum had mentioned *Karthigai Deepam* briefly in his interview, calling it the "Festival of Light." We were able to join them at the Rams' home to celebrate the festival on November 28, 2004. Earlier that day, the Rams invited us for dinner without mentioning the special occasion; only after some time at the Rams' home did we become aware of the festival.

Katherine, Christopher and I arrived at about 6:00 pm and were greeted by Suganthi at the front door. We removed our shoes and entered the living room area where Kumaran, as usual, was playing with his toys. Kart had mentioned on the phone earlier that day that he would be doing all the cooking for dinner so I left my family with Suganthi and Kumaran in the living room and went to the kitchen to greet Kart.

Since it was unusual for Kart to be preparing the food by himself, I asked why he was doing so that night. He explained that Suganthi was menstruating and was thus not allowed to handle any of the cooking utensils or vessels. I realized this was not an ordinary night for the Rams. As the night wore on, I noticed that Suganthi did not participate in any ceremonial festivities. Later, she and Neela told Katherine that menstruating women were considered ceremonially unclean. Kart himself was barred from so much as tasting the food until "after the prayers."

Once the dinner preparations were completed, Kart went upstairs to bathe. When he returned a few minutes later, he was wearing a white, neatly pressed, button-down dress shirt and a *veshti* that was beige in color and trimmed at the bottom with a band of gold. He had with him a tray of 25 tea lights which he then proceeded to light.

As he was lighting the candles, I began asking questions about the festival. Kart and Suganthi did not know the meaning behind the candles or *Karthigai Deepam* in general. They knew only that they were supposed to light an odd number of candles and place them outside and "around the house." They were also able to tell me that on that particular night they were celebrating the second day of a 3-day festival that honored the god Murugan and, they thought, Siva as well.

Wind actually prevented Kart from being able to keep the candles he had placed outside lit, so he decided instead to put them all over the house—on the staircase, behind the stove, on the kitchen counter, and elsewhere. Only about eight remained outside. They lined the pathway that led from the driveway to the front door.

The Rajans arrived at about 7:00 pm. They each had some sandalwood paste on their foreheads. Otherwise, Arum was dressed as I normally saw him—in blue jeans and a button-down shirt. Neela wore a bright yellow sari.

We all sat in the living room and conversed for about 10 minutes before Kart announced that it was time for prayers. He took Kumaran in his arms and began to ascend the stairs. The Rajans, Katherine, Christopher and I followed closely behind.

At the top of the stairs was a loft that functioned both as a home office—complete with computer, desk, and chair—and a *pooja* room. In one corner sat a 2-foot high, wooden end table. Upon the table was an assortment of several small framed pictures and tiny statuettes no more than an inch or two high—these were the household gods.

Kumaran toddled over to the table and picked up a bell that he began to ring over the items on the table. Kart offered a plate of the food he had prepared by setting it on the table and using his hands to waft the aroma towards the gods. He then used a bronze vessel to drizzle a clear liquid at various points on the table. Finally, he lit a small oil lamp and wafted the smoke from its flame towards the gods. Kart then brought the lamp around to each of us. I watched as Arum and Neela placed their hands palms down about an inch above the flame and then wafted the smoke towards their faces.

The *pooja* lasted only about 5 minutes, during which time all except Kart and Kumaran stood about 3 feet away watching in silence. It ended without a word and we all filed back downstairs and picked up the conversations that we had left to do the *pooja*. About 10 minutes later, we all ate together as usual. The celebration ended at about 8:00 pm and we returned home.

Raj and Kali Joshua

I had met Raj and Kali when I visited their church in the southwest Chicago suburb of Hickory Hills in November 2004. After the worship service, Raj had shared with me enough of his and Kali's story to make me want to hear more. They invited me to their home about a week and a half later, on November 24, so that they could tell me the whole story.

Kali's Early Life

Kali was born in Thanjavur, Tamil Nadu, in the early 1970s to devout Hindu parents who nevertheless sent her to a Lutheran boarding school for her early education. She recalled how she came under the powerful influence of the gospel through the school:

> *There I came to know about God, but I was arguing with my friends—I never wanted to be a Christian. But one missionary—he was an evangelist—he preached for us for 3 days. There I came to know about God well and I got saved by his preachings . . . . He, the preacher, talked about God's love, who is the true God, and he talked about the saving grace of God. And he did a healing ministry too . . . . I was not healed [of] anything, but I was touched by the love of God.*

Her family, to some extent, tolerated her new found faith. Although they refused to let her attend a church, they did allow her to pray and read the Bible. Her father, who had become involved with a Hindu fundamentalist organization, did not force her to attend Hindu meetings against her will. Kali explained, "My father doesn't worry or bother as long as I am within the family boundaries."

After her years at the Lutheran school, Kali attended college where she studied electronics. It was there that she befriended a fellow electrical engineering student, Raj Joshua.

Raj's Early Life

Raj was born to a Lutheran father and a Catholic mother in Thuvarankurichi, Tamil Nadu, a small village of about 300 families, in 1970. He described the villagers as "downtrodden people" who "were not economically on the higher level." In an effort to overcome his impoverished background, Raj worked hard in high school and even achieved "state rank." After high school, Raj entered college to study electrical engineering.

Marriage and Beyond

Raj and Kali began their relationship as fellow students in college. As Raj explained, at the beginning, it was purely academic:

> *When we meet outside and talk to each other, out of 2-hour meeting only ten minutes personal things. An hour and fifty minutes will be discussing our subjects, our country, politics, you name it—all subjects. That's the kind of relationship we had.*

Soon, however, the relationship blossomed into more and the two began to consider marriage. Eventually, they told their parents about their plans. "They did not agree," recounted Raj, who remembered that his father was especially opposed to the idea. "He even slapped me. Yeah, he got mad. Because 'til that time, I did not argue with him." Kali explained,

> *I think for his father, for his mom, normally they don't agree dating. You know the Indian culture? The parents arrange marriages for the children. That's the thing [Raj] doesn't like . . . . he wanted to look for love.*

Raj added,

> *[My father] wanted to look for a girl for me. "Not you, I will look for one girl." The thing is not she's a Hindu. That is not the thing. The thing is you decided. No, that is*

> *not acceptable. I had a hard time convincing him—he was not convinced.*

For Kali, the opposition from her parents to her marrying Raj was even stronger. She remembered her father's reaction, "After I met [Raj] in college, he was so mad. And when I said to him that I want to marry [Raj], he was so mad." Kali continued, "He said, 'I will not accept you in my family.' So without their permission I married. They didn't allow us into their house—both of us—into my father's house."

Raj and Kali were ostracized from their parents for 2 years after their marriage until the birth of their daughter brought about a gradual reconciliation on both sides. Over the years, they said, the relationships got stronger and stronger.

After college, Raj worked for the Indian government as an engineer for 9 years, during which time Kali gave birth to their second child, a son. Eventually, Raj's interest in computers motivated him to get into the field of software development. In 2000, after a brief stint working for Singapore Airlines, he landed a job in the Chicago area and immigrated with his family to the United States.

Meanwhile, just beneath the surface, another story was unfolding in Raj's life. He explained to me that although he was born and raised in a Christian family and attended church every week, he was not a Christian "by heart." Raj added, "I was a Christian in the society, but not inside." Only through Kali's influence did he begin to realize this fact. He recalled,

> *One day . . . . when we were coming from another city to our town in a bus, she said, "You are all namesake Christians. God is not in your heart. You are a Christian by name. That's all. You don't know what real Christianity is." I was mad at her. You know why? She was from an orthodox Hindu family and she's accusing me that you are not a true Christian. Naturally I got mad . . . . Several journeys after that, she made me think, "You* really *are* wrong."

Even though Raj knew that something was missing in his spiritual life, he refused to admit it. "I was stiff," he confessed, "Honestly I say I was stiff. I realized, but I did not want to yield. I don't know why, maybe male ego . . . . Something was happening in me, but I was not convinced to show that out." Raj's sense of conviction grew stronger on their wedding day when he watched his bride get baptized publicly in a lake. He recalled his thoughts on that day:

> *When she took baptism, only I started thinking she was stronger than me in Christian belief and Christian doctrine. Definitely she was—still she is. And I started thinking even she is taking a baptism . . . . She is completing something in her mind, so why not me? So it was urging me . . . I cannot explain that feeling.*

It was more than a decade later that Raj finally decided to take action. He said that after they moved to the United States, they began attending a Baptist church. "The messages were good over there," he recalled, "The people, they were good and beyond that, we started praying every day at home. We, in Christian life, started coming together—nearer and nearer." A final turning point came when Raj heard a message preached on the topic of baptism. He explained, "The main thing [the preacher] underlined on that day was even Jesus got baptized. That's what [Kali] said. Then, I'm no better than Him, no way." So on November 26, 2001, twelve years after Kali's wedding day baptism, Raj and his two children were baptized together. "That was my birthday," he said with a smile, "On that day we were born again."

When I interviewed the Joshua family, 3 years had passed since Raj's baptism. They had become active members of Chicago Tamil Church where Raj directed the music ministry.

The Joshuas' Experiences as Worshippers

Although it had been 17 years since Kali had first put her faith in Jesus Christ, I was interested in knowing what she remembered about her experiences of worship as a Hindu and how becoming a Christian had affected her worship life. Kali began by talking about her experiences of worship in Hindu temples:

> *At the end of our street there was a temple. I used to go there every evening and pray. Yeah, we used to leave the lamb in front of the god and pray there—sit down and meditate for some time and go around the temple.*

She went on to describe how she had always felt like a mere "spectator" when worshipping in the temple because "the priest did everything." Furthermore, Kali was never exactly sure of what was going on because the language used for worship in the temple was Sanskrit, which she did not understand. On the positive side, Kali described worship in the temple as involving all the senses. Comparing it to her experiences of Christian worship, she said, "When I was a Hindu, sometimes we used to get together and pray—it was more emotional, more emotional . . . . it was a positive thing."

Kali recalled that as a Hindu, her family would often use devotional songs when they did *pooja*. Smiling, she said, "My father, he's a good singer. He used to sing all the time the Hindu devotional songs. He taught us a lot of songs too—all my sisters and brothers. Yeah, we used to sit down and sing sometimes."

When I asked how worship had changed for her when she became a Christian, Kali replied,

> *After I became a Christian, I stopped going to the temple. I used to pray at home every morning, evening. I think I used to say every time the word* thurtur—*it means "thank you God." I think I said it every minute. I thought there was a constant interaction between me and God after I became a Christian. But when I was a Hindu, I used to go to temple and pray. That was the only time I interact with those gods.*

She went on to describe in depth how becoming a Christian had changed the way she prayed. As a Hindu, Kali focused her prayers on her "worldly life." She explained,

> *I was so materialistic I think. I used to pray for the family's well-being and for everybody's health and for good studies and a good job and something for worldly life—earthly blessings. Though after I became a Christian, though I prayed for the worldly things, but it was not the only motive. My motive was to go to heaven and to tell God to other people.*

Festivals in Tamilian Christian life.

Kali's marriage to Raj brought her fully into the Christian lifestyle of Tamil Nadu. I asked Raj to tell me something about their experiences of worship as Christians in India. He began by describing three Christian festivals: Christmas, New Year, and Easter.

> *The Christmas day is almost equal to* Deepavali. *Crackers, you name it, the fireworks—everything will be*

> there. In individual homes you do it . . . . The main thing on Christmas day is cake. You make or purchase cakes—mostly purchase cakes . . . . We have a grand meal, go to a special service . . . . the Christmas day morning service, you cannot find a seat to sit. You got to go to the church at least 1 hour before to get a seat, because a lot of Christians are coming to church only on Christmas day. The church will be more than full on Christmas day. So Christmas day is a very grand function.

The second biggest festival for Tamilian Christians according to the Joshuas was New Year. The festival, they said, was celebrated in churches with a special "Watch Night Service" which Raj described:

> That is when you get into the new year, you are in the church. That is the custom for every Christian, and everybody will be there. They pray, husband and wife, holding hands and they really kneel down and pray. Even in the churches, no music, nothing will be played and there is perfect silence from 11:58 till 12:00—the countdown—perfect silence . . . . You feel full when you come out of the church.

Easter, Raj said, was not celebrated as grandly as the other two festivals. For example, he said that he would receive gifts of new clothes on Christmas and New Year but not on Easter.

Noting a number of similarities between the ways Tamilian Christians and Hindus celebrated festivals, I asked the Joshuas if they ever celebrated *Pongal* or *Deepavali* or if they had ever considered ways in which a Christian could do so without compromising his or her faith. Kali responded, "I don't celebrate because those things, *Deepavali* and *Pongal*, they are attributed to Hindu gods." Raj added, "If you go with them, maybe you get lost. I'm sorry to say that, but it's true."

Music in Tamilian Christian life.

Raj was more open to Hindu music. When in India, he would often visit the temples in order to hear the *Carnatic* and *Hindustani* musicians perform. "I really enjoy that music, I even played," he said. "They used to play in December. They used to go around the town singing right in the morning . . . . I used to go with them. Go with the Hindu priests . . . playing music for them."

His love for traditional Hindu music styles had an influence on his music ministry at Chicago Tamil Church. With the help of his daughter, Raj had begun writing Christian worship songs based on the *Carnatic* and *Hindustani* styles.

The Impact of Living in the United States on the Joshua' Spiritual Lives

Clearly, coming to the United States had a positive impact on Raj's spiritual life in that he not only grew spiritually together with his wife and children but also in that he had experienced what he described as a spiritual rebirth. Kali also felt that her spiritual life had improved:

> *I will think it's better here. Because, I don't know, maybe it's different for everybody. For me, I found a good church. The people are, I felt, are true Christians. They truly love each other. And they do anything to reach out to Hindu people or other religions.*

Raj added, "That is the great difference between [the church] where we go in India and here. The people who are doing the ministry are really doing the ministry here—no pretending."

The one negative that they mentioned about life in the United States had to do with their social life. Raj explained, "There is no social life in America at all . . . . Coming back from work, we are inside the house. We are not going out. We are not socializing."

Personal Experiences with God

As usual, I brought the interview to a close by asking them to reflect upon their spiritual lives as a whole. I wanted to know if they felt that they had ever experienced God in a personal or life-changing way. Kali was first to respond, "I think there are many times that I felt like that." She went on to describe a motorcycle accident in which she had been involved and how she had "miraculously escaped without any injury." Kali recalled, "At that time, I felt the presence of God . . . . I felt that some supernatural power was holding me without hurting me."

Raj also had a story to tell,

> *I felt God in one moment . . . when I was in Singapore by myself—my family was in India. I was in Singapore for some time. When I was there, I was staying with other guys, other engineers in one house, and one day they*

> *started drinking alcohol at night. I was tempted. I never tasted alcohol. So I was tempted, "Okay, why don't I try?" I almost went to the table—almost. I really felt God—something was intervening—I really did. I did not touch. Came back to my room and slept. I did not pray, did not. But in the morning, I felt something. Somebody was talking to me before I woke up. Might be a dream—I could not explain that, I really could not. Something, some kind of "Well done," "Good job," or something like that. Somebody giving me a pat on the back. I felt really is. Then I prayed. When I woke up, I prayed, "God it is you, I could feel you!" Even to this minute, I've never tasted alcohol.*

Immigrant Tamilian Christians at Worship in Chicago

When I conducted my research, the Tamilian Christian community in Chicago was very small and widely scattered. They had managed to form three small churches that held regular services: Calvary Church of South India in Downers Grove, Chicago Tamil Church in Hickory Hills, and Tamil United Church of Christ in Westchester. I had the opportunity to observe worship services at the latter two.

Chicago Tamil Church: Hickory Hills, IL

My first experience of worship with Tamilian Christians came on November 13, 2004, at Chicago Tamil Church (CTC) in the southwest Chicago suburb of Hickory Hills. The church was renting space at Steeple Hill Christian Life Center where they were holding worship services every Sunday afternoon. CTC also held a special Saturday evening worship service once a month.

I arrived for November's Saturday evening service at the advertised start time of 6:30 pm. Pastor Austin Albert Raj, with whom I had already spoken on the phone, greeted me in the foyer and invited me to sit with him so that we could get to know each other better. For the next 10 minutes or so, Pastor Raj and I spoke together about our respective ministries. He explained to me that CTC was a non-denominational church that he had helped form about 3 years earlier. About eight families regularly drove in from different parts of the metropolitan area in order to attend their services.

The service finally started at about 6:50 pm with about 15 Tamilians seated mostly in a few pews near the front of the sanctuary. As I entered, I was instantly noticed by the assembled worshippers and promptly offered a seat next to a middle-aged Tamilian man and his family. The sanctuary itself, I felt, bore no signs that Tamilians actually worshipped there save the obvious presence of the Tamilians themselves. The pews were arranged in rows facing a stage upon which was a four-and-a-half foot high wooden pulpit that had been positioned squarely in the middle. About ten feet behind it, a baptistery was built into the wall. Above the baptistery hung a black and white banner which read, "My house shall be called a house of prayer."

To begin the service, Pastor Raj, who was holding an electric guitar, and two teenage girls assembled behind microphones at the front of the sanctuary. Raj Joshua, whom I would later interview, sat in the front pew with a small electric drum set resting in his lap. His teenage daughter was on the stage seated behind a piano. Three preteen boys were in a pew to my left where one held a trombone, another had an acoustic guitar, and the third operated an overhead projector which displayed English song lyrics on a side wall.

Pastor Raj began by praying in Tamil. As he did, I noticed that a few women in saris covered their heads with their *ghunghats*, a practice they repeated during each subsequent prayer. Once the prayer ended, the musicians began to play. They started off with six songs that were all sung in English. The congregation remained seated throughout, with about a third of them singing along and a few clapping from time to time. At the end of the sixth song, Pastor Raj gently chided his people, saying in English, "We must learn new songs."

The music continued with songs that were in Tamil. A total of five Tamil songs were played. Some I recognized as English hymns that had been translated but others were unfamiliar to me. Most of the congregation sang and clapped their hands during the Tamil songs, with the exception of the children who seemed to be less comfortable with them. Even the musicians appeared to play the Tamil songs with more energy and skill. During the final song, the congregation stood together. As the music ended, several people raised their arms above their heads as Pastor Raj prayed.

At the end of his prayer, the musicians went to sit with the rest of the congregation and Pastor Raj made a few announcements. He then introduced me to the people as a "very fine missionary" and turned the service over to anyone who had a "special program" to present.

The boys with the guitar and trombone came to the front first and presented instrumental versions of "Joyful, Joyful, We Adore Thee" and "Amazing Grace." They were followed by the man sitting next to me who sang a Tamil song together with his preteen son. Finally, the teenage girls who had been helping to lead music earlier returned to their microphones to sing an English worship song that they had prepared.

Pastor Raj then made his way to the stage and got behind the pulpit. He preached a sermon on the topic of "Success in the Christian Life," in which he frequently switched back and forth between English and Tamil. Throughout the message, he would ask congregants to read passages aloud from the Bible and to answer questions that he raised.

After the sermon, a little boy of 6 or 7 years came around to the pews with a velvet bag into which people placed offerings of money. While this was going on, Raj Joshua's daughter returned to the piano to play and sing another song in English. Pastor Raj then led the congregation in a closing prayer and dismissed them with the words of a doxology quoted, in English, from the Bible.

The service ended at about 8:45 pm and was followed by a "fellowship dinner" that featured traditional Tamilian food for the adults and pizza for the children. People sat around tables in the church's dining hall and engaged in lively conversations while they ate. When I finally left the church at 10:00 pm, the fellowship showed no signs of ending.

Tamil United Church of Christ: Westchester, IL

The day after my visit to CTC, I drove to the western Chicago suburb of Westchester to attend one of the regular weekly services of Tamil United Church of Christ (Tamil UCC) which was renting meeting space from Westchester Community Church. I arrived at the church at 1:00 pm, about a half-hour before the service was scheduled to begin. As at CTC, I had the chance to speak briefly with the pastor.

Pastor Godwin Kanagaraj told me that the church began in 1998 as a merger between Chicago Tamil Koil and United Church of South India, Chicago. Since then, two other Chicago area Tamil churches had formed from among Tamil UCC's membership: CTC and Calvary Church of South India. Pastor Kanagaraj described his church as being "evangelistically-minded" with a special desire to reach Hindus living in Chicago with the gospel. In doing so, he stressed, "We will never hurt."

About twenty people were scattered throughout a dozen pews when the service began promptly at 1:30 pm. Though older than the one in which CTC met, the Westchester sanctuary was similarly designed and decorated. A man named Joe, whom I had met earlier, held a tambourine as he stood facing the congregation at the front of the church. To his left, two women dressed in saris stood behind microphones. On the opposite side were a woman with an electric guitar, a man sitting in the front pew with an electric drum set in his lap, and another man who sat on the floor behind a *tabla*. All the musicians were shoeless.

Joe began the service by praying aloud in Tamil. The musicians then led the congregation in three Tamil songs. I noticed that the people in the pews were energetically clapping and singing throughout all three but remained sitting until the third song began. After each song, Joe would again pray in Tamil.

The singing was followed by what Joe called a "witnessing time." In English, he said to the congregation, "If you have any testimony, come and share it with the church." After a couple minutes of silence, the man who had been playing the *tabla* stood and shared something in Tamil. When he finished, Joe prayed again and then he and the other musicians took seats among the rest of the congregation.

At that point, Pastor Kanagaraj, who was wearing a white robe over his suit and tie, walked to the stage from the pew where he had been sitting and stood behind the pulpit. He asked everyone to stand and began to lead the congregation in singing an English hymn while a teenage girl accompanied on piano. After the hymn, the congregation read a passage from the Bible aloud together. A small boy then went to the front of the sanctuary and stood behind a lectern that was in one corner of the stage. Opening a Bible, he read aloud another portion of Scripture.

After asking the congregation to be seated, Pastor Kanagaraj then took a few minutes to make announcements and to introduce me to the congregation. This was followed by another English hymn that was played and sung as a middle-aged man passed an offering plate among the congregants. The pastor then dismissed the children to go to their "Sunday school."

Once the children had filtered out of the sanctuary, Pastor Kanagaraj began to pray aloud in Tamil. Though I did not understand the words of his prayer, I felt that it sounded incredibly passionate and even seemed to have something of a rhythm to it. Pastor Kanagaraj went on without so much as a pause for a full ten minutes, gradually increasing in volume as he reached a climatic "Amen."

Prior to the start of the service, Pastor Kanagaraj had informed me that on that particular Sunday Tamil UCC was observing its traditional "Preacher's Sunday." He explained that each month, he asked a layperson in the church to prepare to preach. Pastor Kanagaraj felt that it was a good way to train up new leaders for future ministry. So after the pastor's passionate prayer, it was time for Victor Antoniswami to deliver his first sermon.

Victor preached in Tamil from the lectern. His sermon lasted about thirty minutes and from time to time elicited light laughter from the congregation. After Victor brought his message to a close, the congregation stood together to sing a final song in Tamil. Pastor Kanagaraj then dismissed the people with a prayer.

As at CTC, I was invited to join the people of Tamil UCC in a meal following the service. Traditional Tamil food was served along with a large pile of McDonald's McChicken Sandwiches that the children were eager to gobble up. I was warmly received by the people and engaged in several small conversations before I left the church at about 4:30 pm.

Data Analysis

My encounters with Tamilian immigrants yielded data of two basic types. First, by conducting interviews with both Hindus and Christians, I was able to record what Tamilian immigrants *said* about worship. Secondly, through participant observations of 4 Tamilian worship events, I was able to see firsthand what these same people *did* in worship.

Tamilian Worship Described

Seven major themes emerged from a cross-case analysis of the 3 interviews. Six of these themes focused on the role of various expressions in worship. Festivals, community, prayer, music, sacred places such as temples and church buildings, and spiritual teaching were all described as being connected to the worship experience. The seventh theme centered on descriptions of the subjects' personal experiences with God or a god.

The role of festival in Tamilian worship.

One of the most frequently discussed subjects throughout the 3 interviews was the role of festivals in worship. Kart, Arum, and Neela each portrayed religious festivals as their preferred mode of worship—central to their spiritual experience as Hindus. A total of five festivals were specifically mentioned by the 3 Hindus, with *Deepavali* and *Pongal* mentioned as personal favorites. *Deepavali* and *Pongal* were also considered to be the most important festivals in terms of their spiritual significance.

The 2 Christians interviewed also described the observance of religious festivals as significant to their worship experience. Christmas, New Year, and Easter were specifically mentioned, with Christmas and New Year being described as the two most prominent celebrations. Unlike their Hindu counterparts, however, Kali and Raj portrayed religious festivals as playing a more peripheral role in worship. More central to their worship experience as Christians were daily and weekly activities such as church services and private prayer.

A total of five festivals were described in depth in the 3 interviews. As Table 1 shows, the most common characteristics of festivals described as "most important" by the 5 Tamilians (i.e. *Pongal*, *Deepavali*, Christmas, and New Year) are that they involve family, food, gift-giving, decorations, and special worship services or *poojas*..

Despite the fact that certain similarities exist between how Christian and Hindu festivals were celebrated, Raj and Kali were in agreement that Christians should have nothing to do with Hindu religious celebrations. For Kali, her participation in festivals such as *Pongal* and *Deepavali* ceased as soon as she became a Christian because, as she said, "They are attributed to Hindu gods." Raj did not believe that it was possible for Christians to participate in Hindu festivals without compromising the principles of their faith.

Table 1: *Descriptions of Religious Festivals*

Traits	Pongal	Deepavali	Xmas	New Year	Ayutha Pooja
Religious association	Hindu	Hindu	Christian	Christian	Hindu
Described as important family celebration	Yes	Yes	Yes	Yes	No
Theological or mythic background explained	Yes	Yes	No	Yes	Yes
Role of food in festival	Sweet rice prepared, "Pongal sweets" distributed	"Sweets" distributed special meal	Large meal, "cakes" made or purchased	No data	No data
Games or contests described	"Bull-fighting"	None	None	None	None
Gifts received during festival	Money, new clothes	New clothes	New clothes	New clothes	None
Decor described	Cattle decorated with flowers, fine cloths, etc	Colorful lights	Xmas tree	Candles in churches	No data
Use of firecrackers	No	Yes	Yes	No	No
Description of special worship services or poojas	Worship of sun and cattle	Worship of god Murugan	Christmas day service in church	"Watch Night" service in church, families praying together	Worship of tools of trade

The role of community in Tamilian worship.

Closely related to the subjects' discussion of religious festivals was their frequent reference to the role of community in Tamilian worship. All 5 interviewees indicated that relationships with family and friends were to some extent connected to worship. Raj's discussion of the community-worship connection was mostly limited to descriptions of worshipping at home with his wife and children. The other 4 Tamilians, however, had a more expansive view of this connection. They each spoke at length about the role of extended family members, friends, and even neighbors in worship.

For the 3 Hindus, the community-worship connection was so strong that each of them reported that moving away from friends and family to live in the United States had detrimentally impacted their spiritual life. As immigrants, Kart and the Rajans confessed that they were less motivated to observe the festivals and more likely to neglect Hindu religious customs such as dietary regulations, *poojas*, and regularly worshipping at temples. Furthermore, they admitted that their experiences of worship in the United States were less meaningful to them than their previous experiences of worship in India where they had been in close proximity to friends and family.

The role of prayer in Tamilian worship.

Prayer was a key expression of worship for all 5 of the Tamilians interviewed. There was, however, a difference in how the Christian subjects and the Hindu subjects described mature prayer. Kart, Arum, and Neela all felt that they had experienced a maturing in their prayer lives when their prayers moved from petitions for their own personal needs and desires to intercessory prayers for the well-being of others. Arum, for example, described an episode of praying for his mother's health as being one of the most meaningful spiritual experiences he had ever had. On the other hand, the 2 Christians viewed mature prayer as going beyond material concerns altogether and incorporating elements of personal dialogue with God. Kali described this as a "constant interaction" between herself and God that began after she became a Christian.

The role of music in Tamilian worship.

The role of music in worship was considered significant by all the interview subjects. The Tamilians explained that music was used in particular to express devotion to God or a god. Kart and the Rajans said that they continued to use indigenous Tamil music on a daily basis in their worship lives. Raj reported that he was active in composing Christian worship music that was modeled after musical styles indigenous to Tamilians.

The role of sacred place in Tamilian worship.

When asked to describe the most peaceful experiences they had ever had, the 3 Hindus all responded by telling about the sense of peace they experienced when visiting temples. They all seemed to feel that simply being in the buildings was itself an act of worship that resulted in feelings of peacefulness. Raj and Kali did not describe church buildings in the same way. For them, it was the activities that took place in the buildings that was significant for the worship experience rather than the buildings themselves.

The role of discourse and literature in Tamilian worship.

Spiritual teaching in the form of discourse or literature was less important for the Hindus than it was for the Christians. Only Arum mentioned reading as having played a significant role in his spiritual life and none of the three Hindus mentioned being influenced by preaching, lectures, speeches, or other forms of religious discourse. Raj and Kali, however, stressed that literature and discourse had played extremely important roles in their lives as worshippers. They had both been influenced by sermons to make initial commitments to embrace the gospel. Furthermore, they each considered regular Bible study to be foundational to their spiritual lives as Christians.

Tamilian worship and encountering the Divine.

Kart and Arum recounted providential experiences that they attributed to divine intervention. For Kart, his experience of being given the opportunity to work in the United States left him feeling amazed by God. When Arum's mother was restored to health after a prolonged illness, he felt it had been an answer to prayer. None of the three Hindus, however, felt that they had ever encountered God in either a personal or a deeply life-changing way.

Raj and Kali, on the other hand, vividly recounted experiences in which they felt they had personally encountered God. They also each described how their lives had been radically changed through spiritual experiences.

Tamilian Worshippers in Action

My observations of 4 Tamilian worship events resulted in the identification of several elements that were common to Tamilian worshippers regardless of their religious beliefs. In both Hindu and

Christian worship events, interpersonal relationships, feasting, prayer, and the presentation of offerings to God or a god played key roles. Both Hindus and Christians also made special efforts to involve their children in worship practices.

There were a number of differences, however. In the 2 Hindu worship events—both festivals—interpersonal interaction was central to the experience. The majority of the time at these festivals was spent in eating and carrying on conversations. By contrast, the 2 Christian events each devoted only about half the time to interpersonal interaction. Instead, prayer and music were the central components of the Christian events. Also, the Christian events were more structured and, unlike the Hindu events, featured both spiritual teaching and worshipper testimonies about spiritual experiences. The Hindu events, however, were more sensual, incorporating worship expressions that appealed to touch, taste, smell, and sight. As shown in Table 2, a total of 16 elements were identified as being used in a least one of the four worship events.

Table 2: *Observations of Tamilian Worship Events*

Element	Karthigai Deepam	Thalial*	Tamil UCC	CTC
Private gathering for invited guests	Yes	Yes	No	No
Open to the public	No	No	Yes	Yes
Venue	Home	Home	Church building	Church building
Structure of event	Improvisational	Improvisational	Planned	Planned
Ceremonial requirements for participation (cleansing, etc.)	Yes	Unknown	No	No
Ceremonial adornment involved	Yes (optional)	No	Yes (optional)	Yes (optional)
Time devoted to interpersonal relations	Yes (central aspect)	Yes (central aspect)	Yes	Yes
Feasting together	Yes	Yes	Yes	Yes
Time(s) of prayer	Yes (5-minute *pooja*)	No	Yes (central aspect)	Yes
Use of music	No	No	Yes	Yes (central aspect)
Offering types	Food, water, fire	None	Monetary	Monetary
Use of *pratika* (images, idols)	Yes	No	No	No

Table 2 (Continued): *Observations of Tamilian Worship Events*

Element	Karthigai Deepam	Thalial*	Tamil UCC	CTC
Ceremonial use of candles or lights	Yes	No	No	No
Spiritual teaching	No	No	Yes	Yes
Discussion of personal spiritual experiences	No	No	Yes	Yes
Efforts to involve second-generation Tamilians in worship	Yes	No	Yes	Yes

(* Note: Although no *pooja* was performed at the time of my observation, the Rams and Rajans may have done so earlier in the day.)

Part 5: Conclusions

At the end of my interview with Arum and Neela Rajan, with Kart having also joined us in the room, I turned off the camera I had been using to record the session and said to my 3 Hindu friends, "You know, I've been asking you all kinds of questions and you've answered them all honestly and fully. Is there anything you want to ask me?" After a short pause, Arum responded, "How did you get so deep into religious things?"

Just a few hours earlier I had prayed for the interview, asking that God would grant that at the end of our time I would have the chance to share how my life had been changed through a personal experience with Jesus Christ. As I shared my testimony of faith with the Tamilians that night, I could not keep from smiling, knowing that God had answered my prayer.

That evening as I drove home, I was filled with a sense of excitement because I knew that God was at work in the hearts of my Hindu friends. It had become clear to me that it was only a matter of time before they too would decide to follow Jesus as their Lord and worship Him alone. Such a realization helps me to grasp the import of this research project. If it is true that one day immigrant Tamilian Hindus like Kart and the Rajans will embrace the gospel, then at some point—after the initial excitement subsides—they will be faced with all sorts of questions as to how they should go about worshipping Jesus Christ.

Considerations for Contextualizing Christian Worship

So, what should worship look like for immigrant Tamilian Christians of Hindu backgrounds? How can they experience God personally and meaningfully without compromising their new found faith with syncretistic practices? Unfortunately, a comprehensive answer to that question is a bit beyond the scope of this project, not to mention my expertise. However, the time I spent with Tamilians of both faiths in interviews and during their worship events has yielded a number of insights that I believe are worthy of consideration.

What "Going to Church" Should Mean

A week before I began writing this report, my wife and I had the opportunity to take the Rams and the Rajans to a Christmas celebration that was held by Tamil UCC. We all had a great time and the event was clearly a significant one for both couples in their consideration of the gospel. As we left the church, however, Suganthi Ram shared with my wife Katherine that she was disappointed that the event had been held entirely in the basement of the church building. Apparently, Suganthi had been eager to go inside the church's sanctuary. At first, I dismissed this as mere curiosity but as I reflected further on Suganthi's comments, I realized that they had stemmed from a perspective of worship that attributed great significance to sacred spaces.

In the Tamilian Hindu worship experience, simply going to a place that is considered sacred by the worshipper is in itself an act of worship. All 3 Hindus indicated this fact in their interviews. This, of course, differs from the mindset of Protestant Christians who generally attribute little spiritual significance to places of worship such as church buildings. If an expression of Christian worship is to be truly contextualized for Tamilians of Hindu backgrounds, "going to church" must therefore become a spiritual experience through which a Christian can encounter God in a meaningful way. A significant obstacle to this is the fact that groups of Tamilian Christians in the United States will likely be small and able only to afford to meet in private homes or in rented spaces. Thus, the challenge becomes developing a way to transform environments that are associated with common activities into sacred spaces for worship.

Worship for All the Senses

Tamilian Hindu worship involves all the senses. There is music and "bursting crackers" for the ears, feasting and *"Pongal* sweets" for the tongue, and images and idols for the eyes. During *poojas* worshippers commonly "show fire" and use their hands to feel the heat of the flame. In temples, offerings of food, incense, and flowers fill the air with their pleasing aromas.

Beyond this, Tamilian Hindus utilize a wide variety of forms as expressions of worship. Everything from drama and ceremonial adornment to gift-giving and even flying kites has its place in their worship experience.

The Tamilian Christian worship experience is comparatively less diverse both in terms of its expression and its appeal to the senses. However, it is clear from this research that Christian worship is particularly well-adapted for spiritual instruction and exhortation due to the prominence of teaching and Bible study.

There is, I believe, great potential for combining the intellectual appeal of traditional Christian worship with the sensory appeal of Hindu worship into a worship expression that is both Christ-honoring and contextually relevant to Tamilian Christians of Hindu backgrounds. Obviously, there are certain practices (e.g. idol worship) that are incompatible with a Christian worldview and must therefore be excluded. Nevertheless, Christians must experiment with a wide variety of indigenous Tamilian worship forms and even create new forms if they hope to develop an expression of Christian worship that is truly rich and meaningful.

Elevating the Role of Festival in Christian Worship

Perhaps the most glaring distinction between the ways in which Tamilian Christians and Tamilian Hindus worship lies in the importance attributed by each group to the role of festivals. For Christians, festivals are important but merely peripheral to their overall experience as worshippers. To Hindus, on the other hand, festivals are absolutely central to worship. They are, as V. Francis Vineeth explained, sacred times during which a worshipper "moves from this world to the other world and participates in the life of God" (1987, p. 133).

It is important to note that Tamilian Hindu festivals are not just big parties. Occurring throughout the year, the festivals are each observed in specific ways that incorporate a variety of both celebratory and somber worship expressions. Thus, a Hindu who faithfully observes at least the major festivals will experience regular periods of prayer, vigil, fasting, feasting, celebration, and meditation. The result is a spirituality that is actually rather well-balanced.

Therefore, elevating the role of festival in Christian worship is not only a good way of making the Christian experience more familiar to Tamilians of Hindu backgrounds but it could also be a very effective means of promoting spiritual growth among Christians. Traditionally, Christians have been exhorted to practice spiritual disciplines such as prayer, fasting, Bible study, Scripture memory, and meditation. Incorporating a festival system would provide both a framework for the regular exercise of such disciplines as well as a structure of accountability in that Christians would experience these expressions of worship together.

For Tamilian immigrants, considerable freedom exists for the development of a Christian festival calendar. However, Christians should not be afraid to utilize elements of the existing Hindu calendar in the process. Celebrating Christian versions of festivals like *Deepavali* or *Pongal* at the same time as Tamilian Hindus would communicate a sense of cultural affinity that would challenge the centuries-old notion of Christianity as a non-Indian religion. Furthermore, Christian versions of Hindu festivals would provide excellent opportunities for outreach. Particularly in Chicago, where the most cohesive and well-organized communities of Tamilians are the churches, the potential exists for Christians to not only sponsor the best *Pongal* celebration in town but to do so in a way that honors Jesus Christ and communicates His love.

The Horizontal Dimension of Tamilian Worship

In his article on Hindu festivals, V. Francis Vineeth explained that Hindu worship essentially had four goals: union with God, union with fellow-beings, union with nature, and union with oneself (1987, p. 136). Of these four, Vineeth stressed that in orthodox Hinduism uniting with God, which was known as *Utsava* or "elevation," was "understood as the supreme bliss to which man enters" (1987, p. 135). However, in my interviews with the 3 Tamilian Hindus, only union with fellow-beings emerged as a major theme. All 3 Hindus admitted to never having had a significant experience of feeling united with God—at least not in a personal or life-changing way. Moreover, notions of uniting with nature or self were only very briefly discussed. Thus it appears that in the experience of immigrant Tamilian Hindus it is not the vertical but rather the horizontal or social dimension of worship that is so crucial.

The fact is that even without a significant experience of *Utsava*, Kart and the Rajans were consistent in their participation in worship events and rituals as long as they remained in India. It was only when their union with fellow worshippers was cut off through immigrating to the United States that their system of worship began to crumble. In an informal follow-up conversation that I had with Kart, he validated this by confessing, "When I came to the U.S. as a single man, I didn't do anything—no *Pongal*, no *Deepavali*." Only after the birth of his son did Kart experience a renewed desire to participate in Hindu worship.

The importance of the horizontal dimension in Tamilian Hindu worship has significant implications for those who seek to develop a contextualized expression of Christian worship. To put it bluntly, any effort of contextualization for Tamilian Christians of Hindu backgrounds must find a way to incorporate the horizontal dimension into the Christian worship experience. This, of course, must be done in a way that accents rather than overshadows the true *Utsava* experience that only Christianity provides.

A final point is worth mentioning regarding this horizontal dimension of worship. Plenty of room exists in Scripture not only to provide for the accommodation of a social component in Christian worship but perhaps even to make a case for it as a Biblical mandate. One key passage along these lines is found in the first epistle of John: "for he who does not love his brother whom he has seen cannot love God whom he has not seen" (1 John 4:20b).

The Tamilian Church: Obstacles and Opportunities

Unfortunately, the Tamilian church's reputation of being essentially foreign in its worship expression has become something of a tradition as each new generation rehearses many of the missiological blunders of their predecessors. Every Tamilian Christian that I spoke with, whether in formal interview settings or in various informal conversations that occurred at the Tamilian churches, was opposed to the idea of using Hindu festivals as opportunities for Christian worship or outreach. They were convinced that such events were simply off-limits for Christians because the festivals were "attributed to Hindu gods." While the Tamilian church's passion for orthodoxy is to be admired and commended, if this crippling fear of syncretism is maintained, the Tamilian Christians will continue to find it extremely difficult to reach their Hindu brothers and sisters with the gospel.

My research has convinced me that immigrant Tamilian Christians have an incredible opportunity to be used of God to reach Hindus for Christ. The immigrant Tamilian Hindus in Chicago are aware of a great spiritual void in their lives. Not only do they feel disconnected from God but life in the United States has left them feeling disconnected from Hindu spirituality in general because of their separation from a cohesive worshipping community. Like no one else, Tamilian Christians have a chance to address this void. They know the music, language, customs, and common worship expressions of Tamilian Hindus and are thus in a position to create experiences that will help Hindus feel connected to an authentically Tamilian worshipping community. Once these horizontal yearnings are satisfied, Tamilian Christians will no doubt find ample opportunity for helping their Hindu brothers and sisters finally connect with God in a personal and deeply life-changing way.

Recommendations for Future Research

This subject, of course, is far from exhausted. A number of recommendations for future research have come to mind during the course of this project. I will briefly mention four.

Contextualization of Christianity for Modern Folk Hindus

Something of a gap exists between the descriptions of worship in the literature I reviewed, which largely focused on contextualizing Christian worship for orthodox Hindus, and the common experience of my Hindu subjects. There is a need for further research into contextualization issues that are relevant to the experience of modern folk Hindus like the ones featured in this study.

Compelling and Sensitive Missiological Education for the Tamilian Church

Future researchers should take a utilization-focused approach to this subject in order to develop a program for encouraging and training Tamilian Christian in the principles of contextualization. Such a program must be both effective in mobilizing the Tamilian church to put these principles into practice and sensitive to the fact that there is much of value in Tamilian Christian heritage.

Contextualization Models that Incorporate the Horizontal Dimension

As far as the horizontal dimension of Tamilian Hindu worship has been incorporated into the Christian worship experience, case studies should be presented, analyzed, and interpreted.

Larger Scale Study

Finally, as has been previously mentioned, the sample used for this research was quite small, consisting of interviews with just 5 Tamilians and observations of only 4 worship events. Expanding the study to include more interviews and observations would be beneficial. In particular, future studies could consider immigrant Tamilian Hindus who are significantly older, who have been in the United States for longer periods of time, or who live in close proximity to clusters of other Tamilian Hindus.

References

Adinarayan, S.P. (1956). Indigenization of worship and its psychology. *Indian Journal of Theology*, 5(2), 27-30.

Amaladoss, M. (1973). Searching together. In Sister Vandana (Ed.), *Indian spirituality in action* (pp. 35-47). Bombay: R.B. Pinto, Asian Trading Corporation.

Bhajanananda, Swami (1980). Worship in Hinduism and Christianity. In C.M. Vadakkekara (Ed.), *Prayer and contemplation* (pp. 311-329). Bangalore: Asirvanam Benedictine Monastery.

Carner, Gerald L. (1998). Kirthan, the effective means of communication. In Jey J. Kanagaraj (Ed.), *Mission and missions: Essays in honour of I. Ben Wati* (pp. 175-189). Pune, India: Union Biblical Seminary.

Chenoweth, Vida. (1984). Spare them Western music. *Evangelical Missions Quarterly*, 20(1), 30-35.

Consultation on World Evangelization Mini-Consultation on Reaching Hindus (1980). *Christian witness to Hindus*. Wheaton, IL: Lausanne Committee for World Evangelization

Garrett, T.S. (1958). The Indian Church as worship. *Indian Journal of Theology*, 7, 127-133.

Griffiths, Bede. (1973a). Introduction. In Sister Vandana (Ed.), *Indian spirituality in action* (pp. 10-14). Bombay: R.B. Pinto, Asian Trading Corporation.

Griffiths, Bede. (1973b). The Sources of Indian Spirituality. In Sister Vandana (Ed.), *Indian spirituality in action* (pp. 63-67). Bombay: R.B. Pinto, Asian Trading Corporation.

Hedlund, Roger E. (1998). The search for indigenous church models in India. In Jey J. Kanagaraj (Ed.), *Mission and missions: Essays in honour of I. Ben Wati* (pp. 162-174). Pune, India: Union Biblical Seminary.

Lederle, Matthew. (1973). Interpreting Christ through Indian art. In Sister Vandana (Ed.), *Indian spirituality in action* (pp. 130-141). Bombay: R.B. Pinto, Asian Trading Corporation.

Rangaswamy, Padma. (1995). Asian Indians in Chicago: Growth and change in a model minority. In Melvin G. Holli & Peter d'A. Jones (Eds.), *Ethnic Chicago: A multicultural portrait* (438-462). Grand Rapids: Wm. B. Eerdmans Publishing

Scott, David C. (1986). Worship in an Indian Christian ethos. *Bangalore Theological Forum*, 18, 75-84.

Sheth, Noel. (1973). Towards an Indian Christian spirituality. In Sister Vandana (Ed.), *Indian spirituality in action* (pp. 112-121). Bombay: R.B. Pinto, Asian Trading Corporation.

Perry, Cindy. (1990). "Bhai-Tika" and "Tij Braka": A case study in the contextualization of two Nepali festivals. *Missiology: An International Review,* 18(2), 177-183.

Vineeth, V. Francis. (1987). Religio-cultural festival of India. *Journal of Dharma,* 12, 133-144.

Younger, Paul (1993). Hindu-Christian worship settings in South India. In Harold Coward (Ed.), *Hindu-Christian dialogue: Perspectives and encounters* (pp. 191-197). Delhi: Motilal Banarsidass Publishers.

Chapter 4:
Tamilians in Mission History: *Considering the Example of Roberto de Nobili and his Contextualization Efforts in 17th Century Tamil Nadu*

Cody C. Lorance
Pastor / Church Planting Leader
Trinity International Baptist Mission
Carol Stream, IL

From the sultry confines of his prison cell in Madurai, India in 1640, Father Sebastian de Maya watched in wonder as his aged cellmate and fellow missionary Roberto de Nobili continued to energetically minister to the visitors that came "from morning to night." In spite of illness, malnutrition, and otherwise terrible living conditions, as de Maya observed, "Father Robert is constantly preaching the Gospel to them; and all go away pleased . . . ."[1] Such tirelessness and effectiveness, while new to de Maya, were certainly not uncommon for de Nobili whose half century of work in southern India launched a movement that would eventually reach tens of thousands of Hindus for Christ.

Key to this rapid spread of Christianity was that de Nobili, driven by his love for the Hindus, strove to develop a way of sharing the gospel that was both culturally relevant and doctrinally sound. His was not a complete success, however, as lingering elements of his cultural heritage as a missionary of the Counter Reformation continued to shape the mission in a manner that would contribute to its ultimate decline.

Towards Cultural Relevance

In November of 1606, Roberto de Nobili arrived in the south Indian city of Madurai to join Gonçalo Fernandez, a Portuguese Jesuit 36 years his senior, who had been operating the mission there for more than a decade. The mission's stagnation was quickly evident to de Nobili, who was disturbed to discover that in all his years of work Fernandez had failed to make a single local convert.[2] In a letter to his relative and fellow Jesuit, Fabio de Fabiis, de Nobili described his initial reaction to the situation in Madurai, "When I arrived in this city . . . I found that the demon had so well closed the doors against the Holy Gospel that, though we had in this town a residence for the last fifteen years, nothing could be done . . . ."[3]

Something would be done, however. De Nobili's love for souls would not allow him to spend his life in fruitless ministry. He had been sent to Madurai to win the locals to faith in Christ and he was committed to do whatever was necessary in order to accomplish that goal.

Soon, the reasons for Fernandez's failure became clear to the new missionary. Through many conversations with his Tamil language tutor, a

---

[1] S. Rajamanickam, "De Nobili in the Madurai Jail: A Letter of Sebastian de Maya," *Indian Church History Review* 18 (1984): 87-93.

[2] Vincent Cronin, *A Pearl to India: The Life of Roberto de Nobili* (New York: Dutton, 1959), 39.

[3] Ines G. Županov, *Disputed Mission: Jesuit Experiments and Brahmanical Knowledge in Seventeenth-century India* (New Delhi, India: Oxford University Press, 1999), 203.

Hindu and native of the city, de Nobili began to understand the implications that the intricate Indian caste system had on the Madurai mission. De Nobili learned that Indian society was divided into a number of rigidly structured hierarchical groupings called "castas" by the Portuguese missionaries. A person's caste was determined by birth and upward mobility was impossible.[4] In a report to the Jesuit General Claudio Acquaviva in 1615, de Nobili explained that one's caste is of the utmost importance because social rank, profession, and even perceived levels of "refinement and cleanliness [are] peculiar to each class."[5] Furthermore, as caste rules governed a person's diet, dress, social manners, and relationships, any violation resulted in severe consequences ranging from ritual uncleanness to public beatings and the loss of one's caste. De Nobili explains that losing caste was considered "the worst of evils:"

> *Many would willingly undergo death to redeem it, and not infrequently they do! For as soon as anyone is degraded from the order of his clan he becomes an outcast, deprived of all honor and hereditary dignity, thrown out from any meeting held by members of his grade, scornfully denied any fellowship with his social equals and kinsfolk, and separated from intercourse and companionship with his own family members.*[6]

De Nobili discovered that Fernandez's failure was due to an inadequate knowledge of the caste system coupled with what Princeton missiologist Alan Neely has deemed a major "linguistic *faux pas.*"[7] It resulted from a misunderstanding of the word *Parangi,* the moniker the Indians had applied to the missionaries, which Fernandez believed simply to be the Tamil word for "Portuguese."[8] To the locals, however, the word "signified in the most pejorative sense the polluted, uncultured, contemptuous foreigners and their proselytes. Parangis were despised . . . because they ate meat, drank wine (usually to excess), bathed irregularly, wore leather

---

[4] Alan Neely, *Christian Mission: A Case Study Approach* (Maryknoll, NY: Orbis Books, 1995), 36-37, 45-46.

[5] Roberto de Nobili, *Preaching Wisdom to the Wise,* trans. Anand Amaladass and Francis X. Clooney (St. Louis: The Institute of Jesuit Sources, 2000), 62.

[6] De Nobili, 217-218.

[7] Neely, 46.

[8] Cronin, 45.

shoes, and ignored the rules of social intercourse."[9] What made this especially problematic was Fernandez's insistence on using the term as a badge of honor, even using it as a synonym for "Christian." When asking a Hindu to become a Christian, he used the phrase, *"Prangui kulam puguda venumo,"* which would have been understood as, "Do you want to fall down among the outcaste Parangis and become Parangi?"[10] Naturally, the Hindus began to see Christianity as the religion of the *Parangis* and rejected outright any possibility of conversion due to its inevitable consequence—the loss of caste.

Such a revelation set de Nobili on the path of *accommodatio*, the missionary method the Jesuit order had made famous in the generations prior to de Nobili through the works of Matteo Ricci in China and Alessandro Valignano in Japan. Like Ricci and Valignano, de Nobili sought to remove the barriers that lay between the Hindus of caste and faith in Christ by stripping both the Christian message and the Christian messenger of their respective "cultural 'enclothing'"—that which was strictly European rather than "supracultural revelation from God"—thus leaving only the bare essentials.[11] He then adopted a variety of forms indigenous to the Indian culture in order to create a culturally relevant or contextualized expression of Christianity. Essentially this meant for de Nobili and his message a radical conversion from Western European to high-caste Indian. The driving force behind this transformation process was the conviction that the Indian people whom he was growing to love needed the message of Jesus Christ, a message they would accept only if "communicated in the proper way."[12]

De Nobili's transformation was by no means simple or immediate; rather it was a complicated and life-long learning process not without its blunders. Space permits here only a brief sampling of his contextualization method—a process of adaptation and accommodation which targeted the messenger, the message, and Hindu culture.

---

[9] Neely, 47.

[10] Cronin, 45.

[11] Charles H. Kraft, "Toward a Christian Ethnotheology," in *God, Man and Church Growth*, ed. Alan R. Tippett (Grand Rapids: Eerdmans, 1973), 113.

[12] De Nobili, 33.

The Messenger

De Nobili knew that in order to successfully communicate the gospel with the Hindus of Madurai, he would have to not only distinguish himself from the despised *Parangis* but also present himself as a holy man in the Indian context. He soon learned that just as a Jesuit priest would be typically regarded in Catholic Europe as embodying that culture's ideals of piety, so in south India the holiest of persons were those renunciants known as *sannyāsīs*.[13]

Not unlike a Jesuit, a *sannyāsī* took a vow of poverty and devoted his life to prayer, study, asceticism, and training disciples. His appearance was unique: a saffron-colored cotton cloth draped from the shoulders, painful wooden sandals, a bamboo staff with seven knots, and a gourd of water. A *sannyāsī's* head would be shaved and his forehead painted with sandalwood paste. His diet was severe, consisting of only one meal of rice and herbs daily. For the *sannyāsī's* austerities, he would be highly regarded and often sought out for spiritual counsel and instruction.[14]

Such was the life de Nobili determined to live in spite of the protests of Fernandez who felt such radical methods to "be a denial of the gospel."[15] In a 1619 letter to Pope Paul V, de Nobili explained his theory:

> *When I noticed that certain Brahmins* [sannyāsīs] *were highly praised because they led lives of great hardships and austerity and were looked upon as if they had dropped from the sky, I thought that . . . I could, to win them to Christ, conform myself to their mode of life in all such things which were not repugnant to the holiness of Christian doctrine . . . Therefore I professed to be an Italian Brahmin who had renounced the world, had studied wisdom at Rome and rejected all the pleasures and comforts of this world.*[16]

De Nobili therefore proceeded to exchange his cassock for the garb and lifestyle of a *sannyāsī* and move out of the mission and into a private

---

[13] Cronin, 47.

[14] Cronin, 47.

[15] Neely, 47.

[16] S. Rajamanickam, "The Goa Conference of 1619 (A Letter of Fr Robert de Nobili to Pope Paul V)," *Indian Church History Review* 2 (1968): 85.

hermitage in an area of the city populated by high-caste Indians, attempting to embrace the Hindu culture as his own.

Gradually, de Nobili's contextualization efforts began to gain him acceptance and respect among the locals. The label of *Parangi*, while renewed from time-to-time by persecutors, seemed to no longer apply. Eventually, even the Brahmins, the members of the highest Indian caste, began visiting the new *sannyāsī*. In fact, de Nobili gained such popularity among the Hindus that he had to set strict limits as to whom he would allow to visit him. Thus he wrote to Acquaviva, "As I do not want to waste my time . . . I have told [my visitors] clearly that, except for questions and arguments which regard the soul, I do not wish to treat of any other philosophical subject." His superior Alberto Laerzio explained to Acquaviva that it was necessary for de Nobili to not "allow people to see him at any time they please. It is only when visitors have called two or three times and begged his interpreter to let them speak to [de Nobili] that he allows them to . . . have a speech with him."[17]

The Message

The receptivity of de Nobili's Hindu audience was not due only to his personal transformation, however. The Italian *sannyāsī* also managed to adapt the Christian message to the ideas, forms, and languages of India. This difficult contextualization process began with the mastery of languages.

The *lingua franca* of the region was Tamil. This de Nobili mastered so thoroughly that later generations have referred to him as the "Father of Tamil Prose." He also learned and wrote in Telugu and, in spite of Brahmin prohibitions against it, Sanskrit. Sanskrit, he found, held in Hindu culture "the same place as Latin" did in western Catholicism—a language for religious functions and philosophical discourse. By the end of his life, de Nobili had composed numerous works of prose and poetry in these languages including more than forty in Tamil alone.[18]

Learning the languages of Madurai opened a way for de Nobili to enter the world of Hindu religious thought and literature. This he eagerly did having been granted access to the secret knowledge of the Hindu religious texts—the Vedas—by a well-respected Sanskrit scholar, Śivadarma, who

---

[17] Cronin, 75, 80, 85.

[18] Michael Amaladoss, "Nobili, Robert de," in *Biographical Dictionary of Christian Missions*, ed. Gerald H. Anderson (New York: Simon & Schuster Macmillan, 1998), 498; S Rajamanickam, "The Goa Conference," 85.

would eventually become the first Brahmin Christian in the Madurai mission.[19] So complete was de Nobili's assimilation of the language, philosophy, texts, and communication forms of the Hindus that after a visit to the hermitage, Laerzio was compelled to write:

> *The Father* [de Nobili] *speaks the purest Tamil and pronounces it so well that even the most fastidious Brahmin scholars cannot improve on his diction. He has already read many books, and learned by heart the essential passages of their laws as well as many verses of their famous poets . . . Many are the hymns he has learned by heart, and he sings them with such perfection and grace that all listen to him with pleasure and unconcealed admiration.*[20]

Modern scholarship has recognized the excellence of de Nobili's communication as well, noting the unusual clarity and forcefulness of his writings, his ability to integrate Sanskrit with his Tamil texts in the fashion of the Brahmin scholars, and his use of terms etymologically equivalent to the Latin in order to express difficult theological concepts.[21]

It must not be assumed, however, that de Nobili's contextualization of the Christian message amounted to mere external "packaging." While it is true that his message retained its doctrinal orthodoxy and Thomist influences, it cannot be said that Hindu ideas played only a superficial role. Francis X. Clooney has asked a poignant question in this regard, "Is it likely that someone could live for fifty years in a Hindu environment, eat and live and dress like a Hindu, learn Hindu scriptures and philosophy . . . without interiorizing and 'owning' some of that religion and religious truth?"[22] Indeed, de Nobili did seem to have interiorized Hindu concepts that he found to be of particular value in understanding Christianity. For example, de Nobili began to understand and communicate the doctrine of Christ's incarnation through the Hindu concept of "divine guru," emphasizing the significance of Jesus' manner of life and its conformity to

---

[19] Cronin, 110.

[20] Cronin, 81.

[21] De Nobili, 35.

[22] Francis X. Clooney, "Christ as the Divine Guru in the Theology of Roberto de Nobili," in *One Faith, Many Cultures: Inculturation, Indigenization, and Contextualization,* ed. Ruy O. Costa (Maryknoll, NY: Orbis Books, 1988) 26.

His teaching. This concept, according to Clooney, could help "the Christian community throughout the world to see Christ in a new way, more completely than has hitherto been possible in our history."[23] Undoubtedly, it was the idea of Christ as the Divine Guru that led de Nobili to the conviction that the gospel must be communicated in deed as well as in word. It must surely have been his inspiration for writing these words in 1649 to his sister, a leading nun in her convent: "Be careful that you teach nothing which is not, by God's grace, found doubly in you . . . ."[24]

The persecution that arose against de Nobili numerous times throughout his life is enough evidence to demonstrate that his Hindu audience readily recognized the distinct nature of his teaching. Nevertheless, he was able to so penetrate Hindu thought with his message that many caste Hindus, including Brahmins, embraced the gospel. By 1610 de Nobili had seen sixty Hindus become Christians. Two years later that number had tripled and by the time of his death in 1656, the total of baptized believers surpassed 4,000. As a further testimony to de Nobili's success in contextualizing the Christian message, locals began to refer to him as *Tattuva Bodhakar*—or the "Teacher of Reality."[25]

The Indian Culture

Contextualization for de Nobili was not merely a matter of adaptation but also of adoption. Many cultural forms and rituals indigenous to the Madurai Indians were incorporated into the life of the church to complete the construction of a culturally relevant expression of Christianity. For example, de Nobili blessed and distributed the sandalwood paste that the Indians used ornamentally to cover the "nakedness" of their foreheads. During the annual festival of Pongal when the residents of Madurai boiled rice before the idol Vighneś, instead of causing his neophytes the disgrace of not participating in the festivities, he simply replaced the idol with a cross and said a blessing over the rice.[26] Moreover, while de Nobili was careful to teach his congregation that even outcaste Christians deserved love and respect, he essentially upheld the caste system, undoubtedly

---

[23] Clooney, "Christ as the Divine Guru," 28-29, 37.

[24] Cronin, 265.

[25] Cronin, 127, 129, 161, 263.

[26] Cronin, 118-120.

finding it not altogether different from the sharp class distinctions he had grown up with in Italy.

By such accommodations de Nobili won the hearts of followers for he provided them with a way to embrace Christ while retaining their Indian identity. So when the Brahmin Śivadarma was finally baptized on Pentecost in 1609 his sins had been washed away but, as historian Vincent Cronin has commented, "not his colour, nor his nationality, nor all that was good in his former way of life."[27] For de Nobili, the contextualization process was a path fraught with difficulties and much suffering, but because of his love for the Indians it was one worth following in that it was the only one that would bring them to Christ.

Towards Doctrinal Soundness

When Roberto de Nobili, dressed as a *sannyāsī*, defended his radical methods at the Goa Conference in 1619, he was met with fierce opposition. His detractors accused him of the vilest syncretism, of polluting the gospel, and of apostasy. In response, de Nobili declared:

> *I left Rome for Madurai only to preach Jesus Christ. I have not discarded all religious sense; my only wish is to be useful to souls. Without fault on my part and without any shadow of proof you accuse me of inventing a false and absurd method of evangelization. This is unjust, for I preach Christ openly, without fraud or disguise.*[28]

Unfortunately, the majority of those in attendance that day were unconvinced or at least too intimidated by de Nobili's chief opponent, the Archbishop of Goa, to vote in favor of the controversial methods. Nevertheless de Nobili believed and predicted that even if things turned out unfavorably for him that day, he would "find elsewhere more friendly and attentive ears and defenders" of his cause.[29]

He was right. In spite of the innumerable charges of heresy that have mounted against de Nobili's teachings and methods in the four hundred years since he first donned the saffron robes of a *sannyāsī*, he was indeed passionately committed to doctrinal soundness. His orthodoxy, in fact,

---

[27] Cronin, 110.

[28] Rajamanickam, "The Goa Conference," 94.

[29] Rajamanickam, "The Goa Conference," 94.

was affirmed by two popes, the Grand Inquisitor Dom Martins de Mascarenhas, the Archbishop of Cochin in whose diocese de Nobili served, and such prominent theologians as Cardinal Robert Bellarmine and Peter Lombard.[30] In his *Report Concerning Certain Customs of the Indian Nation* (1615) de Nobili forcefully stated the principle which guided his work, "In furthering the conversion of souls and in the matter of adopting or allowing the customs of unbelievers, the preacher of Christ should always comport himself in such a manner as to preclude anything that is in the least sinful, even were he thereby to secure the conversion of the whole world."[31] Clearly, compromising the essentials of the Christian faith was never a conceivable option for de Nobili.

This commitment to doctrinal soundness was in fact a driving force behind many of his Tamil works, such as *Dialogue on Eternal Life* (1610) wherein he proclaims and defends, among other Christian truths, the omniscience, omnipotence, omnipresence, eternality and oneness of God as well as the authority and inspiration of Scripture, the doctrine of the Trinity and salvation through Christ alone. The much shorter treatise *Inquiry into the Meaning of "God"* (c.a. 1610) is entirely devoted to proclaiming the nature of the one true God and denouncing the various gods of the Hindus as false.

As for the criticism surrounding de Nobili's adoption of various Indian forms and customs such as baths, the application of sandalwood paste, and the manner of dress, it is clear in his *Report* that he believed in carefully evaluating each one to determine whether or not they were inherently or primarily idolatrous. Some were, he found, and these were strictly prohibited. An example is recorded of a young Brahmin Christian who observed certain forbidden rituals during his wedding ceremony and was consequently excommunicated for a time from the church.[32] Other forms, however, while having been attributed religious significance by the Hindus, were either primarily civil or essential for life and health. These de Nobili allowed, having removed or reinterpreted their religious significance through careful instruction.

The reason for de Nobili's staunch adherence to Christian orthodoxy may also be deduced from his writings. He was convinced that to compromise the essence of the Christian faith in the name of contextualization would result in a gospel devoid of its power to save

---

[30] Cronin, 206, 223-230.

[31] De Nobili, 195.

[32] Cronin, 201.

souls. As he wrote in his *Report*, such deviation would "ultimately render unstable and altogether unprofitable"[33] the message of Christ. Thus de Nobili's love for the Hindus manifested itself not only in the often painful process of contextualization but also in his unfailing commitment to the truth—both, he felt, were absolutely indispensable for the cause of bringing the Indians to faith in Christ.

Did He Succeed?

Roberto de Nobili was a young and wealthy noble when he joined the Society of Jesus in 1597. His family was among the most powerful and influential in Rome, counting among their relatives popes, cardinals, saints, and even a Holy Roman Emperor. One presumes he might have been able to live the life of his choosing—in prestige and luxury—but he gave it all up, declaring to protesting relatives, "When God calls, no human consideration should stop us."[34] Years later, standing before the magnificently robed Archbishop of Goa, he said candidly, "Let others crave for and seek the temporal goods which I have given up, let others enjoy them. As for me, I have decided to spend my days unknown in some obscure corner and to sacrifice my wretched life for the salvation of souls."[35] This he did, exchanging the comfort of a nobleman for the black cassock of a Jesuit and then that for the saffron robe of a *sannyāsī*.

By the time of his death in 1656, de Nobili was spent and worn out, blinded from years of poring over texts in poor lighting and having faced shipwreck, imprisonments, betrayal, the harshest of criticisms and near continuous illness. He had lived for nearly fifty years on a daily diet of but one meal of rice and herbs and had become so immersed in Indian culture that he had all but forgotten Italian and had to use an interpreter in order to write to his own family. He had poured out his life in an effort to create a culturally relevant and doctrinally sound expression of the Christian message and thus to enable the south Indian Hindus to come into a saving relationship with Jesus Christ.

His success was nothing short of amazing. De Nobili was able to expand the mission to include various other cities, inspiring growth that continued for years after his death. Several Jesuits joined him in his work and dozens more succeeded him. They too adopted de Nobili's

---

[33] De Nobili, 195.

[34] Cronin, 16.

[35] Rajamanickam, "The Goa Conference," 94.

controversial methods of contextualization and by 1740 the number of Indian Christians in the mission had grown to more than 100,000.[36] The experiment de Nobili had begun in a little hermitage in Madurai had fast become a powerful evangelical movement sweeping through south India.

This great success is what makes the letter written by J.A. Dubois in 1815 so disturbing. Dubois had been a Catholic missionary among the Tamil-speaking Hindus in the south Indian region of Mysore for about twenty-five years when he reported on what he found to be the sad state of the church in India. According to Dubois, the number of Christians in India had dropped to no more than a third of what it was in the mid-eighteenth century. Further, he noted, "this number diminishes every day by frequent apostasy. It will dwindle to nothing in a short period; and if things continue as they are now going on, within less than fifty years there will, I fear, remain no vestige of Christianity among the natives."[37]

Dubois describes further a scene not unlike the one in which de Nobili found himself more than two hundred years earlier, "The very name of Christian carries along with it the stain of infamy; and the proposal alone to become a convert to Christianity is considered by every well-bred Hindoo [sic] as a very serious insult, which is instantly resented."[38] He explains that Christianity was now being derided as the religion of the *Fringy* or, as they were called in Madurai, the vile *Parangi*. And so, Christian missions in south India among the Hindus of caste had come full circle. The belief which de Nobili had worked so hard to debunk—that Christian equals outcaste and everything unclean—was again so prominent that the door to Christian missions seemed hopelessly closed. Such a sense of resignation permeates Dubois' letter which sums up the dire situation, "I repeat it with deep sorrow . . . the time of conversion has passed away, and, under the circumstances, there remains no human possibility to bring it back."[39]

Every movement in the history of Christian missions has from time to time experienced periods of slowed momentum, but when such a vibrant movement as the one begun with de Nobili suffers not only decline but a

---

[36] S. Rajamanickam, "The Old Madura Mission: A Chronological Table," *Indian Church History Review* 21 (1987): 130; J.A. Dubois, *Letters on the State of Christianity in India In Which the Conversion of the Hindoos is Considered as Impracticable to Which is Added a Vindication of the Hindoos Male and Female in Answer to a Severe Attack Made Upon Both by the Reverend * * * **, ed. Sharda Paul (New Delhi, India: Associated Publishing House, 1977), 4.

[37] Dubois, 7.

[38] Dubois, 8-9.

[39] Dubois, 23.

complete reversal in its progress, it commands attention. What was the cause of this reversal? Certainly one cannot ignore the impact of the 1744 papal bull *Omnium sollicitudinum* issued by Pope Benedict XIV which, by finally confirming and enforcing an extensive list of regulations against the Madurai missionaries, essentially put an end to de Nobili's methods of contextualization. Neither did Pope Clement XIV help the cause when he issued *Dominus ac Redemptor* in 1773, a brief calling for the suppression of the Jesuits who were the only priests serving in the mission. Causing still more damage was the fact that while Rome was busy re-Westernizing the Madurai mission, English and French forces were warring for control of the Indian subcontinent, giving impetus to the already strong anti-European sentiment of the Hindus.[40] And yet, none of this fully explains the demise of the Madurai missions movement.

The real problem Dubois observed in 1815 was not a matter of papal legislation or Western imperialism. Rather, he knew that the door of salvation was closed to the Hindus chiefly because they still regarded Christianity to be no more than the religion of foreign invaders. In spite of de Nobili's most heroic efforts and even at the pinnacle of the mission's history, the message of Jesus never really became indigenous. The fact is that certain strictly cultural and ultimately detrimental practices were imported to Madurai from Rome, and by none other than Roberto de Nobili himself. Two of the more significant of these deserve at least a brief examination.

When Bartholomew Ziegenbalg, a Lutheran Pietist, completed his Tamil translation of the New Testament in 1714, he was the first do so.[41] A full century earlier, de Nobili had already mastered Tamil, Sanskrit, and Telugu, and by the end of his life had written in the Indian vernacular apologetic treatises, complicated theological discourses, devotional works, catechisms, poetry and more. However, de Nobili never provided a translation of the Bible for the Indian Christians. Indeed Bible translation was simply not given a prominent place in the missionary movement of the Counter Reformation because personal Bible reading was not a part of the spiritual life of most Roman Catholics in Europe. De Nobili was uniquely positioned within the Indian community and certainly well-equipped to make the Bible indigenous to that culture, but this he failed to do, thanks to the lingering forces of his own distinctly Roman Catholic worldview.

---

[40] Claudia Carlen Ihm, *The Papal Encyclicals 1740-1878* (Raleigh, NC: McGrath Publishing, 1981), 141; Stanley Wolpert, *India* (Englewood Cliffs, NJ: Prentice-Hall, 1965), 72-83.

[41] Stephen Neill, *A History of Christian Missions* (London: The Penguin Group, 1990), 195.

Another enduring part of de Nobili's cultural heritage manifested itself in the glaring omission of indigenous leadership among the south Indian Christians. This is not to say that there were no Indians performing ministry in the Madurai mission. Indeed there were catechists and parish workers but even with more than 100,000 Indians in the mission, it was still to the Europeans that one had to turn for theological training or sacramental life. Surviving records show that in 1722 one part of the Madurai mission consisting of 10 chapels and 5,500 Christians was ministered to by only one priest, a European.[42] This, of course, was not unique to the Madurai mission; a similar phenomenon could be observed practically anywhere the Counter Reformation missionary movement spread.

It is little wonder then that in spite of the laudable efforts to contextualize Christianity in Madurai, it remained foreign for neither its Scripture or its leaders were Indian. Thus when the Europeans gradually fell into disrepute during the latter half of the eighteenth century, so did their religion. And missionaries like J.A. Dubois, who spent their careers in India during that time, could do nothing but weep at the resulting apostasy.

A Final Word: Implications for Missions Today

Christian history has provided us with only one perfect model of ministry and Roberto de Nobili is not it. Nevertheless, he remains a model for missions today. De Nobili was willing to sacrifice his comfort, his culture, and his very life in an attempt to remove every unnecessary barrier that separated the Hindu from the Cross. Moreover, his sacrifice was not in vain, for thousands did indeed embrace Christ. Those of us who, like de Nobili, desire to take the message of Jesus to the nations and peoples of the world must also follow in his footsteps by passionately seeking both a culturally relevant and doctrinally sound expression of Christianity. We must also learn from his omissions by striving to make Christianity indigenous to the culture as soon as possible. God's desire and plan for global evangelization will not be accomplished solely through the work of Western missionaries but will occur through the raising up of reproducing indigenous leaders and their churches.

---

[42] Francis X. Clooney, April 20, 2004, personal email message (accessed April 20, 2004); Achilles Meersman, "Some Eighteenth Century Statistics of the Archdioceses of Goa and of the Diocese of Cochin," *Indian Church History Review* 2 (1968): 113.

References

Amaladoss, Micheal. "Nobili, Robert de." In *Biographical Dictionary of Christian Missions,* edited by Gerald H. Anderson. New York: Simon & Schuster Macmillan, 1998.

Carlen, Claudia Ihm. *The Papal Encyclicals 1740-1878.* Raleigh, NC: McGrath Publishing, 1981.

Clooney, Francis X. "Christ as the Divine Guru in the Theology of Roberto de Nobili." In *One Faith, Many Cultures: Inculturation, Indigenization, and Contextualization,* edited by Ruy O. Costa. Maryknoll, NY: Orbis Books, 1988.
— April 20, 2004. Personal email message (April 20, 2004).

Cronin, Vincent. *A Pearl to India: The Life of Roberto de Nobili.* New York: Dutton, 1959.

de Nobili, Roberto. *Preaching Wisdom to the Wise.* Translated by Anand Amaladass and Francis X. Clooney. St. Louis: The Institute of Jesuit Resources, 2000.

Dubois, J.A. *Letters on the State of Christianity in India In Which the Conversion of the Hindoos is Considered as Impracticable to Which is Added a Vindication of the Hindoos Male and Female in Answer to a Severe Attack Made Upon Both by the Reverend * * * *,* edited by Sharda Paul. New Delhi, India: Associated Publishing House, 1977.

Kraft, Charles H. "Towards a Christian Ethnotheology." In *God, Man and Church Growth*, edited by Alan R. Tippett. Grand Rapids: Eerdmans, 1973.

Meersman, Achilles. "Some Eighteenth Century Statistics of the Archdioceses of Goa and of the Diocese of Cochin." *Indian Church History Review* 2 (1968): 97-114.

Neely, Alan. *Christian Mission: A Case Study Approach.* Maryknoll, NY: Orbis Books, 1995.

Neill, Stephen. *A History of Christian Missions.* London: The Penguin Group, 1990.

Rajamanickam, S. "De Nobili in the Madurai Jail: A Letter of Sebastian de Maya." *Indian Church History Review* 18 (1984): 87-93.

— "The Goa Conference of 1619 (A Letter of Fr Robert de Nobili to Pope Paul V)." *Indian Church History Review* 2 (1968): 83-96.

— "The Old Madura Mission: A Chronological Table." *Indian Church History Review* 21 (1987): 130-135.

Wolpert, Stanley. *India*. Englewood Cliffs, NJ: Prentice-Hall, 1965.

Županov, Ines G. *Disputed Mission: Jesuit Experiments and Brahmanical Knowledge in Seventeenth-century India.* New Delhi, India: Oxford University Press, 1999.

Chapter 5:
Tamilians in Spiritual Context: *Considering the Folk Hindu Spirit World and its Implications for Mission*

Cody C. Lorance
Pastor / Church Planting Leader
Trinity International Baptist Mission
Carol Stream, IL

Good News for the Folk Hindu

A critical task for missionaries is to discover in a given culture exactly where sin has taken hold of the society and the souls of its members. It is precisely at this point—where the gospel may be understood by its hearers as *good news*—that the message of Jesus Christ must be vigorously proclaimed. For the innumerable folk Hindus in India and throughout the ever-growing Hindu diaspora, that point is where the gospel offers deliverance from the fear of a capricious and chaotic spirit-world through the powerful and triumphant blood of the risen Christ.

In this chapter I will be examining humanity's interaction with the spirit-world as it is commonly understood among folk Hindus. In so doing, I will specifically explore one of the most common forms of spiritual affliction in folk Hinduism, the phenomenon of *pēy* possession. I will then suggest how Christian missionaries should attempt to make sense of these types of spiritual afflictions. In a final section, I will present a model for mission advance that relies on holistic spiritual conflict as a primary method for making disciples of Jesus Christ in a folk Hindu context.

The Phenomenology of Spiritual Affliction among Folk Hindus

The fact of Hindu polytheism is one that is well-known. Ranging from the high, pan-Hindu deities such as Siva and Vishnu to those more culturally-specific such as Murugan among the Tamilians and Swaminarayan among the Gujaratis, the Hindu gods populate thousands of temples and millions of shrines throughout the world. Analogous to this pantheon, however, there exists an equally crowded world of local deities, demons, malevolent spirits, and ghosts. It is for most folk Hindus an immanent spirit-world relevant to the day-to-day issues of life and impacting the whole of society. Charles Hoole has explained that the common Hindu understands the world as riddled with spirits, "a world full of chaos and terror" (1997, p. 67). Wayne McClintock characterized the spirit world of folk Hindus as consisting of a "vast army of demons and ghosts" (1990, p. 40). By this McClintock meant only that there were an innumerable amount of such spirit-beings. However, the metaphor is a useful one for other reasons as well.

Like the members of an army, the spirit-beings of folk Hinduism can be said to have differing ranks and jurisdictions with corresponding powers and authorities. This hierarchy is detectable in the various ways folk Hindus deal with each type of spirit-being. For example, at the bottom of this authority structure are the numerous ghosts of those humans who suffered inauspicious deaths such as by murder, accident, execution, or suicide. Known as *pēys*[*], these spirits can be captured and controlled by controlled by shamans who use them to perform supernatural feats and to send various kinds of afflictions upon others (MacPhail, 2002, 148). More powerful local deities are often channeled by mediums in order to drive away *pēys* in a sort of power encounter. These same gods, however, are powerless against such roaming deities as the Seven Sisters who are thought to "stalk the countryside decimating the population" by inflicting disease and disaster (Hiebert, 1983, p. 95). The only recourse against such powerful and capricious goddesses is to placate them through sacrificial offerings, ceremonial worship, and the construction of shrines and temples. Reigning atop this spiritual hierarchy are the high gods of Hindu orthodoxy who are sought out for protection from a wide range of evils. In the following diagram, I have attempted to briefly present the structure of the spirit-world of folk Hinduism:

---

[*] Tamilians use the word *pēy* which is derived from the Sanskrit word *preta preta* meaning "departed" (Nabokov, 1997, p. 299). Other names used in the Hindu world for these or similar spirit-beings include *bhut*, *bhootam*, and *bayu*. Because most of my experience with folk Hindus has been among Tamilians, I have opted to use the Tamil word in this article.

Diagram 1: *The Hierarchical Structure of the Folk Hindu Spirit-World*

	Realm of Authority
Pan-Hindu deities	The "high gods" of orthodox Hinduism, authority is over all Hindus everywhere; examples include Vishnu, Siva, Brahma, Ganesh and others
Cultural gods, gods of large movements, famous saints	At least respected throughout the Hindu world but the majority of their following is among specific groups; examples include Murugan among the Tamilians and Swaminarayan among Gujuratis.
Regional or "roaming" gods, regionally known saints	Spirits whose power is generally limited to specific regions or cultural groups; examples include "The Seven Sisters" and the Alvar saints of Tamilnadu
Local gods, village guardians, "installed" demons	Spirits whose power is limited to a specific locale such as a village; favor sought only by those living in / traveling through that locale
Ancestors, apotheosized *pēys*	Spirits of a particular family or clan; generally beneficent
Pēys, "uninstalled" demons, other ghosts	Will typically exert power by afflicting a single victim
	Spirit-beings of Folk Hinduism

In addition to its hierarchical and territorial aspects, the folk Hindu spirit-world is like a "vast army" in at least two other ways. For one, its members will attack in order to protect or advance their interests. J.C. Gamaliel, in his study of popular Hinduism, recounted how when residents of a village of southern Kerala allowed a *Yakshi* demon's temple to fall into disrepair, the demon harassed a local woman until her husband agreed to finance the temple's renovation (1983, p. 72). Furthermore, as in most any army, the spirit-beings of folk Hinduism have the opportunity for advancement. Demons living in trees have been known to attack passersby, afflicting them variously until they have agreed to erect a temple and install an idol in its honor. The newly installed demon will often become regarded as a village guardian or local deity. A specific example is found in the case of Murugan, who was a tribal chieftain before his death. His ghost was eventually worshipped as a local demon by the *Kurinci* people and over the centuries growing popularity led to Murugan's becoming the favorite deity of Tamilians around the world (Hoole, 1997, p. 64-65).

I must, of course, be careful not to push this "vast army" metaphor too far. In the end it falls short of capturing the complexity, the chaos, and the ambivalence of the spirit-world as experienced by folk Hindus. Gamaliel summarized the folk Hindu experience, providing a glimpse of life in a world teeming with so many ghosts, gods, and spirits:

> *The Hindu seeks to appease spiritual forces. Fear and uncertainty surround him everywhere. Evil spirits are real to him . . . . Though abstract speculation may give some intellectual satisfaction, it does not answer the quests of his heart and soul. He moves from one deity to another and from one guru to another. In pilgrimage and meditation he seeks fulfillment* (1983, p. 85).

Clearly, folk Hinduism provides its adherents with a life that is precarious at best. The folk Hindu is in constant danger from malevolent spirits of various kinds. Spiritual afflictions are frequent as thaumaturgical explanations are given for everything from marital problems and alcoholism to fever and small pox. "Every trouble, every suffering we have," said one Tamilian man, "we get only through the evil spirits" (MacPhail, 1999, p. 171). The reality of this precarious life can be seen in one of the most common forms of spiritual affliction, the phenomenon of *pēy* attacks.

The Phenomenology of Pēy Possession and Affliction

As has already been mentioned, the term *pēy* refers to the spirits of people who have suffered inauspicious deaths such as by murder, execution, suicide, or accident. Isabelle Nabokov explained that the word "usually characterizes the spirits of people who remain indefinitely in this liminal state" (1997, p. 298). Such beings are frequently thought to be the culprits in a wide range of afflictions but different explanations are given for why and how *pēys* attack. Different kinds of attacks often result in different kinds of afflictions and call for distinct methods of deliverance. I will examine three of the major types of *pēy* attacks below.

The Wandering and Neglected Spirits of Nepal

In the villages of Nepal, folk Hindus know *pēy* spirits by the name *bayu*. There the victims of inauspicious deaths are thought to be imperfect sacrifices whose cremation rituals are thus inadequate for transferring them into the realm of the ancestors (Gray, 1987, p. 184-185). Consequently, the *bayu* remains in this world, "wandering from dusk to dawn around his former house" (Gray, 1987, p. 179).

The *bayu's* condition means that it is neglected in his or her family's annual rituals of ancestor worship. This can only be tolerated for so long before the spirit will begin to take action in an effort to remedy the situation. John Gray's study of *bayu* exorcism cited an example of a *bayu* who, six years after his suicide, began to afflict his family. Gray noted that the family suffered "a string of misfortunes—sick cows, poor crop yields, and frequent illness among the children of the household" (1987, p. 179).

The solution for *bayu* attacks is usually a *bayu utarnu* ritual. A shaman is contracted to perform a serious of séances in an effort to make contact with the spirit. After family members verify the identity of the *bayu*—as deceitful spirits have been known to impersonate the deceased—a "second cremation" is performed in which the *bayu* possesses a close relative who then dances upon the burning coals of a sacred *om* fire (Gray, 1987, p. 179). As a result, the *bayu* is apotheosized, becoming a household deity that is worshipped on a daily basis (Gray, 1987, p. 179, 187).

Vulnerable Spirits and Sorcery

A second type of *pēy* attack is related to the concept of liminality among folk Hindus. Like pubescent youths or the bride and groom at a wedding, the deceased person is thought to be in a state of transition—a liminal stage. Liminality refers to the "in betweenness" of these periods of life when persons finds themselves lodged somewhere between the familiarity of the past and the uncertainty of the future (Hertig, 2000, p. 579). Such individuals are considered to be particularly vulnerable to spiritual afflictions (Hiebert, 1999, p. 305), and *pēys* are no exception.

The vulnerability of *pēys* makes them an easy target for shamans who are able to catch and manipulate these spirits through various rituals and incantations. The shaman, known by Tamilians as the *mantiravāti*, may then use the spirits either curatively or, as often is the case, maliciously— in *cēvinai* sorcery—to attack individuals through possession and cursed objects (Bergunder, 2001, p. 104-105; MacPhail, 2002, p. 148). Victims of *cēvinai* manifest any of a wide range of symptoms, as is illustrated in the words of one popular *pēy* exorcist who prayed for her clients to be delivered from the spirits that were:

> *causing pains, hand pains, leg pains, nerve and sinew pains, stomach pain, headache, toothache, chest pains . . . preventing them from doing any work, making them weak, causing them loss of money, financial problems . . . . blocks to family progress, blocks to making money, blocks to family unity, blocks to peace and harmony, blocks to good memory, blocks to studying well, blocks to writing examination, blocks to knowledge and wisdom . . . blocking the coconut trees from bearing fruit, blocks to making money, blocks to accounts receivable . . . blocks to good proposals, blocks to proposals from abroad* (MacPhail, 1999, p. 193).

Combating *cēvinai* usually involves a type of power encounter that mixes in elements of interrogation and negotiation.[*] Typically, a *cēvinai* victim will be brought to a *mantiravāti* (presumably one other than the *mantiravāti* who had caused the affliction in the first place) who, for a fee, utilizes *mantras* and tutelary spirits to exorcise the *pēy* (Bergunder, 2001, p. 104-105). The power encounter should be understood as primarily between the *mantiravāti* who initially caused the problem and the one who has been contracted to solve it, as a successful exorcism usually depends on the skill level of each (Bergunder, 2001, p. 104). Also worth mentioning is the fact that it is common during these exorcisms for *mantiravātis* to interrogate the offending *pēy* in order to find out its identity, who it was sent by, and why (MacPhail, 1999, p. 180). At this point, the spirit will often try to argue its case for continuing to afflict its victim, sometimes prompting a negotiation which may lead to efforts to placate the *pēy* through sacrifice or offering (MacPhail, 1999, p. 180; cf. Singleton, 1977, p. 187-188).

---

[*] In addition to the exorcism method described here, many other efforts will commonly be made to arrive at a solution. For example, seeking the favor of a more powerful spirit such as a local deity or a high god is very common in cases of spiritual affliction. Paul Hiebert notes, "If the case is serious, the villagers may turn to several remedies simultaneously in hopes of saving the situation. Thus it is not uncommon for them to seek treatment for an illness from a modern allopathic doctor, a local ayurvedic doctor, and the local village magician or astrologer at the same time and also stop at the local temple to offer a prayer and make a vow" (1983, p. 91).

Brokenhearted Spirits

A final category of *pēy* attacks involves the spirits of men who committed suicide due to some sort of romantic disappointment. Motivated by an irrepressible desire for intimacy, these *pēys* will invariably attack and possess newly married young women, and, in effect, claim them as brides (Nabokov, 1997, p. 298-301). Although the afflicted woman will rarely be aware that an attack has actually taken place, she will begin experiencing symptoms of the possession that are usually directly related to her marriage. Mental illness, refusing the sexual advances of her husband, and infertility are common (Nabokov, 1997, p. 298, 301).

Isabelle Nabokov documented several cases of *pēy* possession among Tamil women and noted that the *pēys* will often try to guard their victims by inciting them to kick and bite their husbands in order to prevent sexual intercourse (1997, p. 301). Nabokov tells of one woman, "Shanti," who after being possessed began to experience mood swings, depression, and a loss of appetite (1997, p. 302). Shanti became "withdrawn, apathetic, anemic, aggressive, incoherent and barren" (Nabokov, 1997, p. 302). At times, she would even run away from her husband (Nabokov, 1997, p. 302).

Treatment for this type of spiritual affliction is usually quite a difficult experience for the possessed woman. It is not unusual for women to be required to stay at a temple or shrine for several days or weeks, participating in various purification rituals before undergoing an exorcism ceremony (Nabokov, 1997, 303). Nabokov recounted how some women were "whipped with freshly-cut margosa leaves to ward off the *pēy*" and required to fast and walk around the temple 108 times a day in the days leading up to the exorcism (1997, p. 303).

The exorcism itself may take a number of forms. Nabokov describes the *pampaikkarār*, troupes of men who use percussive instruments and singing in their exorcism rituals (1997, p. 303). The *pampaikkarār's* rituals rely on using music to induce a trance-like state in the possessed woman so as to more easily communicate with the *pēy*. Communication will center on interrogating the spirit—asking it to reveal its identity, why it had attacked the victim, and under what conditions it would release the woman. In Shanti's case, it was discovered that the *pēy* who attacked her had committed suicide because his parents refused to arrange a marriage for him (Nabokov, 1997, p. 305). Below is an excerpt from that interrogation. Notice how elements of power (in the form of threats) and placation were mingled together by the *pampaikkarār* who performed Shanti's exorcism ceremony:

Pampaikkarār:	How did you die?
Pēy:	*I hanged myself.*
Pampaikkarār:	On what kind of tree?
Pēy:	*A tamarind.*
Pampaikkarār:	Why did you hang yourself?
Pēy:	*They did not want me to marry.*
Pampaikkarār:	So you died. But you must have had a name. What was it?
Pēy:	*Yes, they gave me a name. But I don't know it.*
Pampaikkarār:	Come on, the people here will thrash you. Tell me your name and I'll arrange a proper funeral marriage.
Pēy:	*Will you arrange for my marriage?*
Pampaikkarār:	Yes, I promise.
Pēy:	*My name is Shankar.*

(Nabokov, 1997, p. 305)

Shanti's exorcism climaxed with the *pēy* finally being "chased away" and ceremonially nailed to a tamarind tree. Nabokov suggested that this last act actually had the effect of marrying the *pēy* to the tree (1997, p. 311) and thus the spirit was both overpowered and placated.

A Holistic Analysis of Spiritual Affliction Phenomena

When Christian missionaries are confronted with the phenomenon of spirit attack in the folk Hindu context, how are they to make sense of the experience? Are they simply to uncritically accept the emic interpretations of such events? Or should they regard the indigenous explanations as wholly irrational and mere superstition, seeking instead a more "enlightened" understanding? Is there an alternative hermeneutical approach that will assist missionaries in reaching a more thorough and truthful analysis of spiritual affliction? Anthropologists and missiologists have usually taken one of two basic approaches.

The Supernatural Hermeneutic

One tendency is for cultural observers to focus primarily on the supernatural aspects of spiritual affliction and to see such phenomena as being genuinely thaumaturgical in origin. When Christians take this approach, they will usually reinterpret the experience in light of Biblical revelation; however, there is often much from indigenous interpretations that is retained. For example, south Indian Pentecostals generally accept folk Hindu beliefs about the existence of evil spirits, the power of *cēvinai*, and that most forms of suffering are the result of spiritual affliction (Bergunder, 2001, p. 104; Hoole, 1997, p. 59). The Christian exorcists at *Kōvai Tūya Mariyannai Cepakulam* in Tamil Nadu even accept the notion that *pēys* are indeed the disembodied spirits of the inauspicious dead (MacPhail, 1999, p. 189). Even many prominent missiologists would agree with several folk Hindu concepts such as the belief in spirit-beings that have authority in certain territories and the importance of interrogating spirits during exorcisms in order to obtain important information about the spirit world (Greenway, 1995, p. 21, 23; Weerasingha, 1995, p. 54; Hoole, 1997, p. 60; Wagner, 1989, p. 279).

An obvious strength of this approach is that it takes seriously the reality of Satan and demons and the fact that they can and do attack human beings. No less an authority than the Apostle Paul wanted Christians to clearly understand that they were called to take part in a war against "the spiritual forces of evil" (Eph. 6:12). Roger Greenway has rightly pointed out that Paul "regarded his mission work as an engagement in spiritual warfare . . . . a frontal assault on Satan's dominion" (Greenway, 1995, p. 23; cf. Acts 26:17-18). Missionaries working today among folk Hindus cannot afford to neglect the essential relationship between Christ's call to global disciple-making and the genuine need to engage in spiritual conflict.

The Naturalistic Hermeneutic

A second major approach to understanding spiritual affliction phenomena is to interpret these experiences naturalistically, usually in terms of the physiological, psychological, or sociological factors involved. Nabokov's study of *pēy* possession among Tamilian women is a good example of this approach. Noting that most cases of *pēy* possession in women follow periods of marital conflict, Nabokov argues that the possession and exorcism experience should be understood both as a personal psychological construction and as a social mechanism designed to reinforce certain cultural norms. She sees the possession itself as the result of "female distress," a creative way of indirectly voicing "feelings of loneliness, abandonment, and marital disappointment" (Nabakov, 1997, p. 311). On the other hand, the exorcism ritual is an invention of the culture that forces women to publicly renounce such thoughts by attributing them to malevolent spirits (Nabakov, 1997, p. 312). The ritual thus reinforces "the safety and structure of the patriarchal family fold and women's proper role in it" (Nabakov, 1997, p. 312).

Naturalistic interpretations of spiritual affliction phenomena are valuable because of their ability to identify the underlying social, psychological, and physiological factors that often precipitate such experiences. A careful examination of these factors enables the missionary to see to a fuller extent the brokenness of a culture as doing so inevitably uncovers examples of social injustice, marital dissatisfaction, disease, mental illness, or other forms of suffering.

Towards a Holistic Evaluation

What is imperative for Christian missionaries is that they not strictly reduce their interpretative approaches to either the supernatural or the naturalistic hermeneutic. Rather, a holistic approach should be taken that recognizes that Satan, demons, disease, injustice, familial dysfunction, and mental illness are all painful realities that result in human suffering. It is usually the case that a combination of factors precipitates a given case of spiritual affliction. Only when all of these factors are identified and the gospel has been applied to each can true hope and wholeness in Jesus Christ result.

In the following diagram, I have applied a holistic approach in evaluating the previously mentioned case of the possession and exorcism of Shanti:[*]

---

[*] My diagram is based on one by A. Scott Moreau in which he suggested that factors influencing a supernatural experience fall into the categories of physical, psychological, cultural and social, and spiritual (1995, p. 31). What I have done is simply apply his analytical structure to Shanti's experience as reported by Isabelle Nabokov (1997, p. 301-302).

Diagram 2: A Holistic Analysis of Shanti's Spiritual Affliction

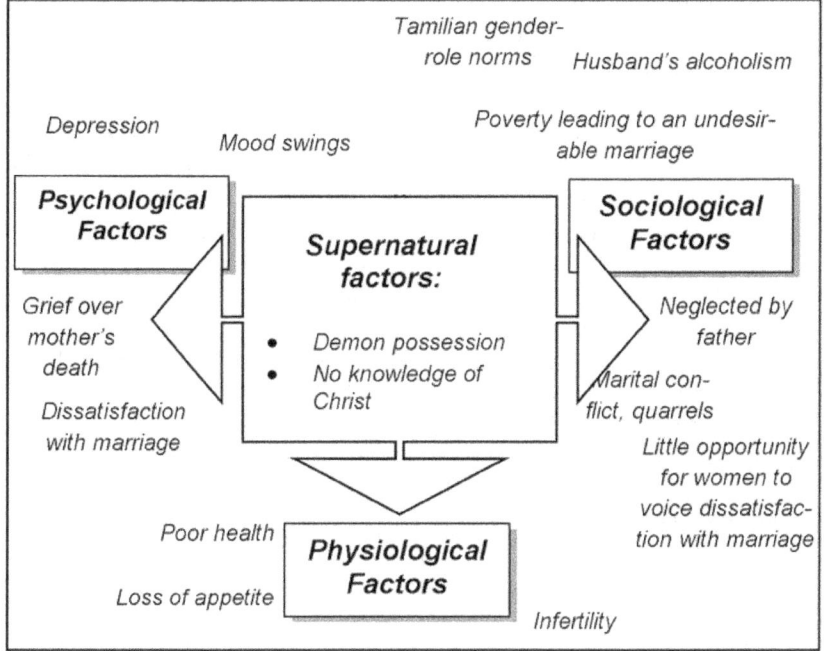

From the diagram, it is clear that simply driving out the possessing spirit will leave many areas of brokenness in Shanti's life. Equally problematic is to address physical, psychological, or social issues without dealing with the spiritual strongholds in a her life, an approach which provides relief for temporary problems while leaving Shanti bound under the power of sin and Satan.

Holistic Spiritual Conflict and Mission Advance

I began this chapter by stressing the importance of proclaiming the gospel precisely at that point where it may be understood by its hearers as good news. Indeed, for Christian missionaries ministering in the context of folk Hinduism, the realization of the good news about Jesus Christ by folk Hindus is an absolutely fundamental goal. This will not occur apart from a gospel message that presents Christ as the one who has come in matchless power to defeat malevolent spirits and to set people free from sin, fear, and slavery.

Of course, this is not a gospel message that can be adequately proclaimed merely through preaching. Folk Hindus who are daily burdened with the fear of an immanent spirit-world will understand the gospel only as they see and experience the power of Christ in the midst of their own spiritual struggles. Therefore, it is as the missionary confronts the phenomena of spiritual affliction with the power of Christ that God's mission of salvation is advanced. Spiritual conflict, in effect, becomes the primary means of spreading the gospel.

I have already argued that spiritual affliction phenomena should be evaluated holistically in order to thoroughly understand how a given person has been gripped by brokenness, sin and evil. This understanding is essential to the development of truly effective approaches to deliverance and healing because it helps the missionary to know where people are bound to demonic powers, where personal and cultural sin has produced brokenness, and what factors hinder people from believing and living according to the gospel.

Once these questions have been answered, every area of suffering must be confronted with the gospel. This requires a holistic approach to spiritual conflict. Holistic spiritual conflict consists of at least three major components: power encounter, therapeutics, and spiritual formation.

Breaking Bonds through Power Encounters

People who have been possessed or attacked by evil spirits are in need of the power of Christ to deliver them from their spiritual slavery. A power encounter is an event that is intended to do just that. It is the pitting of God's power to liberate against the power of Satan to keep people in bondage (Kraft, 2000, p. 775). An example of a power encounter in a case of spiritual affliction is seen in the context of the south Indian Pentecostal movement where one man testified:

> *I had a nervous problem on account of witchcraft* [cēvinai]. *This spoiled my education . . . . As the pastor was praying for me, I felt something coming out of my stomach. It was a lemon, a big lemon. While he prayed, I felt I ought to vomit it out. As they prayed, it came out. Then they prayed and controlled the evil power.*
> (Bergunder, 2001, p. 104).

Scriptural examples of power encounters abound throughout both testaments (e.g. Exod. 7-12; 1 Kings 18:16-40; Dan. 2; Mark 5:1-20, 9:14-29; Acts 16:16-18). No single pattern for them can be identified; however, common elements of Biblical power encounters include displays of supernatural power, prayer, authority statements, a focus on God's glory, the restoring of health or dignity to those afflicted, and the stimulation of faith among those witnessing the event.* A final point for missionaries to keep in mind regarding power encounters in the Bible is that the people God used in such ministries were always individuals of deep spiritual discipline and Christ-like character.†

Healing Brokenness through Therapeutics

Victims of spiritual affliction often suffer from long-term and deep-seated brokenness. Sickness, injury, emotional trauma, or marital problems may either have directly resulted from the attack or else precipitated it. While missionaries should not exclude the possibility of God removing all such brokenness instantaneously through a power encounter, neither should they neglect the fact that God often brings healing through therapeutics.

By "therapeutics," I am referring to so-called "modern" systems of healing. Such systems tend to bring a naturalistic perspective to issues of pain and suffering, focusing on issues related to biological diseases, mental and emotional illness, and social dysfunction. Examples of therapeutic approaches to dealing with affliction include allopathic or homeopathic medicine, psychiatry, and psychotherapy. Therapeutic systems that are integrated into a holistic system of spiritual conflict should not be criticized as "unspiritual." On the contrary, when therapeutic systems are understood as part of God's created order over which He exercises complete sovereignty, they are wholly Biblical.

---

* Examples for the elements I mentioned include: Exod. 7-12, 1 Kings 18:38, Dan. 2:30-45, Mark 5:13, Mark 9:26-27, and Acts 9:18 for displays of supernatural power; Exod. 10:18, 1 Kings 18:36-37, Dan. 2:18-23, and Mark 9:29 for prayer; Exod. 7:4-5, 1 Kings 18:32, 36-37, 39, and Dan. 2:20-23, 27-28, 47 for a focus on God's glory; Dan. 2:24, Matt. 9:33, Matt. 12:22, and Mark 5:15 for restoring health or dignity to people; 1 Kings 18:39, Dan. 2:46-47, Matt. 9:33, Matt. 12:23, Matt. 17:18, Mark 1:27, Mark 5:18-20, Mark 9:24, and Acts 8:12 for stimulating faith or life change; and Matt. 17:18, Mark 1:25, Mark 5:8, Mark 9:25, and Acts 16:18 for authority statements.

† The human agents through which God worked in the power encounters I have cited are Moses (Exod. 7-12), Elijah (1 Kings 18), Daniel (Dan. 2), Jesus (Matt. 8, 9, 12, 17; Mark 1, 5, 9), Phillip (Acts 8), and Paul (Acts 16).

Promoting Spiritual Formation through Discipleship

The last component to the holistic model of spiritual conflict is built upon the presumption that God and Satan have diametrically opposed goals for humanity. It may be said that God's purpose in the world is to glorify Himself by making from sinful humanity objects of His grace and products of His workmanship—a people conformed to the image of Christ (Eph. 2:1-10). Thus, God has committed His Church to the task of global disciple-making (Matt. 28:18-20). Satan opposes this purpose, seeking instead his own glory (Matt. 4:9, 1 Cor. 10:20, 2 Thess. 2:4-9, 1 John 3:8-10, Rev. 13:4). Every demonic attack against humanity must therefore be understood as essentially an effort to impede spiritual formation and thus rob God of His glory.

The Christian missionary must evaluate a case of spiritual affliction in order to discover how the persons involved are being hindered from knowing and growing in Christ. Power encounters alone are temporary fixes and therapeutic treatments essentially superficial unless they are accompanied by a strategy for permanent life transformation (cf. Luke 11:24-26; John 5:14). The following excerpt from a statement by Pentecostal pastors in Tamil Nadu illustrates the problem of spiritual conflict approaches that fail to incorporate long-term programs for spiritual formation:

> *If they experience a healing they stay a while in the congregation but if there is no system to hold them, they go away again . . . . They come just to be healed and then they go . . . . After the healing is over they again are back in their own temples.* (Bergunder, 2001, p. 111).

For the gospel to bear lasting fruit, missionaries who confront spiritual affliction phenomena should prescribe evangelistic discipleship plans as part of the healing process. Furthermore, these plans should be customized so as to address the needs of a specific person. In a folk Hindu context, discipleship prescriptions could focus on helping people to discover the power of Jesus Christ over the spirit-world, to hear God speaking through the Bible, to develop a Biblical view of suffering and evil, and to know the love of Jesus Christ that casts out fear and brings liberty (1 John 4:18).[*]

---

[*] A theology of suffering will be desperately needed for missions among the folk Hindus. Folk Hindus view suffering as essentially evil and its alleviation essential. For this reason, it is common for an afflicted person to try method after

Making Spiritual Conflict Holistic

Holistic spiritual conflict utilizes power encounters, therapeutics, and discipleship prescriptions in an integrated approach to sharing the Good News of Christ. When this approach is informed by a holistic analysis of spiritual affliction phenomena, the two work together to proclaim the gospel as "good news."

Diagram 3: *Sharing the "Good News" in the Face of Spiritual Affliction*

Holistic spiritual conflict involves:
- Breaking bonds through power encounter
- Healing brokenness through therapeutics
- Promoting spiritual formation through discipleship

Holistic analysis answers:
- Where are people bound?
- Where are people broken?
- Where are people hindered from knowing and growing in Jesus Christ?

Spiritual Affliction Phenomenon → Sharing the "Good News" in the Face of Spiritual Affliction → Missionary

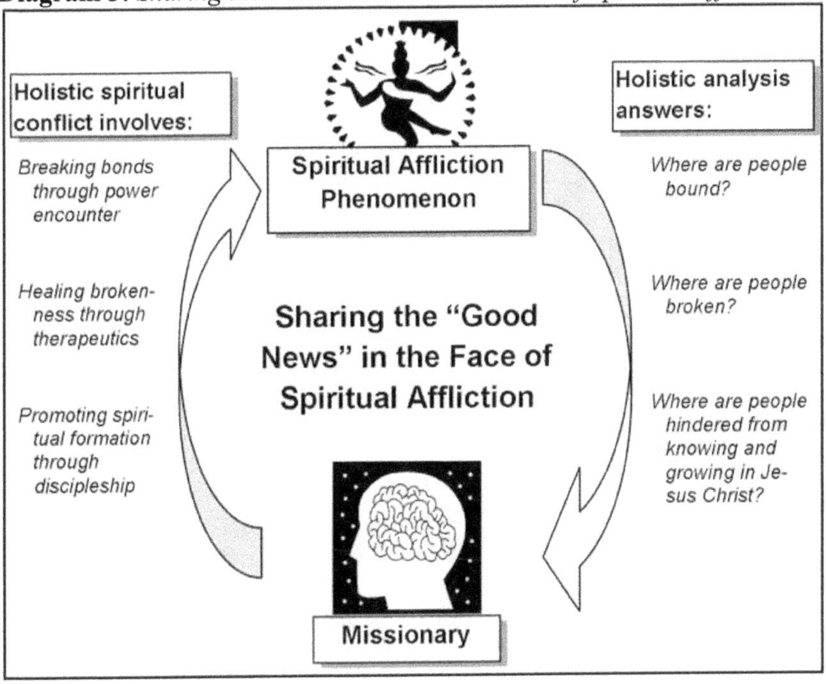

Conclusion

Paul Hiebert and Daniel Galat have rightly said, "We fail if we do not show that the Gospel has meaning for every dimension of life" (1998, p.

---

method and healer after healer until a cure is found. The Biblical worldview provides for healing and restoration but does not guarantee it. Instead, we see God using suffering as a part of the unfolding of His redemptive purposes. Part of the discipleship process among folk Hindus must provide the disciple with the ability to envision Christian suffering as an opportunity for godliness.

16). That failure grows more acute when we miss the dimension of life most in need of Christ's salvation. In the context of folk Hinduism, holistic spiritual conflict informed by holistic phenomenological analysis is the means by which Christian missionaries proclaim the gospel as *good news* where it is needed most.

References

Bergunder, Micheal. (2001). Miracle healing and exorcism: The South Indian Pentecostal movement in the context of popular Hinduism. *International Review of Mission*, 90(356-357), 103-112.

Gamaliel, J.C. (1983). Pattern and processes in popular Hinduism. In Vinay Samuel & Chris Sugden (Eds.), *The gospel among our Hindu neighbors* (pp. 63-86). Bangalore: Partnership in Mission.

Gray, John N. (1987). Bayu Utarnu: Ghost exorcism and sacrifice in Nepal. *Ethnology*, 26, 179-199.

Greenway, Roger. (1995). Missions as spiritual warfare. *Urban Mission*, 13(2), 19-24.

Hiebert, Paul G. (1983). Folk religion in Andhra Pradesh and some missiological implications. In Vinay Samuel & Chris Sugden (Eds.), *The gospel among our Hindu neighbors* (pp. 87-109). Bangalore: Partnership in Mission.

Hiebert, Paul G. & Galat, Daniel D. (1998). Ethnomedicine and medical missions. In Evvy Hay Campbell (Ed.), *Ethical issues in health-related missions* (pp. 3-21). Deerfield, IL: The Center for Bioethics and Human Dignity.

Hiebert, Paul G., Shaw, R. Daniel, & Tiénou, Tite. (1999). *Understanding folk religion: a Christian response to popular beliefs and practices*. Grand Rapids: Baker Books.

Hertig, Young Lee. (2000). Liminality. In A. Scott Moreau (Ed.), *The Evangelical dictionary of world missions* (pp. 579). Grand Rapids: Baker Books.

Hoole, Charles R.A. (1997). Territorial spirits: An Indian perspective. *Stulos Theological Journal*, 5(2), 59-68.

Kraft, Charles H. (2000). Power encounter. In A. Scott Moreau (Ed.), *The Evangelical dictionary of world missions* (pp. 774-775). Grand Rapids: Baker Books.

MacPhail, Richard D. (1999). Finding a path in others' worlds: The emic challenge of exorcism. *Bangalore Theological Forum*, 31(1), 168-204.

MacPhail, Richard D. (2002). Finding a path in others' worlds: The challenge of exorcism. In Selva J. Raj & Corinne G. Dempsey (Eds.), *Popular Christianity in India: Riting between the lines* (pp. 141-162). Albany, NY: State University of New York Press.

McClintock, Wayne. (1990). Demons and ghosts in Indian folklore. *Missiology, an International Review*, 18(1), 37-47.

Moreau, Scott A. (1995). Evil spirits: Biblical and practical issues. *Urban Mission*, 13(2), 25-36.

Nabokov, Isabelle. (1997). Expel the lover, recover the wife: Symbolic analysis of a South Indian exorcism. *The Journal of the Royal Anthropological Institute*, 3(2), 297-316.

Singleton, Micheal. (1977). Spirits and spiritual direction: The pastoral counseling of the possessed. *Missiology, an International Review*, 5(2), 185-194.

Wagner, C. Peter. (1989). Territorial spirits and world missions. *Evangelical Missions Quarterly*, 25(3), 278-288.

Weerasingha, Tissa. (1995). Spiritual warfare in Sri Lanka. *Urban Mission*, 13(2), 53-58.

Chapter 6:
A Case Study of Tamilian Hindus Seeking Jesus through Contextualized Spiritual Festival: *The Passover Healing Ceremony*

Cody C. Lorance
Pastor / Church Planting Leader
Trinity International Baptist Mission
Carol Stream, IL

Introduction

Early in our work as missionaries amongst the immigrant Hindus of suburban Chicago, my wife Katherine and I learned that the typical Hindu's perception of the Christian faith as a non-Indian religion presented one of the most significant barriers to the effective spread of the gospel. Our neighbors, Mr. and Mrs. Ram[*], Tamilian Hindus from south India, described their impression of many Indian Christians as unfriendly and "always shouting." Mr. Ram added that they tended to dress differently, did not go to the cinema like everyone else, and refused to accept food that Hindus offered them during festivals. To the Rams, Indian Christians seemed less than Indian. If we were going to have success in our efforts to reach immigrant Hindus with the love of Jesus Christ, Katherine and I knew that developing an authentically Indian expression of Christianity would be essential. We were convinced that God had charged us with the task of presenting Christ and a way of seeking and worshipping Him that was relevant and meaningful to Tamilian Indians from Hindu backgrounds.

This chapter is an analysis of one of our earliest efforts of contextualization among the Hindus in our mission field. During our first year-and-a-half on the field, Katherine and I spent a great deal of time in ethnographic, theological, and missiological research, seeking not only to understand the various cultures of our Indian neighbors but also to learn how to go about building God's Church among them. Our study provided a rich foundation which significantly shaped the contextualized discipleship event presented here; however, it is important to note that the event itself was essentially a response to an unexpected opportunity we had to communicate Christ with a Hindu family in crisis. Thus, the event was not the product of months of planning but rather days of seeking God's guidance and wisdom and drawing upon the things we had learned through study and experience in order to meet the immediate needs of our neighbors with the immediacy of a culturally contextualized Christ.

The experience itself provides a great example of the importance of missiological reflection, ethnographic research and a prayerful dependence on the Holy Spirit as foundations for missional action. Without having spent months of spiritual, missiological, and cultural preparation, we would have been ill-equipped to meet our neighbors at the point of their need with the hope and wholeness of Jesus in a way that they could understand and respond too.

---

[*] I have changed the names of our neighbors in order to protect their privacy.

Healing Mr. Ram: A Story of Contextualization

A Crisis Arises

Mr. and Mrs. Ram were among the first people we met after moving into our neighborhood in suburban Chicago. They had only just moved in themselves and we soon became friends—sharing meals, backyards, holidays, and family outings. Gradually they became aware of the role that Christ played in our lives and began to see us as people with deep faith and strong prayers. By September of 2004, about a year after we became neighbors, the Rams were ready to admit to us that they believed that God was answering our prayers regarding their one-year-old son's sleeping patterns. Therefore, it was not a surprise when they came to us several months later asking us to pray again.

In early April of 2005, Mr. Ram was diagnosed with a serious health problem. In something of a panic, they asked us to pray. The very next day, Mr. Ram told me that he believed that God had begun to heal him in answer to our prayers. Indeed he did look significantly better. He asked that we continue to pray and that we begin to thank our God for the healing that was taking place. A few days later, Mr. Ram's health was continuing to improve but enough symptoms remained that he again brought up the subject of prayer. This time, he said that he wanted to come over to our house for a time of prayer. Now I knew that something significant was occurring in terms of God drawing this Hindu couple to Himself.

For most Tamilian Hindus, there is a strong sense of territory when it comes to their understanding of the spirit world. The fact that the Rams wanted to come to our house for prayer told me that they wanted to go to a place outside of the influence of their household gods. To them, our house represented the territory of Christ. The fact is, I had never seen them so serious about seeking the favor of Jesus Christ and, to be honest, I wasn't exactly sure how to respond at first. My first instinct was that this was something that should be done as soon as possible, but as Mr. Ram and I talked further, I remembered from previous conversations and my ethnographic field work that the Rams believed strongly in the idea of auspicious and inauspicious days. I realized that my best bet for making this an experience that would resonate deeply with them would be to suggest an auspicious day for seeking Jesus Christ. Since Passover was two weeks away, I suggested we have a time of prayer then. After I explained the story of the Exodus and the fact that Jesus Christ died on the Passover, Mr. Ram excitedly agreed to come with his family on that day.

Preparing for the Passover Healing Ceremony

Over the next two weeks Katherine and I sought God in prayer and fasting and mobilized other Christians to pray as well. We thought through our previous research into folk Hindu spirituality and south Indian culture as well as our own theological understandings of various relevant issues. We consulted fellow missionaries for their thoughts and advice and gradually formed a plan for a contextualized Passover healing ceremony. We decided that the ceremony should focus both on Mr. Ram's healing as well as on celebrating Jesus Christ's work on the cross during the Passover. The latter we decided should be done through a simplified Passover Seder, resembling a Eucharist meal in that it consisted only of bread and wine.

On the day of the service, I went over to the Ram's home in the morning to remind them about the prayer time and to give them a few instructions. I asked Mr. Ram to bring one large piece of unleavened bread and explained its relevance to the Passover. He responded enthusiastically and wanted to know if he could bring more. I explained that he was welcome to bring more bread but that it was significant in the ceremony that we break the bread and share it among ourselves. Mr. Ram also asked if he could bring wine for "the Mass" and flowers and fruits as an offering. I told him that we could use the wine but that the other items were not necessary. I explained that Jesus Christ doesn't answer prayer because we do things for Him, but that it was because Katherine and I had entered into relationship with Christ through His death and resurrection that we could come to Him in prayer. After setting a time with him for the ceremony, I returned home.

We prepared a large room in our house for the service by thoroughly cleaning it and constructing a makeshift altar. The altar was basically a small table that I covered in red cloth. On top of the table, I placed four small cups for the wine, a fifth cup that contained anointing oil, a wooden cross with gold trim, and a plate for the bread. I put four Bibles on a nearby table. After the room was ready, Katherine, our two-year-old son, and I changed into nicer clothes and spent time in prayer before the ceremony.

The Ceremony

The Rams arrived a few minutes after the scheduled time. They were dressed somewhat more formally than they had been when I saw them earlier that day. They removed their shoes at the door and I led them to the room where we would be having the ceremony. Mr. Ram handed me a bottle of Merlot and a bowl containing one *chapatti*. He also held three bags of fresh fruit—one pineapple, grapes, apples, strawberries, and oranges—and a large bouquet of bright orange daisies. After I had poured the wine into the cups on the altar and placed the *chapatti* onto the plate, Mrs. Ram, without waiting for my permission, arranged the fruit and flowers on three paper plates on the floor in front of the altar.

We all then sat on the floor in front of the altar and I explained that the service would have two main parts—one to celebrate the Passover and one to pray for Mr. Ram's healing. I then bowed my head and prayed aloud that God would bless our time and allow His presence to be felt.

After the prayer, I handed Bibles to Katherine and Mr. and Mrs. Ram and instructed them to turn to the eighth chapter of Luke. I told them that reading the Bible was a very important thing for us to do because God says that His Word is like a surgeon's scalpel (Heb. 4:12) that He uses to work in our lives. I explained that not only can we learn from the Bible but as we read it, God's Spirit goes to work in our lives wherever we need Him. We took turns reading several lines each from Luke 8:1 to 9:6, which speaks of a couple of incidents in Jesus' healing ministry. I then paused to see if there were any questions. Mr. Ram said that he thought it was all pretty clear.

I collected the Bibles and then asked Mr. Ram to kneel down before the altar. I told them that it was our tradition to put our hands on people when we prayed for their healing, so I asked Mrs. Ram to kneel beside Mr. Ram and do just that. Katherine then put her hands on Mrs. Ram and knelt beside her. I then explained that I would be anointing Mr. Ram's head with oil and that in doing so I was praying to Jesus Christ—God's anointed one. I dipped the index finger of my right hand in the oil and traced a cross on Mr. Ram's forehead as I said, "In the name of the Father, the Son, and the Holy Spirit." At that point, I gave Mr. Ram the cross to hold and then knelt beside him with my hands on his shoulder to pray. Katherine and I both prayed aloud asking God in Jesus' name to heal Mr. Ram both physically and spiritually. We prayed about the natural and spiritual causes of his illness and asked that God would show His power and love to this family.

Immediately after prayer, I stood again and went behind the altar to serve the Seder elements. The other three remained kneeling before the altar as I lifted up the *chapatti* and said (roughly):

> *On the night that Jesus was betrayed, arrested and then later crucified, buried, and resurrected He celebrated the Passover meal with His closest friends. During the meal,*

> *He took the bread and broke it saying, "Take and eat.*
> *This is my body, which is broken for you."*

I then tore the *chapatti* and handed a piece each to Mr. and Mrs. Ram and Katherine. I said a quick prayer thanking Jesus for dying on the cross and then gave them permission to eat. I then took one of the cups of wine and said, "After the meal, Jesus took the cup and said, 'Take and drink. This cup is the new covenant of my blood which is poured out for you to take away your sins.'" I distributed the cups to each of the adults and then prayed, thanking Jesus for how He had paid for our sins on the cross with His blood. Finally, I told everyone that they could drink. I then brought our ceremony to a close with a final prayer thanking God for the time and the friendship our two families shared.

The Aftermath

Mr. and Mrs. Ram began thanking us profusely for the ceremony and the prayers. I then gave Mr. Ram the cross and told him and his wife that it was theirs to keep so they could use it when they wanted to pray to Jesus Christ. I explained that the cross was not for praying *to*, but they could hold it when they prayed in order to remind them that it was only through the death and resurrection of Christ that we can have access to Him. Mr. Ram then asked, "Is there anything else we should do?" I told them that if they were members of my church I would give them further instructions and asked if they wanted me to do that for them. They replied with an enthusiastic "Yes." I proceeded then to prescribe that they pray each night as a family for the next seven days to Jesus. I told them that it was okay to pray to Jesus just as they would talk to me. I then gave them one of the Bibles that we had used that night and told them to read together one chapter each night for the next seven nights beginning from where we had left off during the service. I explained that God wasn't just interested in working in their physical bodies but in every other area of their lives as well. They indicated that they understood and again thanked us for all we had done. Our two families spent the rest of the evening together eating and enjoying fellowship.

Theoretical Foundations for the Passover Healing Ceremony

As Katherine and I were confronted with Mr. Ram's health problem, we began to prayerfully consider how we might best minister to the Ram family during their time of crisis. A number of guiding principles strongly influenced our thinking as we planned our response. First, even though the

Rams were coming to us with only a physical need, we were committed to responding holistically. Indeed, Mr. Ram's health condition did call for healing ministry, but we also believed that the crisis afforded us important opportunities to address spiritual and even psychosocial issues as well. We were convinced that Mr. Ram's physical health, albeit important, was essentially a superficial problem and that the family had far more important needs related to their spiritual formation.

A second guiding principle related to deciding how we could minister both holistically and effectively. Here we were influenced by the Biblical book of Ezra and the writings of A.H. Zahniser to utilize ritual because of its unique ability to address physical, spiritual, and psychosocial needs in one integrated event and because of its power to disciple people and groups not just through cognitive processes but by creating new spiritual reality.[*]

Finally, we believed it to be essential that any use of ritual in our ministry to the Rams be both culturally contextual and Biblically founded. This meant that every dimension of the religious experience we were developing had to be analyzed in order to determine whether or not it was likely to resonate with Tamil-speaking Hindus from south India such as Mr. and Mrs. Ram. It also meant that we would have to test every element of the ritual in light of careful Biblical exegesis. In the following table, I have listed the elements of our Passover healing ceremony that Katherine and I intentionally incorporated into the ritual. In the table, the elements have been categorized according to the dimension of religious experience[†] they best reflect.

---

[*] The use of ritual in discipleship is powerful because it effectively transfers people from an old spiritual reality to a new one. I explore the issue at length, especially as it relates to the book of Ezra, in chapter 14.

[†] See A. Scott Moreau's *Contextualization: Course Notes* (Moreau, 2005) for explanations of the nature of these dimensions. I have chosen to omit the "Experience" dimension because there was nothing that we intentionally *planned* for the ceremony that fit into that category. Other elements of the ceremony that were not intentionally planned, such as the Rams bringing fruit to offer to Jesus Christ, are not included in the table.

Table 1: *Elements of the Contextualized Passover Healing Ceremony*

Doctrine	Ritual	Ethics	Myth	Material	Social
• The Holy Spirit works in people's lives as they read the Bible • Access to God in prayer is possible only through the death & resurrection of Christ • God has power to heal and often does so in answer to prayer • Passover is an "auspicious" day for Christians • A Christian home is an especially appropriate place for seeking Christ • Physical sickness can have either or both natural or spiritual causes • The death of Jesus Christ paid for sins • God wants to work in every area of life	• Cleaning room • Dressing formally; removing shoes • Rams bring bread and wine • Prayer throughout ceremony • Reading Bible in community • Kneeling and "laying on hands" in prayer • Anointing with oil • Mr. Ram holding cross • Consuming bread and wine in commemoration of Jesus' death on the cross • Instructions for follow-up prayers and Bible readings during the next seven days	• It is not appropriate to pray *to* the cross • Avoided cross-gender touching when "laying on hands" except for husband and wife • No special language or style is needed when praying to Jesus	• Stories of Jesus' healing ministry • The story of the Exodus commemorated in the Passover • The story of Jesus' death and resurrection permeated everything	• Bread and wine • Cross • Altar with red cloth • Bibles • Oil	• Sitting together • Reading Bible together, both men and women • "Laying on hands" and praying together, both Katherine and I prayed verbally • Bread and wine shared among worshippers • Instructed to pray and read Bible as a family • Meal and fellowshipping together after formal ceremony completed

Taken together, these elements reflect a number of values that Katherine and I felt were important in the development of a ritual that was both Biblically sound and contextualized to Tamilian culture. In particular, sacred space, participant discipleship, community, sensory appeal, and a strong Biblical view of God were all areas of specific emphasis. I will now briefly examine each of these.

Sacred Time and Space

From our previous ethnographic research into the worship lives of Tamilian Hindus, Katherine and I had become aware of the fact that they tended to put a high value on sacred space. Hinduism is a religion of temples, shrines, and pilgrimage sites such as sacred cities and rivers. We recalled how during Hindu festivals we had seen the Rams spending extra time cleaning their house in order to make it suitable for hosting sacred activities. The Hindu concept of sacred space is also closely tied to the festival calendar. For Mr. and Mrs. Ram, not only were there good and bad places for worship but also good and bad times.

Katherine and I felt that establishing a sacred time and space in which to perform the healing ceremony was essential if we hoped to be truly contextualized in our ministry to the Rams. We sought to establish a sense of sacred time by choosing to perform the ceremony on Passover (April 24, 2005). I told the Rams that Passover was an auspicious day for Christians because of the Exodus event, which I briefly recounted, and because of the fact of Jesus Christ dying during the Passover. As for establishing a sense of sacred space, we utilized several elements in an effort to convert a room in our house from a common place to a sacred space. First, the fact that the ceremony was going to happen in our home—a Christian home—meant to the Rams that we would be in a particularly auspicious place for seeking Jesus Christ (at least in relation to their own home). Secondly, we thoroughly cleaned the house and especially the room set aside for the ceremony. Next, I cleared out several pieces of furniture and placed a small table in the middle of the room to serve as an altar. Finally, even changing our clothes and taking off our shoes contributed to the sense that we were entering into both a time and a space devoted to sacred activities.

Christians may struggle with the idea of affirming a worldview of sacred time and space in light of the notion of Christian liberty. After all, Paul made it clear that religious calendars were merely a shadow of the fullness found in Christ (Col. 2:16-17) and Stephen went to his death arguing against the notion that true worship must be performed in the temple (Acts 7:2-60). Nevertheless, the early church had a strong affinity for the temple (Acts 2:1, 46; 3:1) and Paul himself affirmed those Jewish Christians who maintained the Judaic religious calendar (Rom. 14:5-6). A key passage on this issue comes from Paul's letter to the church in Corinth:

> *For though I am free from all, I have made myself a servant to all, that I might win more of them. To the Jews I became as a Jew, in order to win Jews. To those under the law I became as one under the law (though not being myself under the law) that I might win those under the law. To those outside the law I became as one outside the law (not being outside the law of God but under the law of Christ) that I might win those outside the law. To the weak I became weak, that I might win the weak. I have become all things to all people, that by all means I might save some.* (1 Cor. 9:19-22)

Participant Discipleship

Tamilian Hindus are not used to coming to a time of worship empty-handed. On the morning of the ceremony, I recalled a time when we had gone with Mr. and Mrs. Ram to a Hindu temple. The Rams had filled the trunk of their car with flowers, fruit, and other items as offerings to be presented to the various gods in the temple. I also recalled my study of a fringe Christian movement in Tamil Nadu, India that had achieved remarkable success among Hindus in part because of the way it actively engaged people who came seeking physical healing or exorcism in their own spiritual formation by prescribing programs of prayer, meditation, and Bible reading. It occurred to me that I should seek to similarly engage the Rams. They should be allowed to be participants in worship and challenged to actively seek God through Jesus Christ. In that motivation, I went to their house several hours before the ceremony and asked them to be responsible to bring the bread and wine for the Seder. It was also in this spirit that we involved them in reading the Bible during the service, allowed them to receive the bread and wine, and prescribed seven days of Bible reading and prayer following the ceremony.

A brief word is due regarding our decision to serve a Eucharistic-like meal to Mr. and Mrs. Ram as professing Hindus. At least in my denomination, it is traditional that the Eucharist be served only to "born again" Christians. To be honest, this is an issue Katherine and I have wrestled with for some time, even before Mr. Ram's health declined. In the end, we felt that the consuming of bread and wine ritual was simply too powerful a vehicle for communicating the gospel to be omitted on the basis of evangelical tradition alone. We could find no Biblical basis for refusing non-Christians the privilege of receiving Seder (or for that matter, Eucharistic) elements providing they do so reverently.* In fact, we found it significant that none of the original recipients of the Lord's Supper were "born again" and one was even possessed by Satan at the time (Luke 22:3, 14-23).

Community

Our research into Tamilian spirituality informed us that on the popular level, Hindu worship puts a strong emphasis on community. This being the case, we knew that this ceremony could not simply focus on Mr. Ram and his illness; rather, this needed to be a time in which one family was ministering to another and when both families were experiencing God together. We sought to achieve this sense of community by reading the Bible together, praying while touching each other ("laying on of hands"), sharing the Seder together, and having dinner together after the formal ceremony was over.

---

* Passages in 1 Corinthians should be consulted here. In chapter 11 of that book, Paul talks about taking the Lord's Supper in an unworthy manner but is addressing Christians only. That is to say, the "unworthy manner" is the Christian who takes the elements in a cavalier manner, not acknowledging the "body of the Lord." As for the Rams, the manner in which they took the elements was far more reverent than what I typically witness in churches by Christians. In 1 Corinthians 10, Paul gets perhaps more to the point (10:21) but again these are instructions for Christians. Again we must consider the fact that Judas Iscariot while possessed by Satan was offered the original Lord's Supper by Jesus and it is hardly conclusive. Clearly a sacramentalist has more of a quandary here than a Calvinist, Zwinglian or an Evangelical—after all, if it is just bread, it's just bread regardless of who eats it.

Engaging the Senses

The most common form of Hindu worship is the *pooja* which happens on a daily basis in the home around the family shrine. Katherine and I have seen Mr. and Mrs. Ram do a *pooja*. It is a feast for the senses. Everyone focuses their eyes on the beautifully fashioned idols on the shrine. An oil lamp is lit and worshippers feel the heat of its flame with their hands and face. The aroma of flowers and burning incense fills the air. Food that is offered to the gods is later eaten by the worshippers. Prayers are sung or chanted by the devotees. The typical American evangelical song and sermon service simply can't compete in terms of sensory appeal.

Katherine and I wanted to create a ceremony that was not merely cognitive; we wanted it to be an experience that engaged all the senses as well. A number of symbols were employed in order to help accomplish this. Thus, instead of simply telling the Rams to focus on Jesus Christ and His death and resurrection, I anointed Mr. Ram with oil to remind us that Jesus is God's anointed and gave him a cross to hold as we prayed. Red cloth was used on the altar because it is the most auspicious color[*] for Hindus and because it represents the blood of Jesus Christ. The physical sensations associated with kneeling and the "laying on of hands" as well as the taste of the Seder elements and the sound of prayers and Bible readings also contributed to the creation of a religious experience of diverse sensory appeal.

Many Protestant Christians have been wary of symbols since Carlstadt took to smashing stained glass windows in Wittenberg during the Reformation. However, the Bible itself is loaded with symbols, particularly in the Old Testament. It is significant that one of the first people in the Bible said to be full of God's Spirit was Bezalel whose chief ministry was in creating religious symbols such as the Ark of the Covenant and furnishings for the Tabernacle (Ex. 31:3). Providing that Biblical meaning is poured into them and idolatry is avoided, symbols can be a powerful means of engaging the whole person in a discipleship experience.

---

[*] Colors have important significance in Hindu spirituality. Red is the color of auspiciousness. It is used for weddings, births, festivals and more. Red is the mark of an auspicious occasion. Saffron is also an important color because it represents fire and thus stands for purity. It is a priestly color. White can symbolize peace and purity as it commonly does among Christians; however, it is most commonly associated with mourning and death.

Communicating the God of Scripture

Of course the main thrust of the ceremony was our effort to communicate the God of the Bible as clearly as we could. Many of the symbols (e.g. the cross, the oil, the bread and wine, the red cloth) pointed directly to Jesus Christ and His death and resurrection. I spoke about the Holy Spirit before we read the Bible. The Bible passage we read recounted stories from Christ's healing ministry. Our prayers were directed to God the Father in the name of Jesus Christ. We wanted to make it very clear that we were not just seeking some general notion of divinity but rather the unique God revealed in the Bible.

Literature Review

Once again it is important to note that Katherine and I developed and implemented the Passover healing ceremony in response to an unexpected crisis experienced by our Hindu neighbors. We did not have the luxury to conduct extensive research into the particular issues of this new situation. Instead, we turned to cultural, missiological, and theological research we had already conducted. The following is a brief survey of several pieces of literature that had significant influence on us as we responded to the Rams' crisis. A number of my own works are included here because they reflect well the foundation of research that we drew upon.

In 1980, the Consultation on World Evangelization Mini-Consultation on Reaching Hindus published a list of barriers to reaching Hindus with the gospel of Jesus Christ. One of the most significant, they noted, was "the Christian way of worship which is predominately non-Indian" (p. 11). The consultation went on to explain: "Western culture has been injected into Indian culture as an acceptable form of Christianity; thus, it appears to non-Christians, this alienates them to a large extent" (p. 11). However, it was only when I personally experienced the "non-Indian" nature of Indian Christian worship while conducting participant observations at Tamilian churches in 2004 that I really began to see the urgent need for contextualization. I recorded the details of these observations in an earlier chapter.

Several works have influenced us in terms of how contextualization should be done among Hindus. Key among these has been my own study of Roberto de Nobili's 17th century mission among Tamilians. De Nobili's strong commitment to both contextualization and Biblical authority served as an inspiration and guide for us.

We had also become very much inclined towards making use of our creative ability in the contextualization process. Two chapters in the 1973 book *Indian Spirituality in Action*, one by Michael Amaladoss and the other by Matthew Lederle, emphasized the importance of creativity and the arts when contextualizing Christian spirituality among Indians.

Our understanding of Hindu religious forms and important areas for contextualization came from several sources. Examples include Swami Bhajananda's "Worship in Hinduism and Christianity" where he provides helpful historical and theological insights into some of the most common forms of Hindu worship (1980). Paul Hiebert's "Folk religion in Andhra Pradesh and some missiological implications" briefly mentions roles of idols and symbols in folk Hinduism (1983). Charles Hoole's "Territorial spirits: An Indian perspective" helped us to understand why the Rams felt it was important to seek Jesus Christ at our home rather than their own (1997). Richard MacPhail's "Finding a path in others' worlds: The challenge of exorcism" illustrated through a case study the effectiveness of participant discipleship in ministry to Hindus (2002). V. Francis Vineeth's "Religio-cultural festivals of India" emphasized the importance of sacred time in Hindu spirituality (1987). Again, my own ethnographic research about Tamilian Hindus proved invaluable in that it alerted us to a number of relevant issues including the importance of sacred space, community, and sensory appeal in worship.

Our desire to respond to the Rams' crisis holistically was stimulated by A. Scott Moreau's "Evil spirit: Biblical and practical issues" (1995) and my work on Tamilian folk Hinduism discussed in a previous chapter. A.H. Mathais Zahniser's book *Symbol and ceremony: Making disciples across cultures* (1997) and my study of discipleship rituals in the book of Ezra helped us to see that the most effective and most contextualized way of responding holistically was through the development and implementation of symbols and ceremony.

References

Amaladoss, M. (1973). Searching together. In Sister Vandana (Ed.), Indian spirituality in action (pp. 35-47). Bombay: R.B. Pinto, Asian Trading Corporation.

Bhajanananda, Swami (1980). Worship in Hinduism and Christianity. In C.M. Vadakkekara (Ed.), Prayer and Contemplation (pp. 311-329). Bangalore: Asirvanam Benedictine Monastery.

Consultation on World Evangelization Mini-Consultation on Reaching Hindus (1980). Christian Witness to Hindus. Wheaton, IL: Lausanne Committee for World Evangelization

Hiebert, Paul G. (1983). Folk religion in Andhra Pradesh and some missiological implications. In Vinay Samuel and Chris Sugden (Eds.), The gospel among our Hindu neighbors (pp. 87-109). Bangalore: Partnership in Mission.

Hoole, Charles R.A. (1997). Territorial spirits: An Indian perspective. Stulos Theological Journal, 5(2), 59-68.

Lederle, Matthew. (1973). Interpreting Christ through Indian art. In Sister Vandana (Ed.), Indian Spirituality in Action (pp. 130-141). Bombay: R.B. Pinto, Asian Trading Corporation.

MacPhail, Richard D. (2002). Finding a path in others' worlds: The challenge of exorcism. In Selva J. Raj and Corinne G. Dempsey (Eds.), Popular Christianity in India: Riting between the lines (pp. 141-162). Albany, NY: State University of New York Press.

Moreau, Scott A. (1995). Evil spirits: Biblical and practical issues. Urban Mission, 13(2), 25-36.

Vineeth, V. Francis. (1987). Religio-cultural festival of India. Journal of Dharma, 12, 133-144.

Zahniser, A.H. Mathais. (1997). *Symbol and ceremony: Making disciples across cultures.* Monrovia, CA: MARC.

Appendix: Case Study Version for Group Study

"Come as you are"

Chris went to bed on Saturday night reflecting on what a big day it had been for the small Indian church which met at his house. Chris was an associate pastor of a suburban church which had done a great job of reaching the mostly white, middle class population by allowing people to "come as you are." When the church directors noticed that several Indians had started attending regularly, they asked Chris to help form a group that would someday become a sister church.

It had only been a few months ago that Chris first met with the six Indian believers. As they shared their testimonies, Chris learned that they were all in their 20s, had been raised as Hindus and had decided to follow Jesus in college or shortly after. Most were children of immigrants and had lived in the United States all their lives. When the group expressed a desire to reach out to the Hindu community (a significant minority), Chris's suggestion of starting a house church was met with enthusiasm. Chris was to lead until God raised up a pastor among the Indians. After some discussion, every other Saturday afternoon at Chris's house seemed to be the best time and place for the group.

The reason for excitement on this particular Saturday was that it had been the first time Hindu visitors had come. Hari, who had been a believer for four months, was the only one of the group whose family lived nearby. Hari's parents were tolerant of their son's new faith and wanted to visit his church. Chris thought their visit had gone well overall, although they seemed to be confused when Chris told them they did not need to take off their shoes or that the fruit and flowers which they had brought were not appropriate on the altar. Well, Chris reflected, Hari's parents did not leave as Christians but they had witnessed true worship for the first time. Perhaps on their next visit they might even realize that they did not need to wear fancy clothes to impress God.

The next night, Chris received a frantic call from Hari, asking that they meet as soon as possible. Chris and Hari met over coffee the next morning. Before Chris could share his excitement about Saturday, Hari blurted out, "My parents were so offended by their visit that they are demanding that I stop coming. In fact, they want me to stop being a Christian completely if all churches are like ours."

Hari went on: "They asked so many questions I couldn't answer. Why do we meet every other Saturday when there's nothing special about Saturdays and if there is, why do we only meet every other week? Why do we meet at a house instead of at a church when there's nothing special about the house? Why do we dress so casually when God wants our best? Why do we leave on our shoes when they bring in dirt and make things unclean and impure? What was wrong with the gift of fruit and flowers my parents brought to God? Why don't the rest of us bring offerings to God other than money? My parents think God does not accept our worship since we ignore these simple things. They think God will be more pleased with me if I worship him the Hindu way."

After a moment, Hari said, "I still want to be a Christian and I still want to go to church, but I want to worship God in a respectful and honoring way. Is there any way we can make our church look more Hindu?" Chris had asked Hari for some time to pray and think about the situation and now lying in bed, he wondered what he should do . . . .

Chapter 7:
Ethiopians in Chicagoland: *Ethnographic Insights for Mission Advance*

Jeffrey Davis & Donna Herron
2007 College Summer Missionaries
Trinity International Baptist Mission
Carol Stream, IL

Part 1: Research Methods

This study employed a blend of surveys, interviews and focus groups in addition to an intense review of existing literature in order to more fully explore the religious and cultural issues facing Ethiopian immigrants in the Chicago area. Before embarking upon the field work portion of our research, we began with an in-depth literature review in order to gain a greater understanding of the background behind our research question: "What needs to be done in order to most effectively reach the Orthodox Ethiopian population of Chicagoland?"

In *The Role of the Ethiopian Church in Affirming the National Identity of Her People,* Barbara Smith brings to the surface one of the most pivotal elements of this research—that the Ethiopian Orthodox Church is a deeply-rooted national institution, intertwined with religion, culture and society to the point that these elements are inseparable. We found this to be a recurring theme as we began to delve into field work, interviewing six members of the Ethiopian population of Chicago.

Research Subjects[*]

- Tariku is a 36-year-old male Orthodox Ethiopian immigrant who came to Chicago four years ago through the diversity lottery and is now a cab driver in the city. He lives in the Edgewater community with a roommate in a rented apartment. His wife remains in Ethiopia.

- Bedelwa is a 36-year-old female Orthodox Ethiopian immigrant who came to the United States six years ago for health reasons and now lives with her daughter in the Edgewater community. She works a night shift job in the city. Her husband lives and works in Sudan through an agency based out of New York City and thus is able to visit occasionally.

- Mekdem is a 47-year-old male who describes himself as a "born again" Christian. He came to Chicago seven years ago to join his wife after she won a diversity lottery five years prior. He is a writer and they live with their two children in a suburb west of Chicago.

---

[*] *All names have been changed to preserve the anonymity of the research subjects.*

- Amsalu is a six year resident of Edgewater since immigrating from Ethiopia as a political refugee. He now works for an Ethiopian agency in Chicago and lives with his wife in the Edgewater community.

- Dawit is a 38-year-old male who came to the Chicago area three years ago as a student to study and later started an Amharic speaking church where he serves as a minister. While he was in Ethiopia he worked with the evangelical movement in the country training Ethiopian leaders. Dawit lives with his wife and two children.

- Zelalem is a 41-year-old male who immigrated from Ethiopia to Chicago fifteen years ago. During his time in the United States, Zelalem attended college in Ohio. Within about a year of coming to the United States, Zelalem converted from the Ethiopian Orthodox faith to evangelicalism. He now resides in Wisconsin, approximately two hours north of Chicago. Each week he makes the two-hour commute to the Chicago area in order to attend an Ethiopian evangelical church.

Statistically speaking, these interviewees may be considered typical of Ethiopian immigrants in the United States in terms of language, marital status, the time they entered the U.S., and their housing situations. According to the 2000 U.S. Census, in a special tabulation regarding people living in the United States who were born in Ethiopia, several commonalities stand out. Most immigrants came to the U.S. after 1990, speak a native language other than English, are between twenty-five and fifty-four years old, are married and live in a rental unit with a spouse and children. These characteristics of the typical Ethiopian immigrant generally apply to our research subjects, making them good representatives of the broader Ethiopian population in the U.S.

The interviewees are also representative of Chicagoland's Ethiopian community in general. Most Ethiopians in Chicago are Orthodox Christian with some evangelical Christians among the population. Our samples are also drawn from various geographical regions of the Chicagoland area; some interviewees live in the Edgewater community while some live in the west suburbs of Chicago. We feel that this sample is representative of both evangelical and Orthodox Ethiopian Christians living in Chicago and in the surrounding suburbs. Most of our interviewees have immigrated to Chicago within the last ten years and identify themselves as either Orthodox or evangelical Christian.

Research Design and Procedures

We collected our data through a combination of qualitative and quantitative research methods. A participant observation at Tensae Church, an evangelical Ethiopian congregation in Glen Ellyn, IL, gave insights into the evangelical worship experience of Ethiopians here in the U. S. There we were able to conduct interviews and surveys with evangelical Ethiopian Christians.

In order to interview Orthodox Ethiopian Christians, we made contacts at local Ethiopian-run businesses and agencies in the Edgewater community of Chicago where many Ethiopian immigrants live. We conducted interviews and surveys with random people who patronize these businesses and agencies.

At times, conducting field work among the Orthodox Ethiopians was quite challenging.

There was not a steady traffic flow at these businesses and a number of people were unwilling to speak with us. Setting up interviews occupied much of our time, as we had to contact and were shuffled between many agencies throughout the Chicago area.

Limitations

Our research into Ethiopians in Chicagoland was hindered by a number of factors. The first of these impediments was the fact that, as first-time ethnographic researchers, our inexperience often worked against us. Another major factor was that most Ethiopian immigrants live in the Edgewater area of Chicago, which resulted in a great deal of travel time for us to go there and meet with people. We were also limited by scheduling and timing difficulties as we attempted to obtain a random sample in the Edgewater area. It was often difficult to make contacts at local establishments since we did not know when the high traffic times were and often had to guess when would be best to encounter people. We also ran into cultural differences about time and scheduling which often made it difficult to pin down a day and time to interview people and thus were unable to complete some of the interviews we would have liked to. Many of the females we approached did not wish to be interviewed but instead deferred to a male. Another difficulty we encountered, as would be expected when working with recent immigrants, was the language barrier. Some interviews were difficult or impossible due to this barrier.

One last roadblock we encountered was the reluctance of agencies to help us contact members of the Ethiopian community, mainly because many of the people that the agencies work with are refugees and there are many security procedures in place to protect those people. Our research could have been more exhaustive, but given these limitations we completed the study to the best of our abilities given our time and resources.

Part 2: Literature Review[*]

As we began to explore the existing literature related to advancing the gospel among Ethiopians in the Chicago area, we found a wealth of information. The existing information only goes so far as most of the existing research is focused exclusively on Ethiopians in Ethiopia. Nevertheless, after surveying dozens of pieces of literature, we have identified several major themes: the impact of indigenous religious beliefs, the uniqueness of Ethiopia and the Ethiopian Orthodox Church, the role of the Ethiopian Orthodox Church in the nation, the interaction of Islam with the nation of Ethiopia, instances and causes of religious conflict, issues faced by missionaries to Ethiopia and the issues facing immigrants to new countries as they seek to maintain their native religions.

Indigenous Religious Beliefs

Many authors focused on describing and explaining Ethiopian spiritual beliefs. One particularly well-researched idea is the belief in the "Evil Eye." Belief of the power of the evil eye is especially strong among the Buda people, one of the minority ethnic groups of Ethiopia. Unlike most of the Ethiopian population who are agrarian, the Buda are skilled artisans (Reminick, both articles). It is difficult to distinguish Buda people from other Ethiopians by mere sight, so other ethnic groups of Ethiopia fear strangers who might be overtly friendly for fear that they may possess the Evil Eye (Reminick 281).

Another topic frequented by researchers addresses the folklore of the Ethiopian people, specifically the Sidama, an idea explored in an article titled "The religious conversion process among the Sidama of North-East Africa." The article explains that the Sidama continue to practice some of

---

[*] *Editor's Note: The following literature review is inadequately cited according to the rules of the APA. I have chosen to include it here for the sake of demonstrating that an attempt to consult extant literature on the subject was made by the authors of this chapter.*

their traditional beliefs, even while attending Christian church services (Hammer, 599). Existing material shows that the Sidama appear to be the only tribe with an indigenous moral code, which they credit as given to them by a god. The Sidama continue to use this long-standing code today, as they have for centuries. From research performed thus far, the only information about the code is that its primary function is to help distinguish the difference between good and evil (Hammer, 601).

One of the other major indigenous beliefs surfacing in extant literature is the belief of two spirits called the Zar and Adbar (Reminick <u>eHRAF</u>). These are spirits that belong to the mother and father of a family which, upon their deaths, are passed down to their eldest son or daughter. The child is then required to appease the gods to keep the spirits happy (Reminick).

The Uniqueness of Ethiopia and the Ethiopian Orthodox Church

Ethiopia is a unique nation within Africa on many different levels. Never subjected to a colonial conquest (not including the brief take over by Italian troops under Mussolini during World War II) and having a continual line of patriarchal rulers during the times when colonial powers carved up the rest of Africa make Ethiopia politically distinct. Add to that Ethiopia's geographical isolation, which is also a factor in her stability and development, and you begin to grasp the country's uniqueness (Tibebu, 1996). This stability and self-governance also facilitated the formation of religion within the country, which in turn has an impact on the society and culture of the entire nation. Barbara Smith looked at this in *The Role of the Ethiopian Church in Affirming the National Identity of Her People.* Her findings show that the development of the national church of Ethiopia, the Ethiopian Orthodox Church, which began in the fourth century and made Christianity the state religion of Ethiopia, was also a major contributor to national development in the fields of independence, social progress, national unity and empowerment, literary development, arts, architecture, music, publication, and declaration of a national language and leadership, both spiritual and military. These advances also contribute towards the idea that national development is interdependent with the well-being of the Ethiopian Orthodox Church. Also cited is the role of the Ethiopian Orthodox Church hierarchy in national governance and its role as the defender of the masses (Wubishet, 1990). However, many consider this intertwining of church and government to be a hindrance to development and modernization within the country. To see the strength of the Ethiopian Orthodox Church, note the fact that it pervades personal, interpersonal and social relationships, is the custodian of education and is one of the main influencers of art and literature (Smith, 1999).

Role of the Ethiopian Orthodox Church in the nation

Again contributing to the strength of the Ethiopian Orthodox Church is the relationship that it maintains with the national government. There exists a great deal of literature regarding this area, which often delves into the importance of the church-nation relationship. It is hard to question the role of the Ethiopian Orthodox Church, as it numbers as many as thirty million members. In its development, the Ethiopian Orthodox Church addressed issues that were specific to Ethiopia and the culture of the people within the nation, thereby solidifying the relationship between the people and the church. Joachim Persoon identifies the strength of the people's dedication and points out the sense of community and security that it inspires among Ethiopian Orthodox Church members. The sense of community also means that religion does not resound with the individual but instead with the community; religion then becomes part of one's natural identity and to break away is betrayal of the community and the religion. Getatchew Haile (1998) highlights this idea in *The Missionary's Dream: An Ethiopian Perspective on Western Missions in Ethiopia* as he emphasizes the rooting of religion in the culture of Ethiopia, expounding on the idea that one is born into the religion. From this deep dedication to the Ethiopian Orthodox Church and the image of the church as a community, it is not surprising that Ethiopian Orthodox Church clergy are strongly opposed to their members converting even to other branches of Christianity. They view conversion as the loss of a family member among the Ethiopian Orthodox Church. This provides some key insights into both the church-state relationship and the failures experienced by missionaries in Ethiopia in trying to convert Ethiopian Orthodox Church members to Protestantism or Catholicism.

Even under the disestablishmentarianism of the Marxist regime, which took a strong hold on the nation in 1974, the strength of the church was obvious. An article in *Evangelical Missions Quarterly* quotes a citizen as saying, "You can take away our politics, take away our food, but if you take away our religion you've got a problem" (Niklus, 355). The regime strongly discouraged most religious activity, but due to the historical government ties and deep-rooted sentiment for religion, the Marxist leadership recognized the inevitability of the role of religion in the nation (Abbink, 117). To avoid intense conflict, the government made concessions in their communistic agenda. While communist restrictions limited some functions of the Ethiopian Orthodox Church, they did not completely take away their religious practices (Abbink and Ostebo). Nevertheless, during the time period of the communist regime (1974-1991) reports show a large number of both evangelical and Orthodox churches closing, illustrating the rise in restrictions that were placed on the churches, which further complicated the relationship between the church and the government (Mumper 70).

Before the communist regime took over, the government used religion as an aid to achieve the goals of the nation and obtain support necessary for national leadership. The leader of Ethiopia before this time was Emperor Haile Sellassie, whom the Coptic church of Ethiopia sanctified to rule the nation (Hussien). Sellassie was an integral part of allowing entry into Ethiopia by evangelical missionaries before 1974. He was a supporter of rural education and sought the development of western medicine in the country, so he invited evangelical Protestant missionaries to come into Ethiopia and set up hospitals and schools. In return for providing these services to the Ethiopian people, Sellassie allowed the missionaries to evangelize to the rural people and try to convert them to their religion (Hamer, 606). The work completed by missionaries also aided in strengthening the emperor's power in the country (Eide, 473).

Islam in Ethiopia

As the Ethiopian Orthodox Church maintained a strong role in the government and development of the nation, keep in mind that Islamic countries surrounded Ethiopia. Even with the strong influence of the Ethiopian Orthodox Church on the core of society, Islam could reach the periphery, mainly tribal and pastoral members of society, before working towards influencing more core members. The peripheral members could more easily understand Islam because it adapted well to the way of life of the people and the religion came to the people by means of peaceful traders who moved to the areas and slowly taught the ways of Islam (Tenna, 1998).

Religious Conflict within Ethiopia

As is often the case when multiple ethnic and religious groups cohabitate the same geographical region, there are instances of conflict among these groups. Ethiopia has been no exception. Most confrontations arise over cultural differences within local villages and outbreaks are often between either Muslims or evangelicals and Orthodox Christians (Ostebo 434). One article cites an event in 2001, when a skirmish occurred between Christians and Muslims surrounding a disagreement on the rights of each to hold religious processions in a small village. The conflict escalated, resulting in the death of members from each group and requiring the use of government troops to regain control over the situation (Ahmed, 17).

Issues in Missionary Interaction in Ethiopia

Sven Rubenson points out that many early missionaries were comparable to colonizers as they came and went from the country at their own will, showing little to no regard for the culture and customs that had existed long before their arrival. These early missionaries tended to seek out new mission fields much akin to the degree with which colonizers sought out new peoples to capitalize upon. This aggressive manner of missions tended to aggravate pre-existing internal conflicts and led to the expulsion of many mission groups. In *Religions of the World*, an illustration of this problem is clear, as during the sixteenth century, Ethiopia expelled Catholic missionaries from the country because they were too aggressive and ignored local customs. Samuel Rubenson also points out in *The Interaction between the Missionaries and the Orthodox: the Case of Abune Selama* that many missionaries to Ethiopia were of the mindset that they were messengers to the heathen. Most early missions were culturally insensitive and tried to force Westernized Christianity, specifically Protestant beliefs, onto a people with fundamentally intertwined culture and religion. As a result, the Ethiopian Orthodox Church and Ethiopian evangelical church as well as other Protestant churches have very strained relationships. In addition, among missionaries, there exists the blurring of the differentiation in the concepts of changes in belief (conversion) and changes in affiliation, which missionaries to Ethiopia often overlooked as they considered a change from Ethiopian Orthodox Church to Protestantism to be a complete conversion (Kaplan, 2004). There also exists a difference in the social perception of religion in Ethiopia; Christianity spread from the core of society (nobles and priests) to the periphery, whereas Islam spread from the periphery to the core. These manners of proliferation of the respective religions shape the way in which Ethiopians view the religions and affect the way missionaries address each (Kaplan, 1986).

Immigrants and the Maintenance of Religion

For many immigrants, the community of faith is a key player in life in a new country. The congregation serves as a reminder of the community from their homeland, providing social and emotional resources.

Reproduction of ethnicity through physical structures, celebrations and even vernacular become crucial for the participation of immigrants. However, the focus on the first generation of immigrants and attempts to recreate culture and the lifestyles of their former homes often has a negative effect on the second generation who may be completely unfamiliar with the homeland of their parents and feel alienated by the congregations that cater to the first generation (Ebaugh, 2000).

Part 3: Findings

As previously noted, the research conducted for this project brought us into contact with two groups of Ethiopians in the Chicago area. We conducted three of our interviews with evangelical Christians while the other three were with members of the Ethiopian Orthodox Church. The participants came to the United States under varying circumstances and all have some connection to the Ethiopian Orthodox Church.

Ethiopian Orthodox Christians

Tariku

Our first interview was with Tariku, an Ethiopian immigrant born into and raised by an Orthodox Christian family. In Ethiopia, he was a high school chemistry teacher and actively involved in his local Orthodox congregation. Tariku came to Chicago in 2002 through the diversity lottery and has lived in Chicago since arriving in the United States. He initially came to and remains in Chicago because this is where his diversity lottery sponsor lives. Tariku now resides in the Edgewater district of north Chicago in an apartment with a roommate and is currently working as a taxi driver in the area. He is married but does not have any family members living in the U. S.; his family, including his wife, remains in Ethiopia.

Religious life in Ethiopia.

Tariku identifies himself strongly as an Orthodox Christian and commented that he went to church every Sunday when he lived in Ethiopia. He says that the Orthodox Church in Ethiopia is a very community and family centered religion, explaining, "My mom, my dad, my grandfamilies, they are Orthodox Church." Everyone has time to go to the church, which is nearby, so families and communities walk to the church together. He also pointed out that there is a very developed organization of the church and that many people attend the churches daily. There is more flexibility with when you can go -- early morning for some or late afternoon for others. He also said that the priests are very available and play a large role in educating the people about the religion.

Religion in the United States.

In Chicago, Tariku attends the Ethiopian Orthodox church located in southern Chicago but he can only go once or twice a month due to his job. When asked about how he came to find out about the church here, Tariku said,

> When I came here, my sponsor told me "There is a community church, we have to go there." Then after 3 days he took me there, introduced me with the community, then I started with the church.

Although Tariku cannot attend the Orthodox church as much as he would like, Tariku maintains the importance of prayer in his daily life, including the role of the veneration of Mary:

> I believe, I pray. It's like people they consider that praying they may say like, "Why I pray every time? What I get from praying?" They say. It's like food. I am growing now my physically I am growing up everything because of the food, so mentally because of praying every day I am alive still now. It's very important... You have to say something, you have to fear something. If you don't fear something, oh God will punish me if I do something wrong, Mary will punish me, that's fine. So it's important for me still.

Changes and difficulties in religious involvement in the U. S.

Here in Chicago, Tariku told us that there is a marked difference in his involvement in the church. As a taxi driver, he must work hours that are not conducive to attending early Sunday morning services. Since the Orthodox church in Chicago is only open on Sundays, he is not able to attend services as he would like to and thus is limited to going once every two weeks or even only once a month. Tariku explained further the contrast between Ethiopia and Chicago,

> *But there, you can go everyday church. Here only they are open on Sunday. Because it is far you don't have time. There we can see a lot of peoples in everyday church. A lot of people come there on the church; you can go, if you want, you can go in the afternoon, 5 pm, 6 pm whatever you like and you can meet priests there and you can come get some education from the churches. But here it's far— once a week or once a month only. That is the difference.*

In addition to the difficulty in obtaining education from the Ethiopian Orthodox church in Chicago, Tariku also stated that,

> *Here there is only one church. It is South Side. It's very far. That's why. It's on 95th. It's very far from, almost South Side. People, they complaining, 'Why don't they make it around here?' A lot of Ethiopians, they live around here. But the priests they say the reason is it is very expensive to buy church around here, that's why. They buy around there; it is less expensive I think that is why they don't buy around here. So because of this, I am sure, if it was around here, I am sure a lot of people can go every day, because of that part a lot of people go once-a-week or twice-a-week, sometimes once-a-month.*

Bedelwa

Bedelwa is an Orthodox Christian, born in Ethiopia, now living and working in Chicago. Bedelwa came to the U. S. with chronic medical problems seeking relief for a seemingly incurable illness. Within a short time after being placed at Cook County Hospital and assigned a social worker, her illness began to improve. At the time of our interview she had completely recovered.

She came to the United States in 2001, leaving her husband and her daughter behind in Ethiopia, and lived with her brother-in-law, also her sponsor, for nine months during her treatment before she could live on her own. Her daughter joined her four years ago. Bedelwa must work a night shift job in order to commit as much of her time as possible to her daughter, who has some developmental problems which have considerably improved in the past few years. Bedelwa's husband works in Sudan for an American NGO based out of New York. They do not live together, but he is able to visit them occasionally.

Religious life in Ethiopia.

Bedelwa is Orthodox like the rest of her family and describes it is a very cultural religion. She even went as far as to say, "You are raised with it, you go to church with your family. It is big trouble if you switch to new religion. " She said that in Ethiopia,

> *There are many people at church every day because you go every day with your family, especially on holidays and Sundays and everyone goes because it is cultural and religion is such a big part of life in Ethiopia.*

Religious life in the U. S.

As mentioned earlier, Bedelwa lives with her daughter, who requires much of her attention. When it comes to church involvement here in Chicago, she would like to go every Sunday, but cannot. Since she works overnight, she gets home when it is morning and must rest and take care of her daughter. Before her daughter came to live with her, she used to go every week. When she goes to church, it is to the Orthodox church in south Chicago because the service is in Amharic. She has been to the Greek Orthodox church in the Uptown community before but the service is in English and she doesn't really consider it "*her*" church." Bedelwa said she found out about the Ethiopian Orthodox church through her brother-in-law who attends there.

Changes and difficulties in religious involvement in the U. S.

Bedelwa said that in Chicago there is not a real community for Ethiopians or the Ethiopian Orthodox Church. Everyone goes to the Ethiopian Orthodox church because it is cultural but people need the proper environment (time and family nearby) to re-create community. In addition, the church is only open on Sundays, which does not help build the community. The community surrounding the church is a large part of what defines the Orthodox Church in Ethiopia, she says, which marks one of the biggest differences between the U. S. and Ethiopia.

Amsalu

Amsalu is a political asylee who has lived in the United States for six years now. After being granted asylum he came to live with a friend in Indianapolis for about a month before moving to Chicago. He then lived with the parents of a friend before renting his own apartment in the Edgewater community. He now lives with his wife and works for an agency that aids immigrants and refugees in the Chicago area.

Religious life in Ethiopia.

Amsalu is also Ethiopian Orthodox Christian and, although he did not expressly state his involvement in the church, he did clearly articulate his feelings toward the role of the Ethiopian Orthodox Church as an institution in Ethiopia:

> *It's very important. It is very crucial in the life and history of that country. Had it not been for that Ethiopian Orthodox Church, Ethiopia wouldn't have existed like it has. It might have been disintegrated. We always have dictators and rulers always dictate because of the church that people come together. We don't have judge, we don't have many courts like here. It is the church that promotes peace, the church that promotes friendship and kind of very cohesive society. That is the role of the church. It has a long history. Three thousand years of history of religion in the country.*

Through his answers to our questions, his sentiments reflect the importance of the connection between the Ethiopian Orthodox Church and Ethiopian society and lifestyle, making it difficult to distinguish religion from culture.

Religious life in the U. S.

Amsalu told us about the depth of his religious involvement here in the United States, saying, "I participate, I participate in Sunday school, and regularly go to church every Sunday and participate in the church services." He indicated that he attends the Orthodox church in south Chicago. An important religious practice for him here is fasting: "There we fast. Here it is not easy. Sometimes you don't find food that you can eat outside, you know." Even though it is more difficult for him to do here, Amsalu still tries to uphold important traditions of the Orthodox Church in his life in the U. S.

Changes and difficulties in religious involvement in the U. S.

Amsalu reflects many of the same feelings as the other Orthodox interviewees about their changes with regard to the church in coming to the U. S. He says,

> *In Ethiopia, people have more time. You regularly to go to church and people attend the full service. Here it is not that easy. People work Saturday in the evening you know Sunday morning and as a social life, it is also. It is not easy to spend the time that you are supposed to spend.*

As mentioned previously, Amsalu spoke about the importance of fasting and how it is more difficult to do here in the U. S. because our culture does not conform to that tradition. He also talked about the importance of community in the culture of Ethiopia, "Here, you know, the culture is different. People are always busy, live apart from each other, don't visit friend every time. There is different."

Ethiopian Evangelical Christians

Mekdem

Mekdem was born in Ethiopia and lived there until he was about forty, when he came to the United States to join his wife who had already been here for five years. He and his wife both came to the U. S. through the diversity lottery and now live in an apartment in a west suburb of Chicago with their two children, who were both born in the U. S. Mekdem is a writer and when we conducted the interview, Mekdem had been in the U. S. for seven years. We asked Mekdem to describe life here in the United States and he quickly described it as an individualistic society where no one really takes part in the community. In response to a question relating to what he misses about Ethiopia, his reply illustrated the importance of family as he stated that he still feels connected to Ethiopia and his family and community that remains there.

Religious life in Ethiopia.

Mekdem was born and raised into an Orthodox family in Ethiopia. However, Mekdem said that he never felt truly connected to the religion. He described it as being too formal and ritualistic, saying,

> *(The priests use) language that is too high, like Latin in the Catholic Church. The laity, like me, do not understand it. It is all a ritual. They say, 'stand', 'sit'. It is like exercise. There is no life in it. The place is holy, but there is no transformation within.*

He called himself a "nominal" Christian, alluding to the fact that he was not very involved in the church or in his own personal beliefs. At one point, Mekdem began to read an Amharic Bible and gained a desire to read the scriptures and learn more. A lady invited him to attend an evangelical church in Ethiopia and he went, for he was battling a sickness that would not improve. After that experience, he began attending the evangelical church more and gradually changed. He still occasionally attended the Orthodox church, but again pointed out that he was a "nominal" Christian at that time.

Religious life in the United States.

Mekdem came to Chicago and attended the Ethiopian Orthodox church in south Chicago for two years before attending a Pentecostal church. He continued to pray for an Ethiopian church as he came to a complete change and was born again and re-baptized. Commenting about his re-baptism, he stated, "You know, I was baptized as an infant, but I don't count that because, you know, I wasn't there. That wasn't me. It was my parents."

Soon thereafter, he was involved in a prayer group meeting in a suburb of Chicago. The group was meeting and praying for an Amharic church. When an answer to that prayer came, Mekdem's family was one of the first to join the new church. They now attend the Amharic speaking church in Glen Ellyn, IL each Sunday.

Changes and difficulties in religious involvement in the U. S.

When discussing the impediments to being highly involved in the church here in the United States, Mekdem offered his personal sentiments. He felt that involvement here depends solely on himself; it all depends on him whether he is highly involved or not. He pointed out that since 1992 (the fall of the communist regime in Ethiopia) he was free to practice his religion, as he desired.

Zelahem

Of the six Ethiopians that we came in contact with for the purpose of interviews, Zelahem has lived in the United States for the longest, although he never stated the reason for coming to the U. S. When Zelahem first came to the U.S. fifteen years ago, he lived in Chicago. Since then, he has moved twice, living in Ohio where he attended college and now residing in Madison, WI approximately two hours from the west suburbs of Chicago. In Wisconsin, he lives in an apartment with his wife and two children.

Religious life in Ethiopia.

Like the other Ethiopians we interviewed, Zelahem grew up in an Ethiopian Orthodox home, where he regularly participated in religious services. In addition to participating in these services, he also followed the Ethiopian Orthodox Church's rules of fasting on every Wednesday and Friday as well as on other holy days. He seemed to reiterate the sentiments of Mekdem by commenting on the Ethiopian Orthodox Church practice of conducting services with a level of language that the layperson cannot understand. He also echoed the idea that the services revolved around many directed movements by the liturgy and the hierarchy of the Orthodox Church, with a pre-set schedule of movements and actions during the services. Although Zelahem does not keep to the practices today that he once did in Ethiopia, he still believes that there are some beneficial values instilled by the church and he believes that the evangelical church should exercise some of those values today, like removing shoes before entering a place of worship and the occasional practice of fasting.

Religious life in the United States.

Shortly after Zelahem arrived in the United States, a friend invited him to attend a service at an evangelical church to pray for an ill family member back in Ethiopia. After he attended that service at the evangelical church, it began a marked change in Zelahem's life as he began to convert from being an Orthodox to an evangelical Christian. Zelahem's conversion was aided by his attendance at both an English-speaking evangelical church as a well as an Amharic evangelical church. He currently attends services at an Amharic speaking Ethiopian church. When asked about his current church he said,

> *My first experiences. I think the smallness of the church gives cohesiveness to the member. I believe and I have witness a lot of love for the people. Love for the people, love for Christ, love to do the Lord's work, to see souls being saved and energy in everything I see was really marvelous.*

This aids in explaining what he believes to be the differences in evangelical and Orthodox practices. Zelahem's religious life in the United States is much different from that in Ethiopia. Zelahem involved himself deeply in his religion in both countries, but he believes that his religion here in America with the evangelical church places much more emphasis on a personal, individualized relationship and that, from the perspective of the church, there is much more concern for the growth of the individual than there was in Ethiopia.

Changes and difficulties in religious involvement in the U. S.

When speaking about the change in his involvement in the United States, the main differences Zelahem indicated were the concerns with helping and caring for those in the church community. He stated, "You want to be involved in calling people, how they are doing, if they are sick you go out and see them because you want to connect to those fellow Ethiopians."

The biggest difficulty that Zelahem and his family face is that they live about two hours from their place of worship. Although there are other places they could attend closer to their home, Zelahem says that there is a strong difference in worshipping in his native tongue that spiritually fills him more.

Dawit

The last member of the evangelical community whom we interviewed was Dawit. Dawit came to the United States as a student to study at a Christian graduate school. At the time of the interview, Dawit had been in the United States for about three years and lived with his wife and children in a suburb of Chicago.

Religious life in Ethiopia.

Dawit was born into an Ethiopian Orthodox family but unlike the others we interviewed, the church trained Dawit to be a committed Orthodox member with the eventual goal of him becoming a local priest. While Dawit was a teenager, a man, who Dawit does not believe was a Christian, gave him a Bible. It was through this Bible that Dawit says he began to convert from an Orthodox to an evangelical Christian. After his conversion, Dawit had many struggles to deal with. He had a lot of mistreatment and misunderstanding from his family members and friends, many of whom deserted him. Now, Dawit is able to look upon those trials as an opportunity to strengthen his new beliefs.

Eventually Dawit started to work with the evangelical church in Ethiopia on a more national level. He spent most of his time as a leader who coordinated church ministry to the rural areas of Ethiopia. Dawit was also involved with local church ministry during the same time period.

Religious life in the United States.

Dawit came to the U. S. as a student, but while he was here he saw a need to reach out to the Ethiopian immigrant population. He assisted in starting an Ethiopian evangelical church in the suburbs. When talking about his religious life in both Ethiopia and the United States, Dawit describes his role here as being similar to what his involvement was in Ethiopia. He was a leader of a church in both countries, but now instead of spending time training people to go to the grass roots to take the gospel message, he is now reversing that role and is himself going out into the areas where Ethiopians are concentrated to work to establish evangelical fellowships.

Changes and difficulties in religious life in the U. S.

The biggest challenge that Dawit faces in the United States is that the congregation here is widespread, which means he has to spend a lot of time traveling. Some members of the congregation live beyond the Chicago metropolitan area, which means to effectively do his ministry requires a great deal of time traveling.

Participant Observation at Tensae Church

The service is in Amharic and attended by Amharic-speaking Ethiopians. Three members of a mission team from Oklahoma, Jeffrey and I (Donna) are the only people in the congregation who are not of Ethiopian background. The service is set to begin at 11:00 AM. Most members arrive around that time with their children, who go to another room in the church for Sunday school while their parents are in the worship service.

Around 11:15 AM, there is music played by a roughly twenty-five-year-old male on a keyboard, which signals the start of the service. The music stops when the pastor takes up the microphone. The pastor, a thirty-five year old male wearing a full suit and speaking in Amharic, stands at the front of the fifteen by thirty foot cinder block room and addresses the congregation with opening announcements. These announcements only last a few minutes and he then prays. There are seventeen people present at this time.

The pastor takes his seat and another man (around thirty years old) takes the microphone, asks everyone to stand and prays again. During this prayer, the music begins again and continues throughout the prayer time. The man finishes this prayer and acknowledges the baptism of a member of the church, which occurred earlier the same morning during the service of Glenfield Baptist Church (also the facility in which Tensae Church meets). The leader returns to prayer, but is silent, as is the congregation, many with hands out, palms upwards as the music continues. The leader then begins to pray aloud with verbal acknowledgements from the congregation. All the members are "dressed" for church in American-style clothing: some in jeans, most wear pants (both men and women), some women wear dresses.

The congregation is a younger group, mainly aged twenty through forty but with some late forties. The prayer continues with the music behind it for around ten minutes. People continue to join the service as the prayer continues. There is a seamless transition into song from prayer. There are no hymnals but everyone sings and knows the words. The congregation keeps their eyes closed as the song begins. They are very animated during parts of songs, but some parts are still and reverent. The song continues for five to ten minutes, then the leader prays again and some members continue to sing during the prayer. After the prayer, the congregation goes back to singing. The leader prays again as the music continues. Again, there are verbal acknowledgements to the leader's prayer. The leader looks to be around thirty-five and is married. He passes the microphone to a younger man who stands at the front of the room; three younger women also join him. The younger man speaks and prays for a few minutes as the music becomes louder and another young man plays the keyboard.

The young man and three young women lead in congregational singing and all four use microphones. All of the song leaders appear to be in their mid-twenties. The music continues, spirited and loud. The congregation has hands raised and there is a swaying motion by many. More people enter the service. An older woman (mid-sixties and the oldest person in the congregation) sits quietly and very still, wearing a scarf to cover her head. A twenty-five-year-old female kneels, praying during the song. The music continues as the song leader prays and there is verbal acknowledgement by the congregation. The music ends and a prayer is led by the song leader. The music starts again as the prayer continues before leading into song. The congregation claps their hands to the beat of the music and they join in spirited song. The service is spirited and fully underway at 11:55 AM. There is lots of movement and some people jump to the rhythm of the music. All sway to the music as the older woman now claps her hands. The singing grows louder and louder and some members even shout. The young man playing the keyboard leaves the keyboard and dances about near the front of the room for a moment before returning to the keyboard (the music is set on a beat on the keyboard, so the basic rhythm continued even though he stopped playing). The music is still loud but the atmosphere calms as all continue to sing.

    The song ends, the congregation claps, all take their seats and the musicians sit in the front row. The pastor takes a microphone and speaks, introducing the visitors (three older men from Oklahoma). In English, he says he will be talking about the love of God from Mark 12:29-30 and then says the same in Amharic. He continues in Amharic and reads from the Bible. Most of the congregation has Amharic Bibles and a few carry English Bibles. The pastor translates what he said in summary; that we are nothing without love. He continues in Amharic and says "Great Commission" in English amidst the Amharic and it is 12:10 PM by this time. The pastor is very vocally and facially expressive and uses gestures. He refers back to the Bible as he talks and rhetorically speaks directly to a member of the congregation. He mentions his children as he continues. He occasionally uses pauses as moments of reflection. The congregation responds to a part of the sermon with soft laughter then again later with more hearty laughter. The congregation occasionally responds with "Amen". The pastor says, in English, "We have to love God more than anything. Nothing is worth more than the love of God, which is immeasurable." He returns to speaking in Amharic and there is the occasional "amen" response. The pastor instructs everyone to turn to a person near them and say "I love you," which they all do and exchange handshakes. Everyone turns in their Bibles at the prompting of the pastor, who switches to English to tell the non-Amharic speaking people to turn to Deuteronomy 5:10 and says, "We have to love God", then returns to speaking in Amharic. The pastor walks around the podium (a metal music stand) as he continues to speak. He returns to the Bible and speaks again. There are light chuckles amongst the congregation as he continues. Everyone turns pages in their Bible as the pastor reads a verse in Amharic.

He raises his Bible, speaks, continues to read from it then speaks again. In English, he briefly states, "We have a choice to love or not to love," before speaking again in Amharic. All the members rise to stand and the pastor again speaks in English to say, "We will declare our choice to love God and our neighbors," then returns to Amharic.

There is a responsive prayer in Amharic then the pastor is the only one praying, as there are "Amen" responses from the congregation and he continues to pray. The pastor continues to pray and the prayer lasts around ten minutes in total. At one point during the prayer, all members of the congregation raise their hands, with palms up. The pastor continues to pray and two women bring in communion trays, which are traditional gold communion trays with a cross on top. The pastor instructs everyone to sit and speaks about the communion then prays, speaks again, prays again and during this time all members remain seated with their eyes closed. As the prayer ends, music begins as a man and a woman walk to the front of the room and the man takes the microphone and prays. Some members begin to sing, so there is soft singing as the music continues quietly and the man finishes his prayer. The man and woman pass out the communion bread and wine (juice) together as the congregation continues to sing in a soft, reverent manner. The pastor then takes the microphone, speaks softly and prays. The singing resumes after the prayer. Everyone then takes the bread at the pastor's instruction (which he also says in English). He then raises his cup, prays and everyone takes the juice. The congregation continues singing softly after taking communion, then the pastor prays again, which is received with more "amen" responses. The music stops and the pastor speaks (possibly acknowledging the baptism that took place earlier, since he pointed towards the man who was part of the baptism that morning). The congregation all claps then the pastor continues to speak, with the congregational "amen" response following. He finishes and puts down the microphone, picks up his Bible from the music stand it was resting on then returns to his seat. Two members of the congregation gather the communion cups as the young man who plays the keyboard takes the microphone and leads a prayer and the taking of the offering follows. The pastor returns to the front, speaks without the microphone reminding the congregation of a barbeque after the service the next week, and emphasizes the opportunity for fellowship there. He continues with announcements and at one point, motions toward a member of the congregation, who stands, and the members all clap. The man returns to his seat, the pastor finishes speaking then leads the congregation in a closing prayer and the service ends at 1:20 PM.

After the service ends, all the members gather with their children in a thirty by forty foot room outside their worship area and begin to talk.

Some of the women bustle about with thermoses and trays. They fill the trays with bread and the thermoses are steaming as they put sugar and Styrofoam cups out on one of the tables in the middle of the room. Everyone begins to congregate around the table, eating the bread and preparing beverages. The steaming liquid turns out to be tea, which the women serve to everyone with healthy amounts of sugar added to the tea. The men and women stand around, talk, and enjoy their bread and tea as the children run about playing with each other while eating some of the bread and stealing sips of tea from the adults. In general, the women converse with the other women, continually ensuring that there is enough bread and tea to go around, while the men talk amongst themselves. There is a strong sense of community amongst the members of the congregation whom are all chatting and friendly with each other, mainly in Amharic. Once all the bread and tea is finished, the women clean up and put away the thermoses for next week as parents gather their children and slowly filter out. The pastor and his family are the last to leave and they retire from the church around 2:00 PM.

Data analysis

Throughout the observation and in our interviews, we noted several recurrent themes brought forth by our research subjects, both Orthodox and evangelical Christian. Among these themes were the interconnectivity of the Ethiopian Orthodox Church and the government of Ethiopia, the role of community in faith and society, the role of family in faith and the importance of staying within a certain denominational boundary.

Interconnectivity of the Ethiopian Orthodox Church and the government of Ethiopia

All of our interviews involved a conversation on the role of the Ethiopian Orthodox Church as a part of the nation and everyone said that the two are intricately connected, but each had a different sentiment about that connection. Mekdem described the Ethiopian Orthodox Church as not being merely a church but as being a part of the country that is closer to the leaders than to the people. He feels that the church acts in a manner that seems as if it owns the country and that if you are not a member then you are not a part of the country. Mekdem believes that the Ethiopian Orthodox Church does not have a positive role in Ethiopia. Bedelwa, on the other hand, says she is glad to have a national church to which everyone can belong. Amsalu is very clear in his sentiments about the church, saying, "It is very crucial in the life and history of that country."

His comments reinforce his idea that the Ethiopian Orthodox Church has a positive role in the nation. Dawit, however, feels that the level of connectivity with politics in the nation was a disadvantage to the Ethiopian Orthodox Church. He believes that if the church was not as involved with the government that they could become more missions oriented and reach out beyond Ethiopia. Tariku talks about the high level of trust that Ethiopians place in the church and how most Ethiopians have a very positive view of the church as a whole. However, he goes on in a later comment to say that the church must be a better steward of humanity and battle poverty and fight for peace; the church must be more proactive.

The Role of Community in Faith and Society

Through our various interviews, we came to realize the importance of community to the people with whom we were speaking. They all said that one of the things they missed most about Ethiopia was the sense of community and family. Bedelwa says that the family culture was the thing she misses most about Ethiopia; for Tariku, the lack of social interaction in Chicago is most difficult. Amsalu points out a lack of being able to come together with friends and family while Mekdem feels nostalgic when thinking of the large family with whom he lived in Ethiopia. Dawit comments on the differences in the community between the U. S. and the community in Ethiopia. The American community is more of an individualist community, whereas, in Ethiopia people are more interconnected and support one another. Zelahem misses the community he shared with his family. In our observations of Tensae Church, we also noted the importance of community as instead of rushing home after the service, everyone stayed in the building, socializing and eating together.

The Role of Family in Faith

When asked about their past religious experiences, the interviewees all made mention of the role of the family in one's religious formation. Amsalu clearly reflected the importance of family when he said, "What I am is what they are, from my parents. So, everything comes down from my parents. You can see my parents in me. "
Tariku commented that he is Orthodox because his parents are, and their parents were, and he even goes on to talk about future generations, saying, "If you believe something, you have to believe for your son, too. If you believe, you have to pass forward your son. "
Although he is now evangelical Christian, Mekdem says that he was raised Orthodox because he was born into an Orthodox Christian family.

Bedelwa, too, was born into an Orthodox family and remains Orthodox. Dawit speaks of his family and the community and the importance of being a strong teacher of biblical virtues such as honesty and faithfulness to friends and family and fearing the Lord.

The Importance of Staying Within a Certain Denominational Boundary

Each of our interviews included a conversation about converting to a different denomination and there is a clear division in the answers between the Orthodox and evangelical interviewees; everyone with whom we spoke was born into the Orthodox tradition, meaning those who are now evangelical converted at some point to evangelical Christianity. Among the Orthodox community, there lies a strong sense of loyalty and connection to the Orthodox Church and there is a negative sentiment toward those converting to another denomination. Bedelwa clearly stated, "It is big trouble if you switch to new religion." However, the evangelical interviews looked at conversion with a different perspective. When asked about his feelings if a family member were to convert to another religion, Mekdem pointed out that conversion is gradual and said, "Your son is your son no matter what happens. All we can do is continue to pray and try to persuade them back into the Light."

Part 4: Conclusions

We began this research by keeping in mind the question of how to bring the gospel to Orthodox Ethiopians in the Chicagoland area. Throughout our interviews with both evangelical and Orthodox Ethiopians, we came across several interesting themes that lead us to our conclusions; however, these conclusions are not exhaustive given the nature of our research and the limited scope within which we had to work. There is still room for continued research, but we feel that our findings and conclusions provide a solid foundation from which to begin.

Community

When considering how to best reach the Ethiopian community of Chicagoland, one of the most important and recurrent themes throughout our interviews was a lack of a sense of community. In Ethiopia, most of our interviewees commented, there is a great sense of community. Most families are large and the church serves not only as a religious establishment but also as a gathering place for the entire village. They went on to say that this integral part of their lives has been lost since coming to the United States. Some say that distance and the fact that there is only one Ethiopian Orthodox church in Chicago diminish the role of the church as a place to find other Orthodox Ethiopians. Even the evangelical Christians with whom we spoke acknowledged that many of them miss the large families and ease with which they could have fellowship in Ethiopia. Thus, the establishment of community, through church and social events in areas that are convenient to Ethiopians, will aid in bringing together the Ethiopian community and further the establishment of more Ethiopian churches in the Chicagoland area.

Proselytization

Another important finding in our research was a major factor for the Orthodox population, while not as important among the evangelical interviewees. Many of our Orthodox interviewees commented on their feelings about the Protestant-Orthodox relationship as not being a positive one. They felt that Protestants viewed the Orthodox community as a mission field and considered them non-Christian, thus making their focus one of proselytization instead of fellowship. Therefore we conclude that when working with the Orthodox community, there must be work to establish a fellowship and community, which may eventually lead into a deeper sharing and understanding of the gospel only after establishing a strong relationship. Orthodox Ethiopians must not perceive contact and communication by evangelicals to be simply conversion work.

Language

One of the major motivations for Ethiopians in the Chicago area to make a trek to the Ethiopian Orthodox church in the South Side or to Tensae Church in the suburbs is that these services are in Amharic. Each of the surveys we conducted generated answers in which the respondents were very likely to go to services that were in their native language. When working with this people group, keep in mind the importance of their national language, both as a communication tool and a cultural identifier and work to incorporate their native language into as many aspects of your work as possible.

Location

Although it seems like the most obvious factor in reaching any people group, we must iterate here in our conclusions the importance of location.

The largest concentration of Ethiopians in the Chicagoland area lives in the Edgewater community, north of downtown Chicago. In this community, several restaurants, stores and community agencies are Ethiopian-focused, proving that this is the hub of activity for Ethiopian immigrants in the Chicagoland area. However, the only Ethiopian Orthodox church is in south Chicago, some twenty or so miles south of Edgewater. In order to most effectively create a much needed sense of community and fellowship and to make church attendance more feasible, there must be an Ethiopian church, with services conducted in Amharic, located in the Edgewater community. There already exists a strong communication network within the community, so once the church is ready to open, the news will quickly spread among the Ethiopians in the area. Ultimately, establishing an Amharic speaking Ethiopian church in Edgewater will be one of the most effective and feasible ways of reaching the thousands of Ethiopian immigrants living in Chicagoland.

Recommendations for further research

This research focuses mainly on Orthodox and evangelical Ethiopians in the Chicago area, but there is obviously room to delve into many other facets of the religious life of Ethiopians in this area, some of which we suggest below.

Protestant Perception among Orthodox Ethiopians

One possible area of further research is the question of how to improve the Protestant-Orthodox relationship in the Ethiopian community. Most of the immigrants we spoke with were willing to discuss their sentiments about other denominations openly, so a possibility of forming focus groups to research how to improve the relationship could result in great strides forward in reaching the Ethiopian Orthodox population.

Muslim Ethiopians

There is a growing number of Muslim Ethiopians both in Ethiopia and in the United States, which researchers should investigate further in order to understand this people group and learn how to spread the gospel to a people often overshadowed and ignored due to the power and influence of the Ethiopian Orthodox Church.

Ethiopian Orthodox Church Observation

A very pertinent area of research that further research can investigate is the Ethiopian Orthodox Church, specifically the church in south Chicago, to understand how they form community, reach out to immigrant Ethiopians, what is specific to the Orthodox Church worship style and so on. Time and travel restraints prohibited us from completing research in this area, but it is a very viable resource for further information.

Larger Scale research

This research investigated mainly middle-aged, first-generation immigrants from Ethiopia in the Chicago area. This obviously leaves a great range of other demographics that further research can consider. One could investigate second-generation immigrants, a younger or older age demographic, specific socioeconomic groups or a very large sample of the Ethiopians in Chicagoland to obtain greater and different findings about the Ethiopian community.

Tailoring the church to U. S. lifestyle while maintaining cultural identity

Among the subjects we interviewed, many of them commented on the harshness of the U. S. lifestyle, especially that of living in a large city, and how that prevented them from being as involved in their church as they would like to be. This provides a key insight into an area for continued research. Further studies can investigate the factors pertinent to the U. S. lifestyle that affect immigrants and see how to tailor the church to work around those factors while still maintaining the cultural identity of the immigrant population.

Ethiopian Ethnographic Supplemental Materials: Data Matrices

Table 1: *Data Analysis Matrix: Experiences and Values of Worshippers*
The following matrix organizes responses of six Ethiopian immigrants to interview questions related to worship:

Subject of question	Tariku	Bedelwa	Amsalu	Mekdem	Zelalem	Dawit
Time in US	4 years, 8 months	6 years	6 years	7 years	15 years	3 years
Married	Yes	Yes	Yes	Yes	Yes	Yes
Children	Not mentioned	Yes	Not mentioned	Yes	Yes	Yes
Career	Cab driver	Not mentioned	Social worker	Writer	Not mentioned	Minister
Religious identification	Ethiopian Orthodox	Ethiopian Orthodox	Ethiopian Orthodox	Evangelical	Evangelical	Evangelical
Importance of religion	High	High	High	High	High	High
Amount of Religious involvement (US)	Low	Low	High	Average	Average	High
Religion from family	Yes	Yes	Yes	No	No	No
Change in religious involvement in US	Less involved	Less involved	Less involved	More involved, religion more personal	More involved	More involved with the grass roots of ministry
Level of religious tolerance	Average	Average	Average	High	High	High
Devotion to religion	High	High	High	High	High	High
Religious involvement in Ethiopia	High, Ethiopian Orthodox	High, Ethiopian Orthodox	High, Ethiopian Orthodox	Low, Ethiopian Orthodox Some, evangelical	High, Ethiopian Orthodox	High, Ethiopian Orthodox High, evangelical
Ease of involvement in Ethiopia	High	High	High	High	High	High

Subject of question	Tariku	Bedelwa	Amsalu	Mekdem	Zelalem	Dawit
Ease of involvement in US	Low	Low	Low	High	Somewhat Low	High
Conversion sentiment	Slightly negative	Negative	Negative	Positive	Positive	Positive

Table 2: *Observation Matrix, Tensae Church*
This matrix illustrates the key descriptors of a Sunday morning worship service at Tensae Church.

Tensae Church	
Open to public	Yes
Held in a church building	Yes
Homogenous congregation	Yes
Service in Amharic	Yes
Pre-structured service	No
Obvious church hierarchy	No
Responsive readings	No
Prayer	Yes
Music	Yes
Involvement of congregation in service	High
Spirit in service	High
Offering taken	Yes
Preaching from Bible	Yes
One Pastor	Yes
Congregational age range	20's-50's
Musical instruments	Keyboard, singing
Technological equipment	Microphones, keyboard/synthesizer
Sole congregation using facility	No

Table 3: *Comparison of religion and culture between Orthodox and evangelical Ethiopians*
This matrix analyzes the importance of central topics across the two main Ethiopian religious denominations, Ethiopian Orthodox and Ethiopian evangelical.

Importance of topics	Orthodox	Evangelical
Prayer	High	High
Saints	High	Low
Fasting	High	Low
Sunday Worship	High	High
Priests	High	Neutral
Church education	High	Not mentioned
Community	High	High
Family	High	High
Physical church location	High	Neutral
Church hierarchy	High	Low
Bible	High	High
Evangelization	Low	High
Personal Spiritual Growth	Low	High
Veneration of Mary	High	Low

References

Abbink, J. (1998). An historical-anthropological approach to the Islam in Ethiopia: issues of identity and politics. *Journal of African Cultural Studies*, 11 (2), 109-124.

Beck, Author Rosalie, & Hendon, David w. (1993). Notes on church-state affairs. *Journal of Church and State*, 35, 439.

Cheyne, J. R. (1991). Southern Baptist evangelism of Coptic Christians: Is it proselytism. *Transformation*, 8 (0) 23-24.

Clapham, C. (1993). How many Ethiopians? *Africa: Journal of the International African Institute*, 63(1), 118-128. Retrieved June 11, 2007 from JSTOR Database.

Costea, P. (1990). Church-state relations in the Marxist-Leninist regimes of the third world. *Journal of Church and State*, 32 (2) 281-309. Retrieved June 14, 2007 from
Academic Search Premier.

Crummey, D. (1998). The politics of modernization: Protestant and Catholic missionaries in modern Ethiopia. In G. Haile, A. Lande, S. Rubenson (Eds.), *The missionary factor in Ethiopia: Papers from a symposium on the impact of European missions on Ethiopian society* (pp. 85-100). Frankfurt am Main: Europäischer Verlag der Wissenschaften.

Ebaugh, Helen & Chafetz, Janet (Eds.). (2000). *Religion and the new immigrants: continuities and adaptations in immigrant congregations.* Walnut Creek, CA: AltaMira.

Eide, O.M. (2001). Political dynamics in the wake of missionary efforts within the realm of human rights: The case of Ethiopia. *Swedish Missiological Themes*, 89 (4) 473-485.

Haile, G. (1998). The missionary's dream: An Ethiopian perspective on Western missions in Ethiopia. In G. Haile, A. Lande, S. Rubenson (Eds.), *The missionary factor in Ethiopia: papers from a symposium on the impact of European missions on Ethiopian society* (pp. 1-8). Frankfurt am Main: Europäischer Verlag der Wissenschaften.

Hamer, J. H. (2002). The religious conversion process among the Sidama of North-East Africa. *Africa* 72 (4), 598-627. Retrieved June 14, 2007 from EBSCO.

Hussein, A. (2006). Coexistence and /or confrontation?: Towards a reappraisal of Christian-Muslim encounter in contemporary Ethiopia. *Journal of Religion in Africa*, 36(1), 4-22.

Hussien, S. A. (2007). Islam, Christianity and Ethiopia's foreign policy. *Journal of Muslim Minority Affairs*, 17 (1), 129-139. Retrieved June 14, 2007 from Academic Search Premier.

Kaplan, S. (2004). Themes and methods in the study of conversion in Ethiopia: A review essay. *Journal of Religion in Africa*, 34(3), 373-392. Retrieved June 12, 2007, from ATLA Religion Database with ATLASerials database.

Kaplan, S. (1986). The Africanization of missionary Christianity: History and typology. *Journal of Religion in Africa*, 16(3), 166-186. Retrieved June 13, 2007, from JSTOR Database.

Messing, S. D. (1957). Ethiopian folktales ascribed to the late nineteenth century Amhara. *The Journal of American Folklore*, 70 (275). 69-72. Retrieved June 13, 2007 from JSTOR.

Melton, J. Gordon & Baumann, Martin (Eds.). (2002). *Religions of the world: a comprehensive encyclopedia of beliefs and practices.* Santa Barbara, CA: ABC-CLIO, Inc.

Mumper, S. E. (1985). Ethiopia continues to impose restriction on the church. Christianity Today, 29(14), 70-72.

Niklaus, R. L. (1983). Ethiopia: Religious at heart. *Evangelical Missions Quarterly*, 19 (4), 355-356.

Ostebo, T. (1998). Creating a new identity: the position of Ethiopian Muslims in contemporary perspective. *Svensk Missionstidskrift*, 86(3) 423-451.

Perry, T. (1999). Southern Baptist Ethiopians focus on evangelism. *Christianity Today* (23), February 1999.

Persoon, J. (2005). New perspectives on Ethiopian and African Christianity: Communalities and contrasts in twentieth century religious experience. *Exchange,* 34(4), 306-336. Retrieved June 13, 2007 from ATLA Religion Database with ATLASerials database.

Reminick, R. A. (1974). The evil eye belief among the Amhara of Ethiopia. *Ethnology,* 13 (3) 279-291. Retrieved June 13, 2007 from JSTOR.

Reminick, R. A. (1975). The structure and functions of religious belief among the Amhara of Ethiopia. *Occasional Papers Series Committee on Ethiopian Studies* 3, 26 – 41. Retrieved June 13, 2007 from eHRAF.

Reminick, R. A. (1976). The symbolic significance of ceremonial defloration among the Amhara of Ethiopia. *American Ethnologist*, 3(4), 751-763. Retrieved June 13,
2007 from JSTOR.

Ruebenson, Samuel. (1998). The interaction between the missionaries and the Orthodox: The case of Abune Selama. In G. Haile, A. Lande, S. Rubenson (Eds.), *The missionary factor in Ethiopia: Papers from a symposium on the impact of   European missions on Ethiopian society* (pp. 71-84). Frankfurt am Main: Europäischer Verlag der Wissenschaften.

Rubenson, Sven. (1998). The missionary factor in Ethiopia: Consequences of a colonial context. In G. Haile, A. Lande, S. Rubenson (Eds.), *The missionary factor in Ethiopia: Papers from a symposium on the impact of European missions on Ethiopian society* (pp. 71-84). Frankfurt am Main: Europäischer Verlag der Wissenschaften.

Semaan, L (1988). *Ethiopia.* British Columbia: Victoria International Development Education Association. [Microfilm].

Smith, B. (1999, Spr). The role of the Ethiopian Orthodox Church in affirming the national identity of her people: Historical observations. *Journal of the Interdenominational Theological Center*, 26(2), 169-189. Retrieved June 12, 2007, from ATLA Religion Database with ATLASerials database.

Stevens, W. D. (2004). Spreading the word: religious beliefs and the evolution of immigrant congregations. *Sociology of Religion*, 65 (2), 121-138.

Tenna, Sebhat. (1998, April). Ambassadors of Christ: A missiological study of Eritrea and Ethiopia (Erithio). Unpublished doctoral thesis. Western Seminary, Portland, Oregon, USA. Doctorate of Missiology. [Microfilm].

Tibebu, T. (1996, March). Ethiopia: The "anomaly" and "paradox" of Africa. *Journal of Black Studies,* 26(4), 414-430. Retrieved June 13, 2007, from JSTOR Database.

U.S. Census Bureau. (2000). *Statistical abstract of the United States. Special Tabulations (STP-159).* Washington, DC: U.S. Government Printing Office. Retrieved June 25, 2007, from www.census.gov/population/cen2000/stp-159/STP-159-africa.pdf.

U.S. Department of Justice. (1993). *Profile series Ethiopia: The status of Amharas since 1991.* (INS Publication No. PR/ETH/93.001). Washington, D.C.

Wells, J. (2005). Ethiopia: "The country blessed by God". *Christian History and Biography* 87(11), 11.

Wubishet, G. (1990, Sum-Fall 1990). A novelist's perspective on the role of religion in
Ethiopia. *Journal of Religious Thought*, 47, 42-51. Retrieved June 12, 2007, from   ATLA Religion Database with ATLASerials database.

Young, A. (1967).Varieties of Amhara graphic art. *The Bulletin of The University Museum of the University of Pennsylvania,* 9(4), 1-11 Retrieved June 13, 2007 from eHRAF.

Chapter 8:
Raw Data on Ethiopians in Chicagoland

Jeffrey Davis & Donna Herron
2007 College Summer Missionaries
Trinity International Baptist Mission
Carol Stream, IL

Editor's Note

For purposes of information and review, I have chosen to include several pieces of raw data gathered by Jeffrey Davis and Donna Herron during the course of their work on this project. It is my hope that these resources will be found helpful in future research and data analysis efforts. Only minor editing has been done in order to better preserve the original transcriptions and to maintain the privacy of interviewees.

Interview 1: July 13, 2007 with Amsalu at the Ethiopian Community Center in the Uptown community, Chicago, IL

Jeffrey: Alright, um, first of all I want to thank you for helping us with this research.

Amsalu: You are welcome.

J: And before we get into this right here, if I could just have you tell me your name and spell it for us just for our notes and everything.

A: Ok, my name is _____

J: Ok, alright, and we can jump right here into our questions with this. First question is how did you come to Chicago and how long have you been here.

A: I have been here for six years

J: For six years? And how did you come to Chicago? How did you end up living in Chicago?

A: I am a political asylee, political asylee. I sought asylum here and then I got approved. Started living here.

Donna: Did you come directly to Chicago?

A: Yes

J: Ok, with whom do you live, if anyone? I mean, do you live by yourself or?

A: Now or when I came?

J: Uh, when you came in and now.

A: With a friend

J: You came in with a friend. How about now? Do you live with a friend or do you live on your own?

A: I lived with a friend for about 2 months, 3 months. And then I rented an apartment.

J: Ok, and you still live by yourself now?

A: With my wife.

J: With your wife. Ok, can you describe the neighborhood that you live in? I mean, the area that you live in. An apartment building or is it in the suburbs?

A: Here, in north Chicago, northeastern Chicago, in Edgewater

J: In an apartment or a townhouse?

A: In an apartment.

J: Apartment? Oh, yeah, I think you may have said that. What do you like about Chicago or what do you not like about Chicago?

A: It's better to tell you what I like. The diversity. That's what I like. I feel comfortable and see people of different color, different backgrounds and that is the most important thing. What I don't like about Chicago; life is hectic and expensive.

D: What about the weather?

A: The weather is okay for me

D: Even in the winter?

A: Yeah, for me it's not bad. But it's expensive, a parking space, and it's not easy to live in Chicago for immigrants; it's for the rich people.

D: Do you think that is specific to Chicago or do you think that's kind of how it is in all the major cities?

A: I think all the major cities but what is special about Chicago is, you know, the pay is low but the expense is high. If you know the pay is better than the other the smaller cities at least people can afford living here.

J: Okay, what do you miss about Ethiopia?

A: My parents, the homeland, friends, the coming together and the going with friends, the families, relatives.

D: Other than your wife, do you have any relatives here?

A: Yeah, my brother, my younger brother.

D: But it's not the same, is it?

A: No, it's not the same

J: Does your brother live here in Chicago?

A: Yeah, in Chicago.

J: Ok, what is your past religious involvement if any?

A: Ethiopian Orthodox Church.

J: Okay. Maybe, what is your involvement with the church. I mean, you say that, but are you extremely active in it?

A: I participate, I participate in Sunday school, I participate in Sunday school, and regularly go to church every Sunday and participate in the church services.

D: Do you go to the one in South Side?

A: Yeah, you know the priest is here in this building.

J: You have been involved with the Ethiopian your entire life?

A: Yeah.

J: What do you see are any changes if any from the Ethiopian Orthodox Church in Ethiopia compared to here in the U.S.

A: *Difference. Here people have more time, I mean there. In Ethiopia people have more time. You regularly to go to church and people attend the full service. Here it is not that easy. People work Saturday in the evening you know Sunday morning and as a social life it is also. It is not easy to spend the time that you are supposed to spend.*

J: Um, and with that do you see any changes in your personal worship style from Ethiopia to here?

A: *No.*

D: Were you more involved there since you had more time than you are here or has that changed a lot?

A: *Yeah, that's changed. Here, less time. Go to school, raising kid. You know, and other activities. There you just work one job, that's it. You have time always.*

D: Was there anything specifically that you were involved with in the church in Ethiopia that you don't have time to do or that you can't do here maybe that you did then that you would like to still be able to do, you just don't have time?

A: *Fasting. Fasting there we fast. Here it is not easy. Sometimes you don't find food that you can eat outside, you know.*

D: What are the specific rules? Is it two days a week that you are supposed to?

A: *Wednesday and Friday throughout the year and there is one long fasting season that is fifty days that is common. Not that we aren't eating for fifty days. Until maybe close to 2 to 3 o'clock in the afternoon we don't eat.*

D: So it's not all day.

A: *In fifty days you don't eat dairy product, you don't eat no meat, no milk, no egg for fifty days, no butter, no fish.*

J: And that's the whole time? I mean, the whole time?

A: *Yeah, fifty days*

D: But then you say that's until 3 o'clock. Then after that you can have bread, vegetables that sort of thing but still no dairy or anything for the whole fifty days.

A: *No. And there is a lot of fasting periods.*

D: That's the longest one?

A: *Yeah, that's the longest one.*

J: And those rules apply also just for the Wednesday/Friday?

A: *Yeah.*

J: You had already mentioned it earlier, you go to the Ethiopian Orthodox church on the South Side.

A: *Right, South Side.*

J: Um, how did you come to find out about the church and what were your first experiences there?

A: *Friends, from your relationships, from Ethiopians they tell you the church is located South Side, they give you ride, take you there. People are very friendly. And they help you in different aspects and you start going there.*

D: You said that when you came you lived with a friend. Did you know them before you came or did you find them when you got here?

A: *My friend?*

D: The person you lived with.

A: *My friend, he was my high school friend. He was in Indianapolis. Yeah, I lived there for one month then I came here. I know, a lady, I know her parents and I stayed with her for a month, two months before I rent my own apartment.*

D: So you didn't come here all alone without knowing anyone.

A: Some people come without knowing anyone. They come here and say, we are Ethiopians you have to help us. This morning for instance, I had to take a couple to the train station to the bus station. They had to go to Minneapolis, they don't know anything. They don't speak the language.

J: That would be interesting. How do you feel about the role of the Ethiopian Orthodox Church in Ethiopia?

A: It's very important. It is very crucial in the life and history of that country. Had it not been for that Ethiopian Orthodox Church Ethiopia wouldn't have existed like it has. It might have been disintegrated. We always have dictators and rulers always dictate because of the church that people come together. We don't have judge, we don't have many courts like here. It is the church that promotes peace, the church that promotes friendship and kind of very cohesive society. That is the role of the church. It has a long history; 3000 years of history of religion in the country.

D: Three thousand years is impressive for anything to last.

J: There is very few things that have lasted that long.

A: So, it has passed the test of time; it has passed the challenge.

J: What is your perception of a Protestant or evangelical church in the US?

A: I know every little but they are more liberal than those in Ethiopia. Those in Ethiopia they are very straight and they tell you, "Don't go to Orthodox church, don't do this." They are really damaging the relationship

D: The Protestants in Ethiopia?

A: Yeah, but here it is just Christian, Christian, it's good. They are kind of very very radical and that's not good to promote, to spread Christianity. Instead of preaching someone that doesn't have any belief or instead of preaching a pagan, they preach Orthodox Christian to convert to Protestant and many Ethiopians don't like that. Like they are Christian already, why don't they work with us. Why don't we, you know, preach the Bible.

D: What about Catholic in Ethiopia? Are there a lot of Catholics?

A: Their number is not that big but they are much better than the Protestants in that regard. They work closely with the Orthodox and they don't say, "You come to our church." They don't say that. You can go but you know they don't tell you, "Forget yours. That's old very traditional, doesn't go with this." They don't do that. Catholics they are good in that regard. But here very relaxed, it's more of social than of [unclear].

J: What are some of the most important Ethiopian religious traditions that your parents passed down to you?

A: I don't know if it's tradition. Let's see, you know, fasting and you know, to follow the rule of the God. To be friendly to people; to be nice to everybody regardless of their economic status, color or whatever. And to, besides that, the Ethiopian Orthodox Church also always teach the unity of the country, that that country should always be united and be protected and that's also good. I think that helped a lot for us too. We didn't have problem like Somalia. I think the church has played a great role in that regard.

J: Is there any other traditions that your parents may have passed down to you besides the religious stuff, I mean, any other type of traditions or anything?

A: That's very difficult. Everything. What I am is what they are, from my parents. So, everything comes down from my parents. You can see my parents in me.

J: And looking at these traditions now, were they important in the past and how important are they now. Or, I mean, are they still very much the same or do you think they have changed?

A: There are things that are important in Ethiopia but when you come here they lose their value. Like being very polite. Ethiopians they don't speak about themselves you have to be very quiet. Less aggressive than people in this country, to be less assertive. I think that's a, maybe a value appreciated in Ethiopia, but when you come here that can play negative role on you, on immigrants. They have to be very aggressive and you have to speak loud, say, "I know this, I can do this, I can do that." It's a different culture, so that's what that is the challenge for the immigrants. Find a lot of immigrants, well educated immigrants, that can do a lot of things but only because they can't tell they can do this and that, they don't get the job.

J: Do the majority of those that do come in like that, I mean do they end up just going with how often do people come in that are very well educated with the higher jobs in Ethiopia, coming here into the U.S., how many of them are actually able to break into those same fields here?

A: Very very few. Maybe in the medical field, you can find some, otherwise no, you see a lot of cab drivers most of them. Master's degree, some medical doctors, PhD holders.

J: Is a lot of that just because of language barriers?

A: Language is one thing and the other is the culture. They don't know the American culture. Let's say if it is a managerial position. It is very difficult for someone from Africa to be in managerial position because he doesn't know how to deal with people in this country and that is one reason. Another is that they are stereotyped. When you tell them you are from Africa, people think that you don't know anything. So that's very difficult. Some people don't put their…I was advising one of my friend here on his resume not to put Ethiopia to that extent. He has great experience, work experience and education but, when people know that he is from Ethiopia, oh who is this guy. At least they give him a chance if he doesn't mention Ethiopia, and then they [unclear].

J: Ok, going back to where we were focusing on the religious stuff. Suppose someone invites you to a worship service that is not of your own religion. What is your reaction?

A: I don't know. What makes it different from my own. I am going to church, why do I need to go to the other one, what makes it different? Is there any other thing they can get from there? Is God closer there? I don't know. When they ask me I don't mind going anywhere but I should see something tangible. And I don't need to anyone who go against my own religion.

J: Suppose someone suggests that your religion or your beliefs are flawed. What is your response or how do you defend your stance and what's your response to that?

A: Yeah, I refer to the Bible, I refer to the Bible.

J: Suppose a member of your family converts to another religion or denomination. How, if at all, does your relationship with them change?

A: Oh, it depends, it depends, if he lives his own life I don't mind but if he tries to disturb my family or other things or if he always say something against my religion maybe there will be a problem. But as long as he follow his own that's not a problem.

J: How do you perceive the Ethiopian Orthodox Church community here in the U.S. as compared to Ethiopia?

A: It is a strong community. I think it is the church that brings people together. There is not any other way to bring almost all Ethiopians together other than the church so it's a unifier. It's a major institution in the U.S. or in a foreign country for all Ethiopians to come together share ideas. Sometimes to express their frustrations and sometimes when they want to help their country or to come together, to contribute money. When there is, let's say, famine. So the church plays a major role and solve conflicts sometimes when there is tribal conflict at home and people you know try to reflect that. It's the church that tries to help solve the problem.

D: Do you think that community is a stronger community in Ethiopia or here? I know it is larger community in Ethiopia...

A: No, in Ethiopia. Here you know the culture is different. People are always busy, live apart from each other, don't visit friend every time. There is different. It's a kind of [unclear] relationship.

J: What do you see that might be able to be done to make that community stronger here in the U.S.?

A: Stronger here? To strengthen the church, to help the church. Let's say, because we don't have enough money, we build the church on South Side. You don't see any Ethiopians living in South Side. It's about 25-30 miles from here. Most Ethiopians live in this neighborhood but they can't afford to buy a church or to rent a church in this area so they have to build that far apart. So if they help, let's say if they make Sunday school stronger it's good to discipline the youth, children. They can teach them morale so you don't see children in the streets. So the church could do a lot of thing because it's poor. They didn't pay their mortgage for long because people maybe they make $7 an hour $8 an hour, most are very low paid, supporting families. From that contribution they [unclear] the church. I *think to make the community strong it's possible by making the church strong.*

D: And a question that is kind of related to that. You say it's in South Side and most Ethiopians live in Edgewater. How hard is it for people to get to the church?

A: We give ride. We give ride. If you know your neighbor or someone who can drive. And after service, everyone comes together and eat lunch there

D: Is it an early service? Is it hard for people to get there early, or is it kind of later?

A: You can go earlier if you want, but if you like, let's say, you want to go earlier, few people can do that. Some start late, maybe you have a kid and you have to take some time and sometimes you're late. I think everybody can get a ride if they want.

D: Just because I am not familiar with that location, does public transportation go there?

A: Yeah, but it takes a long time, you have to take the train and then the bus. You have to take the train to the last stop for red line, then take bus.

D: So it takes a long time?

A: Yeah. And it may not be safe.

D: Is it in a bad part of town?

A: Yeah, South Side area, it's almost abandoned. So it's not safe.

J: What do you perceive are the differences in the Ethiopian Orthodox Church and an evangelical church here in the United States?

A: I don't know. The difference you know, we give much much respect to the saints, Saint Mary, Saint Gabriel, the others., Well, that's my perception. I think the evangelical church, the Protestant, they don't give that regard to the saints and I think because of that the Orthodox church follows some [unclear]. Because you know we respect Mary, she's the mother of Jesus Christ, she should be respected. Yeah, the others they say, "She's like any other lady" and because you know people get annoyed when you say that. That's the only difference, otherwise, we all believe in Jesus Christ, same Bible.

J: Are there any changes you would like to see made in the Ethiopian Orthodox Church?

A: Ethiopian Orthodox Church maybe to open more schools to teach Bible. And if they can afford to train more priests.

D; Kind of going on that, in Ethiopia are there a lot of schools that teach.....

A: Yeah, traditional schools. We start learning our alphabet in church. Our [unclear] Ethiopian, you learn in church.

D: Is it a very long alphabet?

A: Yeah.

D: I saw it one time on a poster and thought there were more than 26 there .

A: It's very easy to write, you don't make any spelling errors once you know it. One hundred percent correct. Very basic.

D: How many are there?

A: I don't know, these are all extensions. These are the basic ones.

D: And these are each kind of like them?

A: These are kind of the vowels. Ha hu he ha he hu ha, lu hu mu. See, it's just extension with the vowels. It's very systematic. Very very systematic. No spelling errors, one hundred percent perfect. Even a third grader or second grader can spell one hundred percent.

D: Does it all sound like the same as it is written?

A: Yeah.

D: It's not like English.

A: In English, sometimes you write what you don't speak, what you don't read, but here it's not. It's a very very long history. Maybe close to three thousand years old. And we have our own calendar too.

D; And it's a few years different, right?

A:, Yeah, the millennium will be September

D: So its seven years back.

J: Out of curiosity, do you know of any people that like speak English how long it's taken them to learn Amharic, I mean is it very tough for them to learn it?

A: It's difficult to learn English than...to learn the English, to write English down. This is very systematic. If you want you can learn in maybe for, it maybe takes, learning this and writing, maybe in one week

D: No way.

A: Yeah, you can do it. It's just systematic. This is ha always. All the extensions, it's very systematic.

D: Oh, so you memorize these?

A: Instead of writing one u, you just put the extension.

D: So that extension is the same for all of them?

A: Right, this is ha, this is hu, this is, la lu, me, mu, se su, re ru.

J: That makes a lot of sense, I have had some classical Latin training so that makes sense from that...

A: What's your name?

J: Jeffrey.

A: Jeffrey? Je-Fu-Ri. See? [Illustrates how to write "Jeffrey" in Amharic]

J: That is, I like that.

A: How many letters do you use in English?

J: Uh, seven.

A: In Amharic, three . . . .

D: So do you start with what we would consider to be the consonant and then the addition is like the vowel, like the a, that goes with the d, then you find the d and the a.

A: Yeah, these are almost constants and these are the...the consonant plus vowel. This is ha, hu, he, ha, same thing, l-u, m-u.

D: That is very simple. It makes sense too.

J: Yeah.

A: Maybe we can adopt this for the future, so that you don't make spelling errors.

D: How hard is it to learn to write those, for like little kids?

A: It's very easy. These are the numbers. The numbers are even shorter. This is one thousand, this is ten thousand.

D: So going back to the church, it teaches children how to read and write?

A: How to read and write, Bible, church music, the church movement, what goes with the music. It's a very long church education sometimes it takes 20 something years. Very long.

D: So in Ethiopia, the church teaches them the whole way through.

A: It depends. Sometimes. Most of the time these days they learn alphabet, how to read and write, then go to modern school, grade school.

D: Is it government school?

A: Government school. But sometimes you continue your study in the church, you become deacon, priest and maybe more than that; expert in Bible, expert in music, expert in the movement, the church movement to the music. Very very complex, it's not that easy. And there are different departments you can specialize in. History of the church is one I think.

The, our church, our priest here, he has PhD from University of Chicago. He is a monk.

D: What is his doctorate in?

A: Theology. One of the maybe best educated church leaders in Ethiopia. He has been here 30 years. He was very close to the king and when the king was deposed by the military government, he left the country. He has been here since then. We had a military government at all post of the church. They say, "What is your religion?" Communists. They tried to destroy the religion...Any other questions?

D: That's about it.

A: Tell me the purpose of... can I get a copy of your questions?

J: Of the questions?

D: I have a clean copy.

J: I started to use this for another interview I was doing. It's the only copy. I thought I had another copy with me, it's just...

A: If you need I can copy

D: I actually have one.

A: I hope your study will bring something that will bring us together and help. Yeah, if it's. I always ask myself, why Christians don't come together and solve this. It is minute and stupid for us. We can work together to make peace and to help a lot of poor people and to preach the Bible. The others, the Muslims, they are spreading much much faster in Africa.

D: I read somewhere that there were thirty percent Muslim in Ethiopia. Are there that many?

A: It could be, it's increasing, it's increasing.

D: That it was approaching the number of Orthodox that were there.

A: It could surpass. Because you know the church is poor, the church is poor, but it's all about money.

D: In the past the church and the government were very connected, but does that help the church with money at all?

A: Yeah, they it's like salary. They give them land, a plot of land for the priests and the deacons and that's how they make a living or else nobody would support them. But when the military government took power, they confiscated all the lands that belonged to the priests and they didn't have anything to eat. They have to leave, they have to leave the area of the church and go to the cities and become [unclear] and they didn't educate the kids, teach the kids to become deacon. Deacon?

D: Deacons. yeah.

A: So that's what happened. They need some kind of support either from the people or the government. They played the role of the government. If the government failed to create peace or bring people together, some problems the church do that. Thye are important, they need to be supported. So your research, that may help in that regard.

D: Would you mind, just, for qualitative we have the questions but for quantitative, would you mind doing, really quickly, we have a survey.

A: Yes, since I am a student, I understand.

Interview 2: July 8, 2007 with Mekdem in a suburb of Chicago.

[We were invited to attend a barbeque with a suburban Ethiopian evangelical church. It was held at the home of two members and we went directly after church and were welcomed into their home. There were only four non-Ethiopians, including us, in attendance. It was a very relaxed atmosphere with children playing, people cooking and eating and everyone socializing. After eating and chatting a while, we interviewed some of the men, as the women were all indoors, deep in conversation, coffee making, cooking and cleaning.]

How did you come to live in Chicago, how long have you lived here and with whom?

Mekdem came to the US seven years ago. His wife won the DV lottery 12 years ago and came here and he joined her five years later.

Describe the area where you live and what you like/do not like about where you live.

He lives in Lisle with his wife and two children in an apartment, which is in a suburb that he says is very individualistic where no one is really part of the community. There is no good public transportation so everyone has to take their own cars and don't get to interact with other people, making it very individualistic.

What do you miss most about Ethiopia ?

In Ethiopia, he was raised with a large family and lacks that here. He still feels connected to Ethiopia, misses his family there, and feels nostalgic when he thinks about it.

What is your past religious involvement?

Mekdem was raised as a cultural Christian in an Orthodox family but doesn't feel connected to God with the Orthodox Church. He went to an evangelical church some in Ethiopia.

What are the differences in worship from Ethiopia to here?

In Ethiopia, in the Orthodox Church, there are clergy and prayer books, but they speak in "language that is too high, like Latin in the Catholic Church. The laity, like me, do not understand it. It is all a ritual. They say 'stand', 'sit'. It is like exercise. There is no life in it. The place is holy, but there is no transformation within." He feels that all the worship is superficial. Here, in the evangelical church, Christ is the center, the Holy Spirit is the guide. Mekdem reads the Word of God on his own and has a personal connection with God. In the Orthodox Church, there are many angels, not God. There are many rituals and to go to the Ethiopian Orthodox church here involves too much travel and leaves him empty. Mekdem leaned toward evangelical church but went to the Ethiopian Orthodox church here for two years then went to a Pentecostal church. He then prayed for an Ethiopian church and was born again and rebaptized. "You know, I was baptized as an infant, but I don't count that because, you know, I wasn't there. That wasn't me. It was my parents." Now Mekdem says he is a passive worshipper, but he is a poet and writes and has begun to write lyrics for gospel songs. He spends more time reading, praying and going to church here.

What affects your involvement here?

He believes that it all depends on him to be involved. Since 1992, he has had the freedom to go to church (before that the communists did not encourage church attendance. It was not banned, but they made it hard to attend).

Where do you attend church now and how did you find out about it?

He now attends an evangelical church in Glen Ellyn. There was a prayer group meeting in a family home in [a suburb of Chicago] and out of that group came the church. They prayed for an Amharic church and they got a pastor. Mekdem's family was one of the first to join the new evangelical church.

How do you feel about the role of the Ethiopian Orthodox Church in Ethiopia?

In Ethiopia, the church is a part of the establishment. Before 1974, the king was anointed by the church, which was part of ruling the nation and was very political. The church was closer to the kings than to the people. Then under the military regime, there was a lot of persecution but the church stayed quiet. Opportunists were not spreading the Kingdom of God. The evangelical church was more persecuted by the Ethiopian Orthodox Church than by the government at that time. The Ethiopian Orthodox Church thinks they own Ethiopia and they ostracize those who are not Ethiopian Orthodox Church members. Last year, a mob killed an evangelical who was working to build a new church and the mob was lead by an Ethiopian Orthodox Church priest. They do not have a positive role in the country and they think they own the truth.

What is your perception of the Protestant/evangelical church in the US?

Mekdem looks at Acts 2 when he thinks of the Protestant church and emphasizes the importance of trusting the Holy Spirit. He notes that the Holy Spirit guides Protestants and he points out that the Bible is the same for Orthodox, but that it is the role of the Holy Spirit that sets the two apart.

What important religious traditions were passed down to you from your parents?

He said that there were no religious traditions passed to him by his parents that he felt were important. They emphasized the importance of fasting (every Wednesday and Friday), but he began to question these practices once he started reading Scriptures for himself. He realized that the traditions were hollow and that following them doesn't make you a better Christian. He did stop to say that there was one important thing he learned from them: the fear of God. He said, "They always said, Mom and Dad may not see you, but God does. And I will tell my children that. That is the one thing that I remember."

Suppose someone invited you to a worship service that is not of your own religion. What is your reaction?

When asked whether he would go to a service that was not of his own religion, he said it depends. He needs to know what they believe. He doesn't care about the nature of the worship, but he won't go if it is not the same beliefs, the same basic doctrines. He said he can usually tell if they have the same beliefs by the kind of person that invites you.

Suppose someone suggests that your beliefs were flawed. How do you defend your beliefs and what is your response to them?

Mekdem also said that he is open to questions about his beliefs and religion. He thinks that the Scriptures should back up your beliefs and that if someone has an argument against his religion and they bring that argument from the Scriptures, he will take it in.

Suppose a family member converts to another religion/denomination. How, if at all, does your relationship with them change?

He says that if a family member converts to another religion or denomination that it should not be a surprise, because conversion is gradual. He feels that if people are taught right, they won't sway from their beliefs. If they do chance, prayer and love are all that you can do. "Your son is your son no matter what happens. All we can do is continue to pray and try to persuade them back into the Light."

How did you come to know the Lord?

It was a gradual change. He had an Amharic Bible that he read and there was something inside of him. He had the knowledge of God and a fear of God. He got very sick once and went to an Ethiopian evangelical church with a lady that invited him to go with her. He saw them cast out demons at the church. From his experiences there, he developed a love of the scriptures and more desire to read them and went to the evangelical church more and gradually changed. He still went to the Ethiopian Orthodox church occasionally as a "nominal Christian" but through the evangelical church and reading the scriptures, he gained a "spirit of repentance" and stopped smoking and drinking. "I was a social drinker and I smoked, like, a pack of cigarettes a day but then I quit. No one told me to. I just read the scriptures" and learned about the body as a temple. There was no special day that he changed. Exposure at the evangelical church set off his change. The lady that took him to the Ethiopian evangelical church was instrumental because he wouldn't have gone on his own. He heard many negative stories about the evangelical church through growing up in the Ethiopian Orthodox Church, that they didn't love Mary and the saints. It took the lady taking him to the evangelical church to begin his gradual change toward loving the Lord himself and being guided by the Holy Spirit.

Interview 3: July 7, 2007 with "M" @ Peacock Café in the Edgewater Community, Chicago, IL.

[Interview took place at a restaurant, so interviewee was dining while we conducted the interview.]

Donna: Please, continue eating while we do this.

Man: How long it takes?

D: 15-20 minutes. Not very long.

M: Okay, okay.

D: Okay, um, how did you come to live in Chicago and how long have you been here?

M: Uh, I have been here almost, almost uh, four years and eight months. Yeah, around that.

D: And you came here directly from Ethiopia?

M: I came directly from Ethiopia to Chicago. And I came Chicago. Uh, I win a visa lottery. You have an idea about the lottery?

D: Mmhmm.

M: *I win the lottery and my sponsor was here. Because of my sponsor is in Chicago, I came to Chicago. Now I have been here almost four years and eight months.*

D: Was your sponsor an agency or a person?

M: *Oh, he is a person. Just a friend.*

D: Okay.

M: *You have to have somebody, you know, because by the time we arrive here they will mail to us the green card and social security you know, so you have to have somebody to come. So if my sponsor was in New York I am gonna go there. That's why I came to Chicago, as a friend.*

D: And do you live here with any family or by yourself?

M: *No, I am married. My wife, she is back in home. But I am living now with a roommate. Just no family, friend.*

D: Do you live around here?

M: *Yeah I am living around here just one block from here.*

D: And do you live in an apartment neighborhood or a...?

M: *Uh, it's a condominium, condominium. I live in a studio with my roommate.*

D: Okay, um, what do you like about Chicago and what do you not like about Chicago?

M: *Yeah, in Chicago in fact, it's a big city, uh, it's, you know, uh the weather is very hard for us. When I came here it was wintertime and it during the wintertime it is very cold for us. Especially for immigrants. But it is very cold weather. But, uh, the people of Chicago is very nice people. It's a big city, the city is also very nice. We can live, uh, in a very affordable apartment rent. Big city but it's ok. We can live uh, all these things, like I like Chicago.*

D: Is there anything that you miss about Ethiopia?

M: Yeah, in Ethiopia and here it is a big difference especially you know, here you know you have to be strong, in America, you have to be strong you have to work hard you have to pay the bills you have to send money for your family you have to cover everything. But, no time to relax for everything because we used to live with family with mom with dad with sister with brother. Now we are alone. Everything socially in our country everything is ok because I have work there. Socially you can interact with a lot of people with the family, with the cousin with everything, but you are alone. But here it is hard that is the difference.

D: Being from Ethiopia, do you have any past religious involvement? Were you involved in a church there or are you involved in one here?

M: Yes, I am Orthodox Christian. I am Orthodox Christian. Yes, I went every Sunday church there. Here also there is there is a community church in South Side. It is very far. Sometimes when I have time because we don't have time here. When I have time, when there is some holiday when there is some, we go with friends together there.

D: Um, do you see any changes in maybe the worship that you did at the Orthodox church in Ethiopia compared to the one here?

M: In Orthodox Ethiopia and here. Here we can see the difference. You know the structure organization everything is the same the Orthodox Church there and here. But here, there you can go everyday church. Here only there are open on Sunday because it is far you don't have time. There we can see a lot of peoples in everyday church. A lot of people come there on the church you can go if you want you can go in the afternoon, 5 pm 6 pm whatever you like and you can meet priests there and you can come get some education from the churches. But here it's far, once a week or once a month only. That is the difference. Because the church is far. Also, you have to drive. There you know it's every interval [unclear] the church can get to church immediately but here it's hard.

D: Has, you've said it a little bit, but have you changed any in your involvement in the Orthodox Church. You say you go a little less now. Is there any other big change?

M: Yes, in fact, I am Orthodox Christian. My family they believe that, most Ethiopians believe that, you know. I pray just, praying, you know, I *pray every time in my home, with a Bible book. Just to my family to my country to my, just everything. But when I compare there and here and there even my involvement decrease here in this country. It's very, involvement back home. There you can go every time. There is every day ceremonies there. Church ceremony you know. You can get every time. But here, one, I am busy to work, I have to work hard. And I am tired then you don't have time. Only once two weeks or once a month, you go to church to see the priest. Because the priests are going to give you some education, some you know, the preaching. But the involvement compared here and there I am sure it's less here for me.*

D: Is it just that it is hard to get to and that there is only one church?

M: Here there is only one church. It is South Side. It's very far. That's why. It's on 95th . It's very far from, almost South Side. People they complaining why don't they make it around here. a lot of Ethiopians they live around here. But the priests they say the reason is it is very expensive to buy church around here that's why. They buy around there; it is less expensive I think that is why they don't buy around here. So because of this, I am sure if it was around here I am sure a lot of people can go every day, because of that part a lot of people go once a week or twice a week, sometimes one a month.

D: And you go to that church here just occasionally?

M: Occasionally. I am not going every day. Now I am driving a cab. Before I worked at the hospital. Because I am driving a cab, you don't know if you work Saturday night you are busy, you have to sleep morning.

D: How did you find out about the Ethiopian Orthodox church here?

M: Yeah when I came here my sponsor he took me there, my sponsor. When I came here my sponsor told me there is a community church, we have to go there. Then after 3 days he took me there introduced me with the community, then I started with the church

D: Is your sponsor also Ethiopian?

M: Yeah, he's from Ethiopia. In this country because we [unclear] comes from Ethiopia, most of the sponsors are. If it is by DV diversity visa. , sponsors are Ethiopians. The Ethiopian has the responsibility to guide you to everything where the church is where the community is, where the social security is, where everything is going to be.

D: How do you feel about the role of the Orthodox Church in Ethiopia?

M: Yeah. The people of Ethiopia, Ethiopians we are ancient Christian people. Long time ago we are Christian. Even the people, they trust the priests. They trust even the leader of the country they believe on the leader of the church. If the leader of the church or the priest say something for the community they accept it. That's why most of our families there are Christians, they are very religious people. So, we believe in Jesus, Mary, in everything so, most of the people you know ancient people is illiterate or not educated people but they respect the religion that's why we have a very good feeling of the Orthodox Church, we have a very trust early in Orthodox Church. Now even the youngsters believe in the Orthodox Church. But not every person is Christian in my country. There are Muslims also.

D: What is your perception of the Protestant churches here in the US?

M: I think in Ethiopia too there are Protestant churches but before they think that the Orthodox Church Orthodox because they, the Protestants, they don't believe in Mary. The Orthodox Church they believe in Mary. So they think that in Orthodox Church the Protestants they don't believe in Mary there is big fighting even between the two church with the two people. Even if one person is Protestant from one family, the family they ignore him because it is very tough. Because what is the people complaining about us. What happened to your children. It's a big a big issue especially for twenty years...ten, ten, fifteen years after the new government established in the country every person had right to believe in whatever he like every person you can believe Protestant; you cannot control his mind. So they have their own church, they have their own freedom, they have their own everything but from time to time here people changes. If there is a big Orthodox community something coming from outside, it is a big revolution. That's why from time to time now there are Protestants also in my country there are Protestants, a lot of Protestants in my country. But before it was like they consider like the devil if one oh they don't believe in Mary, oh like the devil because they're like that. But then from time to time, people change, oh there is also another religion. The only religion is Orthodox. The other religion is nothing because they're like that but from time to time people changes. Now a lot of Ethiopians here Protestants a lot Ethiopians, Christians [unclear].

D: What is the feeling towards Catholics since they venerate Mary?

M: Oh, Catholics are ok in my country, I think Catholic they believe in Mary. So in my country, there is northern part of the country, Eritrea, in northern Ethiopia most of the, there are some part Catholics. Even the great [unclear] Catholics and Orthodox they have no big difference. The people they don't no complaints with them. The complaint is with Protestant so Catholics in my country they have their own big churches they live together, they can get marriage with each other. But with Protestant they cannot get marriage. Orthodox and Protestant it is very tough. They marry Protestant and Protestant...the family because, somebody, trust is very tough you cannot change your mind within one night you take more time, so this is the big difference.

D: What are some of the most important religious traditions that your parents passed down to you?

M: Orthodox Christian Church. Orthodox Christian Church. My mom, my dad, my grandfamilies they are Orthodox Christian Church. So even the problem is don't have most of them don't have deep knowledge about. Just only they believe. In Mary, they believe in Jesus, they believe in God but you have to know what the Bible says inside, you know. So even though my family they don't write they don't read but they believe. If you believe something you have to believe for your son, too. If you believe you have to pass forward your son. So they finally realize we understand what the church, what the preacher says. And finally we have Orthodox Church.

D: Is the involvement in the Orthodox Church still very important for you?

M: Yes, it is very import for me because still I believe in Mary, still I believe in Orthodox Church because there are the ten commandments of the God everything. I believe, I pray. It's like people they consider that praying they may say like, why I pray every time what I get from praying, they say. It's like food. I am growing now my physically I am growing up everything because of the food, so mentally because of praying every day I am alive still now. It's very important. You have to believe something. If you don't believe something. Like in America here you cannot be [unclear]. You have to say something, you have to fear something if you don't fear something, oh God will punish me if I do something wrong, Mary will punish me, that's fine. So it's important for me still.

D: Suppose someone were to invite you to a worship service or a church service that wasn't at the Orthodox church. What would your reaction be?

M: Yeah, do you know, there is something in our country we have things I have worship things here. Protestants, even they invite us go to church with them. But you know I don't blame them because they believe in Orthodox Church. They believe you know you can go. Sometimes they call me in [unclear] I went there with a [unclear] or something but I don't want to agitate me or to talk to me about religion or to change my mind. Just because as a friend I respect them they have their own attitude I have my own attitude. So sometimes we can talk, have dialogue. Because why Mary, why you don't respect Mary. Mary she is a human person, a lot of things. If one person believe in this one you cannot change his mind so I believe in that. I have no negative attitude to on other people. As long as you think about this, religion is supposed to be about peace. You think about peace. So why you blame. I have no negative attitude towards a person, so I don't have any negative action.

D: Suppose someone said that something you believe was wrong or flawed. How do you kind of defend your belief and your religion to them?

M: To defend that's why most of the Ethiopian people they don't have very basic knowledge of Orthodox Church. If somebody defended them, you can't defend him that's why you can't change it. You have to have basic knowledge. If you went every time to church, if you went every day, every week church- you can get from the preacher you can get basic knowledge. You can get basic about the background of the religion. So if you want to defend him you can defend him. If you don't have knowledge you have to accept him. So we can't defend him because if you believe with somebody, if you trust with something, you have to defend it in peaceful way. This is why religion this is a concept of that.

D: What are the main differences between the Orthodox Church and the Protestant church here?

M: For me, the main difference is on, they believe on Jesus, we believe in Jesus, but they don't believe in Mary. So we believe in her. So even they don't this is a big difference I think to me. So that's why as long as Mary, she is the mom of Jesus, so we have to believe her we have to [unclear]. This is a basic difference. That's why maybe there is a lot of things but as for me I know this is the one thing I see.

D: What are the differences you see in the Orthodox Church community here versus in Ethiopia?

M: As a group the Orthodox community here and Ethiopia versus is one, in Ethiopia, the Orthodox community in every neighborhood in everywhere there is a church. Every people, every Sunday at least they have wearing dress. People when they go to church they are not wearing like jacket or something, They have cultural [unclear] dress. They went there, this takes hours for hours and the preacher they gonna give them. Weekdays too, afternoon shift they can go there. There is a way of getting people with each other every month. For instance, they believe in every day there is Michael saints day, Mary saints day. For instance, they consider in one month they are different days. Saint Joseph day, Saint Michael day, Saint Mary day like a lot of things. So the people, they get together every month. Because of this there are twelve people in each house. This month we are going to celebrate at this house, next month this house, next month that house. By thinking Mary's day, because of this there is a big connection society, but here no. You just go to church. You have also plenty of time back home. You don't have to use car, taxi, train. Just by walking you can get around there. So this is a big, the versus is that a lot of everyday you can celebrate there the process, but here, in America, people is busy getting to jobs mostly it is busy. Only you can go there, you cannot get enough basic education here too because only the priest, they also have their own job. So this is a difference between the two.

D: Are there any changes you would like to see made in the Orthodox Church either here or in Ethiopia?

M: Yeah. Even in my country we need, supposed to be you know go...we need a big change because most of the people, they trust the priests. Or they trust. Within one month there are thirty days. And each thirty days there is different religion, different [unclear] Saint Joseph days, different days. So people they make to celebrate every day those days. So on this day if you celebrate, you don't have to go to work, you have to celebrate the holiday. So such we need a big change, we have to give attention for work. There is holiday and people are not doing to work, just church. So within 30 days, within one month and there are different holidays there are different so you have to believe in this church but you have to also big change for development, big change for war, big change for you know fighting against poverty, fighting for Ethiopia. This is why the priest has a big respect in our country. If he say, if you work for instance, there is in every one month, for instance, June 21, July 21, August 21 every 21, 21, 21 that is Mary day, so people are not going to work. And the next day there is Joseph day or St. Joseph day, like that. Different day of respect. So you don't have to work, just have to celebrate, a lot of people they celebrate like this. So we have to work. If they change like this it is ok. Religion also should fight against change, you know against change. Against poverty, against peace. This is the difference and the change.

D: Do you think there is anything different that the Orthodox Church should do different here, that they should make any changes?

M: Yeah, the structure everything, the same everything here and here. The only difference, the only difference here, I don't know. You can't go every day only once. Myself, I only go once a month, once two weeks, once three months, because of far, it's not near, because of the church south, the priests are also busy. They don't give you some basic [unclear]. These are differences.

D: Ok, would you mind, this takes about two minutes, it's just read the question, circle. It's like how often do you go to worship, read the Bible, that sort of thing.

M: Yeah. Yeah.

Interview 4: July 7, 2007 in Ras Dashen Restaurant in the Edgewater Community, Chicago, IL.

[This interview took place at Ras Dashen Ethiopian restaurant, where a family (wife, husband, and two children) were dining in the traditional Ethiopian restaurant. Our waitress introduced us to them after we told her about our research project and she told us that they were both originally from Ethiopia. However, the husband was only visiting, as he works for an American NGO in Sudan, so he deferred to his wife to give the interview since she actually lives in Chicago. Since they preferred the interview not be tape-recorded, we simply took notes.]

How did you come to live in Chicago and how long have you been here?

She came to Chicago to leave her family because in Ethiopia when you start to get sick and lose weight, people wonder what is wrong with you and start to talk. She had bad ulcers that would not heal so she came here to get away from her family. When she arrived in 2001, she got a doctor and was sent to Cook County Hospital and was assigned a social worker and put on medicines that healed her illness.

With whom do you live, if anyone? Describe your neighborhood. What do you like/not like about the city?

She came here with her brother-in-law as her sponsor and had to leave her husband and child in Ethiopia. She lived with her brother-in-law for 9 months before she moved to Kedzie/Oak Park where she now lives alone with her daughter (who has developmental problems and is 6 years old). She loves living in Chicago, maybe because it was the first US city she stayed in, and feels connected to it. The people are nice and she has never had a negative experience.

What do you miss about Ethiopia?

The US is nothing like home at all. There it is a family culture which made her first 2 years here especially hard since her husband and daughter were at home in Ethiopia.

What is your past religious involvement, if any?

She is Orthodox, like the rest of her family; it is a very cultural religion. "You are raised with it, you go to church with your family. It is big trouble if you switch to new religion." Now there are more people with different religion because of changes in the country, government. But here, there is not enough time. In Ethiopia, there is time for other things because you don't live alone, so when you come home from work, someone already has cooked dinner, laundry is done, the house is clean, so you can all go to church together. But here, when you live alone, you come home and still have to do all those things, then you are very tired and do not have enough time to go to church.

[Interview was at restaurant, and family was having coffee and offered it to us. This began a discourse on Ethiopian coffee. It is a very social event to make coffee, especially during the holidays or when guests are visiting. They call this a ceremony; the beans are roasted, ground and boiled in the home, using a traditional clay pot. There are usually three rounds of coffee. The first round is very strong and for the next rounds, water is added to the pot, but not more grounds, so it becomes weaker as the rounds pass. Many people join in and it is a social event that gives people the chance to talk about politics, religion, community life, etc.]

What affects your involvement here as opposed to Ethiopia?

In relation to church involvement, she would like to go every Sunday, but cannot go because she works overnight, so when she gets home it is morning and she has to rest and take care of her daughter. She used to go every week before her daughter came to live with her.

Where do you go to church here?

When she goes to church, it is to the Orthodox church on S. Commercial because the service is in Amharic, but it is far away. She has been to the Greek Orthodox church on Hollywood Street before but the service is in English and it is not really her church.

How did you find out about it?

She found out about the Ethiopian Orthodox church here because her brother-in-law attends there and he has been here in the US for 20 years, so she went with him and his family for a while. However, here the Ethiopian Orthodox church is only open on Sundays, which is very different from Ethiopia.

How do you feel about the role of the Ethiopian Orthodox Church in Ethiopia?

She is very glad to have a national church, but it is not the same here. In Ethiopia, there are many people at church every day because you go every day with your family, especially on holidays and Sundays.

What is your perception of the Protestant/evangelical church here?

As for other religions, she doesn't have an opinion about Protestants because she doesn't think you can ever judge another religion because that is what someone believes and everyone has their own beliefs.

What are some of the most important religious traditions passed on to you by your parents?

One of the most important traditions from her parents is the celebration surrounding Christmas. It is very different from Christmas in America; no gifts are given, but everyone goes to church with their families on Christmas Eve and they stay at the church all night then come home to have a family meal that everyone shares in.

Suppose you were invited to attend a worship service that was not of your own religion. What is your reaction?

If invited to a worship service of another religion, she would usually not go. She once attended a Baptist service out of respect for the friend who asked her to go.

Suppose someone suggests that your beliefs are flawed. How do you defend your beliefs and what is your response to them?

She says that you must know what you believe in order to defend it. "If you know the Bible, you can defend your beliefs. If not, you can't argue with them." You just have to accept that that is what they believe and know what you believe and you cannot push your beliefs on them.

Suppose a member of your family converted to a different religion. How does your relationship with them change?

Religion is very important in Ethiopia; so much so that in the past it was unacceptable for an Orthodox Ethiopian to convert to another religion. Should a family member convert, there would not be a good relationship between them and the family anymore and even neighbors would no longer respect the family. Now things are changing and it is a different situation, but it is still frowned upon to convert from being Orthodox.

How do you perceive the Ethiopian Orthodox Church community here in the US as compared to Ethiopia?

Here in US, there is not a real community for Ethiopians or the Ethiopian Orthodox church. Everyone goes to the Ethiopian Orthodox church because it is cultural but people need the proper environment (time and family nearby) to re-create that community. In addition, the church here is only open on Sundays, which doesn't help build the community.

What do you perceive are the differences in the Protestant churches and the Ethiopian Orthodox Church here in the US?

She thinks that other religions get more benefits (help from the church) than does the Ethiopian Orthodox Church community.

Are there any changes you would like to see in the Ethiopian Orthodox Church?

She also believes that it is up to the believer to make their faith strong; the Bible, the church history and structure are already there and so it is up the individual. Now that there are many other religions coming in, it is even more important that the believer make his/her faith stronger.

Interview 5: July 8, 2007 in a suburb of Chicago.

[This interview was conducted at a family picnic being hosted by an evangelical Ethiopian church. Before the interview was conducted I had the opportunity to sit around a table with several Ethiopian immigrants, one being the gentleman I interviewed. At the table we were able to talk a little about the backgrounds of the people and where they live now—which will help to explain a few of the statements that are already known before the interview.]

Jeffrey: How did you come to live in Chicago and how long have you been here?

Zelalem: [hesitation and thinking] 15 years now

J: 15 years. I know earlier you said you actually live in Wisconsin, in Madison

Z: I first came to Chicago

J: Ok you first came to Chicago

Z: Then went to school in Ohio

J: You went to school in Ohio, you said. Where did you go in Ohio?

Z: Bowling Green State University

J: Bowling Green OK I am familiar with it. Ok um when you first came to, who did you live with or um?

Z: First hotel then Ethiopian friends

J: Ethiopian friends - um how about now -- do you live with family or by yourself or who?

Z: Now?

J: Yes

Z: Married with 2 children

J: Ok where you live right at now what is the neighborhood like that you live in, apartment?

Z: An apartment in suburbs

J: Living outside of the Chicago area what do you like about living around the Chicago area?

Z: Well you know it's like I came here so I came to know people, Ethiopian people and my sister lives here and you kind of get used to the people around here and the surrounding, sometimes to adventure to move to different states you be a bit reluctant so I like utmost knowing people

J: You said your sister is here as well

Z: Yes

J: And does she live with you or

Z: No

J: She does not live with you

Z: No by herself

J: Ok what do you miss about Ethiopia?

Z: Relatives, sisters and brothers, cousins, nieces, nephews, umm working there, just the area itself, the fact that is it my country, that I miss a lot

J: With Ethiopia what is your past religious involvement that you've had before?

Z: *I have been an Orthodox Christian*

J: Orthodox Christian

Z: *Yeah the Russian type or Greek type, whatever it is you call it*

J: Was it part of the Ethiopian Orthodox Church?

Z: *Yes*

J: What was your involvement like with them?

Z: *I mean you know family grows up, mother and family were Orthodox, just like being born in a Muslim family would be a Muslim. I go on Sundays, holy water is sprinkled on you and until 7 years old partake in Lord's supper after that you not allowed because now you know right and wrong, maybe you need to confess to a priest just like in catholic and then you would partake in that, so you say I am young and will not do that so that is my involvement with that, just going on Sundays*

J: Just Sundays. Ok what do you see are changes if any in your worship style from Ethiopia to America? Do you see any changes in how you worship or anything like that?

Z: *There is a difference in the Orthodox worship and the evangelical worship which is the American style so to say, but in Ethiopia it is more of a Mass like a Catholic where the priest do liturgy and things like that. Your participation is when the liturgy says something and you say something and you sit down and listen too and they say it in a different church language so we don't understand it, just like in Catholic if they do the Mass in Latin and most people don't know Latin right, but now in American I became to know Christ and you are more involved in yourself worship in praise and saying hallelujahs free style so it's a dramatic difference*

J: And you said that you came to the evangelical church in the US?

Z: *I came to Christ as my personal savior and Lord in the US*

J: So when you came to America you were still Orthodox ?

Z: *Living as the more I do, I will get into heaven, so more into the works*

J: Ok and this is kind of what I asked a minute ago have you experienced any changes in your involvement at your place of worship and if so why?

Z: *You mean here?*

J: Yes here or Ethiopia, either one.

Z: *Here, here. Yes I can see changes because personally you are involved in the church in different areas. I personally don't have time to be involved because we live in two different places personally, but still getting together when I have time for Friday pray nights or some of the pray times and also get-togethers in environments like you see now. [We were sitting to the side of the backyard of a house where there were several Ethiopian immigrants gathered around in small groups talking and eating, children running around in and out of the house and most of the women inside talking.] A few months ago, a month or two one of our friends got married and we had a praise time here and everybody brings something and prays and that is kind, it is really close, that is the difference*

J: What affects your involvement here in the US as it did when you were in Ethiopia? I mean how or is there something that really affects? You said you are a little more involved here in the US than you were with your Orthodox religion in Ethiopia.

A *Yeah because it may be that Ethiopia is my country and so you have a lot of things to do when it is your country. Here you tend to connect to your fellow citizens here and one of the best connections here is the church right, so it makes you more involved and more connected. And the other most important thing is in Ethiopia the church is lead by the Orthodox archbishop and the others so it is a top down type of thing and you are a spectator in those cases. But here once you have accepted Christ as your savior you want to do something's not ---- but you want to be involved in calling people, how they are doing, if they are sick you go out and see them because you want to connect to those fellow Ethiopians. Not because we don't want to integrate into the*

American society but you still want to talk sometime in your own language and to find out if someone visit. For example last year we were in Ethiopia for a visit and hopefully we will go this year, God willing. And then when you come people will come, "Hey how is it? How are the people over there? How are the relatives? How is the city?" You know, so just for that even you want to connect to the people, so that is what it is.

J: Ok we know that you go to Tensae Church here and how did you come to find out about the evangelical church here?

Z: Which one?

J: The evangelical church.

Z: Evangelical church?

J: Yes Tensae. I am sorry.

Z: I used to go to the American church and this evangelical church start up. My sister E---- was involved with the pastor and what not. When they found the church and they say, "Hey would you mind come to?" Oh I would love to, that is wonderful. So whenever we have Sundays here we love to worship in our own language, we would love to worship and sing in our own language. Kind of you can see I can speak English and understand English well and understand it well but when I hear it in the Ethiopian language, not the sermons but the praises and singing it gives me more meaning in the praise because I grow up in that. So that is how I joined the church.

J: Ok what were your first experiences at Tensae?

Z: My first experiences -- I think the smallness of the church gives cohesiveness to the member. I believe and I have witness a lot of love for the people, love for the people, love for Christ, love to do the Lord's work, to see souls being saved and energy in everything I see was really marvelous.

J: You said that you had went to an American church as a Protestant church before you found the Protestant church or before you found the evangelical church

Z: Protestant

J: Baptist church ok

Z: In the Ethiopian Orthodox Church, the predominate church I believe in Ethiopian because of their long standing history, but being involved as a member of the Ethiopian Orthodox Church, now when I think about it I think they lack teaching the people about the gospel and the that----- Christ has done every single thing is paid in full. Our response is simply to accept by faith Christ as Lord and savior and be born again as the Bible says. They don't really emphasize and teach that because they do it in a liturgical language. They don't teach that so I feel sometimes that more people are being lost because of that so I would love to see and pray to see that there is more teaching the people about the gospel.

J: Ok what is your perception -- what is your perception of the Protestant/ evangelical church in the US? How do you feel and what do you see -- actually I am going to skip this question -- user did not understand question. What are some of the most important religious traditions that your parents passed down to you?

Z: I would say honesty, integrity, respect and the love of God and prayer—prayer, even as Orthodox those were passed down from my dad and my mom.

J: You talk about some of that -- is that stuff still important. You said these were important to you in the past. Are they important today?

Z: Oh yes very important today

J: Very much important.

Z: These are things that do not change even in the evangelical church because that is what Christ teaches: be humble, be loved, if you want to be first be last, if you want to be a master be a servant, respect, integrity, not stealing, not killing, all these things.

J: Was there anything else besides? I know you said, "Honesty, integrity, love of God" -- that type of stuff. Is there anything else that was passed down tradition wise through your family -- anything like that, religious practices or traditions?

Z: Well which I don't practice them now, but for example in the Orthodox Church as we grow up until I came to know Christ Wednesdays and Fridays are fasting days. Fasting by that, people do fasting different ways, but Wednesday, Fridays in Ethiopian Orthodox Church means you don't eat meat, don't drink milk, you don't drink water, you don't eat chicken, everything that has blood in it you don't do. So most of the time eat lentil salad, tea or coffee and that is it Wednesday and Friday. And also during the Lent time, Easter time for 40 days the same fasting would continue for 40 days -- you don't eat milk, eat meat so I used to do that all the time too. And in those cases you don't eat until 3 in the afternoon so that is a tradition that I kept for so long until I came to Christ. I still wouldn't mind doing that 'cause I think it has value today

J: So do you still practice fasting occasionally?

Z: Occasionally

J: Occasionally you do

Z: But not as strict as Wednesday and Friday. But yeah and the other tradition was that when we go to church, they still practice it because I have visited [another Chicagoland] Ethiopian church too -- when you go to church you take off your shoes on the step of the door, when you go into the church, signifying Moses and the burning bush, you've got to take off your shoes. That I think it is also good. I believe if the Protestant churches in America, evangelical church we do, if we take off our shoes and get into the worship room, I think I believe that this tradition to, you are dignifying the Lord and you know that you are in His presence so out of respect you do it. Those are the traditions that . . .

J: Ok suppose someone invited you to a worship service that is not your own religion. If somebody invited you to a Catholic or Orthodox church or maybe a Muslim mosque, what would your reaction be to that? How would you respond to that?

Z: Today I wouldn't mind going to a Catholic I would mind going there I wouldn't mind going to the Orthodox too because I have gone to Mormon church, you know. Mormon -- you know Mormon?

J: Yes

Z: *I have friends who are Mormon and they invited me to see their temple, because they call it temple. I went because I believe that by connecting to people by ---- I will have the chance to share the good news too or to challenge their assumption or to challenge their beliefs too, allowing them to challenge mine. I am not afraid of defending mine because I don't believe being selfish, but I still believe that the work of God withstand any test so and I do ... but the Muslim maybe I doubt it, I don't know, but visiting a Muslim mosque – "I would want to come to your church but would you mind coming and seeing my mosque?" -- I wouldn't mind going there too because I don't see any other way of bringing people to Christ.*

J: You take away, you know, say I will do this if you turn around and visit…

Z: *I wouldn't mind. Otherwise how would you ask them to come to yours because he is already believing passionately that his is true and you telling him that his is trash -- how are you going to show him the truth?*

J: Okay. Suppose someone suggests that your religious beliefs were flawed. How do you defend your stance and what is your response to them? Do you understand the question?

Z: *Yeah*

J: Ok

Z: *Well it depends on the circumstances, but I believe that God has given me the answer to both circumstances but I would start saying this: how would you explain the existence of all these things that we see, visible world, the sun, the moon, whatever you touch, even ours -- the voices -- how do you explain that without saying and admitting that there is some power that really created this ---- to challenge ---- because my thinking is that everything really outweighs the existence of God then towards any existence of God. Like radio waves, for example, I speak now right, this thing is recording, no one sees my voice but you hear it, but you can see, but still it records. So how would you explain that you know, how would you explain that radio waves but you can't see but it exist -- the fact that you can't see the waves does not mean it does not exist. So I would start out by that.*

J: Ok suppose a member of your family converts to another religion or denomination. How if at all would your relationship with them change?

Z: *God forbid I would feel sad because I have sin in my life now I love my sister came to the Lord, my brother came to the Lord, my youngest sister came to the Lord and I take that seriously an answer to my prayer. So if someone changes religions or something, I still love them but I will still pray hard and believe God will bring them to the truth. But I came to a realization that I have tried talking to people, that the only person that can change any one side is only God. It took God 30 years for my brother to come to Christ because he kept say, "I am Orthodox and that's my father and mother's religion and I am sticking to it." But when God touched him, he changed himself.*

J: Ok how -- these are probably a little more personal questions -- how did you come to know the Lord?

Z: *Ok let see, almost 14, 15 years ago, I came here and I was Orthodox Christian but I got saved. Fasting Wednesday and Fridays, I consider more myself a Pharisee, a religious people, Pharisees, so I pray and I do a good thing like... But my mom was sick in Ethiopia and I was really alone, was she going to die, I can't go see her. And a friend of mine who came to Christ, "Why don't you come to church and pray for her too?" And I said ok because I can go to the Orthodox church but they do the liturgy. I go there and the teaching is in Amharic and singing is in Amharic and start praying and my heart gets calm and things like that. It is through my mother sickness and that trial that I came to know the Lord.*

J: So through your friend inviting you to come and pray, that is when you came. And how long did it take from, I mean from...

Z: From Orthodox to...

J: From Orthodox to come into evangelical?

Z: *Well it doesn't take me long to come and just see the church to convert*

J: Yes to convert that would be 6 or 7 months. 6 or 7 months. Ok, my last question you have already answered, so what do you like about Tensae?

Z: *I feel right now, I know that I pray that God keeps the spirit the way it is and even more, because I sense the Spirit of the Lord there when we worship and other times and I see the love. So if each and every one of us really keeps that in perspective and always live for the Lord, that is what I love about the church*

J: Ok I am going to go back just a little bit. You know how I was asking about how you came to know the Lord. Was that a Baptist church I'm assuming?

Z: *Yeah, yeah*

J: I know from earlier you said that you --

Z: *There is another Ethiopian church, in [location], it is an evangelical church*

J: It is an evangelical in [location]. That is ok

Z: *Now they built another church. I guess I used to go to that church*

J: So do they, this other church, do they do their services in --

Z: *Amharic*

J: Amharic. Ok so you didn't actually go to a, well I am going to say, an American Baptist church. You went to an Ethiopian.

Z: *I went to an American Baptist church*

J: Ok you did attend one

Z: *This friend of mine goes to an American church, so in the morning we go to a little church by roadway in Chicago called Faith ------ Church. So we used to go there and you can check it out on the website and in the afternoon we would go to the Ethiopian church. We were like 20, 25 people there, maybe sometimes 15 or 17.*

J: Ok so was it a combination of both the American church and the Ethiopian church that aided in your conversion?

Z: *That brings me to see the light, yeah*

J: Ok

Z: *You know what after all I yes can pray on my own after all I knew Christ died for me after all whoever believes in his heart and spoken in his mouth that Jesus is the Lord is going to be saved, that's what I should be doing.*

J: Ok I think that brings me to the end of your questions and thank you for helping with this.

Interview 5: July 8, 2007 in a suburb of Chicago.

[This interview was conducted at a group study room at a library.]

Jeffrey: First of all I would like to start off with you stating your name and spelling it

Dawit: My name is "D"

J: Ok and first I would like to ask: how did you come to live in Chicago and how long have you been here?

D: I've been here for 3 years. I came here to study at college

J: You said you came here to study at the college. Were you already in the US when you came here or did you come from --

D: I just came from Ethiopia

J: You came from Ethiopia to study here. And when you first came to Chicago who did you live with or stay with?

D: In an apartment

J: In an apartment. Was it by yourself or --

D: With a friend who came with me

J: A friend came with you from Ethiopia?

D: Yes

J: Ok and now, who do you live with now that you are here? You've been here for 3 years -- who do you live with now?

D: *With my family -- my wife and the kids*

J: And your wife is also from Ethiopia

D: Yes

J: She is. How about the kids? Were they born in Ethiopia or were they born here?

D: *Born back home*

J: They were both born in Ethiopia

D: Yes

J: And where do you live now? What type of setting do you live in now?

D: *You mean in the city or --*

J: Well do you live in a house, an apartment?

D: *A house*

J: And what do you most like or not like about living in the Chicago area?

D: *Well I don't know, I like most of the things. [laugh] Well I like, hmm, do you want*
me to compare it from Ethiopia?

J: If you would like. Actually my next question is kind of a contrasting question: what do you miss about Ethiopia? So what do you like and not like about Chicago and what do you miss about Ethiopia?

D: *Well I like Chicago. The cold, the snow is a bit of a challenge -- the cold season, the snow is not something that is challenging and the extreme hot of the summer is another challenge. But I like that it is a multicultural setting. At least people are not noticed, outsiders are really part of the society and you don't be really spotted if you are black and in an exclusive white or black community. I don't know, in a white American community I would be easily picked out so this is multi-ethnic. I like it*

J: Ok and actually I am going to jump to a question here. What is your, now knowing you a little bit, I know a little bit of your story from [before], how did you come to know the Lord?

D: *I came to know the Lord through reading the Bible in my mother tongue. And then I meet some people who knew the Lord and they helped me to understand my Bible. Basically I read the Bible and that is basically what happened in my life*

J: How did you, was the Bible given to you or how did you find the Bible?

D: *Yeah a guy gave me the Bible. Actually I don't think he was a Christian*

J: You don't think he was a Christian, the guy who gave it to you

D: *Yeah he was not a believer. He just gave it to me. I think he liked the Bible, I think, but he was not a believer*

J: Ok and the Bible was given to you in Ethiopia while you were there

D: *Yeah*

J: Anything else that you feel really is important in how you came to know the Lord?

D: *Yeah, in coming to know the Lord is not really a one day experience. It was a process for me so... It is not easy for me to understand the Bible, it took me quite a while to figure it out and I think it is important to be patient to some people when they are struggling to understand the Bible*

J: Did you have anybody when you were trying to read it to kind of help you interpret and understand what you were reading with it or --

D: *The first couple of years, not really*

J: The first couple of years not really

D: *Yeah then I came to get just connected with people who really understand the Bible. They really helped me*

J: Ok going back to some other questions: what, before you came became a Christian, what was your past religious involvement?

D: *Well I was in the Ethiopian Orthodox Church. My families are from the Ethiopian Orthodox Church so I grew up in the Ethiopian Orthodox Church, practicing the religious part in the Ethiopian Orthodox Church and also, you know, we had syncretism I guess to add some more gods, local gods like superstitious things, witchdoctors. So it's not uncommon for me if I get sick my mom goes to the witchdoctors. So that is my religious experience my Orthodox class the African tribes you not religion which is worshiping other gods.*

J: Ok how long had you been involved with the Orthodox religion until you became a Christian?

D: *By the time I become a Christian I was a teenager*

J: Teenager -- just kind of approximation with the years?

D: *Maybe 15 years, 15 or – 15, different my, from childhood to 15. And yeah I was by early in my childhood, I was trained to be a committed Orthodox and I was going to the local priest to study the Orthodox religion so that is my history*

J: About, you said, for about 15 years, so you were about 15 or 16 when you came to know the Lord

D: *Yeah you know so that is why I don't have any one day experience. So that is why it is a process*

J: Yes well that is an age, kind of helps give an idea of what that is. What do you see are any changes, if there is any changes you, of your worship, of how your worship style from Ethiopia to America -- do you see any changes in that?

D: *In our church you mean*

J: Well yeah within Christian church

D: *Within Christian church or Ethiopian church? Are you comparing Ethiopian?*

J: Well were you involved with a Christian church in Ethiopia?

D: *Yes I did*

J: Actually a little bit of both, style of worship, maybe a little bit of both of your Ethiopian Orthodox church when you were involved in the Ethiopian Orthodox Church and your church here but whatever Christian church you were involved with in Ethiopia, I mean, do you see any different styles with the worship?

D: *Well no. Most of my time, I spent most of my time in the Ethiopian evangelical churches. The style of worship is a kind of mixture of traditional and contemporary in my opinion, not very contemporary but there is some contemporary elements in the evangelical realm and the Ethiopian Orthodox Church is more of traditional. But the young people enjoy the contemporary worship while the old generation is uncomfortable of the contemporary so my personal preference is more of contemporary, but our music is a little different from the American music. So when I come to American the American music in the church is a little bit calm so that is one differences. We are more loud and of the style is different, that is the only difference I can see as may be an issue. But with the Ethiopian Orthodox Church the Protestants are more of contemporary and loud and a little informal. The Ethiopian Orthodox Church liturgy is really rich and I don't know, and the other side is the young people doesn't really understand that and that is a challenge.*

J: They don't understand the traditional

D: *The traditional is a little bit, you know, it needs some more of training, more of -- it's a lot like the whole culture is the folk music, Ethiopian folk music. What you hear on the daily mass media outlets is more of contemporary. The Ethiopian Orthodox liturgy is more of ancient so that would be the gap.*

J: Ok have you experienced any changes in your involvement at your place of worship and if so why?

D: Here?

J: Yes that's what I mean, from Ethiopia to here -- have you experienced any changes in your involvement?

D: In my personal life?

J: Yes in your personal life

D: Well in Ethiopia I was a minister. Here I am also in ministry. Maybe there I was more of on a national level. Here my involvement is working with immigrants so that would be a little bit different. I have always been a minister and here a minister so ministry was in, minister in both settings. But here I am in local church and reaching out to individuals and this is a scattered community, so different setting there

J: You said you are more involved with individuals here. What were you more involved with in Ethiopia?

D: I was there training people, training [unclear], recruiting missionaries, sending them. I spent more with ministers. Here I spent more with congregants

J: Ok so you were kind of more working with the leaders over there whereas here you kind of taking their role and working more with the lay people

D: Yes

J: Ok what affects your involvement with that? What affects your involvement here as opposed to Ethiopia? I mean why is it you are more involved with the people here than with what you were doing in Ethiopia?

D: There the people whom I was working, they just go to the grass root. Here I am the person who is organizing so the difference is just the logistical difference. Even there I spent time, I was the pastor of a congregation, but most of my time I was working with leaders. Here I am working with people because I am planting a church. I am a church planter, I have to be involved more with the people.

J: This question, knowing you a little bit is kind of, it says: where do you go to church here? I know [where]. The question is how did you find out about your church here and what was your first experience there? I was wondering if you could on the latter part of that just tell me a little bit about your first experiences with your church?

D: Well as you said I go to [my church]. I used to go here and there. I am sorry, I used to go actually most of my time to the Evangelical [unclear name] Church here -- a white church, English speaking American church -- but in due time I saw the need to reach out to Ethiopian. So we started. My experience with my church is I enjoy it personally, I enjoy it living in America pastoring an Ethiopian church. For me going to American church is not a big problem because I understand the language and the culture is not a huge issue but I feel that I have to start this church because this, you in an American church, well trained, very nice pastors, you can just sit down, get good sermons and good for you personally life. It's not disadvantage but for your mission and reaching other people I feel that I need to start this church so I started this church. It is quite a lot of responsibility and I enjoy the worship. I like it that is the difference, I like, I just easily get connected with that church, the worship, the style and as a minister I try to deliver the message other people. So my first experience as the church started in my own home it's a, it's interesting to see people enjoying their music, enjoying the culture and after church, like as you have seen, we just stay there for a while connecting, talking, discussing. So that is my unique experience, I like it, I like it that way and I feel happy about that because we just give the community to the people. There is a community and in the process of preserving that.

J: Some of these questions are a little related with religious but also some political issues too. How do you feel about the role of the Ethiopian Orthodox Church in Ethiopia? I know that they tend to play a little bit of a political type role with some things. How do you feel about the role they play in Ethiopia?

D: Well it's a -- the Ethiopian church has a long history so commanded by a [recording unclear] might not be fair but I -- the Ethiopian Orthodox Church historical has its own positive and negative side as a state's church until the 1974 Ethiopian revolution. As a state church it used to serve the [recording unclear] of being the political arm of the government is there and it used to be that way. So I think that was a disadvantage to the church not to reach out to our neighbors like the *neighboring nations and the Middle East. We have not significance present as the Ethiopian Orthodox Church and even today the Ethiopian Orthodox Church is not free from political involvement or that is hampering the progress of the church. And the Ethiopian Orthodox Church also used to be historically not a good friend of evangelicals, that is another issue. And the Ethiopian Orthodox Church has been serving a more involved in politics so that also has its own disadvantage in the relationships between Christian and Muslim members. I don't know it is more of a historical issue but I feel that the Ethiopian Orthodox Church is more of -- it's my personally feeling and I think the Ethiopian Orthodox Church is not really mission oriented church beyond Ethiopia.*

J: Ok you alluded a little bit to conflicts between the Ethiopian Orthodox Church and the evangelicals. Could you expand on that maybe a little more?

D: *Well the feeling of the Ethiopian Orthodox Church members is that they are not comfortable towards evangelicals because the Ethiopian Orthodox Church just believe that evangelicalism is a western religion and they had a very difficult time to recognize the evangelicals as Christian sect as part of Ethiopian. They used to identify with ideology, Western ideology, simply because it is mainly started with Western missionaries and also because evangelicals convert Orthodoxes. Historically I think that some of the Western missionaries' intent was not to convert Orthodoxes to evangelicalism but due to the prayer from the Ethiopian Orthodox Church on the teaching of the Western missionaries, evangelicals came out of that. So, yeah the Ethiopian Orthodox Church feelings towards evangelicalism is not really friendly. There are so many persecutions and ups and downs in our relationship but I think we have to mend it and we have join hands and work together.*

J: Are there any advantages in Ethiopia to being associated with the Orthodox Church as compared to being associated with the evangelical church?

D: *Well the challenge is always wherever you are, whether in America or Ethiopian, the majority, being part of the majority, you enjoy some privilege. At least you're not outcast. That is why people normally just tend to in [recording unclear] majority culture even though they are not feeling comfortable to follow. The Ethiopian Orthodox Church at least until recently or until today is a majority church, a majority religious group because it also used to enjoy a set of privilege. So when you are a Orthodox in the community you are just accepted but when you are a Protestant you are -- your friends, your families, the community start pushing you out. Some of the privileges, some of the cemeteries were not allowed. In some place even today you may not get the place to bury you're a -- if somebody died from your family or you may not be able to enjoy the social, the community, the advantage in the community. You are considered to be an outcast, considered to be a Westerner, considered to be who is not really patriotic. Some people think that we don't love our country because we are evangelicals so that's no [recording unclear] that more of a conceived idea not related so there is a whole lot of struggle. You get persecuted, some time beaten, kicked out of your family. So many things happen.*

J: Ok, you were saying that in Ethiopia that the evangelicals were kind of an outcast from the community. Do you feel that in the US, since the evangelicals are more of the majority, that the Ethiopian Orthodox, that the people that are here in the US are kind of treated as an outcast group here in the US?

D: *I don't think so because in America the cultures is different. American cultures is more of primarily individualistic: the individual has all the right and I think if you become, now your family is Christian and you want to be [recording unclear], I don't think that they will outcast you. Here in America you have, that is your right, but the danger is in communal cultures and communities. If you are not with the community, automatically you are considered an enemy of the community. But here the philosophy is different, it is more of democratic. That why democracy and collective society sometimes collide. You know until the community embraces the balance of individuality, it's a challenge so that I don't think the Ethiopia Orthodox believers are outcast here. Of course they don't get some of their food or water for the fasting foods as much as they get in Ethiopia so they have to be selective in their fasting season. I don't know, better to ask a, I hope you ask Orthodoxes how they feel, but I feel, they don't ask us, but they don't get all the privileges, all the things that are automatically available as a community back home.*

J: Ok and also going back to the thing where you said that between the Orthodox and evangelicals that there's some tension between the two.

What do you believe might be able to be done to relieve that tension where the two might be able to get along more side by side?

D: *We both read the same Bible, we are both Christians, so to serve our differences I believe dialogue and discussion would be the best way. And the other thing is we have to promote unity and also part of the individual views. You know if the individual is accepted as an individual the things that you would be relieved in the individual should be allowed to be himself or herself in a community. But dialogue discussion I think is a good thing to vent our opinions and we don't have to go beyond that.*

J: Ok what is your perception of the Protestant/evangelical churches in the US?

D: *Well Protestant evangelical?*

J: Well, it's, some people relate more to one term than the other.

D: *Yeah I mean the Protestant, evangelical church, whatever you call it, in the US is diverse so it is not very easy to really give a general comment on that but it might be better if you give me some of the areas you want me to comment. Like in what areas, even in the best, weak areas it is not easy to comment on the evangelicals in the Americas. It is a wide, wide spectrum but generally there are so many appreciable values and so many appreciable things. Commitments among the cultures in America, we can see that in many ways a commitment for missions, a commitment for peace, a commitment for a mutual understanding, all these things and it's good in American church. American Christians anyways are contributing to a lot of missions, that's good but I am afraid that many things are being taken for granted and American churches are receding in its commitment for missions. Commitment for truth because of the so many works going on in this land.*

J: Ok what are some of the most important Ethiopian religious traditions that your parents passed down to you?

D: *Well so many good things. Most of the biblical virtue I was trained to accept as a child like [recording unclear] honesty, faithfulness to friends and family, and fearing the Lord. The fear of God has been implanted in my heart as a child. The only problem is I have to sift, my Orthodox families, they are committers, they love God, they love people, they respect people, they care for people. I am, they have a lot of qualities. The only problem is they were not trained properly to follow the Biblical truths, especially when it comes to worshiping only one God. So reading the Bible, helping me to really know the Lord, but the 10 commandments, all this good things from the Bible, the Lord's Prayer, everything I knew by heart when I was a kid. So that helped me a lot in that regard. The Ethiopian Orthodox Church has done a lot but the problem is that they are not missionally trained in many ways. It was not really concentrated on discipling believers.*

J: Ok you said that honesty, faithfulness, the kind of virtues and that type stuff -- were those more taught to you by your parents or by the church itself?

D: *In the community, like hospitality, respecting the elders and caring for poor people and helping each other -- all these things, part of the, we live in a community, more than the priest. In the community, you see a lot because you may not see the priest teaching you or teaching the kids or whatever but the community, just really you know you just live together. If you violate one of the virtues anyone in the community can instruct you and rebuke you or even correct you or even spank you. Then that's how we grow.*

J: Ok with what you are talking about that was taught to you as a child -- are those still important? I realize they were important to you in the past -- are they still important to you today as they were in the past?

D: *Very important, like honesty. And as a Christian the way I do, the reasons I do, might be, might have gone to a higher level. But honesty, as a kid if I get hundred dollar over here on the street, I would then take it then, just give it to somebody and tell them that I got it and the community would find who the owner is. So faithfulness, honesty is just part of my, so some of the virtues, most of the virtues are still with me. So for that I just really appreciate my family and my community.*

J: Are there any that you think were important as a child that your parents may have taught you or you learned from the community that are not as important today? Do you feel any of those have wavered away for the importance of them?

D: *Yeah there are some cultural things that you just consider to be universal. When you move out of your community they are no longer* universal. So many minor and major things like, what can I say, like some of the things you have to really be part of the community. Like it or not, you have to really respect the community and you have to suppress your personally opinion, view that might not be really right in all circumstances. So at this point I don't really follow that, I don't take that absolutely I have to you know.

J: Ok suppose someone invites you to a worship service that is not of your own religion. What would your reaction be?

D: *It depends. Like if it is a peaceful Christian kind of things, I feel more comfortable. If it is a group that's not really, after I would think about it. Like even if I am in America I still feel I have to be carefully for my security. I don't go to any temple without any suspicious, I would be suspicious for my personally safety, not for indoctrination things but for me personally safety. I don't go with any one whom I know but if that person is trustworthy and that group is peacefully it doesn't matter for me but if it is out of my will, if a radical Muslim group invited me I would be carefully not to really just jump in and go there. So that is how.*

J: Ok since you have converted to an evangelical Christian, how do you think you would react if you, someone invited you to go to the Orthodox church? Do you think you may have a different response to that since you grew up in it?

D: *Going, just going there?*

J: Yes, to attend maybe a worship service or something -- how do you think you would respond to that?

D: *I don't mind but the issue is, I mean I personally am planning to attend at least once in a year. The issue is only the time. I once in a while, I just want to go there and see you know. At some points I just feel at home at some Orthodox worship. I am not against that, I would not be disturbed, that is ok for me. But if a person is just jumping here and there I would tell him to just stop and think about his life and if he really is with the truth or not, that if he gets the truth in going there it does not matter to me if he goes to the evangelicals. It does not matter if he, if gets the truth. I feel that there are some Orthodox who really know the Bible and know the Lord in personally way.*

J: Ok suppose someone suggests that your religious beliefs are flawed. How do you defend your stance and what is your response to them?

D: Dialogue, discussion, because I, many times ever since I started reading the Bible I converse with many people who discredit my faith or challenge me. I like, I mean it doesn't disturb me. What disturbs me is people just say. "Ok it's good, it's good, everything good. The Muslim is good, the Orthodox is good, the Protestant is good." I have a problem with that. If someone says you are not right, I want to talk with him. I want him to tell me where I am wrong. I like dialogue so I want to discuss it.

J: Ok suppose a member of your family converts to another religion or denomination. How if at all would your relationship with them change?

D: That also depends. I have a standard. Like when you say denomination, if it is a Protestant denomination, it doesn't bother me at all because he's just, I believe that if he is going from a Baptist to Pentecostal or Pentecostal to Baptist, that's very simple and I would say go ahead, it doesn't matter. If he is changing to something else that I feel is untrue or something that is not Biblical, I would stop him and want to discuss. The communal society, we love to be together but if that is his choice, I would continue to discuss with him. I would continue to try to tell him, to teach him but still the decision is still his or hers. But I would pray and try hard like I do to understand the truth and I would try to tell the truth, to share the Bible.

J: Ok with that same thing, I know that you have converted from an Orthodox to an evangelical religion. How did any of your family members treat you any different when you changed or what is some personally experience with that?

D: Well a lot of mistreatment, lot of misunderstanding. Many of my family's friends, they just deserted me and I passed through a lot of challenges. But that didn't make me less committed -- that made me more strong in my faith and that helped me to really question myself and check my attitude. It's harmful and sometime painful too. I mean it's not an easy journey but it's not really completely disadvantages. It's people in [recording unclear] gives you more momentum but those people, when dozen and dozen people stop you that is all to your advantage.

J: Ok just a few other questions. Just kind of finish this right here. Going back to earlier, I know that you said you came 3 years ago. Ok and did you all come as immigrant status or were you looking for a --

D: We came as students so what do you call that, immigrant?

J: Well I am not sure but you came as a student. I know there is the lottery for coming to --

D: No that's not me.

J: Ok I believe that should be most of the questions, so thank you for your time.

Chapter 9:
Ethiopian Immigrants in Social Context: *The Impact of Immigration to the United States on Gender Roles in Marriage*

Talargie Y. Tafesse
Trinity International Baptist Mission
Carol Stream, IL

Abstract

This chapter examines the impact of immigration on gender role separation among two Ethiopian immigrant families in the Chicago area. Interviews and observations of various social events were conducted to determine how and to what extent moving to the U.S. impacted the culture. Impact of family, community, religion and role models and how they contribute to shaping the views of both men and women are here discussed. The perception of both men and women on changes initiated by the Derg government have been incorporated. The view points of both men and women informants before and after they moved to the United States are discussed. Areas of research and strategies of intervention to be considered are suggested. The chapter addresses the impact of the legal system, the need to enlighten both sexes and the necessity of creating equal opportunity for sustainable change.

Part 1: Introduction

Ethiopians received gender equality in a package with other issues of the socialist revolution. Therefore a certain proportion of the traditional communities still equate the issue of women's equality as a destructive ideology initiated by communists. Unfortunately, gender equality was introduced by the socialist government together with many other anti-cultural and anti-religious views and as a result, many still associate it with the negatives of the Derg time that is known for its horrific changes like godlessness, property confiscation, forceful revolution and other dreadful events that led the nation into a state of confusion and assaulted cultural norms.

Ethiopia ranks at the bottom of the Gender Development Index and gender inequality affects the lives of women and girls in all areas, stalling the achievement of government development goals. For example, the HIV epidemic has a very strong gender dimension and the persistence of traditional practices such as marriage by abduction and female genital mutilation seriously affects girls' chances of completing school (Benn, 2005). The 2005 UN Human Development Report ranked Ethiopia 170th out of 177 on the Human Development Index, 99 out of 103 on the Human Poverty Index, and 134th out of 144 on the Gender Related Development Index (UNDP 2005).

This study is conducted with the objective of identifying factors that contribute to a high degree of gender role separation among Ethiopians and investigating positive experiences that have helped to break the barriers of gender equality among the Ethiopian families through investigating the responses of immigrants. The results of my research clearly indicated that the culture of gender role separation adopted during early childhood has significantly shaped the adult behavior of both sexes. Role models and exposures to a different culture also proved to be crucial factors in both the shaping and changing of gender role-related behavior.

Definition of Terms

- Gender Related Development Index (GDI): A composite index developed by the United Nations that measures inequalities between men and women related to life expectancy and health, knowledge, and living standards. The index is calculated based on gender inequalities concerning life expectancy at birth, adult literacy rate, combined gross enrollment ratio for primary, secondary, and tertiary schools, and estimated earned income (UNDP 2005).

- Human Poverty Index (HPI): Also developed by the United Nations, the Human Poverty Index is calculated based on the following indicators: probability at birth of not surviving to age 40, adult literacy rate, number of people without sustainable access to an improved water source, children underweight for their age, and the total population below the income poverty line (UNDP 2005).
- The Human Development Index (HDI) is another United Nations tool that focuses on three measurable dimensions of human development: living a long and healthy life, being educated, and having a decent standard of living. Thus it calculates life expectancy, school enrollment, literacy, and income to provide a broad view of a country's development (UNDP 2005).
- Gender role: The role a person is expected to perform as a result of being male or female in a particular culture.
- Gender identity: The individual's sense of being male or female, resulting from a combination of genetic and environmental influences.
- Derg: The name of the communist government that ruled Ethiopia from 1974 until 1990. Derg was the Coordinating Committee of the Armed Forces, Police, and Territorial Army during the 1974 Ethiopian revolution led by military officers which ruled the country from 1974 until 1991. Most Ethiopians have used it as a pejorative nickname for the communist government.
- Culture: Understood in this chapter as the shared beliefs, values, heritage, customs, norms, and rituals of a community.
- Husband: In this chapter "husband" refers to the male partner in an officially certified heterosexual marriage.
- Wife: In this chapter "wife" refers to the female partner in an officially certified heterosexual marriage.
- UNDP: The United Nations Development Programme (UNDP) is the largest multilateral source of grants for technological and developmental assistance in the world.

Part 2: Literature Review

The Place of Women in Ethiopian Society

Traditionally men are assumed to be the provider and protectors of the family and thus granted more authority in Ethiopian society. The role of women is typically limited to the area of home-making and domestic activities. Despite a limited number of comprehensive studies regarding the impact of gender role separation on women in Ethiopia, governmental and non-governmental bodies agree that Ethiopian women suffer hardships in their day-to-day responsibilities. Some of their burdens include carrying loads, manual grinding of corn and cereals, raising children, cooking, firewood collection, fetching water, shopping, and also participating in farming—especially during harvest and weeding seasons. Women in Ethiopia are stereotyped as inferior to men and suffer from injustice. As Richmond-Abbot (1992) indicated, "Stereotypes permeate all the institutions of society: family, religion, the educational system, the economic system, and the political system" (p. 11). There is ongoing discrimination in providing educational opportunities, employment, right of ownership, access to political power, and opportunities to serve in the religious systems. Due to an inefficient legal system coupled with the trend of focusing on drafting policies and making decisions on various levels without much concern or effort for their practical applications, gender equality seems to be a remote possibility in Ethiopia. As an ancient nation with centuries of tradition, constitutional fiats and propaganda may not be enough to bring the necessary changes to this culture of gender inequality.

Traditionally a woman's worth is measured among Ethiopians in terms of her role as mother and wife. The 1974 communist revolution was the first large-scale institutional confrontation against the deeply rooted ancient tradition of gender inequality. In regard to gender, the communist era waged war on the male dominant system and was able to shake its foundation by constitutionally approving equal opportunity in all spheres of life and providing education for a large proportion of women. However, the movement was more sensational, reactionary, and forceful than it was a strategic, transformational approach and it did little in terms of penetrating the culture of the people. Although women were organized at all levels during the communist period, instead of addressing the core gender issues, women were used as political instruments to promote the communist ideology. The communists exploited the women's movement to promote their own political agendas. Similar trends have been observed in the current government as the focus has been on promoting political interests, pleasing donor nations, and attracting funding agencies instead of changing harmful traditions.

The Status of Gender Inequality in Ethiopia

Considering the Government's Strategies for Change

Gender inequality is still prevalent and deeply rooted all over the nation of Ethiopia. Even in the face of numerous global, continental, and national efforts on behalf of women, gender inequality and injustice toward women seem to be as common as ever. This continues in spite of the fact that the government drafted a constitution and policies in favor of gender equality. What seems to be consistently overlooked is the fact that gender-based discrimination and oppression is rooted in the culture. Religion, community, and family are the most powerful influences on gender role development with religious leaders, community members, and parents inculcating often unjust and oppressive beliefs and values to the next generation. Moreover the legal and justice systems are very weak and do not provide adequate practical support for women in need of it.

The emphasis, both during the communist and post-communist eras, seems to focus on *blaming* men and trying to force them to accept gender equality while portraying women as the victims of male dominance and oppression. This strategy and outlook has resulted in men becoming increasingly defensive about their own roles and resistant towards change. Women, on the other hand, have little opportunity to even understand these issues. The majority of women in Ethiopia still do not have access to informational and educational systems without the permission of men. In the case of girls' education, the only party who has the right to send girls to school is the patriarchal family unit. The current strategy seems thus crippled by the government's failure to convince men to willingly join the movement and support gender equality—a movement that many men view as antagonistic to their own interests as men.

If, however, we adopt a perspective that views the society as one inclusive system, we are able to see both genders as victims of the culture's embedded gender inequality. A holistic approach should take into consideration the fact that gender inequality affects the whole society, including men. The resulting strategy focuses on persuading and involving men as allies of a movement that will benefit all, rather than alienating them by regarding them as agents of oppression. If the movement is clearly communicated, building a better society is less likely to be perceived as a threat. As a parent the father should feel that gender equality positively affects his own life as well as all the male and female members of his family. A compartmentalized and segmented approach is merely a modified replica of the old tradition which pits one gender against the other. Instead of threatening the patriarchal system, those who advocate for equality should assert why and how both sexes benefit from the movement.

Gender Role Views and Practices of Ethiopians

The subordination of women is rampant in governmental, religious, and other social institutions. For instance, men and women sit separately in the Ethiopian Orthodox Church. Women's ordination is unthinkable. There are no women deacons, let alone priests and bishops. "Although there is mention of women deacons in ancient Ethiopian texts, there are none in the church today" (Oriental Orthodox-Roman Catholic Theological Consultation, 2003). Moreover, women are prohibited from entering certain parts of the church, such as the buildings where the Ark is located and the Holy of Holies. They are also prohibited from entering any church during their menstruation period. The situation is similar among Ethiopian Muslims, if not worse. The evangelical believers are in a somewhat better position when it comes to gender role separation. However, the culture of male dominance can often be found there as well.

While many educated Ethiopian women oppose male dominance and role separation, the significant majority of the uneducated and those who are unexposed to other cultures seem indifferent or even opposed to changes in gender role. It is not uncommon to travel in the countryside of Ethiopia and encounter women who advocate the importance of the traditional role because that is the way they have grown up and that is the norm they know. One can hear an Ethiopian woman blaming God for creating her female and wishing that she was a man. By that she means she would have assumed the role of a man, had she been created male.

It is rare to meet men and women who question the cultural norms. The assumption is that the norms were there from the beginning of life and will remain forever. That is why there is a tradition of men praising God for creating them male. One of the most famous stories in Ethiopian culture is about a man who gave a threefold thanks to God: the first for being created male rather than female, the second for being a priest rather than a layman, and the third for being the bishop rather than an ordinary priest.

It is not surprising to witness men struggling, unable to cross the "red line" of gender role separation. They grew up with experiences and stories reinforcing their distinctive role. The culture accepted the authority of the bishop, the priest, and the man to be unquestionable. As a result subordinates are required to believe everything from them to be the truth. Due to this belief the tradition has developed in the Ethiopian Orthodox Church that if an ordinary believer ever questioned the teaching of the religious leaders, the one who questioned was automatically considered a heretic whatever the content of the teaching was. Everyone assumed the religious leader was always right and should not be confronted. If anyone questioned the tradition of the church in any aspect, that person was considered heretic. The same culture assumes men's view to be always superior to women's. By the same merit women cannot question the authority of men.

The broad wisdom tradition of Ethiopia emphasizes the vices of women so that women will be seen as needing to subject themselves to men's rule (Presbey, 1999). Men's work consists of soldiering, plowing, and mercantile affairs, while women labor in all other categories, including agricultural work, reproduction and raising of children, and work in the home.

Women are often subjected to female genital mutilation and early marriage to minimize the potential of promiscuity and violent behavior. Some harmful traditions are practiced out of fear of being dominated by women and in order to protect male honor. Most people groups in Ethiopia agree that women are a source of contamination unless they perform cleansing rituals after childbirth, menstruation, and sexual intercourse. Due to this belief system, in the twenty-first century, among some ethnic groups a woman has to go into the bush to deliver her baby by herself and wait a week before returning home.

The Impact of Past Efforts to Change Gender Inequality

As Presbey (1999) pointed out, "more than official institutional change is needed to challenge negative views of women . . . a change is needed on the micro-level, on the level of individuals' attitudes as they are shaped by language and other practices of culture." The freedom and equality of women require an approach that would enable people to understand the benefit. Moreover, workable strategies that would transform the culture need to be developed together with the community rather than imposing changes from the top which only frustrate the society.

Presbey (1999) reported that "divorce instigated by women is on the rise in the Amhara communities, and this is made possible partly by women's economic independence" and legal protection. This finding, although credible, should not be taken as a strong positive indicator of freedom for women. Rather, this is an indicator of the reaction of men and women to gender issues. This approach raises friction by encouraging divorce as a radical solution, instead of promoting reconciliatory strategies. It motivates women to react against inequality for the simple reason that they have a constitutional right to divorce. Out of frustration both genders might take divorce as an alternative. However, divorce has its own consequences affecting the family. One should not underestimate the effect of divorce in spreading sexually transmitted diseases like HIV/AIDS and in threatening family life. Divorced women face more frustration and stereotyping from the same culture and worldview that condemns unmarried women. Triulzi (1973, p.67) pointed out:

> *A divorced woman usually moves away from her husband's village, and going back to her parents would be rather dreary and would force her to remarry soon. Therefore she often decides to move to a bigger town . . . the question of prostitution comes up.* [They] *have to accept makeshift arrangements . . . working in a bar and prostitution.*

After two decades of forceful revolutionary measure of the communist government and another fifteen years of "democratic" measures, there has been very little progress in transforming the people of Ethiopia to accept gender equality in particular and avoid harmful cultural practices in general. For instance female genital mutilation has been a controversial issue for more than three decades and yet the level of change in the society has been insignificant. It is time to ask why. There is broad agreement that a problem exists. Stakeholders need to admit the failure of past strategies instead of putting all the blame on the change-resistant nature of the culture. Blaming the culture is yet another reactive effort to justify failures instead of accepting responsibility. It is essential to reflect on how to devise successful strategies instead of repeating the same old strategy with different styles.

Mosley (2004) reported:

> *Ethiopian girls are vulnerable to culturally sanctioned violence including abduction, particularly when fetching water or fuel wood. Girls are usually abducted in order to be forced to marry, often by being raped so that her family will be pressured to let her remain with her new husband rather than returning in disgrace. The practice of female circumcision . . . puts girls at risk in Ethiopia. This practice is perpetuated by women, but justified in gendered terms. It is commonly held that without having been circumcised, a woman will find it difficult to marry or will be difficult for her husband to control.*

Mosley's report was indicative of the complex nature and multiple strata of gender oppression -- it is rooted in the culture and accepted by all members, including women. Intervention strategies need to consider cultural issues in order to initiate sustainable transformation, addressing the different level of hidden reactions from the society. In the context of Africa, due to the coercive nature of leadership, government policies and programs may normally gain "unanimous approval" on the surface but face unanimous rejection in implementation. Change that does not transform the belief system of the targeted community, so as to enable it to act out of conviction, will be unsustainable.

The socialist government officially denounced the inequality of women and described the practice as double oppression on women as they suffer both gender inequality and all other oppressions as citizens. That government took large-scale forceful revolutionary measures to break the tradition of male superiority. Instead of persuasion they used propaganda and coercive political power which led the society to "accept" the change with little real change. The only significant change during that time was that men were careful not to beat their wives when there were witnesses present. Instead, they did it at home and in the dark. The communist efforts also opened doors for women to file for divorce. However, one has to note the endless chain of bureaucracy women have to confront with the male dominated court and police. Further, as we have seen, life after divorce is often extremely difficult for women as divorced women are considered to have the status of prostitutes.

Part 3: Research Methods

Description of Research Subjects

The purpose of this study was to determine in what ways and to what extent moving to America has affected the degree of gender role separation in Ethiopian families. The individuals interviewed were Ethiopians who lived as married couples in Ethiopia and later immigrated to America. Four Ethiopians—two married couples—were interviewed. Both families had their first child before they came to America. One of the families had lived in United States for 22 years and the other one for almost 18 years. All the informants grew up in families where their fathers and mothers lived together in the typical Ethiopian tradition of large gender role separation.

As a researcher and native of Ethiopia, I had opportunities to participate in social events like weddings, graduations, religious fellowships, and family events where my observations made me interested in inquiring more as to what extent gender role separation is affected after moving to America. Most of the time I watched with curiosity to understand the differences and similarities in the role of each gender in the two environments. While I was able to see some basic similarities, I felt there was an unstable rhythm in the way men and women responded to their traditional gender roles. My impression was that the regular rhythm of gender role separation was disturbed in its manifestation in the American social setting while the core assumptions remained intact.

The basic selection criteria for my informants were to be married couples who lived in both environments so as to have first-hand personal experience in both cultures. The sample was randomly picked from available options. During the interview process I found that the couples represented the viewpoints of four different Ethiopian ethnic groups as both marriages were inter-ethnic. Both couples had extremely rich insights and experiences of gender issues in various contexts as they lived in different parts of the country. Both families were warm, welcoming, and transparent about sharing their views and struggles in facing the issue of gender role separation in various contexts. While in Ethiopia both husbands were government employees and the women were housewives. After they moved to the U.S. both husbands and wives were working outside of their homes as employees for companies.

Research Design and Procedures

I conducted in-depth personal interviews with the husbands and wives in the presence of their spouses. There were also informal discussions with both the husband and wife together as well as individually on various occasions. Except for one of the male informants, whom I interviewed in my home, all the interviews were conducted in their homes. In addition to the interviews I was able to have extensive informal discussions with all the informants. The concept of network analysis was applied as the interviewees shared about their experience with other fellow Ethiopian immigrants struggling to adjust in the new environments. Moreover, the visits to their homes provided opportunities to conduct onsite observations regarding how women controlled the kitchen.

Delimitation

The sample size is delimited to only four individuals due to time and resource constraints.

Limitations

Some of the basic limitations were that the research was unable to include the views of government and non-governmental agencies involved in addressing the issue. Similarly some other voices that may have different views were not included due to various constraints.

Part 4: Findings

Case Study One: Desta and Alemitu

Desta and Alemitu were married in Ethiopia and lived in many places, traveling together to the south, north, southwestern and central parts of Ethiopia as a couple. Desta was a government employee while Alemitu was housewife. Despite some differences regarding the level of freedom for women, both Desta and Alemitu had similar views of the role of women and men. During the sample identification process it was somewhat difficult to find the right kind of couples who had experience as a married couple in both Ethiopia and the U.S. A friend referred me to Desta and Alemitu as the right candidates for the interview and he gave me Desta's phone number. The first day I phoned, Alemitu answered the call and I was somewhat unprepared to talk with her. I gave a short introduction of myself and then asked her if they would be willing to be interviewed regarding gender role issues. Her response was positive and she told me to call Desta. For people from a high context culture, that could mean either a positive or negative response. Curious about it, I called Desta a few days later and mentioned my interest. In the meantime my friend who referred me to them told them about the study. I had to wait for sometime without a clear understanding of their response. One evening I got a missed call and immediately I phoned and talked with Desta. We fixed a date to meet at their home and he asked me if I needed a ride. I thanked him and told him I would drive myself.

On that beautiful afternoon of November 10, 2005, excited and curious about the kind of people I was going to meet, I drove to the interviewees' home in a western suburb of Chicago. After 35 minutes I reached their home. Desta opened the door with a big smile and extended warm greetings. After big hugs, I took off my shoes and immediately was escorted into the living room. Both Desta and Alemitu extended warm welcomes. The house was beautiful and clean. Everything was in order and well managed. The living room was adjacent to the kitchen. After a brief introduction I sat down on the couch. After about ten minutes of chatting on various issues I expressed my appreciation for their time and willingness to share their stories. Their response was encouraging. Alemitu commented that as far as they could be helpful for the study it was their joy to talk on anything relevant to the issue. Desta also expressed his positive gesture. Then I put on the recorder and posed the first question. The discussion on gender role separation commenced.

Life before Coming to the United States

Desta lived with his parents until the age of 18 where he had never done anything that was classified as "women's work." He said, "All the time I stayed with my parents I had never cleaned a single cup, let alone cooking food. It was unthinkable and unheard [of] for males to do any kind of kitchen work." Desta explained:

> *I had never seen my father in the kitchen. Not a single day. If you consider my case, I tried kitchen work after I came to the States. But my father had never washed a single cup in his life. You may not believe me if I tell you that all the time I lived in many provinces of Ethiopia including the capital, Addis Ababa, either before or after marriage I had never washed a single dish. How in the world men wash dish? That is shame. I either eat in a hotel or someone has to cook for me. Nobody can claim seeing Desta washing a single cup. I also lived in Asmara and it was the same thing there. In all the provinces a man can't wash dish. That is shame. He will be stereotyped as 'the dish washer,' 'the cooker,' and so on. Then he is no more an honorable man.*

Desta paused with a smiling face and recalled a true story about a man in the village in which he grew up. He remembered how the villagers (both men and women) talked about a shameful act this husband committed one day:

> *Guests came to that family and the wife started arranging the food for the guests. She brought* injera, *the national bread and* wot, *the national sauce. Then she went to the kitchen to bring some more food while the husband and the guests were sitting around the table. Unfortunately she stayed a long time and the husband felt the guests waited too long without starting to eat. Instead of waiting for her to come and serve the food, he opened the pot,*

> *picked up the spoon and put the* wot *on the* injera *to serve the guests. Then the shocked guests spread out the news to all the villagers that this man opened the pot which was a shame for men to do. Then he was nicknamed "the pot-opener" and stereotyped as dishonorable man.*

Desta commented, "Every man in the village was careful not to be labeled. See! Let alone cooking, touching the pot and serving the already made food was shameful. The culture was so strict."

Alemitu added,

> *From the time we knew each other, Desta was a government employee. When I married him I was young and the only knowledge I had about married life was what I saw what my parents had been doing. What I knew from the culture was the husband should not enter the kitchen. If he just shows up in the kitchen I used to feel uncomfortable. Moreover, labor was cheap and you have home maids. They work for you the whole day and they do everything. That makes the men lazy. There is no reason for the man to come into the kitchen. And the women don't have a reason to complain. By then I had no idea that there was a problem in the culture. As a matured person now as I look back in retrospect I think the primary problem is in the culture. Second to that women had no work outside the home while men work outside. So that gives justification for men.*

Alemitu said she was fortunate that her husband had been kind to her and had never beaten her unlike other men in that culture. However, she pointed out, "In that culture many husbands are mean to their wives. They don't think women can get tired and need to rest and eat. Their tongue was stingy. They don't understand even their own daughters." Alemitu considered her marriage unique and herself lucky in that her husband, being a health professional, was helpful. She appreciated that he trained her how to handle the baby as she was living far from her parents and it was impossible to get her mother's help. Therefore, "Desta was unique compared to Ethiopian husbands," as Alemitu said .

The culture molds women to obey their husbands without questioning anything, shaping them that way from early childhood. Alemitu was no exception. She recalled her experience:

> *When we were in Ethiopia I used to agree to Desta 100%, not 90%. I didn't question his view. Whatever he said, that was perfect and I did accept everything as he presented. At this stage that is changed. When growth comes, you add your own opinion in a healthy way. You grow up.*

Desta and Alemitu fled from the communist government to Sudan, where Desta lived six months by himself until later Alemitu and their son joined him. Desta found the degree of gender role separation in Sudan to be even greater than that of Ethiopia, a fact that pleased him. He had a fond memory of the large gender role separation and communal way of life in Sudan. Although I was amazed to hear about a culture more communal and more male-dominated than Ethiopia, Desta's face was radiant as he shared stories about joyous community life in Sudan–eating together with friends so that, as a result, he did not need to bother about cooking for himself while alone without his family. Desta shared how Ethiopian immigrants and the Sudanese mistreated and oppressed their wives in Sudan. He added, "Sudan is more difficult for women. The temperature is hot making kitchen work extremely difficult in that condition."

Desta explained the reason why Ethiopian men believe in oppressive and harsh treatment for their wives,

> *I think it is running in the blood. Especially uneducated men resist any kind of change. There is a strong belief that a woman must listen and obey her husband. She must do what she is told. If she failed to do so she will get the consequence–beating which is the norm. Generally that is what they believe in that country.*

Alemitu added, "There is ignorance. Their belief is that the wife loves and respects the husband if he beats her, becomes strict on her, and gets angry at her." Both Desta and Alemitu agreed that their marriage was exceptional in that Desta did not believe in beating and abusing his wife. He said, "I have never beaten my wife. I saw husbands beating their wives. I am different in that case. She can tell. I have never been dictatorial in our relationship. I don't know why I am not like that. I am glad about it."

"Your father was also like that. You had never seen him doing such a thing on his wife," added Alemitu. Desta agreed,

> *I had never seen him verbally abusing and beating his wife, his children, and even his servants. He ordered and*

> *commanded everybody. Since I grew up within that setting, I had never wanted to look on my wife as inferior and treat her with contempt. He had never entered the kitchen. I did what my father did and I did not do what my father did not do.*

Desta attributed his good behavior to his experience with his parents. He remembered that boys help outside the home taking care of various things.

Alemitu, however, explained that her upbringing was quite different,

> *I grew in a different environment. Desta did not see his father speaking harshly. I grew hearing bad stuff. My father beats and insults my mother. What I saw was dictatorship of man. He gets angry at, insult and beat the wife and abuses. I had seen that. Then if I were a man I might have imitated and practiced the same thing. Education and living with my husband helped me to change. Before I got married I thought the same thing will happen to me. I expected every man would do like that. Husbands in my province were very difficult and my family was not an exception. While he beats her, if my mother say anything or argue he would beat her more.*

After Coming to United States

When he came to the United States, Desta went through a difficult time of cultural shock in regard to gender role. He said,

> *Life in America requires you to change a hundred percent. You can live easily in Ethiopia. The first few weeks I felt as if I were in a hell. Because we arrived during the night our sponsoring family welcomed us and the husband was administrator of a big company and the very first morning I saw this honorable man washing dishes and cooking breakfast while his wife was dressing her hair. In the morning as we woke up he was washing dishes. My immediate reaction was, 'Is this man normal or have some abnormality?' It was surprising, he was washing dish while she stood arranging her hair. I asked myself, 'What kind of crazy world did I come to?'*

After a loud laugh and a pause Desta continued:

We stayed with them for about two months and he was doing the same thing every day. I had never washed a single cup during all those weeks. Because I came with a mentality of shame ideas, I felt ashamed to do kitchen work. After two months we moved to live by ourselves. Our son was four years old and my wife get pregnant. I started work and she was staying home. Now I started to understand that I need to help her for she couldn't manage everything. I asked myself, 'She is getting tired and there is no one helping her. Why don't I wash some dish?' I started washing one or two cups. Then I began to hate just to sit down and eat. I decided to work. Finally I started washing dish and I entered to that world without my interest. I really was forced and obligated by the situation. I felt as if it was forced on me by police with a court decision. I did not do it willingly.

Gradually, Desta started to learn cooking and at the time of our interview he said, "I am a good cook." He learned cooking from his wife and reading recipe books. However he admitted it is impossible to compare him with Alemitu. He said, "I can't cook like her. I stand and watch how she cooks. What she can do in a short time may take an hour or two for me." After 22 years of struggle Desta was still incompetent at cooking efficiently. He defended himself, "That is because I started late. If I started as a child I may have been good enough by now." Alemitu commented, "I think it is the problem of men. We women can cook two or three foods simultaneously, but men are incompetent and cook just one food at a time."

Desta mentioned how he was always surprised as Alemitu cooked a variety of things while he couldn't do a single dish from what was available in the kitchen. He even asked her, "Where did you bring all this? How couldn't I think about it? I don't know why I become blinded and fail to be creative many times."

Alemitu said,

Women are good cooks. They imported the culture and they want to work themselves. They don't want men to come and mix up in the kitchen. At the same time you hear them complaining. They don't encourage and give opportunity for men to cook. Men need appreciation when they work. Even if it is not good enough, we need to

> *appreciate the effort. We have to thank them when they make simple things such as tea. If the wife told him he may break the kitchen material and things like that, the next morning he will not go to the kitchen. How come you discourage them and yet expect improvement? The other problem is women comparing one's husband with another better performing husband. We women have a problem of too much comparison.*
>
> *We also need to have boundaries that limit interference. I remember I used to prepare everything and make even sandwiches for him when we were in the same shift. He tells me, "I don't know how to do it. Please make one for me." I had been doing so. When my shift was changed, I couldn't do that for him. Then he started to do it for himself. No more waiting for my help. He started making the sandwich the way he likes. We need to give opportunity for men.*

Regarding what her response would be if others said that Desta was a very good cook and skilled husband helping her in the kitchen, Alemitu commented,

> *If it was before I moved to the States I would have been unhappy. I would feel embarrassed and be ashamed. While my friends' and neighbors' husbands don't do things like that why should my husband do it? However, after I got matured now I really wouldn't care about others' opinions. Now he prepares food and goes shopping. There is big change.*

Desta added, "When I evaluate myself, there is big change. Compared to our country here gender role is upside down. I don't care if there are people or not. I just help my wife." As Desta and I sat on the couch, Alemitu was working in the kitchen. Later, I asked Alemitu, "What would be your feeling if you had guests and Desta comes to help you in the kitchen leaving the guests by themselves?" She responded, "I don't have any problem if he joins me in the kitchen while there are guests here." Then after few minutes of reflection she said, "But sometimes I am not happy. The culture is with me still intact." Then Desta interjected, "I do love to be around her and help. However, she orders me, 'Go, sit and talk with the guest.' She insists, 'Why don't you sit there?'" She agreed with Desta's point and commented,

> As we discuss now I felt self-conscious about my action. Usually Desta like to be around. He says it doesn't matter. But my response was "Why don't you sit and talk with them?" At that time I prefer him to leave the kitchen. I tell him I want to work by myself and ask him not to disturb me.

I asked, "Do you think it is because you feel that the guests would look down on your husband?"

"No, that is not the reason. I just feel comfortable when I work by myself. I can do what I want. When he comes I feel he is taking my space," responded Alemitu. She emphasized, "It is not because I am concerned about the opinion of the guests." Then immediately, she asked. "But on this issue, why is that when a woman comes to help me I don't feel she is taking more space? Why when Desta comes? When a woman comes I feel happy about it and at the same time when he comes I assume my space is taken." She couldn't give the final answer for these interesting questions.

Desta and Alemitu agreed that in America there are incentives that encourage men to change. They believe the lifestyle and the culture are important change factors. The equal opportunities in employment, economy, education, and in political spheres were mentioned as positive contributors to gender equality. Moreover, Desta mentioned, "the kitchen set up and the availability of processed food that men can easily fix" are important things that encourage men in kitchen work. Alemitu, however, commented that, "There are many things men can do in Ethiopia. But they don't have the interest and the willingness to help the women."

Both Alemitu and Desta recognize their faith as a crucial factor in crossing barriers and exercising equality. Desta affirmed that being evangelical Christians played a key role in shaping their view. He believed that the Christian concept of marriage life enabled them to appreciate one another as a special gift from God and have a unique perspective on gender equality. He added, "We learn Christian values from the Bible and that changes us a lot. We read, reflect, and practice it. We believe it is the command of God for us to respect one another."

Perception of the Gender Equality Movement in Ethiopia

Both Desta and Alemitu experienced the women's equality movement during the socialist revolution. Desta commented:

> *When women's equality was proclaimed by the socialist government, I was very critical of the issue. I remember how people were negative towards it. Our conviction was that women were moving to the wrong place–taking the male role. I was not happy about the political movement on women's issues. However, in the hospital, I used to work with women respecting their equality. There was much criticism. But people did not speak openly because of the political measures.*

Alemitu's response was somewhat different. She explained:

> *I don't remember much about it. At any level change always disturbs. Change can shake families and communities. The problem was not the change, rather how it came. I think they did not educate the people and even the elite were not equipped on how to go about it. That is why it did not succeed. I think in our country it is essential to educate the people. Women also have to be intentional and practical rather than just talking about equality. If you claim equality you need to be responsible.*

Dinner with Desta and Alemitu

I found that Desta and Alemitu were open and interested in discussing this issue in depth. We had three hours of discussion responding to the interview questions and then an informal discussion continued over dinner. I suspected that the delicious food might not have been cooked by Desta and in the process of the discussion it became clear that Alemitu was the one who cooked it. I was amazed how the culture of cooking traditional food and honoring guests was still preserved after 22 years of stay in the States. In the midst of the feasting I expressed appreciation about the delicious food Alemitu cooked. Desta also shared that Alemitu was a great cook and that he tried to learn from her. We laughed at ourselves as Desta shared his struggles to adapt to the kitchen environment which he still is passing through even after this long period.

Chapter 9: Ethiopians in Social Context   Tafesse

Case Study Two: Yaqob and Senite

Life in Ethiopia

Yaqob and Senite were married in Ethiopia and had lived in various areas before they moved to the States. Yaqob had moved around a lot as a student and later as a government worker. Most of the time they lived in the north central highland part of the country. The demarcation of gender role was clear for both of them. They fled from the communist government to Kenya and ended up in a United Nations refugee camp where things started to change in their roles.

Yaqob had never crossed the line of gender role separation while in Ethiopia. In retrospect Yaqob recalled and explained his view,

> *During my childhood I had never learned how to cook food and I consider cooking and all the kitchen work to be the wife's role. In Ethiopia we had maids and even my wife was not working in the kitchen. The maids were responsible for the kitchen. Everybody had a maid. Whether your salary is big or small, it is affordable to hire a maid. Senite and I used to be served together. Even if I occasionally wanted to join my wife just to talk around the kitchen it was impossible because of the fear of being stereotyped. It was unthinkable for men to enter the kitchen. Culturally, if I am a good man I can't shop and talk with the maids about kitchen issues. People even think I am controlling my wife and the maids if I try to be involved in women's roles. They would think I am a mean person. My role was to provide the finances when requested. I just go out to work and come back, eat the prepared food. Then I go out and spend my time with friends. I was 100% outside any kitchen work. Regarding food my role was to provide and then eat. There was no way to think about washing dishes. All my friends and the people who lived there did the same thing. That was what we saw and what we did. That was what the society accepted and approved. As a man, you don't go to market and shop for yourself. If you do that you will lose your reputation. That sends a negative signal to the society. No one would perceive that as a positive gesture. The cultural norm was to provide and then eat the cooked food. I observed my father doing that and later I*

> *practiced what I saw. He was a farmer and his role was 100% outside the home. He worked at various things in the field depending on the season. Everything that had connection with shopping, washing clothes, cleaning, and kitchen work was my mother's role. I had never seen my father doing any of these things. As he was the provider of the family when I get married I took the same role.*
>
> *In the region I grew up it is unthinkable to cross the gender role and do women's work. You can go and see the real rural villages. In the setting the wife is also just like a maid: she cooks, takes care of children, and also during harvest season assists the men in the field. They equally work in weeding.*

During the course of our discussion Yacob's description and list of women's jobs was endless. He explained:

> *The assumption is that men's work is more tiresome than women. Of course, men work long hours in the field, especially during the farming season. However, in addition to the kitchen work women take care of children, walk long distances fetching water and firewood, and then walk home carrying it on their back. I don't know, I think men's responsibility is harder, especially during the farming season. During the weeding season, I think it becomes very hard for women. In the dark while men rest, enjoy the coffee and eat, women still continue to serve men. They also assist in gathering the crop. They carry grain on their back. During the non-farming season in some areas men are advantaged.*

Life in Kenya as Refugees in Transition to the USA

After they left Ethiopia Yaqob and Senite lived in Kenya for about two years before moving to the United States. Reflecting on how he started to change, Yaqob asserted:

> *It was not America that changed me. I started to change after I went to Kenya. When we arrived in Kenya, Senite started applying the cooking knowledge she inherited from her mother and grandmother. Back home she was not really working. But she is a woman and she kept the*

> knowledge in her mind. She used to work for holidays and special occasions. She had not been cooking all the way through from starting to the end of making a dish. In Kenya it was too hard for Senite to cope up with refugee life. When we were in a UN refugee camp, they give us grain, vegetables, and other raw materials. Because there was no maid, no one to help her, I started to share responsibility. I knew nothing about kitchen work. She had not been cooking by herself without assistants. I started there due to life's pressure. In the UN camp there was job sharing among the refugee. She couldn't do everything. So I had to participate in helping her. Because of my love for her and also due to the pressure from the situation, I started to change my role. In the camp I did not want her to feel sad. We were away from our family and it was harder for her. I started cooking there. I think I was good in cooking some meals like porridge.

Regarding other Ethiopian men in Kenya, Yaqob commented, "There were men who cook better than women. They bake *injera* and prepare many kind of delicious sauces. I can't compare myself with them."

Life in the United States

"After we came to United States," Yacob explained, "you might be surprised, I am not directly involved in cooking." He continued,

> My wife is very good in cooking. She likes to cook. I think she is gifted in it. If I cook, I know she will not eat it. She is not interested even to hear that Yacob cooked wot. I can fix sandwich. Occasionally I help to do minor things in the kitchen. She doesn't expect me to work in the kitchen. My responsibility includes shopping, cleaning the rooms, vacuuming, cleaning the toilets. She doesn't like shopping. She gives me the grocery list and I do all the shopping. That is my responsibility. At times, unconsciously I feel cooking is Senite's role. But I help in cleaning and shopping.

Yacob mentioned that they do not categorize work on the basis of gender, as sometimes he washed the dishes and she also helped in cleaning. He considered himself as an ordinary cook and asserted, "I can cook *wot* if it is for you and me, but she is very particular and I even don't try to make national dish for her. That requires more competence." Yaqob admitted:

> The fact that both of us work eight hours a day and it was too much for Senite to do everything at home forced me to change my paradigm. Both of us come home tired. Then I completely understood she doesn't necessarily have to cook for me while I am sitting. Then I became compassionate and started to help. If I have time I want to do more than what I do now. I believe it is necessary to avoid dominating my wife.

Yaqob commented, "What makes America special is that both work, come home tired, both have equal contribution, and are equal at home."

Asked what his experience looked like in comparison to other Ethiopians who lived here and how they were changed after coming to the United States, Yaqob said,

> There are many who don't do what I do in my home. There is personality problem. The situation forces you to change. When you are a Christian you understand the weakness and strength of the others and care for them. Some men, especially non-believers, although they are in United States, they seem living in Ethiopia. There are husbands that have the role of the typical traditional husband. They expect their wife to prepare everything on the table and then eat from there and go to bed. If she fail to do so they would complain and get unhappy. I think my faith is the basic factor in changing my behavior/attitude. Because of my faith I couldn't sit down and command her to work hard, serve me, and suffer. I believe she is my equal and co-inheritor of the Kingdom of God. The Lord helped me to change the belief I inherited from my parents.

Contrasting women's life in Ethiopia and America, Yaqob asserted,

> In the U.S. the contribution of women and men in the economy is recognized, both genders are equally exposed for information, they are equally informed about husband-

> wife relationship, they have access for media. There is no external influence. They do whatever they are convinced to do. In Ethiopia women are obligated to obey their husbands. Here women are not afraid of their husbands. If there is misunderstanding between husband and wife, you can't threaten and beat her or abuse verbally to forcefully change her decision and obey you. The law doesn't allow men to do whatever they want on their wives. In America there is legal protection. As for me the law of the land and my Lord made us equal. In the Ethiopian culture from the foundation everything seems prearranged to fit for women. For instance the kitchen is at the back corner of the house where guests and men can't see and access it. The market system and carrying many things fit for women. Here the setting of the market and the environment encouraged me to shop. You see honorable men, well dressed husbands, shopping by themselves. You don't feel bad about shopping; instead you get motivated. Here the kitchen materials like microwave and oven facilitate cooking. It is efficient and easy. As a result of this there will be less tension between husband and wife. Economic development, technological advancement and the environment encourage men to participate.

Senite's Thoughts

On one occasion, I had the opportunity to interview Senite alone. Senite assumed that there might be some difference between believers and non-believers in regard to treating women. She commented:

> Maybe Christians are treating their wives better. In general there is big pressure on women. It is believed that women shouldn't speak equal with men, can't argue with men, and always she is expected to be homemaker. Even if there is maid it is the wife's responsibility to train the maid and offer hospitality to guests. I am talking about the majority culture where a wife is expected to do what her husband tells her to do. If she disagree with what he said that is considered wrong. As for me, before I came out of Ethiopia I was very young. I did not understand much about issues regarding married life and the role of

> men and women. It is after arriving to the States I was able to understand the difference. I really started to feel sad about my mother and became compassionate for her. Before I came, when my mother gets disappointed and feels bad about her situation, I used to think that was unnecessary and I even sided with my father supporting him. It is after I came here that I started to realize that what men did back home is wrong. I think that is because I started to get more matured and grow . . . that means I knew the issue. Then I wrote to my father not to oppress my mother. There it is not wrong for men to have extramarital partner and I wrote him not to hurt my mother in that way. I beg him. I don't remember all the detail now. Then later he thought I am passing through a difficult time here. His assumption was that I was writing because of passing through difficult circumstances. The reason I did that was because I understood the difference.
>
> When I grow my father was always out of home and we had to wait for him to eat together. We do not eat if he doesn't come. He is always out of home and even after he came, he didn't stay home after eating. I had never seen him sitting at home and helping. I never know any occasion that he helped in the home. I had never seen him taking a glass of water by himself. He had never touched any women work.

Reflecting on what her reaction would have been if she had seen men working in the kitchen, Senite responded:

> I don't know. What I knew was that it is shameful. Sometimes if there is a man who spends his time at home we question what kind of odd person he was to stay there just like a woman. Let alone coming near to the kitchen, staying at home during the day was a questionable habit. That was considered very bad.

Regarding her experience with her brothers, Senite shared a story that she heard from her family back home:

> When my mother got sick my little brother tried to help her and he made her tea as she was sick. What happened was another elder brother beats him, getting angry that

> *this little boy went in the kitchen to do women's job. The elder brother always gets angry at and beats the little boy. Finally he warned and threatened him, "In the future I never want to see you in the kitchen." For this little boy loves his mother very much, when she gets sick he used to make the tea hiding from his brother.*

Senite said, "It would have been okay for boys to make tea. But my brother's position was, 'Why do you make tea like a woman? It is embarrassment for us and we will be insulted by others.' I was surprised when I heard this incident." Senite explained that the beatings in this case were motivated by a desire to preserve the family's honor and to keep the younger brother from being labeled as feminine.

I asked Senite how she felt coming to the U.S. impacted gender role attitudes. She responded,
"It is hard for Ethiopian men after they came to the States. There are some who don't want to help in the kitchen. Even after coming here there are men who are unable to come out of their culture." She added, "Those who want to help also help out of duty—just like obligation." Senite continued:

> *Their motivation is not that both work eight hours and she gets tired too. Rather the woman insists for help. There is no maid or neighbor to help . . . child care, cooking, baking. How can she do everything by herself? It is a lot of struggle here for women. We work outside and inside the home in this country too and the husband helps because she tells him she is tired . . . men don't have the culture to work in the kitchen and they are stressed. I think they are not free here too. Their culture pulls them back.*

It was surprising to here Senite portray life in the U.S. as even more difficult for women than life in Ethiopia. Senite explained, "Life in America is harder for Ethiopian women. Back home you have a home maid to help. Here we work outside and also the kitchen work is ours anyways. Here it is hard for the women especially. If you have good income, life is very easy in Ethiopia."

Senite spoke of her changing views of gender roles,

> *[When we were in Ethiopia] I wouldn't want him to enter to kitchen, because I had no problem to employ maids. Now I have some knowledge and if we go to Ethiopia we will help the maid*

> and if he enters to the kitchen to help I don't mind. Now, right now . . . if it were before we came I don't think I will allow him.

She explained, "In our family everything at home is the responsibility of my mother and the maid. I had never seen or heard my father talk or have concern about anything in the home. I used to help a little."

She also reflected on her possible reaction if her brothers tried to help in the kitchen during the time she was in Ethiopia and then responded:

> I don't think I would allow my brothers to work in the kitchen if they were interested to do it. If my brother comes to the kitchen, I think I would tell him, command him to go away from the kitchen. Because it is the culture.

As for her own children, Senite said, "Now I am changed. When they get married, I want my sons to help their wives in the kitchen."

I asked Senite to sum up her thoughts on how coming to America has impacted gender roles in her marriage. She responded,

> I feel happy to get help in some areas. I want [my husband] to do the cleaning, shopping, and things like that. When I cook I am not satisfied of his level of cooking and he can't cook a delicious injera and wot. Rather than cooking, I would prefer him to wash the dishes, vacuum, and clean the house. I enjoy that. I don't think that is even easy for him. From experience I have seen that it is not easy for Ethiopian men to help their wives. The culture captures them, and as much as they can they try not to go closer to where women are working. There are some women in both extremes. Some go over and do everything for their husbands and other tell them, "Cook for yourself, this is America." Both views will create tension in an Ethiopian marriage.

Senite became an evangelical Christian a number of years ago and indicated that her new faith had a big impact on her view of family relationships. She said, "Without faith it might be difficult to understand one another and stay together in life. Our faith encourages us to have mutual understanding and love. We believe in God. That has big benefit for our marriage." Senite, herself a former Muslim, continued, "Islam puts more burdens and pressure on women." I asked if she felt that the Ethiopian Orthodox Church was any different. She responded:

> *I saw Orthodox Christian marriage which is better, because in Islam one man marries four wives. They have wives everywhere, they have children everywhere. They can't care for all these families. Very few, like one percent, may be faithful to their marriages. The majority claims that the Book permits multiple marriages. They don't have respect. I don't think they treat the wives well. They expect the women just to listen. They believe she can neither ask nor answer. When he marries another wife, she has to accept whether she liked it or not. The wives live as neighbors and it is very disappointing. Moreover there will be many children. My mother never accepted the idea.*

Reflecting on the possibility of change in gender role Senite was concerned that it is very hard to introduce something new. Indicating that the culture is conservative she commented, "In our tradition if something is good but foreign to the culture it is not welcomed. If something bad and harmful happened and yet agrees with the culture it is accepted and people use all means to justify its acceptability."

Perception of the Gender Equality Movement in Ethiopia

Senite remembered the issue of gender equality from the communist era. She shared her memory of the movement:

> *I used to hear wives claiming, "Derg told us that we are equal." I don't think that is true equality. Because it was not equality based on love and understanding. It would have been good if it was based on love. It was a command imposed on the society. The man was obligated and the woman did not understand the concept of equality. The perception of the women was that they had to confront their husbands, insult him. If he asked her where she was going her response was, "It is not your concern." I don't call that equality. That is disrespect. They did not understand the true sense of equality. If the women knew how to respond and men knew how to treat women, and then if both were knowledgeable with love to one another that would have been good. But it was not like this. I remember that both the educated and uneducated women*

> talked about women's equality claiming they are equal. Especially in Islam during divorce the man was allowed to take 80% and the wife would take only 20%, and Derg stopped this practice. That was correct action for me. But there was a lot of chaos and wife-beating followed with unnecessary divorces.

Data Analysis

The responses of all four of the informants showed that family and community had significant roles in shaping the view of both boys and girls to accept their cultures' ideas of gender role separation. All four made up their minds during early childhood and they admitted that it was very difficult to break the culture and change roles.

The communal lifestyle reinforced these values as community members condemned shifts of role. Policy makers and implementers need to understand and apply wisdom to mobilize and empower communities to initiate change within the community instead of importing a good but foreign idea to this conservative culture.

It was interesting that none of the four informants questioned the appropriateness of their cultural practices of gender roles until they came out of that environment and experienced different cultural norms. In fact for some of them, especially for Desta, it was a shocking experience to see men crossing the boundary of gender role separation.

Discussing the history of attempts to change Africa, Willcox and Short (2005) pointed out, "A hundred years of education had resulted in little positive change in Kenya." It is time to question the approach instead of assuming the culture is change-resistant. To introduce major changes, even in a small way, and break the ground to lay the foundation might demand deviation from tradition. One should not necessarily expect the deviation from the targeted community. The question is—Who should deviate? Should it be only the targeted community? Policy makers and implementers need to be willing to deviate.

The interviews revealed that the culture of gender inequality was acceptable for both the female and male informants. Mosley (2004) also reported similar findings. All four of the informants pointed out that ignorance and lack of education had significant roles in the continuity of the problem. Imparting change requires identifying and addressing the source rather than concentrating on treating the symptoms like forcing men to change or motivating women to revolt. Both female informants had negative impressions about the revolution Derg proclaimed against gender inequality. What they remembered were the conflicts and problems of the movement instead of any positive, transformational impact.

The fact that the informants came from four different ethnic backgrounds, lived in various parts of the country, and had similar experiences with high gender role separation and a male-dominant culture supports the idea that this tradition is deeply rooted and prevalent throughout Ethiopia. Despite their different backgrounds there was agreement in their experience and perceptions of issues like women's equality, role models, honor and shame, and contributing factors for the prevalence of the gender inequality.

The study revealed that both women and men had negative perceptions of the communists' gender equality approach and were critical of the regime's use of coercive power instead of persuasion to convince and educate the people to change the culture. Society has to be enlightened about the interdependence and unity of human life as a system. The fragmentalist and particularistic attitude which assumes exploitation and subordination can benefit a certain segment of society and which legitimizes such practices must be challenged as a view that is harmful to the whole system. The practice ultimately destroys the system and exploiters are equally affected in the long run. By a similar logic, if women are disadvantaged and denied opportunities to thrive as part of the society it should not be assumed to be a women's issue. Rather it is a problem that affects the whole society.

Governments and organizations working towards addressing the problem have missed the target on many occasions. It is easy to be deceived in understanding the dynamics of cultures. Agencies and individuals working in cultural transformation need to understand the cultural dynamics more than their strategies. I think Mohandas Gandhi's assertion, "A nation's culture resides in the hearts and in the soul of its people," is a wonderful lesson for those who have the discipline to listen to his wisdom. Those who address the symptoms seek superficial "results" and popularity as opposed to initiating lasting change which can take generations to see the fruit. The philosophy of Jay Forrester mentioned by Peter Seng in his book *The Fifth Discipline* is worth noting:

> *Jay Forrester, a computer pioneer, had shifted fields to develop what he called "systems dynamics." Jay maintained that the causes of many pressing public issues, from urban decay to global ecological threat, lay in the very well-intentioned policies designed to alleviate them. These problems were "actually systems" that lured policy makers into interventions that focused on obvious*

symptoms, not underlying causes, which produced short-term benefit but long-term malaise, and fostered the need for still more symptomatic interventions.

The excess number of maids available for cheap employment has been just the tip of the iceberg indicating one layer of gender inequality. Close observation of this matter magnifies the hidden problem rooted in the culture. All the informants pointed out that having maids is a norm in the society. They consider it as a factor for the continuity of gender role separation. Yaqob's statement, "Everybody had a maid. Whether your salary is big or small, it is affordable to hire a maid," was basically what all four informants mentioned in a similar manner. Until I started studying the puzzle, I fully agreed with the informants' justification that men do not enter the kitchen because there are plenty of maids. The big questions that deserve to be answered are: "Why is there plenty of cheap female labor?" and "Where do all these maids come from?" Rather than being a factor for gender role separation and serving as justification for the continuity of the problem, the cheap labor is itself a product of gender inequality. Inequality, role separation and cheap maid labor are part of a chain of contributing factors that form a destructive cyclical system—one phenomenon perpetuating another and fueling the continuity of the injustice.

Figure 1: *The Vicious Cycle of Gender Inequality: Cheap female labor & gender role separation.*

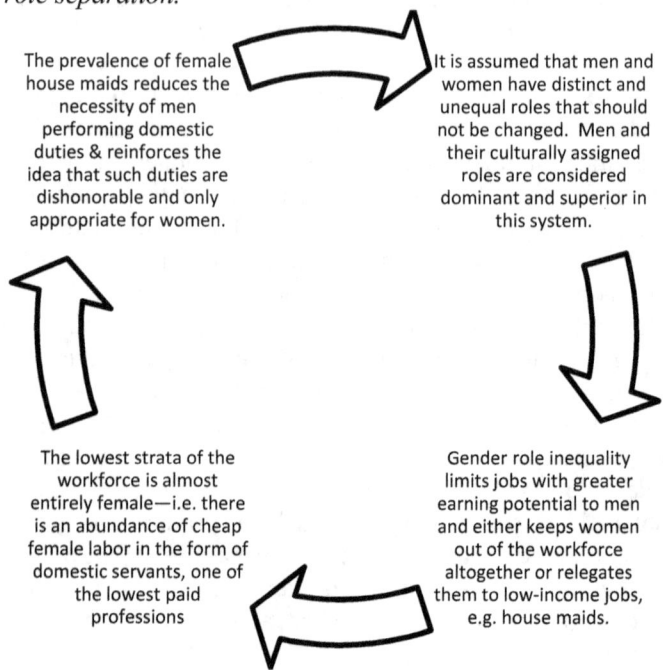

Concerned governmental and non-governmental bodies need to create empowering and conducive environments for transformation. Decision-making and empowerment issues on gender role have to include both genders for sustainable implementation.

It is strategic to focus on children to impact the next generation, which in turn requires involving family and community members. My research indicates that building up the culture involves the whole community including men, women and children. Indeed, any approach should include all stakeholders to introduce meaningful and sustainable change. If a project or program is constantly failing to convince a father (or husband) to understand the harmful aspects of a woman (such as his daughter or wife) being abused by a system that degrades her dignity, people should diagnose the problem(s) in the larger system, not only the problem in the man. For instance in a system where there is no meaningful intervention to protect abduction of girls, it is difficult to avoid early marriage which is a traditionally accepted means of protecting the girl from the worse fate of abduction.

Creating a positive synergy between the two sexes and involving men in the movement towards gender equality is essential in building a positive picture of women and building mutual confidence. Political, legal, and socio-economic action alone, without efforts to transform culture holistically, has and will continue to fail.

Part 5: Conclusions and Recommendations for Further Research

The findings of this study revealed that gender equality is still a remote possibility in the context in today's Ethiopia. Constitutionally, Ethiopian women have equal rights. In practice, however, it is unrealistic to exercise that right and access the opportunities. It seems that there is a lack of proper models and strategies to implement sustainable transformational change in a manner acceptable to both women and men. Property rights, protection from harmful cultural and religious practices, and the rights for justice are not easily accessible for women. Moreover, the standards of the justice system and legal protection do not enable victimized women to claim full protection.

Instead of forceful interferences to bring change in rapid manner, it is essential to strategically expose the society so as to initiate sustainable change. Creating an atmosphere conducive for learning and change seems more fruitful. In real life situations there are unavoidable factors governing a process. Gender inequality is rooted in the culture which means the process of transformation requires proper intervention through the removal of factors which interfere with change. This study also illustrated the importance of helping both genders to understand the issue and work together for the common good.

The struggle to bring gender equality should not be assumed as benefiting only women. Intervention strategies should make it clear that both genders -- the whole society -- will benefit from it. Trust has to be built up and men have to be convinced and come to an agreement that a better society is not a threat for them. It is essential to help men to feel secure about a society with educated and influential women where both sexes will use their full potential for the sake of their common good. Albert Einstein taught, "All that is valuable in human society depends upon the opportunity for development accorded the individual." It is essential to open doors of opportunity for women to benefit from their valuable contribution to society.

In Ethiopia more attention has been paid to combating the symptoms of gender inequality with approaches that lack the creativity needed to change cultural assumptions. While policies and regulations on paper seem sound and send positive signals of progress in gender equality, certainly the legal and justice environment is discouraging in that these systems are operating in a particularistic society where the executors are male chauvinists. The impact of the legal system remains unreliable until transformation is initiated within and beyond that system. Research on how to transform the stakeholders in the legal and justice sphere would be an asset to combat the injustice on women.

Contemporary policy makers and change implementers seem indifferent or at least not serious about the importance of integrating religion with cultural change. Religion can be either a vehicle of change or an obstacle to change. Ignoring religion while the society is religious opens the door for the society to either ignore or reject the proposed change. History has proven that religion can serve as a powerful force either to liberate or oppress society depending on various factors. The tendency of marginalizing religion from change strategies seems an unreasonable approach in the context of Ethiopia. Worth considering is Mohandas Gandhi's claim, "The human mind or human society is not divided into watertight compartments called social, political and religious. All act and react upon one another." It would be helpful to study the impact of religion in effecting change. Most harmful traditions including gender inequality operate in the context of religion. All the major religions inherently support gender inequality. In some cases they promote it from their pulpits. However they are neither legally accountable for their actions nor officially participating as strategic partners.

The study revealed that ideas about role separation start from early childhood. Concerted effort in educating and training children and youth might be a promising field as they are less change resistant than the adult community. Conducting further research on how to identify effective strategies to build role models, convincing men to be part of the solution, creating equal opportunities at all levels, and enlightening women would be helpful to enhance sustainable transformation. Study of the positive and negative effects of the forceful and coercive movements on gender equality, and identifying the crises and benefits of the approaches would be highly beneficial for future intervention.

It would be helpful to conduct further research on cultural, institutional, legal, economical and structural barriers for gender equality, and to carefully examine the insiders' view in order to introduce appropriate gender-sensitive and inclusive strategies for effective mobilization of the whole community.

The danger of particularistic cultures is the challenge to build a justice system that treats everybody equal. The society does not sympathize and handle all victims equal. Research on how to design a strategy that can convince the society to perceive the importance of gender equality to each individual and for the whole community may be helpful to bring change.

References

Benn, H. (2005). What is changed in twenty years? *The International Development Magazine,* 30. Retrieved November 25, 2005 from http://www.developments.org.uk/data/issue30/ethiopia-now.htm

Mosley, J. (2004). Gender and daily life in Ethiopia. *Contemporary Review,* 285 (1663), 97-101.

Presbey, G. (1999). Should women love "Wisdom"? Evaluating the Ethiopian wisdom tradition. *Research in African Literatures,* 30 (2).

Report on Oriental Orthodox-Roman Catholic Theological Consultation. St. Nersess Armenian Seminary, New Rochelle, NY; June 9-10, 2003. Retrieved Nov. 15, 2005 from http://sor.cua.edu/Ecumenism/20030626OORCConsultation.html

Richmond-Abbot, M. (1992). Masculine and feminine: Gender roles over the life cycle (2nd ed.). New York: McGraw-Hill, Inc.

Senge, P. (1990). The fifth discipline: The art and practice of the learning organization. New York: Doubleday Currency.

Triulzi, G. (1973). Women factory workers in Ethiopia. Eva Zabolai-Csekme (Ed.), *Leadership Development for Women* (p. 67) Lutheran World Federation Department of Studies, Geneva: Switzerland.

UNDP (2005). Human Development Report, 2005. Retrieved Nov. 25, 2005 from http://hdr.undp.org/statistics/data/country_fact_sheets/cty_fs_ETH.html

Willcox, S. & Short, A. (2005). Cutting flowers: Female genital mutilation and Biblical responses. Addis Ababa, Ethiopia: SIM Publishing.

PART II: NEXT GENERATION RESEARCH IN CHICAGOLAND

Chapter 10:
Art Students at Chicago Loop-Area Colleges: *A Compilation of Field Work*

Luke Burton and Michelle Yu
2007 Summer Missionaries
Chicago Metropolitan Baptist Association
Chicago, IL

Editor's Note:

Since no final written product was completed by the Burton / Yu team, I have chosen to include here much of the raw data from their field work. The data here consists of interview transcripts and compiled survey data. I have also included some brief comments of Burton and Yu that they have provided as reflections on their research findings.

Interview Transcripts

Student Interview #1 – Seung Huh
Date: July 6, 2007   **Major: Painting**
Time/Location: Noon at the Art Institute   **Year: Undergraduate**

Michelle: So, can you tell me a little about yourself.

S: Uh, myself?

M: Yeah.

S: Like what about myself?

M: Like maybe your school, major, where you grew up and stuff like that.

S: I am Korean and I grew up in Korea until I was 17 and then I came to the States and went to an art school in Boston and yeah, came to art college. So, I am majoring in painting but used to be film and video.

M: Wow! So how did you decide to focus on painting rather than filming?

S: Well, um at this school it's much easier to pick painting and to just go ahead and do it. But film, I'm not rich. I don't have money to afford to do it.

M: So, do you feel that you are part of the arts community and if so, how would you describe the arts community?

S: The arts community, how would I describe it? Sometimes I feel that I am a part of it and sometimes I don't because of my nationality maybe. I feel like I'm part of it because I've been going to the school and I am part of the arts community when I go to school.

M: So how would you describe the arts community as a whole?

S: Um, compared to the non-arts community? Maybe uh, um, I... [unsure of question asked]

M: Maybe like specific words you would describe the arts community with . . . like are arts people, like I don't know. How would you characterize arts students as?

S: Um, um. Lunatics. [Both Laugh] Or pretend to be lunatics. Or hipster. Um. Yeah, that's about it. I can't really think of more.

M: Okay, so what do you think are some of the major needs of the art community?

S: Major needs. Uh, in the arts community. They need to actually have community and have communication with each other because often times artists are very isolated and uh yeah. Maybe these days, maybe the arts community needs more seriousness because they don't really take anything serious anymore. So, maybe that and yeah.

M: Um, what areas do you think they do take seriously?

S: Um. Um.

M: Well, how about yourself. What areas of your life do you take seriously?

S: Areas in my life that I take seriously are living as an artist, living making money, living life with making art. That's the only serious part of my life.

M: It's just really pursuing what you're painting or...

S: Yeah what I'm painting and keep doing it after school and yeah it's a lot of pressure.

M: Um, do you spend time in the Loop like this area other than when you're in class?

S: Um, I'm usually at home. I never really go outside. So, I uh, go to uh, I don't really like hanging out here.

M: Um, what kind of music do you like to listen to?

S: *I haven't really listened to any music for years and uh I basically listen to every genre there is but I don't really buy or collect music at all anymore.*

M: Okay, um. Do you consider yourself to be a spiritual person?

S: *Very much so, yeah.*

M: Okay, how do you express that? How do you express being a spiritual person? What does spirituality mean to you?

S: *Spirituality is like a taboo word for artists because they, we, are very careful of using that word. Because sometimes for other people spirituality can mean like Kenny G or like New Age music, or mediation, or yoga class. But to me, it's uh, um, it's definitely not those things. But uh, it's something, spirituality is something that I, it's really hard to talk about isn't it.*

M: Yeah.

S: *Because one of my source is, it's a big question mark. What is spirituality? Like, I feel it every day in everyday life like when I'm painting or when I'm sleeping or yeah, um.*

M: Um, we kinda spoke yesterday a little bit about how you grew up and your parents being Christian and Buddhist and Christian -- did that affect your spiritual life at all?

S: *It destroyed me. [laugh] I used to believe in God, I used to go to church every Sunday when I was young. I started not to believe in God. I was leadership in church.*

M: Oh wow.

S: *Yeah, I just started, didn't trust them anymore and then I came to the States and I started believing in Buddhism and my family did too. And when I got back home they were Christians again. [chuckles] But each time, they were very serious about what they do. And like, I don't believe in religious institution anymore. But I know that I, I feel very close to*

God. I'm very close to God I think. I can't stand the restrictions and rules that they put up. Like the people in church, Buddhist temple, the people, I don't think I can be part of them.

M: And is that just for the Buddhist temple you went to or is that for also, for the Christian churches you went to back home?

S: *I feel it is more the Christian church. Yeah. I got out of church again in America because the preacher was saying something really aggressive about homosexuality and I just got up and left the church.*

M: So what exactly about Christian churches or even your Buddhist temple and the rules and regulations they place, really just like turn you away from church? Like are there specific things, maybe like, the aggressiveness of homosexuality or other areas that they just push you away from church as well?

S: *Um, a lot of things that I can think of. I'm really skeptical about whatever they say. And sometimes they speak very political and they talk about war and I don't really want to hear that in church. And how they quote the Bible, and talk the Bible and the things they used to talk about in the Bible, I don't think uh it really relates to these days. And uh, they're conservative. They're really conservative. And I'm partially scared of it. And yeah, I just don't agree with most of the things they say. I just like when they don't say anything but uh, like when they pray and sing, I like that but I don't like [unclear]. It's scary.* [Both laugh]

M: Um, could you kind of elaborate what part of that is scary. The fact that it is so conservative or --

S: *Like the people are usually like, if you don't act this way, I mean it's obviously that I will be eliminated by the people there. I'll never be part of it and --*

M: So, what would you like to see for churches to change that would appeal to you as an art student or other artists?

S: *Um, I don't really expect much from church so they can do whatever they want to. But, um, I think uh that if it's a Korean church or an Asian church, they concentrate on it being really tall or gorgeous church rather than really helping people and that really ticks me off that they can do that. Or, taking the idea that if you don't believe in God, you will go to hell. That really bothers me. That makes me want to puke. And if they are more open minded about other religions too, it seems like they're denying everything besides Christianity and every human business and every other culture. They're denying it. And it really bothers me. And I personally don't like to believe in 'white' Jesus because I'm Asian and, and yeah.*

M: So, um, these feelings you have towards the church and the institutions -- how do you perceive Christians in general?

S: Uh, I am really judgmental. I have big prejudice towards them and my sister is a really serious Christian. I feel like I have to be really careful about what I say and I can't really be critical about anything. They are happy people. I mean happy but scary like monster. They are happy within themselves but I feel like sometimes you really know like what you believe in and they can't filter whatever they hear and... [laughs]

M: So do you think Christians have anything in their lives that you would want in your life?

S: They seem very stable all the time and like, how they believe something beyond the material world. I think they are spiritual but not everyone is actually. Some people are but not everyone. I think they just go to church for their own sake or it's something like small events in their life. And like the way they depend on God. Yeah.

M: Um, would you have to give up things in your life in order to be a Christian? Like if you wanted to become a Christian again. Like are there things in your life you would have to give up for that?

S: Yes. Uh, I want to be Christian sometimes but I'm scared that uh, the inspiration and the ideas and the critical mind would go away because I would be too happy. And the kind of lifestyle, it uh would have to change. And yeah.

M: Have you had any memorable experiences with Christians? Whether good or bad and can you explain one of those experiences you've had with them?

S: Uh, um. I remember having a fight with my sister. [laughs] Because we were talking about, my parents were talking their church and their priest and God basically and they were drinking and my sister said that "God wouldn't like you if you were talking about him while you were drinking," and they started fighting about it. That's one of the more recent memories I have. And I have a lot of negative and positive memories. And I guess positive memories coming from God and me directly and not from regular people. But it was usually negative. When I was at church.

M: Um, okay. That's good. How do you perceive Jesus?

S: Jesus. Uh. I think he's a really cool guy. I understand why people say that, who, wish to be like him. I understand that. I think it's cool. Except one thing that bothers me is that he is white.

M: Does that make it hard?

S: Yeah, it makes it hard. Well, whoever he is, I think he's a really good guy.

M: So, um. Going back to some of your religious background, when you were growing up as a Christian, what were some of the things then that you really, kept you being a Christian and didn't turn you away from that?

S: I like the mutual, or, the uh, [unclear] that I was feeling that I was loved by so many other people and that. Until I realized that people are just people and until you get to close to them they get jealous and they fight and they will yet and they are just people. I get disappointed with them. And the priest was a good guy but he liked money and one of the turn offs was that he built a new church and when I walked out, there was a homeless man and I just couldn't understand why he wouldn't let him in, let him into church or let him sleep. I don't remember doing any volunteering or spiritual work and that was one thing that really bothered me. Yeah, but the way I uh, the way I was feeling at church.

M: Do you feel that you are loved by the people around you now?

S: Uh, no. [laughs]

M: No.

S: Yeah. Yes and no. Sometimes yes. Sometimes no.

M: And are there specific reasons why you feel that, I mean?

S: *It's because I'm self conscious about . . . it's because I want to feel loved by other people. It's like I want to be the center of attention, their attention. And it just doesn't happen anymore.*

M: Um, how can people show you love in a practical way?

S: *Um . . . just stick with me when I am in trouble and be sure to help me.*

M: How would you describe your friendships with other people?

S: *Um, very minimal. I only have a few friends that I can actually talk to. Otherwise, there just, I don't really have that many friendships. How would I describe my friendship? I don't know.*

M: Okay, um, I actually think that's all the questions that I have for you. Is there anything else that you would like to share about your own experiences with Christians or with church? Or things that people could do to help reach out to the artists in the community here?

S: *I think that it's, it's pretty . . . people, artists are scared to talk about Jesus and Christianity but they are really open minded to religion and there are so many, it's like trend. It's really trendy to use um, their own religion or practice in their art. But not Christianity. I haven't seen many students show that subject in their art. It's like once you actually say that, you can't get out of it, they will eat you alive. I know they are really against Christianity. Because part of the reason is, that I think, they just stop doing what they used to do and uh in ancient times like Christians. But we have to feel like we are, we are living in uncertainty and our self as the creator and um, yeah. And it's not that we don't*

Student Interview #2 – Jiyoon Cheng
Date: July 11, 2007   **Major: Painting**
Time/Location: 12:15 p.m./ Art Institute   Year: Undergraduate

Michelle: Please tell us about yourself.

J: *I'm from Korea. My Mom is Christian and my Dad is Catholic. I chose to become a Christian after attending church, school, and Bible study.*

M: Do you feel that you are part of the arts community?

J: Yes

M: How would you describe the arts community?

J: Depressed, sad, violent, unhappy. I can tell the difference of being a Christian in an art school. My art is much happier than non-Christian. In my class right now, there is a lot of sad and violent arts. One painting is of a girl holding a dead, bloody rabbit.

M: Okay, what are some practical ways that you think other people could help the arts community?

J: Don't force religion on people.

M: Do you spend time in the Loop other than for classes? If so, how do you spend that time?

J: No.

M: Tell us about the music you listen to.

J: I listen to anything. I think that art students perceive church as old fashioned and so music is old fashioned. Possibly due to Bible being old.

M: Do you consider yourself to be a spiritual person? If so, how do you express that?

J: Yes. I do not express it through art though. It's hard to combine religion and art together.

M: Do you feel that you have a purpose in life? If so, tell us about it.

J: Trying not to be sinful and trying to go to church.

M: Do you feel loved by the people around you?

J: Yes and no. I still feel lonely but will pray and read the Bible for comfort, calmness, and happiness. It's hard sometimes because students will get drunk and do drugs and I feel lonely.

M: How would you describe your friendships with other people?

J: *My friendships are deep and easy to talk to friends. My friends know that I am a Christian and they tolerate that.*

M: Tell us about your religious background, if you have one.

J: *I grew up in a Christian home and had Christian schooling.*

M: If you were at a religious service, what would you want it to be like?

J: *There should be more art to explain the history of religion. They should play more modern day songs like Hillsong, Chris Tomlin, and Shane & Shane.*

M: Okay, tell us about how you perceive Christians.

J: *Christians are not consistent because everything they do is depending on circumstances.*

M: Tell us about how you perceive Jesus.

J: *He is my Savior. He died for us even though it was hurtful for Him. He was holy and born with human body. He is the way to get to heaven.*

M: What are some ways you think Christians can reach out to the art community?

J: *Invite them to church because it's less threatening. Maybe to have a concert or to use art to explain religion.*

[She opted not to be recorded with the micro cassette. Therefore, the answers above were written down. At one point in the interview, she told me about a conversation several other students were having in the classroom. It was about religion but she was too scared to talk about religion with them and join them. She was telling me how there are not many Christians in the art program and so she doesn't say anything. But she did mention that the students are more open-minded and tolerant of religion. She also told me that being in college is much different. Being from a Christian high school, all her friends were Christian but here not many are at all. She expressed how it's hard for her not to sin and do sinful things like smoke but she wants to try.]

Student Interview #3 – Nabiha
Date: July 6, 2007 **Major: Photography**
Time/Location: 1:00 p.m. / Art Institute **Year: Undergraduate**

Michelle: Do you feel that you are part of the arts community?

N: Yes.

M: How would you describe the arts community?

N: Versatile.

M: What do you think are some of the major needs of the art community?

N: I think there needs to be more general awareness of art in the community and people need to have a more worldly reflection of past and present art.

M: Okay, do you spend time in the Loop other than for classes? If so, how do you spend that time?

N: Yes, I live in the Loop. I like to shop in the Loop.

M: Tell us about the music you listen to.

N: Everything.

M: Do you consider yourself to be a spiritual person?

N: Yes.

M: How do you express that?

N: Through my art.

M: How would you define spirituality?

N: Spirituality is being aware of possibilities in life and different possibilities of answering the questions of why and how and where.

M: Do you feel that you have a purpose in life?

N: Yes.

M: What would that purpose be?

N: My purpose in life is to live my life and to exist.

M: Do you feel loved by the people around you?

N: Yes.

M: Tell us about your religious background, if you have one.

N: My parents are Muslim. I don't label myself a specific religion. I take bits and pieces from each religion and have my own.

M: Okay, tell us about how you perceive Christians.

N: My experience of Christians are actually through my mom. After 9/11, it really affected my mom a lot. She was hesitant of wearing her traditional clothing; however, as she wore it, people, I assume Christians, would walk up to her and tell her that "God loves you." When my mom told me this, I was directly affected and it has now changed the focus of my work to focusing on my own culture.

[Due to time constraints, these were the only questions that were asked of Nabiha. I have attempted to contact her again to ask more questions but have not received a response.]

Student Interview #4- Alex Bailey
Date: July 13, 2007   **Major: Painting**
Time/Location: 1:15 p.m. / Park   **Year: Undergraduate**

Michelle: Alex, could you give me maybe a one to two minute background information about yourself?

A: Um, yeah. I am 20 years old and I'll turn 21 in two weeks. I'm from Virginia Beach, Virginia. I moved here to the Chicago Art Institute, because I wanted to study art, not specifically painting but that's where I ended up I guess. And I'm pretty stoked about it. I was Protestant, raised Methodist. My dad was a Catholic but he didn't really like Catholicism or religion, he isn't really a religious person. He used to be a chemist, so he's very science. I don't know. And yeah, um but I didn't grow up in a very religious background. I don't know if that's what the interview is about but like maybe that's a good opening.

M: Okay, do you feel that you are part of the arts community here?

A: Um, that's kind of difficult to say. Um, it depends on, like, I'd say an artist community is sort of multi-layered. Not only by your medium of choice but also by, I'm definitely not part of any gallery sort of community. Or, because I don't work at any gallery or show at any gallery really because I don't really want to do that at this point in my career. Um, but uh yeah, I'd say there is a community. I'm attracted to people who like to work and I'm attracted to people who are interested and who have the same kind of fetish for objects that I have. Which is kind of interesting. So, I think I am definitely part of an art community. I don't know if it's the art community. But I think, yes. I would say that most of my friends are artists.

M: Okay, so how would you describe the arts community, like, as a whole?

A: Um, I don't know. It's sort of a weird mishmash of people. I'd say that at this stage of the game, a lot of kids in college are sort of, hmmm . . . It's sort of difficult to say because as you get older, a lot of the older artists here are teachers, they're kind of dorky and all they care about it is art. And they're over their sort of hipster posturing. And they're not all trying to be the cool guy anymore. I'd say in undergraduate level, especially kids from L.A. or New York who come, there's sort of an elitism that runs, that courses through an artist community. And it's got very neat layers to it. There's elitism to what you wear and how you dress, and your work, you know if you make good enough work. It doesn't matter what you do, or it doesn't matter anything you do, you could be an asshole and make really great work and everyone's like, "That guy's an asshole, but he makes really good paintings." And you know, and there's sort of respect given to that, and I don't know if it should be but maybe it's all right. Like, I, I'm not sure about that. I'd say at least here, I hear it's different in other places, it's kind of difficult as an artist community because it's competitive. It's just a competitive place. You end up in these small cliques. I'd say that, um "a bunch of guys who paint clique," and you know it feels kind of like a boys club but you know there's few girls in there. And you know, there's people who are my friends who go to parties.

The sort of party scene at art school is really, I don't know if it's different from other places. There's only 2,000 people at this school and there aren't like giant parties. It's not that anonymous. You end up seeing the same people all the time. You know who's doing coke all the time, you know who's drinking a lot or not, or who, you know. It's kind of like this weird dysfunctional family, where you know everybody's everything but you don't really know anyone that well. It's a good way because people are, most people seem really like, I don't know if it's recent or if it's always like this, but there's sort of like a, being sort of timid is a cool thing, like being quiet to be really cool. Like you're cool because you're quiet, which is fine but then you're not meeting anybody at any real level because you're too scared that if you talk to someone you're opening up too much and like, yeah, I obviously don't have this problem. But yeah, it's something that I feel a lot especially at, in certain ways.

M: What are some, like, key words you would use to describe the arts community? Like you know when you were saying people are timid to be cool. What are other words would you use to describe the arts community?

A: Hmm . . . key words. Self-reflective. I think, I want to think experimental or progressive but I'm not actually sure that's true. Um, hmm . . . I, you know, I think those are the three I can think of. The people I like are diligent and maybe crazy. There's maybe an essential sort of aspect of insanity, crazy. It's hard, I don't want to say that because no one's Van Gogh here, no one's cutting their ear off or anything. I think there's a general, I don't know if you got this, a lot of people, it might be just Chicago, seem really upset a lot because they're being self reflective and they're realizing, "My art, why am I doing art?" There's a lot of questioning of why you do art in the first place and that you know, it's good because people are self reflective and they're like, "This is why I've chosen this path" but some people, after spending $40,000 a year or more are like, "Shit, I don't want to be doing this. This isn't what I do. I spent so much money to find that out. I don't like art. I don't like looking at things. It doesn't appeal to me in that way." I guess that's not really an answer to your question really. But I figure there are a few words you can use.

M: Okay, what do you think are some of the major needs of the arts community? Especially the undergraduates or the graduates.

A: Um, I don't know. Ah, man. Um, I wish there were more galleries. I wish there were more stuff to see. I personally, I can't speak for the whole community. But I would say there's generally a feeling that Chicago doesn't have enough. I mean the Art Institute is great and a lot of people don't take advantage of it like they should. I think there are really amazing, fresh, contemporary artists that don't make it there. Except for like maybe some hip artists like Kadagumta [spelling?] or other hiring galleries in the West Loop that are sort of still second hand New York but not quite. And they never will be but sort of like an equivalence to that. I think the other thing that I personally need is, I really wish there were more nature. Just being in the city, this isn't enough. It's sort of a prescribed way of trees placed in Millennium Park and Grant Park. It just seems really fake and artificial. It's just not enough I think. I'd say those are the things that they need. Maybe exercise or something. Maybe they should quit smoking.

M: On that note, do you smoke?

A: No, no I don't.

M: Have you seen a major trend with artists smoking? Is it just something that they do or…

A: Yeah, right when they're born, it's like they're given a cigarette and that's how they know their path and it just makes it easier to choose. No, I don't know. Well, yeah. When I first moved into the dorms, I think a lot of people started smoking. I never, really, I don't know. My mom used to smoke and I thought it was weird and I didn't like it, and when we were kids we'd make her quit. So, I never did it. So, I'd just sit out and eat like Goldfish or something. You know, smoking is really great because it lets you look cool because you have something in your hand. Because you're rolling your tobacco, because it's too expensive to buy, like a pack. You're lighting it up and you're smoking it. By the time you're done, you've spent six minutes looking cool and it's perfect. Smoking is really great unless you don't want to smoke because you want to run or do anything. I think people definitely pick up smoking a lot more. I'm not sure why. It's like why do people wear tight pants at art school, you know as smoking becomes taboo in mainstream culture. It will stay as a pleasant vice that artists indulge in.

M: How would you describe an artist just by physical appearance? Like a general, stereotypical, even for yourself, how would you describe them?

A: I think generally smaller build than most people. Not all the time. I'm actually one of the bigger artists and I'm not really a big guy. Generally we're sitting at a studio, we're not at a gym. There's no sports teams at art school. I'm a vegetarian. There's a lot of vegetarians and most people I know are vegans. They are really health conscious too in a sort of organic food way. And of course there are people who rebel radically against that and like do it the opposite way. So, say you've got your. It's like at art school, there's definitely art school types and, but there is a different spectrum. There's like the kids from L.A. who are really lanky and tall and androgynous. They look kind of like elves and wear vests and belts over their V-necks, and wear super tight pants that go into boots. And they have long hair on the sides and the back is sort of a mullet. And they kind of look like aliens. But they look really good too. I think there's something really attractive. Maybe it's that they work in numbers and they make sure that they look good. Um, there's cohesiveness to the style that's not. I prefer it to the pop collar frat boy look personally. There's those kids and then there's the kids which are '90s throw back clothing, then there's kids who come from hard core scenes and punk scenes and have always tight pants, a trucker hat and camo cut off and Converse shoes. There are a lot of things that are really specific but they're not really specific to artists. You know, if you're in that punk scene, your art reflects it, like you may be into stencils and you might be into hard core music. Or if you're an elf kid, you might be sort of into trendy drawing that's sort of come out of Providence in the last ten years. And not necessarily -- people are always surprising. There are people who fit these categories pretty closely where you're like, you're just into being cool in every aspect of it. And that can be important to someone and give someone a purpose.

M: Okay, um, do you spend time in the Loop other than for classes?

A: Yeah, I like to ride my bike down the lake shore path. I actually don't like the Loop that much. I'd rather be -- well, I'm actually not sure where I'd rather be. I actually spent more time in Wicker Park but I don't actually enjoy it that much really. I spend most of the time at home or on my bike riding around. The Loop is good. There's really great libraries. We have the library here and I really like the museum.

M: Um, do you feel you have a purpose in life?

A: Yeah, um. You know what, I think yes and no. This is yes or I think it's less a purpose or more that I'm excited about, I like the idea that I can change my life at any point less than I have a purpose. I like painting and I believe in it, you know, but it's weird to say and I know it's just you're putting goop onto a cloth and you know that's all it is and it's not that important but there's sort of a weird ineffable quality to not being able to explain an abstract painting and that's really exciting to me. Um, and certain objects and things like that, which goes back into the fetish thing probably. I um, I also think the purpose is I want to have adventures. I want to do wilderness training, and I don't know. I like the idea that I can end up in Panama and marry some Panamanian woman and have no idea how I got there. Or you know. But you know, we're just waiting for 2012 when the apocalypse comes so it's not even a problem. [unclear] I'll just be ready. I'll train in martial arts the year before and lead a revolution.

M: Do you feel that coming to art school here, do you plan on doing art after you're done with college?

A: Yeah, I can't not make it. It's not something I think. That's what people who stop realize, is that they don't. It's not that I want to make art -- it's that I have to make art. I think about it all the time. I don't know what situation I'd have to be in that I couldn't think about it. And I guess if that happened, and I was just "I really want to be, stop making something." Because we've, at my job I work with so many materials. I don't want to work on painting, I start writing because I have to be doing something. So yeah, long story short. Like I'm gonna continue making art. I'm interested in doing galleries and stuff like that. I'm ambitious to a large extent and I'm also interested in making something really great for myself. I like, don't want to say that because that will probably just end up being really hypocritical in the end. I'll probably just sell out. And yeah, I definitely will be making things for the rest of my life. It's the only thing that keeps me going, you know.

M: Do you consider yourself a spiritual person and how would you express that spirituality?

A: Yeah, I think there's a yes and I think I express it by sort of being immersed in nature especially. I think it's sort of a transcendental or German romantic feeling towards nature. That nature is an expression of God or whatever. It is what it is and I like it. I think being overwhelmed by the sublime is how I really feel any sort of spirituality.

M: Do you feel loved by the people around you?

A: Ah man, yeah. I sometimes, it's not so much. Not so much as at home sometimes. It's hard to say. Yes, I do. I think. [laughs] My roommates are the best friends I have in the world. So, I feel like I've lived in a house that has a lot of love. I think there's a lot more tension between one or two of us and since we're living together now, it's just me and him, the tension is going up a little more. I think so, sometimes I feel a little less. I'd say yes but when I think about the people I feel loved by it's actually a lot fewer than the people in my immediate circles. But it's still enough.

M: What are some practical ways someone can show love towards you?

A: Um, man I don't know. They could, I'm not really sure. That's a really tough question. I'm much better for the art questions I think. Um, practical ways someone could show love towards me. They could hug me. I don't know. When you want someone to show love towards you is when you're down. You want to think that someone is going to be there for you. And I feel that way to a large extent. I'm not down that often but when it happens I'd like to think that there would be people that would not just tell me what to do or what I'm doing wrong or to prescribe some solution. And just say, "Hey, I'm here." I feel like part of me is that I want to figure it out for myself. But I do just want to know that you're there and I don't need advice so much as much as just knowing you're there.

M: Do you feel that with your roommates or any other people here in the arts community who can do that for you?

A: Yeah, I have a lot of friends who are like my painting friends, which is when class is over some of my roommates, who are my friends primarily through painting classes, and all we talk about is painting and girl problems. And you know, and how they relate which is really weird. Like if you're timid at making a painting maybe you're like that in relationships. Which is like you know, really bad gross analogies that somehow make sense of the world. I feel like sometimes painting does that for us. It's sort of a philosophy to it that's sort of a way of conveying. You're not mimicking the world so much as how to translate it into a different language. I feel like we talk about that and then I usually feel better about whatever it is by relating it through that.

M: Okay, that's really cool. Um, so how would you describe your friendships with other people?

A: Ah man, in life in general. I think the best friendships I have are ones that I always want to hang out with them and I'm always willing and I respect them a lot. I'm impressed by them -- you know I don't worship them, but I think I've had a lot of friendships in the past I felt are really parasitic. A lot of people who are sort of on the darker side of things. I used to have a friend I guess from third grade, but recently who was singled out in Virginia after the shootings. They looked for kids who were suspect. So, he was singled out as a suspect and he was definitely dark. I still think that it was horrible that it happened. He's actually, seen in another place he'd be seen as a dark romantic, gothic sensibility in the German tradition or something. And maybe he doesn't make anything but he could be an artist in his own right if he did. I find myself in a lot of friendships with a lot of people who are constantly sad. I don't really like that very much. Who are constantly needy and I feel bad because I want people to be there for me when I'm needy, but at the same time I feel very often that some of my friendships are quite draining and I don't like that because I can't just cut them off. I'm kind of cold that way. My friends back home I haven't talked to in months. I don't talk to my family. I don't have Facebook or AIM or myspace. I don't keep connections with people. I sort of cut people off. So, my friendships are not dispensable but I like them to be in memory more than drawn out than it should be.

M: Okay. And would you say that for a student here, is that the kind of the same trend you see? Or does it just depend?

A: No, it just depends.

M: Okay, okay. Could you tell me a little bit more of your religious background? I know you started off with some of that in the beginning.

A: I was born. I'm a Methodist I guess. I didn't go to church very often. When I was younger, I really liked praying, especially after my grandmother died. I used to pray a lot as if I were talking to her. And then uh, so I don't know if it was praying or mild schizophrenia. I used to, I think there's something about spirituality and religion that's really attractive. I was raised that way and at one point, I don't know if it was puberty or learning to masturbate or whatever or feeling awkward about God because of that and the sort of physical aspect of life. But also sort of a, in here, in art school, when someone is religious they chose to be religious. When you're in art school, most people aren't religious and you had to make some sort of a choice. That you did believe in something and *not everyone else is going to believe in it but you deciding to believe in it. Whereas in Virginia, it's really conservative and it's in the Bible belt and a lot of people didn't make that choice -- they were sort of born into it. And I think it's fine. A lot of people don't make a lot of choices about their life. They sort of just go with the flow and that's not necessarily a problem but like I said, that's not how I, my purpose is that I, this sort of freedom to decide things. And I guess at one point I just felt like, I thought about Christianity really hard and it just wasn't the choice I felt like making or I felt like really appealed to me completely. I felt like there are great things and I think for me I always felt that Christianity actually, especially recently, prevents a lot of bad experiences. You're not gonna have sex with a lot of people and get chlamydia. Or you know, feel really terrible psychologically or emotionally. You're not gonna deal with that sort of thing if you don't have sex before marriage, or if both people don't. But uh, and you know being circumcised is a good thing you know, if you don't want bacteria there or whatever. Beyond that, the teachings, I'm not really so well versed. A lot of the things are good ideas but I never really felt that I needed the ritual that was inherent in the churches I went to. And it's a little unfair because they were like newer rituals so I didn't feel like the rituals had been carried out like for a long time, like if you go to a Catholic procession and they wave all those things. I'm actually more attracted to that. It appeals to me a lot more -- a ritual that is ancient because it's, I like the idea of things being passed down. That's kind of why I'm a painter too. Sort of a thousand years old or more. I'm connected with cave people now because I just smear paint onto things. But that was a really long answer again. But yeah, I. I have definitely a strange relationship with the church back home. I feel very much like, a less a part of the way I live, I think the Christians I know are great. They chose their path and they're smart about it and they're not preachy to me. I respect them very much and I think some of them are like happy, really nice people. Some of the nicest people I know. So, you know as the whole church you know, I felt alienated. It never felt right to me.*

M: Do Christians have anything you want in your life?

A: Um, it's hard to say. I don't think so. Yes, yes the idea of being a Christian. There are certain things I like. I don't know if I need something bigger than me because I think the world itself is big enough for me, or bigger than me enough, and I'm not really attracted to the idea of truth and it might be sort of a postmodern condition. I think most of the people here do not believe in essential truth in a lot of ways. Maybe it's like that but not really. I like the idea that it's all up for grabs and I'm an anarchist at heart. A community would be nice. Christianity, I think that's what I would want. Christianity is a great way for people to connect on one thing and I think art almost could be but it's competitive. People don't . . . painters don't respect performance artists; video artists don't like painters. So, I think no one likes ceramics even though ceramics is awesome and probably cooler than all of them. As people will find out later. So, I think a sense of community would be great though. I think, I don't know how you build that. I don't know how you start something fresh and new that has tradition enough to get people together. I don't know if we have to build elf villages in the west, a tree town or something. I think that's one of the best parts of Christianity. It's just sad that I always felt alienated from that community and I could never feel a part of it.

M: And why did you feel alienated from it and separated from it?

A: I don't know. It's very hard to explain. I uh, I'm not sure. I think maybe because I always felt like all these people were going with the flow and it's just also, it didn't, I think, being alienated is maybe a part of why I'm here or why I do what I do. It might be why I'm an artist. I don't know. I'm not a very group person and I'm not out to make myself look eccentric or, I actually would like to, you know, as far as appearance goes, to be normal enough and artsy enough, and not too much of either. And I think that's a good, a certain sense, I said I want community but at the same time I feel a little weary or scared of community and the implications of a group of people in being that sort of mentality. And I think Christianity, I think, because I think it's definitely different in Virginia too. I'm not gonna be into certain things that everyone says and I need people who are more dogmatic and a lot more self righteous. And I'm not interested in self-righteous anti-Christians or Christians. It doesn't interest me at all. It doesn't seem like a very thought out way to view the world since it's so layered in my opinion.

M: Could you explain to me or describe to me a memorable experience with a Christian, whether it be good or bad?

A: Ah man. Um. Yeah, it's a lot of them. Yesterday I talked to my friend Joey Jax about your survey and it was great talking to him because he is such a charming person and very sweet. I remember specifically a kid in my science class when we were studying evolution, he was yelling about, that the bones uh, were all placed, so that uh, he was getting really angry and I just remember like if you're getting all heated and yelling and it just,

I just think that in an argument if someone is yelling, they're losing the argument. I just feeling really weird about that. I think I remember an experience with a church. I was just working with this church. I just remember going there and everyone was so into what was being said and people who were singing were so into it. I just remember being a little scared because I just couldn't get into it. I couldn't get into it but a part of me wanted to into it. So like, when my school won the homecoming football game I was there and everyone ran up and like hug all the football players, I just didn't care about football enough. You know, it's not that I don't want to feel the spirit. It sounds great. It sounds awesome. I'd love to feel the spirit. Sort of like uh, you know, not being able to have an orgasm or something. It's a really weird comparison. But it's like, I feel like, "Oh yeah, of course, that sounds great. I would love that. It sounds awesome but at the same time I feel really alienated seeing the spirit being felt. And I think those experiences, being in a church, and seeing everyone into it, I remember when I was a kid and I was really into it. I remember when I was a kid and I remember I was like, "Whoa I can feel something, I can feel the energy and it was like [weird noise]." For me the energy, I don't know if it's God, or a group of people that come together and believe something, and it just happens between people you know. There's an electricity when people believe in something together. Whether they're rioting or at a church and I think it's exciting. And I think it's something I remember and I think it's scary, because rioting and praying aren't actually that different to me in a weird way.

M: So, how would you um, how would you describe a religious service or a church service that would appeal to an arts student?

A: I'd say uh, I'm really not a fan to answer your question. It might be out of negativity or something. I'm not a fan of like TVs in churches. I'm not a fan of the mega church atmosphere. Christian rock is bad. The gospel Christian music is better. I, my great grandmother is 96 and she died recently and I went to her service in a Catholic church and it, I'm not specifically into Catholicism, but I really liked the ritual aspect of it. I liked the Latin. I liked how foreign it seemed but I liked how well everything was made there. I liked the church itself. I think that all really appeals to me. It's a unified sensibility. It's still weird that everyone comes in their SUV to come to church. At the same time the formal aspect of it I really like. That actually really appeals to me as a sort of uh, I mean I can only view it as a performance. But it has so much more when it's tradition of thousands of years. I think the Catholic traditions are mixed with older pagan traditions too. They have that feeling of all those mixed together to create this sort of swinging of the smoke thing and the motions and the range of motion and the standing up back and forth. I much prefer that to the sort of "We're really cool and we're trying to make church fun!" I mean that's good too but you gotta get your subscribers however you can.

M: Okay, um, tell me how you perceive Jesus.

A: I perceive Jesus as probably being a pretty fun guy. Probably pretty nice. Uh, good to have at a party because he could turn water into wine. He can walk on water -- that's pretty extreme. I mean, I guess you know, I think, you know, he sounds like a great person. I'd love to meet him. Um, I think he had it tough. But then he also had it easy. He knew he was Jesus. The angel came and was like, "You're Jesus." And he's like, "Oh yeah." So he had his purpose in life. It was already set out and we don't have that. I think Jesus is a great guy and I think that it's sort of tragic. At the same time I think, you know, even though knowing you're gonna die, there's something easier about that. About then you know, well something that's harder about being in this world is that you're not sure whether you can believe in a god or anything. You're not sure what is truth or if there is truth. You don't believe in anything or, so I think you know he's great and uh, I don't know. Him and Buddha would hang out or whatever.

M: You were talking about earlier, when you were younger you were really into church because you kinda grew up in it with your family and everything and now not so much. What in your life do you think you would need to change for you to maybe into church again, or do you even have a desire?

A: I don't really have a desire for church specifically. I mean, I uh, Christianity. There might be a way to get into that. But church itself, I don't think. Church is a weird thing to me because there's morals and ethics involved, and there's beliefs and there a lot of things for me are left out. Things are changed formally about churches, the way they look. They sort of have TVs and they have, you know, there's not, maybe there's some, there's not an emphasis of ecology in church. Which maybe is not the church's job. But I'd like to go to a church where not everyone is driving a SUV you know. Because I feel like that's a moral choice or even buying clothes off people in South America who are getting paid nothing. Or any amount of things we are connected to that don't really seem to come into a lot of congregations that I think are really important. And I think everyone wants to be a good person and I think actually most people are. But I mean, to me it's like you know, we live in a country that is pretty exploitative to weaker countries. Somehow I would want to be part of a church that took that in account more and took our place in the world into account and not like, wasn't defensive about, "We use a lot of gas and we're still good people." I don't know, sure, everyone is a good person. Like, you now, if you look at the Nazis. Well, not to compare the church to Nazis. But like a Nazi soldier who probably had a kid who was probably a good dad, a good husband. Or he was a Nazi but he was a dad, a husband or so and so. And everyone is like that. Everyone has these different layers they fulfill. Like I'm an artist, I'm a brother, I'm a white male beneficiary of a capitalist system of exchange and that's not necessarily bad but that's what it is. We're all these different things and I'd want to be in a place to take into account the implications of certain things. Spiritual, even in a secular world I think that these other things need to be taken into account for me to be interested.*

M: I had a question for you while you were talking but I forgot it. So, while I think about that, is there anything you want to share with me or any questions or comments?

A: Um ,no. I can't make up a question and have you answer.

M: Okay, well I think that's all I have for you. So, thank you.

A: Okay, no problem.

Student Interview #5 - Danna
Date: July 12, 2007   **Major: ?**
Time/Location: Email   **Year: Undergraduate**

Luke: Please tell us a little about yourself: hometown, family, etc.

D: I'm 26, single. I'm from a small military town in Tennessee called Clarksville. I have a mom, sister and 9 year old nephew that live there. I don't know what else to say about that.

L: Do you feel that you are part of the arts community?

D: Not so much.

L: Do you spend time in the Loop other than for classes?

D: No.

L: Tell us about the music you listen to.

D: *Punk, outlaw country, Oi...*

L: Do you consider yourself to be a spiritual person?

D: *I do.*

L: How do you express that?

D: *I don't express it much, but I talk to God sometimes and ask him or her what I should do.*

L: Do you feel that you have a purpose in life?

D: *Yes, I do. I think God gives us all talents and weaknesses for a reason and we must follow the signs to the correct path in life.*

L: Do you feel loved by the people around you?

D: *I guess I feel loved by my mom, even though I am the version of her when she was my age and my one year older sister is the version of her now at age 55. So we don't all do things together much.*

L: If not, why not?

D: *I guess I feel a lot of distance from my family because well . . . maybe because I am an emotional person and I don't show them my emotions because they don't understand it and our ideas of right and wrong are different. But mostly I feel like they judge me and that they have no right to do that because I am the better person.*

L: What ways do they show you love that are meaningful to you?

D: *My mom always helps me out when I need and she tells me she loves me.*

L: How would you describe your friendships with other people?

D: *I have acquaintances. I have a select few friends that I don't even talk to, but they know I'm there with one call and they would do the same. I guess our lives are just too busy for each other now.*

L: Tell us about your religious background, if you have one.

D: *I just found out that when I was little and my sister and I would fight, my mom would threaten us with overnight Bible camp. Ha ha, we didn't know what it was, but it sounded really scary.*

L: If you were at a religious service, what would you want it to be like?

D: *I love the traditions of the Catholic religion: the symbols and saints and rituals, but the sermons are usually VERY boring, so maybe more upbeat singing or more involvement of the worshipers.*

L: If you were at a religious service, what would make you uncomfortable or offend you?

D: *That depends, I guess. I think the Bible is a lot of folk lore and most of it is offensive to me. The way women are portrayed is a small portion of evidence that the Bible was written by men and men with power will say and do anything to keep it. Therefore it can be corrupted. Not only that, if Jesus was really the Messiah, don't you think he would have traveled a lot further to spread his message? European countries didn't even become Christians until 400 years after Christ and that was only because a Roman emperor waged a war in his name. The Jesus I've read of would never visit someone in a dream stating, "Conquer in my name."*

L: Tell us about how you perceive Christians.

D: As a generally unhappy to content person I wonder if my life would be "fuller" if I had more faith in God and Jesus. I see those "do-gooder" Christians that are so hardcore their lives are the church and they always seem glowing with happiness. They claim to be so happy because they are filled with the Holy Spirit. Sometimes I wish I could be like them, but then I think that they are just happy because they are just filling themselves with a false sense of security and ignorance. Example: when something bad happens it's not the Lord working in mysterious ways. It's life. It's supposed to be hard.

L: Do Christians have anything you want in your life?

D: The blissfully ignorant happiness I mentioned above.

L: Would you have to give up things that you value in order to be a Christian? If so, what?

D: Premarital sex? I think if I did that I would never have sex again. I do not confuse true love with my feelings for God and nature. I am like-minded with the Catholics on this one. I believe you may have as many vices as you wish as long as your want or need for them do not cause you to do anything that would break God's laws.

L: Have you had any memorable experiences with Christians, either good or bad? If so, tell us about it (them)?

D: The only thing I can think of really is my experience with the Southern Baptists in Arkansas. They owned everything and controlled everything. No beer, liquor, MTV. MTV was completely removed from the cable package. Even if your parents (the cable buyer) went down to the office and requested MTV, they refused as if it didn't exist. Skating at the skate rink was a sin after 10 pm. I think you get the idea.

L: Tell us about how you perceive Jesus.

D: Jesus was a man. Whether or not he was the Messiah, I don't know. I do know that regardless he was a very good man who had many great things to teach us. Then again so did Gandhi, Buddha, Martin Luther King. I find all religions to be fascinating and I believe there is great benefit in extracting the best aspects of all religions to create a nameless, global religion. Because that is God to me -- a nameless, bodiless entity that makes the universe function. I hope this does you some good. Sorry I kind of rambled on a bit.

Student Interview #6 – Eric
Date: July 12, 2007   **Major: Fine Art**
Time/Location: 1:00 p.m. / Bennigans   **Year: Undergraduate**

Luke: This is an interview with Eric. It is Thursday, July 12 at 1:00, and we are at Bennigan's. Eric, could you just tell me a little bit about yourself, where you're from, all that kind of thing.

E: I'm from Missouri originally, 32 year old male, Caucasian, 6'4" 160 lb., a little underweight for my size. I'm an undergraduate here at a university in Chicago majoring in art, fine art. I'm here with my daughter.

L: Ok, first question: do you feel like you're part of the art community?

E: Yes, there are a lot of divisions of that community, but as far as just with the school, then yeah, I'm in that community . . . my major . . . participation.

L: How would you describe the art community? I know that's kind of an open ended question.

E: Yeah, it's under development right now. I mean the art community of Chicago . . . the professional art scene is sort of lacking to a degree. Really conservative in the sense that there isn't much new work happening. Art right now . . . it's cyclical in nature, but it's also, at this point, it's just kind of searching, going back in history, and repeating history and redefining it and moving forward. The community at the school is actually . . . I'm excited about next year. The previous year was more active than it was my first year at school, so it's changing and it's an exciting time.

L: What do you think are some of the major needs of the art community?

E: Motivation. With the school being defined the way it is, there are no grades, so a person could come in and they could put off doing their homework until the night before, and just get by and still get a grade whereas you work on it for weeks and months. You have to actually critique their work, because they did do the work. You know, they might not have put any thought into it, but you have to let them know whatever, however you feel about it. So, I feel like there's a real lack in motivation for a lot of people and I ran into that a lot in my classes. And as we were speaking before the interview, you were saying that people don't want to hurt other people's feelings. I run into that in my critiques a lot too, where I don't get any feedback because someone's afraid to hurt my feelings. I would rather -- I had a class last year where I disagreed with everything everyone said just so I would get -- even negative feedback's better than no feedback. So people would gun for me when I would come up for critique, but hey, I want an honest passionate answer about my work and if that's not going to be given to me I'm going to search it out.

L: What are some practical ways that you think that other people could help the art community?

E: Other people outside the art community or inside?

L: Yeah, outside the art community.

E: I don't know, I don't know that the art community . . . I mean funding, I guess, would be always nice. Artists generally, unless you're really fortunate to have a financial backing, then that's not an issue. But as far as the community, I think that art is changing. From a fine art appreciation, it's changing into more of a commercial, it has more of a commercial influence. I don't know of many people from my home town who go to the museum to see a Picasso or anything. They're all more like media, what's on TV, new design, the iPod, or the iPhone. The fine art community would be helped more by more active involvement by the community, and I don't really see that that's the community's responsibility as it is an artist's responsibility to engage the community.

L: Do you spend time in the Loop other than for classes?

E: Oh yeah, I live down here.

L: Ok, I was going to ask how you spend that time, but I guess you kind of live your life. Tell us about the music you listen to.

E: *Everything from -- mostly jazz and blues. I listen to some electronica, art -- like Aphex Twin, created sound that's all samples. More instrumental than lyrical.*

L: Ok, do you consider yourself a spiritual person?

E: *I do.*

L: Ok, how do you express that?

E: *In my work, through my artwork, and through the materials I use. I express it through my art. I experience it through nature and express it through art.*

L: What are some of the criteria that you meet to be a spiritual person?

E: *For me to be a spiritual person is to be in touch with myself and my inner voice and my environment and to be engaged with people and to help people, because I feel like you reap what you sow.*

L: Ok, do you feel like you have a purpose in life?

E: *To live.*

L: To live? Ok, anything beyond that? No? Ok. Do you feel that you're loved by the people around you?

E: *Yeah I do. Actually, the place that I'm staying, a friend of mine is letting me house-sit his house this summer while he's at home. I don't know how to explain it. Yeah I do. I have some really great friends and I know if I'm in need they're there, and if they need anything I'm there.*

L: That's really important to have.

E: *Yeah, it is.*

L: What are some of the ways that those people show you love that are meaningful to you.

E: *Well, for example, my birthday was just July 3rd, and my friends just made a party for me. I didn't ask for it and they didn't ask if I wanted it. They just made me go and they paid for everything. We had a blast, sang karaoke. Really giving people. Just listening to me gripe sometimes too. They're just there. If I need anything they're there. That's important to me.*

L: How would you describe the nature of your friendships with other people?

E: *The nature of my friendships?*

L: It's kind of an ethereal question, but --

E: *Yeah. What's the word I'm looking for? Reciprocal. Not necessarily 100% of the time, but the nature is of the helping hand. I know I don't know everything and no one else knows everything, but together we know a lot more than one person. So it's just a help, as a helper, an aid in life.*

L: Cool. Tell us about any religious background you have, if you have one.

E: *Yeah, I was raised Pentecostal, then evangelical, then Baptist, and I stopped attending services regularly with my family when I was about 12 or 13.*

L: Sounds like you've been through the whole spectrum.

E: *I've had some nice rides. Catholicism, I'm not really. My father's Catholic but he never really talks about any religious anything, so I have some experience with some religion.*

L: How do you feel like those experiences impacted your life?

E: *I feel like they educated me on my future beliefs and my attitudes toward people and religion in general.*

L: Ok, in like good ways, bad ways, a mix?

E: *Both. Both. I mean, it depends, everything's intertwined, just a mix. Negative in the sense of blind faith and followership with non-questioning attitudes – that was just my personal experience and I try not to project on anybody my . . . which is what I expect in return from others. I've had these types of conversations with my cousins for years and years up until the last three years --*

L: I'm sorry. I didn't understand what you said.

E: My cousins, speaking on my family --

[waitress interrupts]

E: My cousins would always question my faith and my beliefs and try to make me believe what they believe rather than accepting what I believe as I have accepted what they believe and not try to convert them as well. Accepting me as a person and loving me as a person rather than loving me because I believe what they believe.

L: You know, personally, I'm a Christian and I do try to share with people what I believe, but one of the major, major things that really hurts me is when I see other Christians who are talking to people and it's like it's not even a person. They're not loving on that person. It's just like it's a trophy they're trying to collect. That really upsets me. It's like, "What are you doing? You're making all of us look bad and you're hurting that person."

E: I have friends also that make the same argument. They say, "Christians just want to do this, they want to do that." I'm like well, how can -- you can't generalize any group of anybody as being one specific way. You just can't.

L: You, for example. I wouldn't have expected to find an art student who had been in the Navy. You're not your prototypical art student.

E: No, I'm not. And I have the advantage of being out in the world and experiencing a little more of life than some other people, so I feel fortunate to have those experiences, good or bad. They've made me who I am today and I love myself.

L: I think you're one of the few people I've ever had tell me that directly.

E: I think it really comes with age, with life experience. When I was younger, I didn't. I didn't when I was your age. For me it's been just acceptance. I had a really hard time just accepting life for life and me for me and the sky for being blue.

L: And all those insecurities you have at my age, "Who am I?" and "Why am I here?" and all that kind of thing -- you've gotta resolve all that.

E: Come to some type, whatever that is, for the individual. And I think that's the power of religion. It gives the person that. They don't have to figure it out for themselves, because it's just there. You can either accept it or reject it.

L: If you were to go to a religious service, what are some things that you would like to see and what would be some things that would really make it enjoyable for you?

E: Well, there was a church in St. Louis I used to go to with my cousin. It was a nondenominational church. They met in a high school gym and people were just . . . I always felt at home there. The praise and worship was great. It was just like the band was up there and everybody was involved and the Spirit was there and was alive. That's what's enjoyable to me: a non-questioned acceptance of individuals come together for one common purpose and it's not about money and it's not about social status and it's not about any of these things, but just enjoying this moment that you have together.

L: Kind of conversely, if you were to go to a religious service, what would be some things that would turn you off or make you uncomfortable?

E: The first thing that turns me off is . . . there's a man that stands out, and I'm sure you've seen him if you've been walking around the Loop, over by Old Navy on State Street. And he stands with a megaphone – "You can't go to heaven smokin' cigarettes, you can't go to heaven doin' this, you can't go to heaven doin' that." Setting these boundaries and limits and -- scare tactics, that's what turns me off. Immediately, my brain just shuts off. I'm not listening.

L: We have a guy like that on the OU campus. He tells the sorority girls that they're going to hell because their skirts are too short.

E: I was surprised when I first got to the school and saw that there's a really big Agape group here.

L: Is that like a Christian group?

E: Yeah, they get together and do Bible studies and I think it's great, but it just kinda surprised me. That broke my stereotype of art school right there. I had to take a step back and realize that we are in the Midwest, but it just surprised me.

L: As far as my perception so far, it seems like Chicago is one of the most postmodern, liberal cities that you'll ever end up in. Is that fair?

E: Not the most, but more so for the Midwest, yeah.

L: Kinda the same question, you mentioned scare tactics, are there any other things that would make you uncomfortable or make you be like, "I don't want to come back"?

E: If it's dead. If there's no life in the church. I went to, I don't remember the church. I went with one of my friends who was an RA in the residence hall with me last year. I went with her to a service. I hadn't been in probably 5 years. I go in, sit down with her. It's a Sunday afternoon, they read the book of Revelation, they're not telling me anything, they're not speaking to me anything that I can't open a Bible and read for myself. The man would read. He read through half the book, stopped, took a drink of water. Everyone sang some hymns, passed around the plate for money, then he finished reading. I could have done that myself. Why would I go to church? Church in the Bible is two or more people praying to God. I can do that at home. I don't need to go to church if that were important. And that's where I have a problem with religion – it's man made. I don't want anything to do with it. I'm a spiritual person and I can experience my beliefs on my own.

L: I guess another question that occurs to me out of that: is there anything that would get you into church, that would make you want to go?

E: I'm sure there is, I don't know what that would be. I have such a preset idea of what church is and what it has been in my life that I don't necessarily ever want to go back, to be involved in a congregation. It doesn't appeal to me at all.

L: Tell me about how you perceive Christians.

E: How I perceive them? As a group of people that believe the same ideology. I view Christians the same way I view Buddhists and I view Muslims -- just a group of people who all believe the same thing.

L: So do you have any emotional response, positive or negative in any way?

E: Honestly, it really depends on the person. Like the gentleman that stands on the corner and shouts things out. It's a judgmental one on my part: oh, you're ignorant, just shut up, [unclear]. As far as a whole, I have a neutral -- because I grew up in a Christian home, and I understand the ideal behind it. I have friends that are very judgmental.

L: Who are Christians who are judgmental or judgmental toward Christians?

E: Well both, both toward Christians and that are Christians.

L: In general, do Christians have anything in their life that you would want in your life? No?

E: No, I'm not, I mean, no. I'm happy. Some days I'm not, just like everyone.

L: Yeah, those days you get out of bed and you're like, man I do not want to go to work today.

E: True school.

L: Have you had any memorable experiences with Christians?

E: Yeah, my best friend is my role model in life. I think he dipped tobacco once or twice when he was like 6 or 7. He waited until he got married and lost his virginity to his wife. Just a really upstanding person and never once did he try to convert me or question me because of my beliefs. He just accepted me for me and that was a huge thing in me not being judgmental as well. He taught me.

L: In that, it makes me sad, because for me, when I read the Bible, that's what Jesus was like. He said, "I have this truth and you can come and I'll tell you about it," but at the same time he just was friends with people and loved people and wasn't like, "Ok, now you need to change now." In fact, in some ways, he was more like . . . people would come to him and he would not reveal everything to them. He'd say, "You're not ready yet." It kinda makes me sad how I see quite the opposite of that in our culture today. Oh dear, I may have just prejudiced this next question, but tell us about how you perceive Jesus.

E: That one I don't necessarily know if I've hashed out completely. I understand that he is a man who walked the earth. I feel that, as Buddha, he had a lot of enlightening things to say. I don't know that I believe historically everything in the Bible, just because of translation. I lived in Italy for two years, and I speak the language, and I know that even when I translate, even from Italian to English, a lot of meaning is lost. So when you translate Hebrew to, I think the first language it was into was, I don't even remember now. And so, English is like the third translation, and then you have a translation of a translation, and then you have all these different things, when Jesus was a person. I feel that he was a very disciplined individual.

L: You know, with the translation thing, though, you're right. That's how it was done originally. But these days, they're using the original Hebrew text and Greek text, so hopefully we've eliminated some of that inaccuracy that comes through two or three translations. But the King James version and stuff like that, they were translating from manuscripts that had already been translated.

E: And I have a problem with that. Who is King James and why does he have a Bible?

L: Yeah, I think he paid for it or something.

E: Yeah, well that's just my opinion on it.

L: Yeah, I don't know much about King James personally, but my dad, we have often had theological disagreements with some of the King James hard-core people and my dad always brings up the fact that he doesn't think that King James was a very Christian person. And I'm like, well, maybe not.

E: Well, and what is that? What definition of a Christian person? That's kind of something that could be even relative to what religion you are.

L: Well, I've ended up with all the questions I have written down. I do have one more question. The reason I'm doing this research project is because I personally am a Christian and I'm interested -- here in Chicago and other places, societies have gone from initially being Christian societies to what we see know – pluralism and postmodernism and stuff like that and I'm just interested to find out what some of the underlying reasons are. So do you think you could tell me anything that might be helpful in that?

E: I don't know. I could give you my opinion, but I don't know. I came to the conclusion, years ago when I stopped going to church, that religion is a way to control the masses and it was probably naïve. And a lot of the reasons why I came up with that, but that's still kind of stuck with me. The things that are taught. And I feel like the idea of faith to a lot of people is absurd. To just believe something because you're told is dangerous. I feel like a lot of people, that's a big, big issue. And with science being what it is today, and being able to prove something a lot, I feel like a lot of people need that proof in order to believe something. But that's just my personal opinion and I can't speak for [unclear].

L: I guess this is kind of a shot at the same kind of thing, but I think if you look at society back then, they really felt like they needed Christianity, that they needed a religion. Why do you think that some of the students today feel like they don't need that?

E: Because I feel like their god is in science now. I just said that people don't believe in faith, but I get contradicted by saying, "Well, you have faith that when you flip the light switch the light's gonna come on." Even historically, looking at art, and I've been thinking about this too when I was going through my Art History classes, the church used to be a big [tape ends]

[He went on to talk about the relationship between art and science. I expressed surprise, saying that I looked at them as opposites. He denied this and said that he considered them intricately intertwined. That was the end of the interview.]

Student Interview #7 – Zac Skinner
Date: July 7, 2007
Time/Location: Email

Major: Painting
Year: Graduate

Michelle: Do you feel that you are part of the arts community?

Z: Yes.

M: How would you describe the arts community?

Z: Eclectic.

M: What do you think are some of the major needs of the art community?

Z: *To connect with the masses, because currently art is not communicating to a large audience.*

M: What are some practical ways that you think that other people could help the arts community?

Z: *By coming to more contemporary art shows, and with an open mind, talking to the artists.*

M: Do you spend time in the Loop other than for classes?

Z: *Yes.*

M: If so, how do you spend that time?

Z: *In my studio, and working at a gallery, and eating.*

M: Tell us about the music you listen to.

Z: *I like to listen to a selection of music from around the world, and also from many time periods. It is an eclectic selection.*

M: Would you consider yourself to be a spiritual person?

Z: *Yes.*

M: How do you express that?

Z: Through my meditation/prayer, my artwork, and also through communication with other people.

M: What makes you a spiritual person?

Z: The belief that there is more to my life than my egocentric perception and identity.

M: Do you feel that you have a purpose in life?

Z: Yes.

M: Tell us about it.

Z: I don't completely understand my purpose, and I also believe that textual/ verbal language is not capable of expressing my purpose. Even the word "my" is deceptive because the purpose that I have or seek must transcend my "self."

M: Do you feel loved by the people around you?

Z: Some people yes, some no.

M: If not, why not?

Z: Not all people want to love me.

M: How can people show you love in a way that's meaningful to you?

Z: I can't imagine a world where all people show me love.

M: Do you feel like you have a lot of friends?

Z: "A lot" is subjective. I have enough friends to satisfy my need for friendship.

M: How deep are your friendships?

Z: Some are so deep that I lose touch with my sense of time and place. I feel ecstatic.

M: Tell us about your religious background, if you have one.

Z: *I have gone to Protestant church several times, and I am interested in it, and also interested in Buddhism.*

M: If you went to a religious service, what would you want it to be like?

Z: *I would want it to combine the discourse of many religions.*

M: If you went to a religious service, what would make you uncomfortable or offend you?

Z: *People asking me if I believe in one dogma in its entirety. I like to contemplate, as well as doubt. And I don't understand why people want to hear the answer to that question. Like I said before, words are incapable of expressing the essence of some things . . . and for me, one of those things is my spiritual beliefs, which exist as a feeling (even this word is inadequate). To say it in words, that oversimplifies, and cheapens the essential truth.*

M: Tell us about how you perceive Christians.

Z: *I have many different perceptions of Christians. I don't have any stereotypes of them. My girlfriend is my favorite Christian☺*

M: Do Christians have anything you want in your life?

Z: *I don't know.*

M: Would you have to give up things that you value in order to be a Christian?

Z: *Yes.*

M: What?

Z: *A different perception of God.*

M: Have you had any memorable experiences with Christians, either good or bad? If so, tell us about it (them)?

Z: Yes. I went to mass in Hong Kong, and the mass was in Cantonese. There was one American family there, and the father of the bunch was volunteered to translate the mass for me. As the mass proceeded, it was obvious that he had no idea what was being talked about. So he would say things like, "Now they are saying something about faith."

M: Tell us about how you perceive Jesus.

Z: He set great examples for being compassionate, and for believing in something greater than the "I" that we all know, or understand (or don't understand). I believe in him. I don't know him well though. There is so much history, and belief, and human interpretation that it is likely that my perception of Jesus is perverted.

Professor Interview #1 – Christian Rieben
Date: July 6, 2007   **Occupation: Professor**
Time/Location: 12:40 p.m. / Art Institute   **Age: 39**

M: Could you please tell me a little bit about yourself?

R: Well, I am an artist. I'm a painter. I got my master's degree here at the Art Institute of Chicago. I lived all over the world and now I'm back in the city I was born in.

M: Okay, how would you describe the arts community?

R: In Chicago? Uh, well I don't. My impression of it is that it is divided somewhat into different camps based on schools in the area. The Art Institute has the biggest alumni group probably and people are probably attracted to the schools, graduates they know and that sort of thing.

M: Are there specific words that come up to describe artists in the community? Like characteristic words that come up?

R: Compared to other communities? Eh, I doubt it. I think that one thing that's not specific to this city or these people are artists who are not in New York are often times insecure about that. So, that would be characteristic but that is not exclusive to Chicago.

M: Okay, what do you think are some of the major needs of the art community?

R: More money. I think there is also a concern in Chicago is that the gallery scene isn't the greatest. There's not a lot of buyers in Chicago. Umm, yeah so.

M: And, what are some practical ways that you think others could help the arts community here in Chicago?

R: Well, I think that um, again this probably is not exclusive to the Chicago phenomenon, but art possibly needs to be demystified for the general populace so it seems more accessible and less of a rarified sort of thing and I think that probably comes down to education. And yeah, then it's kind of a whole slippery slope you get onto.

M: Um, in your opinion, do you think arts students value spirituality and how so?

R: Yeah, I don't think necessarily you can use that word, spirituality. I think that artists generally think of the uniqueness of themselves and their phenomena and I think that can be tied into an idea of spirituality and the uniqueness of the universe and all that.

M: So, how have you seen your students in particular express their uniqueness?

R: Well, I try to make them paint or draw or whatever. To what they care about and people don't always know what they care about. So, that is one of my objects as a teacher is to really analyze their own ideas and feelings and to somehow get to know themselves better and thus make art that is profound.

M: Um, could you please describe some aspects of the lifestyles of art students that you know of? Do you see any generalities do you see in art students?

R: I think generally they are pretty progressive notions of society and generally pretty open minded. I think that is all good.

M: What would you think a religious service that would appeal to an arts students look like?

R: Really that's hard for me to say. I'm not religious myself. I'm sort of anti-religious. Or anti-organized religion and I think people's own spiritual beliefs, to me they are really better served on an individual basis than in community. So, I could not imagine what that would entail that would appeal to arts students.

M: Um, do you find it a trend that arts students, or even yourself and even the people you're with, are against organized religion and organized institutions of religion?

R: I don't think it's a trend. I think it has to do with the psychological makeup of people who are creative, you know. I don't think it's something that we're responding to in contemporary society. I think it's part of us that drives us to make things that's also somehow tied in to our feelings of individuality versus authority and that sort of thing.

M: How would describe the interactions of art students with each other and also with those not of the arts community?

R: Uh, I think they would probably reflect interactions of general society pretty closely.

M: You were saying earlier that you, yourself, are not a religious person. Could you describe maybe an experience that you had with Christians in particular, that was either good or bad?

R: Um, well my father's father was a preacher and I guess a lot of that experience was about exclusion and sort of saying there's only one way that people should be and people who are not that way are wrong and that view, when you are wrong, you are eternally wrong. And that's absurd to me. But not very specific, but that's sort of a general feeling that I have about it.

M: And um, do you have any feelings towards the church in particular? Like your father's father, like the church that you went to or did you go?

R: Okay, I've been to it but we didn't regularly go. We weren't part of that church. Yeah, there's good people within it and yeah um, I don't devalue their sincerity and all that. Um yeah.

M: Okay, do you feel that arts students have a purpose in life and what would that purpose be? From your being a teacher . . . yeah, art students.

R: Their purpose in life, well their purpose in life is uh, to learn the techniques and the materials and the ideas about art, both contemporary and both past. Like if a student were interested in biology it would be their purpose too.

M: Okay, and do you feel that learning all these things serves a greater purpose for them when they're done with school?

R: Oh, of course!

M: And how would you describe that?

R: Well, I think that, you know, artists, like I was saying earlier. The more they know themselves, the more profound the art. And art serves the general population by maybe tapping into the feelings which are less easy to express, which are maybe not being expressed right now in the general population. They offer relief for the general population. They offer hope. They can make life richer. They make life maybe easier too.

M: Okay, those are all the questions I had for you. Do you have any other comments or --

R: Nope.

M: Okay, thank you.

Editor's Note:

Burton and Yu managed to collect 95 completed surveys from art students attending colleges in the Loop. Below is the related data beginning with a copy of the survey template used.

Art Student Survey

Gender: Major: Graduate/Undergraduate

Please rank yourself for each statement

1. I have been satisfied with my life in the past three months.

1	2	3	4	5	6
Strongly Disagree	Disagree	Moderately Disagree	Moderately Agree	Agree	Strongly Agree

2. I would describe myself as a happy person.

1	2	3	4	5	6
Strongly Disagree	Disagree	Moderately Disagree	Moderately Agree	Agree	Strongly Agree

3. I prefer not to depend on other people.

1	2	3	4	5	6
Strongly Disagree	Disagree	Moderately Disagree	Moderately Agree	Agree	Strongly Agree

4. I feel that my life has a purpose bigger than me.

1	2	3	4	5	6
Strongly Disagree	Disagree	Moderately Disagree	Moderately Agree	Agree	Strongly Agree

5. I would describe myself as a spiritual person.

1	2	3	4	5	6
Strongly Disagree	Disagree	Moderately Disagree	Moderately Agree	Agree	Strongly Agree

6. I have positive feelings about Christians.

1	2	3	4	5	6
Strongly Disagree	Disagree	Moderately Disagree	Moderately Agree	Agree	Strongly Agree

7. In the past three months, I have had positive experiences with Christians.

1	2	3	4	5	6
Strongly Disagree	Disagree	Moderately Disagree	Moderately Agree	Agree	Strongly Agree

8. I have positive feelings about Jesus.

1	2	3	4	5	6
Strongly Disagree	Disagree	Moderately Disagree	Moderately Agree	Agree	Strongly Agree

9. If I had the opportunity, I would go to a religious service/church.

1	2	3	4	5	6
Strongly Disagree	Disagree	Moderately Disagree	Moderately Agree	Agree	Strongly Agree

10. I have positive feelings about going to a religious service/church.

1	2	3	4	5	6
Strongly Disagree	Disagree	Moderately Disagree	Moderately Agree	Agree	Strongly Agree

Survey Results

Responses were gathered from a random sampling of male and female, graduate and undergraduate art students enrolled in colleges in the Chicago Loop. When known, specific majors are noted.

Q1	Q2	Q3	Q4	Q5	Q6	Q7	Q8	Q9	Q10	Major
4	4	6	5	3	2	2	4	3	4	Painting
5	4	6	6	2	4	2	6	2	2	No answer
5	5	6	4	2	4	3	2	3	2	Graphic Design
4	4	4	4	1	4	4	3	1	3	Illustration
5	5	4	0	6	4	5	5	1	1	Graphic Design
6	6	4	5	5	6	6	6	6	6	Illustration
1	5	6	5	6	4	4	6	2	3	Performance
4	5	5	5	3	3	4	4	2	2	Architecture
5	4	5	6	6	5	5	6	6	4	Art/Technology
5	5	3	5	3	3	5	4	1	3	Writing
6	6	5	5	2	2	4	1	2	2	Painting
5	5	5	5	4	4	4	4	4	4	Art Theory
4	4	6	1	1	1	4	2	1	1	Film

Q1	Q2	Q3	Q4	Q5	Q6	Q7	Q8	Q9	Q10	Major
5	5	5	4	2	0	5	5	2	0	Fine Art
6	6	3	6	5	6	6	5	0	5	Painting
4	4	5	3	4	5	4	4	2	4	Multi Media
4	4	6	2	1	2	3	4	1	1	Visual Communication
6	5	3	5	3	6	6	4	4	5	Illustration
4	5	6	4	3	4	4	4	3	5	Video Performance
6	6	5	6	1	3	3	2	1	1	Photography
6	6	5	3	5	6	6	4	5	5	Painting
4	4	4	6	6	5	5	6	1	1	Art Criticism
3	3	4	3	2	3	3	3	2	2	Fine Art
5	4	2	4	2	2	2	1	1	1	Animation
5	5	4	2	4	4	0	4	2	4	Sculpting
3	3	4	4	4	5	5	5	5	5	Fiber
6	6	4	4	4	4	0	4	0	3	Fine Art
6	6	4	5	4	4	5	5	3	4	Fashion Marketing
5	6	6	1	3	1	3	1	1	1	Fashion Marketing
6	6	4	5	6	2	3	5	4	4	Visual
4	3	6	4	5	5	6	3	5	5	Fiber
6	5	4	5	3	4	4	4	3	3	Painting
6	5	6	6	6	3	4	6	3	4	Painting
6	6	5	5	4	4	2	4	4	2	Painting
5	5	6	6	6	6	6	6	6	6	No answer
4	5	5	3	2	1	3	3	3	3	Print Media
4	4	5	2	1	2	1	1	1	1	No answer
3	3	6	5	4	3	5	4	5	5	No answer
3	5	6	6	4	5	5	5	2	3	Interior Design
3	4	5	4	6	6	6	6	6	6	Performance
6	6	6	4	4	4	4	1	1	1	Ceramics/Neon Design
6	6	4	4	5	2	2	1	3	4	Film making/Writing
5	5	4	4	6	5	6	6	3	3	Film Video New Media
6	4	5	6	2	2	4	4	2	1	Visual Critical Study
5	5	6	4	4	5	6	4	3	3	Fine Art
4	5	3	5	4	4	6	6	4	4	Illustration/Animation
5	5	6	3	4	2	3	4	4	4	Art
5	3	4	5	4	3	4	4	4	4	No answer
6	4	6	6	6	6	6	6	6	6	Fine Art
4	5	3	6	6	5	5	6	6	6	Photography
5	5	2	5	6	4	4	4	2	4	Animation

Q1	Q2	Q3	Q4	Q5	Q6	Q7	Q8	Q9	Q10	Major
5	3	4	5	1	1	1	1	1	1	MFA Painting
6	6	3	5	1	1	1	1	1	1	MFA Painting
5	5	6	6	5	3	3	5	5	2	Art Ed/Photography
5	5	5	4	2	5	5	4	2	2	Fine Art
5	5	4	6	6	5	4	5	5	5	Painting
2	3	6	5	6	5	2	5	4	4	No answer
5	6	5	6	6	6	6	6	6	6	Illustration
5	5	3	6	6	6	6	6	6	6	Art Ed/Fiber
4	2	6	6	5	2	3	5	4	5	Painting
4	4	6	6	4	1	1	1	2	2	Art Ed
5	5	6	6	6	5	3	5	3	3	Film/Video/Performance
3	4	5	5	5	6	5	6	6	6	Figure Drawing/Painting
5	5	5	4	2	4	4	4	2	1	Painting
6	6	6	6	6	4	5	5	5	5	Fashion
2	2	5	5	4	3	4	4	2	2	Fashion
5	4	6	6	6	5	5	6	4	4	Film
5	5	6	5	5	5	4	6	3	3	Painting
5	5	5	5	3	5	5	5	3	3	Fiber
6	6	6	6	5	4	5	4	4	4	Sculpting
5	5	6	6	4	4	4	5	3	3	Fine Art
5	5	1	6	6	6	6	6	6	6	Vis. Art Communication
6	6	6	5	1	2	3	2	1	2	Photography
3	4	5	2	1	2	1	2	1	1	No answer
4	5	5	5	4	5	5	5	5	5	Drawing/Painting
5	5	4	5	6	4	4	6	5	6	No answer
6	5	6	6	4	3	5	5	2	2	No answer
6	6	4	4	3	5	6	5	3	4	Film Video New Media
5	5	6	4	3	3	4	3	2	1	Photo/Print Making
4	2	6	4	4	3	4	4	3	4	Installation
4	4	6	5	6	5	4	5	4	3	Fashion Design
5	5	5	5	4	4	4	5	5	5	FMM
4	5	6	4	3	3	3	2	2	2	Visual Communication
4	4	4	5	4	4	4	5	5	4	FMM
5	5	5	5	4	5	6	6	5	6	Fashion Marketing
5	5	3	3	2	1	2	4	2	2	Writing/Visual Arts
5	4	4	4	4	4	3	4	5	4	Painting
6	6	5	3	1	3	4	3	1	1	Painting/Drawing
5	5	6	6	4	4	5	4	2	2	Accessory Design

Q1	Q2	Q3	Q4	Q5	Q6	Q7	Q8	Q9	Q10	Major
2	3	2	6	6	6	5	6	6	6	No answer
5	3	6	6	6	3	2	4	6	5	Illustration
5	4	6	2	1	1	2	3	1	2	Painting
5	4	6	5	5	6	6	5	6	6	Painting/Sculpture
6	5	3	4	4	4	3	5	5	4	Painting/Drawing
4	3	4	4	4	4	6	6	5	5	Fashion Design

	Q1	Q2	Q3	Q4	Q5	Q6	Q7	Q8	Q9	Q10
Ave:	4.7	4.6	4.8	4.6	3.9	3.7	4	4.2	3.2	3.3
STDEV:	1.0	1.0	1.1	1.3	1.6	1.5	1.5	1.5	1.7	1.6
Count 1:	1	0	1	2	11	8	5	9	17	16
Count 2:	3	3	3	5	11	12	9	6	20	16
Count 3:	7	10	9	7	11	15	15	7	16	14
Count 4:	21	22	21	22	27	26	26	28	12	21
Count 5:	39	41	24	31	11	20	20	23	15	14
Count 6:	24	19	37	27	24	13	18	22	13	13

Correlations:				
Q1/Q2	0.63	*Significant*	df=93	r(93) = .195 (p<.05)
Q6/Q8	0.64	*Significant*		
Q9/Q10	0.82	*Significant*		

Survey Data Graphs

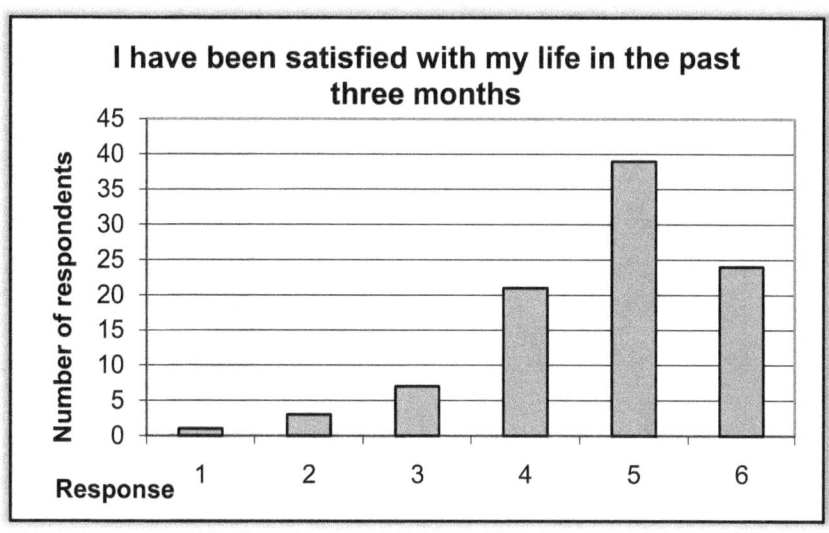

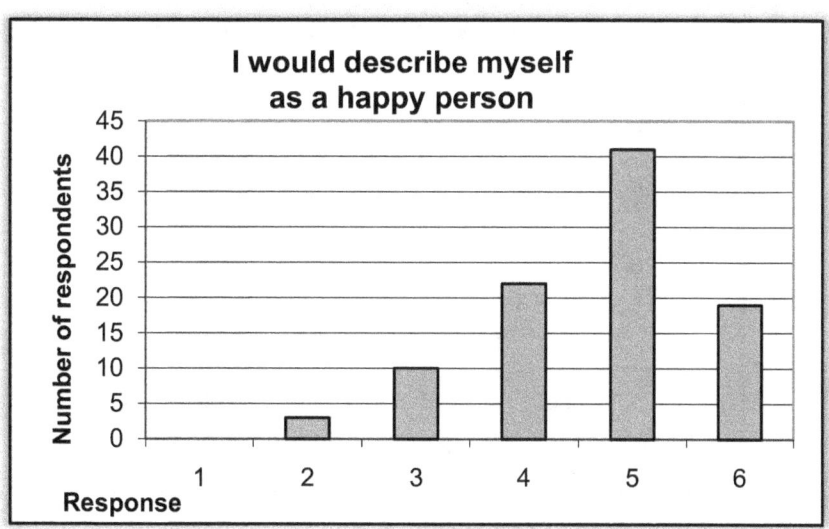

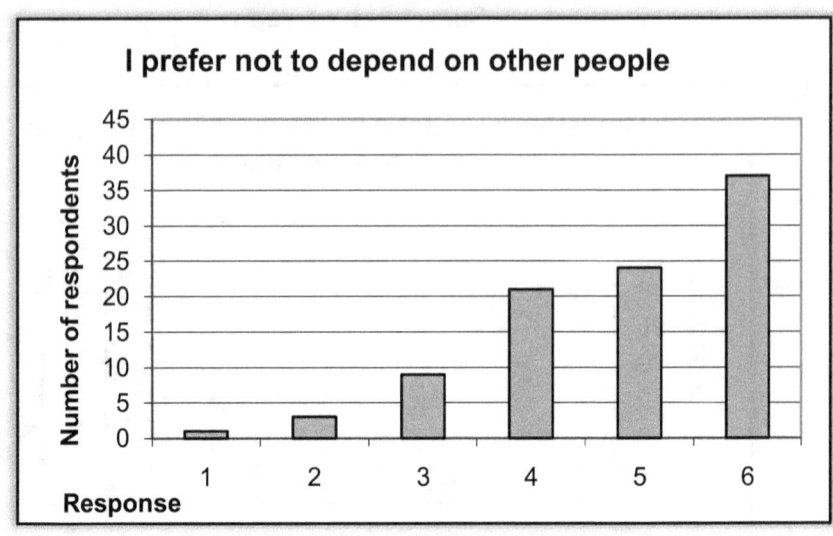

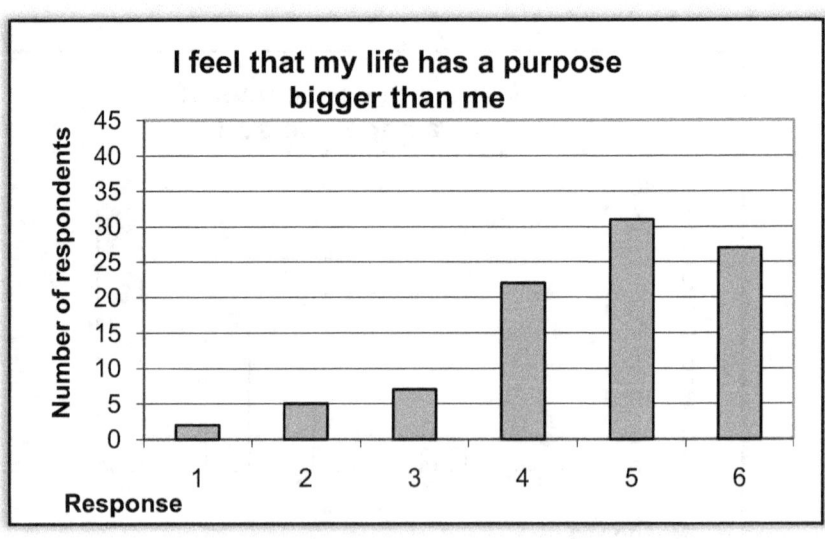

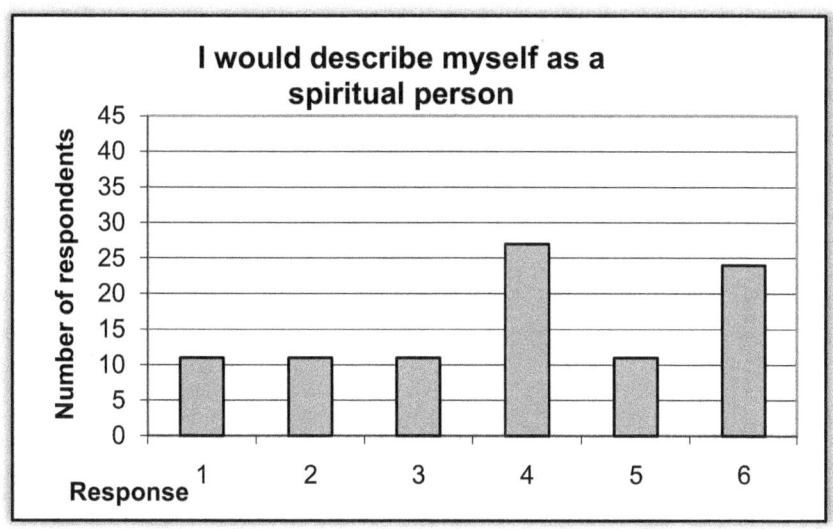

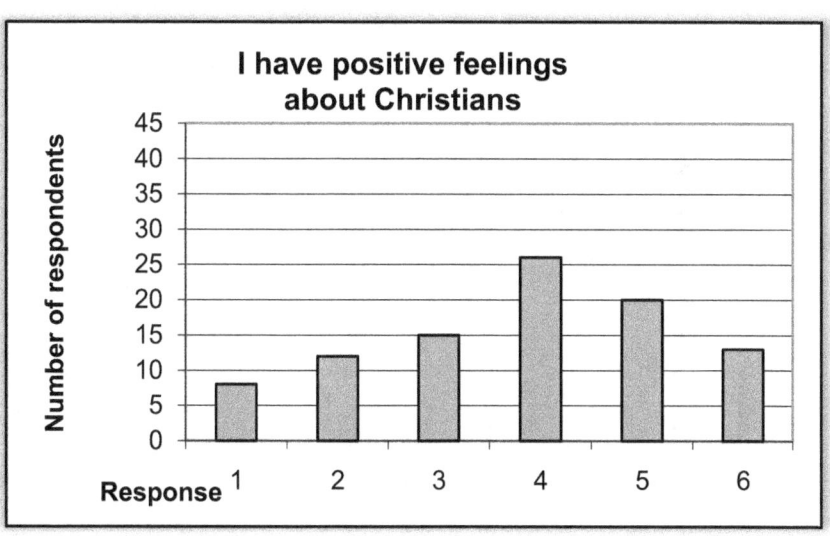

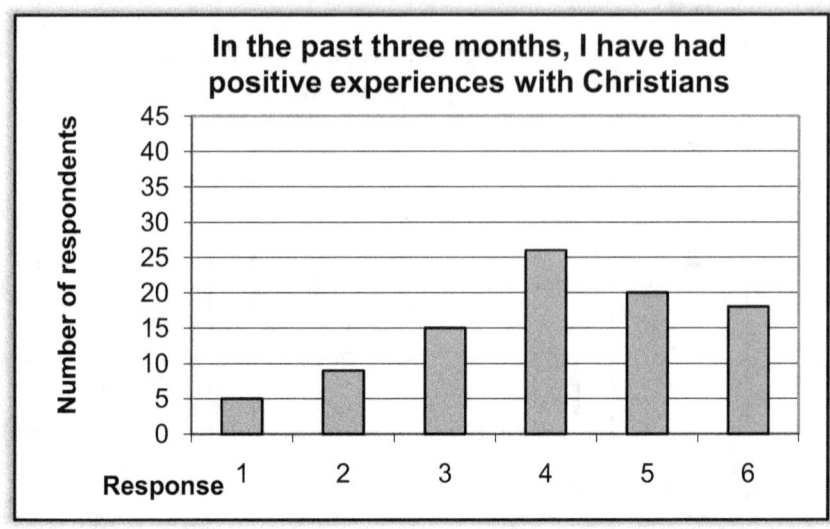

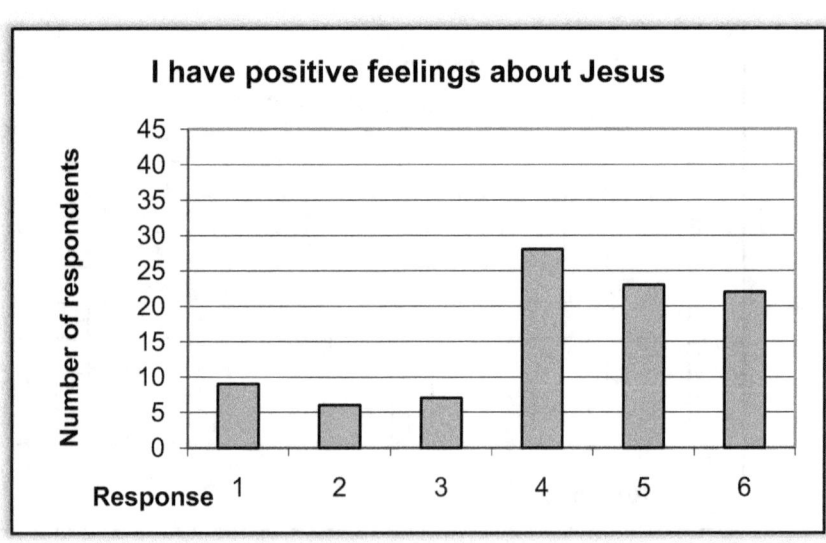

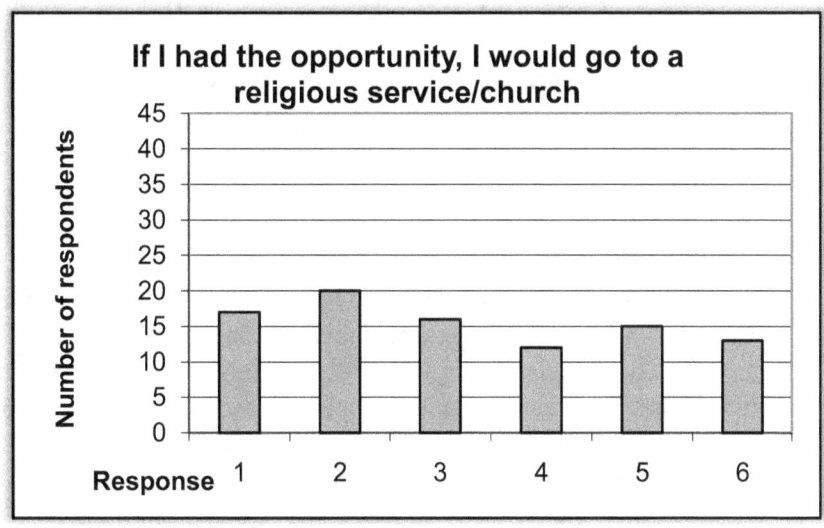

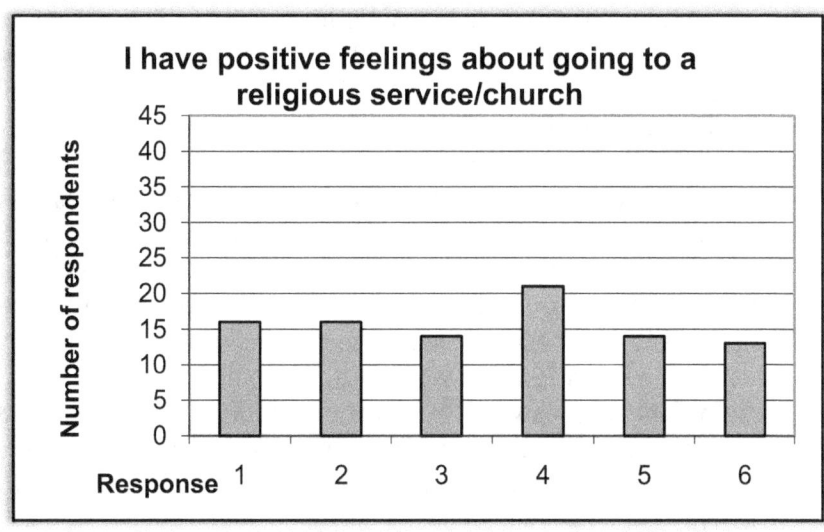

Statistical Reflections on Survey Results

With a total of 95 participants who completed our survey, it is calculated that our degree of freedom is 93 and the critical r value with p <.05. In order for a correlation to be considered significant in this study, our observed value must be larger than the critical value of r (lue of r(93) = .195).

While conducting the surveys, there were several questions asked that had interesting correlations. The first correlation we wanted to research further and analyze was between questions 1 and 2 of the survey. The correlation between respondents' "satisfaction with life in the past three months" and "happiness" was found to be 0.638. This is clearly much greater than the critical value of r; therefore it is a significant correlation. Looking at the bar graphs of the data, it is evident that the majority of responses favored moderately agreeing to agreeing with the statements in questions 1 and 2 of the survey. There is a positive and significant correlation between "satisfaction in life" and "happiness."

Another correlation we wanted to further research was the correlation between respondents' feelings towards Christians compared to their feelings towards Jesus Christ. These were questions 6 and 8 of our survey. The observed r value was 0.649, which again is greater than the critical r value of 0.195. Therefore, this is a significant correlation. Whether it is a positive or negative correlation, we do not know as of yet. However, the averages indicate that participants generally moderately disagreed or agreed to varying extents with the statements. However, we would like to analyze more of the individual answers to these two questions because the data from the surveys seem to suggest that many participants had positive feelings towards Christians yet negative feelings towards Jesus or vice versa. It would be interesting to explore the reasons why. With the given information we cannot make legitimate conclusions from that. However, we know at least the correlation between the two questions results in a significant insight.

The last set of questions for which we found a significant correlation was with questions 9 and 10 of our survey. These questions focused on opportunities to go to a religious service/church and having positive feelings about going to a religious service/church. The answers to both questions had a positive correlation. Those who would not go to a religious service if given the opportunity also did not have positive feelings about going to one and vice versa. The averages for the answers to the two questions however, were leaning largely more toward moderately disagreeing with the statements presented in questions 9 and 10 of the survey.

Chapter 11:
Observing Art Students: *Reflections on Participant Observations of Two Art Student Events in the Chicago Loop*

Tony Romero
2007-08 Semester Missionary
Chicago Metropolitan Baptist Association
Chicago, IL

Editor's Note:

During the fall of 2007, Chicago Metropolitan Baptist Association assigned Tony Romero, then serving the association as a semester missionary, the task of conducting two participant observations of art student events in the Chicago Loop area. What follows are Tony's reflections from those events. I have provided only minimal editing. Please note that Tony had not received any formal training in qualitative research methods prior to conducting these observations.

Reflections on Observation 1: September 21, 2007

I was given the opportunity to observe at an art gallery in September. My friend Kate had an exhibit there and the entire experience was very interesting. I arrived at the venue on Jackson Street in downtown Chicago. There were several people out front, all of which appeared to be college-aged students. All of them were smoking and expressed in their clothing a sense or longing to be individual. Every aspect of their appearance desired nothing more than to be prideful about standing out. I went inside and climbed a couple flights of stairs. I walked into the art gallery which had gray floors and solid white walls and ceilings. There were two art exhibits taking place and I spent the majority of my time in the one labeled "Not a Self-Portrait." The room for the art exhibit was like a maze. I thought it was small at first, but to my surprise there were many side rooms and other places to display art. Inside the gallery, the people had a similar appearance. For the most part, the attendees consisted mainly of college-aged students, many of whom expressed their individuality in their hairstyles and apparel. I began to observe the social setting of this gathering and found some common results. Of those attending, almost everyone was in groups of two or three. Many wandered around on their own, gazing deeply at the different pieces of art. There was a high Asian population there, almost half or more. People remained quiet, but it was not looked down upon if a group began to get noisy. After walking around staring at art and not understanding it, the gallery closed and I left with my friend.

I believe that the art community is focused on being extraordinary or oxymoronic in the presentation of their work. For example, the art show was named "Not a Self-Portrait" yet all of the productions were pictures of the artist. They however were not self-portraits but pictures of the artists portraying someone or something else. I think that artists are determined to be radical in their methods. They desire to express themselves in a way that no one has ever done before. There is a lot to think about when seeking to find out what "church" should look like for this community. Because of their desire to express themselves as individuals, worship/celebration would be something always in flux. There would be an obvious need to not form any kind of traditions in their celebration. It might be a good idea to have an overseer who allows members in the congregation to take turns leading people in various types of worship. There would be an obvious need for the gospel to be expressed in an artistic and contemplative way. The mystery of the gospel might intrigue them more than its other aspects.

The way the students gather in groups is significant as well. It seems to me that a cell group setting would be appropriate for this community. Because they only gather in groups of two or three at social events, these groups might prove to be uncomfortable if they were larger than a certain amount of people. There would need to be some type of gauge to find when that limit was being reached.

Reflections on Observation 2: December 8, 2007

After having observed at an art gallery, I was invited to a lecture session. The setting was very different than that of an art gallery. The place in which this event took place was a lecture hall. It reminded me of a movie theater in the way the seats were placed and the walls being black. There were no windows because there was a large screen in the front of the room with which light would interfere. Rather than sharing their art with the community, the artists had ulterior motives in showing their art this time. They were to prepare a lecture from which they could receive a $5,000 grant towards their work. The room was not filled with people, but rather there were about 30 people present. The majority of them were Caucasian. It seemed also that most people were wearing very dark colors. The artists would project their art onto the screen and narrate to the listeners the inspirations and methods used in their works.

One artist took photographs of imperfections on white surfaces, such as soap scum on the white surface of the bathtub or crumbs on the kitchen floor. This made me draw the conclusion that it is essential that an artist be original in every aspect of his or her work. It also appeared to me that the artists are trying to find art in things that they do not usually find artistic. An artist said that he did not find cars artistic, so he decided to add car themes into his work. Also I observed that some artists try to establish distance between themselves and their work. One man had tried to make every picture look as though a pigeon had taken it in order to establish that distance from his work. Another artist created a myth and made pictures to support this myth's validity. Her presentation however was much more important than the photographs. She had to create an entire back story as well as a new terminology to describe the different practices involved in this myth. The myth revolved around a religious community and I found it interesting that she made this community matriarchal.

There was a common question asked by the audience. The question was, "What's the importance of truth?" It seemed that with every depiction there is a sense of truth as well as deception. When confronted with this type of question it was clear that each artist's cultural perceptions affected his or her ideology and products.

Chapter 12:
Law Students at Chicago Loop Area Colleges: *A Compilation of Field Work*

Felicia Schwake & Sean Watson
2007 Summer Missionaries
Chicago Metropolitan Baptist Association
Chicago, IL

Editor's Note:

Since no final written product was completed by the Schwake / Watson team, I have chosen to include here much of the raw data from their field work. The data here begins with a literature review and list of reviewed sources. I have also included a number of interview transcripts and some brief comments made by Sean Watson as he reflected on his research among law students.

Literature Review

In examining the topic of graduate law students in the Chicago Loop, it is important to look at scholarship that details law students in general as well as the religiosity of college students. In addition, it is important for Christian missiologists who desire to know the issues involving these students' barriers to relationships with God to also learn from scholars who have already researched how college students' religiosity affects their personal outlook and identity. In our survey of this scholarly literature we identified six common themes: the impact of lawyers in the world today, the reasons students choose a career in law, the unique personality traits of law students, the emotional well-being of law students, the religiosity and spirituality of college students, and the researched effects of introspection on identity, morals, and values.

The Impact of Lawyers on the World Today

Many authors believe that areas concerning lawyers' influence through their jobs are important sources of power to initialize an impact for good. For example, Brennan suggests, 'Take these three years to learn how to do law well; even more, learn that the point of doing law well is to do good; still more, learn that doing good through law is about using power to achieve love's ends" (2002, p.19). Brennan also believes that instead of talking about where law can rule good and evil or for life or for death, the place law has in love or vice versa should be talked about (2002, p.20). On a more practical note, Lindholm seems to focus on the belief that future lawyers will "influence the nature and quality of society for many years to come" (2006, p.510). Brennan concludes that law that does good is looked at as very beneficial even to a diverse population (2002, p.21).

The Reasons Students Choose a Career in Law School

We have found studies that show many students have a variable amount of reasons for choosing law school while some have no idea whatsoever.

Schleef mentions that, "Students' accounts of their decisions to attend elite professional schools, although typically couched as preferences, actually reflect deep class-related constraints" (2000, p. 155). Schleef also believes they choose their degree for reasons such as "professional status, intellectual interest, and an upper-middle class lifestyle" (2000, p. 155). This study also found that some students choose law school as a way to discover if they really want to have careers in law (Schleef, 2000, p. 158). When students do have a clear understanding for why they went to law school, reasons mentioned by Lindholm include "an interest in issues of justice, as well as a desire for intellectual growth" (2006, p.514). Lindholm has also found that most students that had a desire for money and position lost sight of the intellectual gain from the law school experience; "[t]hose who choose legal careers primarily for purposes of material gain and prestige tend also to be least motivated by intellectual aspects of the work" (2006, p.515). This study also found motivations for one's job seemed to differ with gender. Lindholm writes. "Women legal career aspirants are generally less materialistic or prestige oriented, favoring instead a commitment to public service" (2006, p.515).

The Emotional Well-Being of Law Students

We found in a study that there are four major emotional complications among law students that cause abnormal predicaments: alienation, dissatisfaction, anxiety and depression.

Alienation

Carrington states, "The essential attitude of the alienated student is disinterest or disengagement" (1977, p. 890). The student who feels alienated does not value his association with fellow law students and doubts that they even enjoy his company (Carrington, 1977, p.891). The study indicated no correlation between sex, age, ancestry, political views, family type or family income with feelings of alienation (Carrington, 2007, p.891). Carrington writes, "Focusing on the immediate consequences of alienation, we can say with greater confidence that the presence of much alienation in law students does detract from the quality of life at the law school" (1977, p.892). In an updated article, Carrington implies that students who were highly alienated did not feel accepted or active in a caring association (1978, p. 1036). Studies presented two aspects of alienated students as being impatient with academic presentations of law and having a negative outlook on their fellow peers at law school. As Carrington writes, "highly alienated students in our surveys expressed impatience with academic presentations of the law that did not clearly relate to their own vocational needs" (1978, p. 1040). Carrington says, "Alienated students see their peers as markedly more negative and cynical than is actually the case. The alienated believed that their peers would lie to secure financial aid or would alter their transcripts to get a better job" (1978, p. 1040).

Dissatisfaction

Studies insinuated that students who feel dissatisfied often view the pressure to be successful law students as a hindrance and eventually resist and rebel against such responsibility. Carrington implies, "At base, dissatisfied students seem to be resisting the pressure that they feel is placed on them to measure up to some abstract standard of performance in law school. We also found a significant tendency for dissatisfaction to fade over time, and by doing so the third-year students appear to be distinctly less dissatisfied than first-year students" (1977, p.894). Also a huge encounter in this reading was that Carrington mentioned, "It appears that dissatisfied students are more likely to consume larger amounts of mind-altering substances" (1977, p. 895).

Anxiety

We found that studies found anxiety among female law students to be higher than male law students (1978, p.60). To summarize how anxiety is connected with law students, Carrington says, "While law students appear to have somewhat elevated anxiety prior to law school, levels are even higher among samples of law students in school. Across studies and measurement instruments, law students almost always reported higher levels of anxiety than comparison groups, including medical students" (1978, p.63).

Depression

Carrington's study shows that there is no difference in depression among female and male law students, but that third-year law students reported more depression than first-year law students (1978, p.65). Carrington concludes depression data among law students as a replication to the anxiety data that was gathered. He stated that the results suggest that self-reports of depression by the law students tend to be higher than the comparison groups and even medical students (1978, p.67).

The Religiosity and Spirituality of College Students

Multiple works were found that described the degree of religiosity and spirituality of graduate and undergraduate students. One study carried out by Hunsberger in the late 1970s attempted to determine if the frequently reported liberalization trend in college was true (1978, p. 159). The only finding that the study could statistically support was that seniors attended church less frequently than freshmen (Hunsberger, 1978, p.163). A more recent article by Lindholm addressed the notion that religiosity's decline during the undergraduate years has been well-documented empirically (2006, p. 513). However, spiritual growth has been found by some to increase for traditionally-aged college students (Lindholm, 2006, p. 513). In a study specifically done on graduate students, it was believed that church attendance during graduate years would follow a "U" curve (Greeley, p. 36). In a paper written by Cook, the perceived differences in the definitions of religiosity and spirituality were studied. The researchers believed that it was important to understand what college students meant when speaking of these terms (Cook, 2000, p. 136).

The Researched Effects of Introspection on Identity, Morals, and Values

Many authors have supported the study of religious beliefs and how they affect students. Others have concentrated more on how looking introspectively and contemplating existence would impact students. One study by Greeley examined the effects of students' religiosity on academics (p. 35). The study did not find evidence to support a conflict between the students' beliefs in science and religion (Greeley, p. 36). They also did not find evidence of emotional strain on students who proclaimed religious beliefs (Greeley, p. 38). Lindholm noted a study that supported the idea that "the intensity with which individuals pursue answers to existential questions could be directly linked to overall mental and emotional health" (2006, p. 512). This existential pursuit was defined as a spiritual quest in searching for acceptance or rejection of religion (Lindholm, 2006, p. 512). It is also stated that how serious these students view their spiritual quest affects positive identity development (Lindholm, 2006, p. 513). Additionally, research has shown that:

> *Developing people's abilities to access, nurture, and give expression to the spiritual dimension of their lives impacts how they engage with the world and fosters within them a more meaningful sense of connectedness that promotes*

altruism, social justice, and individual passion (Lindholm, 2006, p. 513).

References[*]

1. Type: Article Author: Newcomer, Mabel. Title: PROFESSIONALIZATION OF LEADERSHIP IN THE BIG BUSINESS CORPORATION. Citation: Business History Review 1955 29(1): 54-63. ISSN: 0007-6805

2. Database: CSA Sociological Abstracts Title: Does Acceptance of Corporate Wrongdoing Begin on the "Training Ground" of Professional Managers? Author: Yu, Olivia; Zhang, Lening Affiliation: Dept Criminal Justice, U Texas San Antonio Source: Journal of Criminal Justice, vol. 34, no. 2, pp. 185-194, Mar-Apr 2006 ISSN 0047-2352

3. Database CSA Sociological Abstracts Title: A Deservingness Approach to Respect as a Relationally Based Fairness Judgement Author: Heuer, Larry; Blumenthal, Eva; Douglas, Amber; Weinblatt, Tara Affiliation Dept Psychology, Barnard Coll, New York, NY Source: Personality and Social Psychology Bulletin, vol. 25, no. 10, pp. 1279-1292, Oct 1999 ISSN 0146-1672

4.PubMed ID: 17412022 Publication Type: Journal Article
Title: Costs of a medical education: comparison with graduate education in law and business. Author (s):Kerr, Jason R; Brown, Jeffrey J Source: J Am Coll Radiol 3 (2) : 122-30 2006 Feb

5.PubMed ID: 17552349 Publication Type: Journal Article Title: Overcome business culture barriers for successful working relationships. Author(s): Wagner, Jeff Source: Mater Manag Health Care 16 (5) : 48 2007 May Language: English Address: MidMichigan Health, Midland, MI, USA. Citation Subset Health Administration ISSN: 1059-4531 NLM Unique ID:9304859 Country: United States Date Created:07 Jun 2007

6.Title: ASSIMILATION, CHOICE, OR CONSTRAINT? TESTING THEORIES OF GENDER DIFFERENCES IN THE CAREERS OF LAWYERS. Author(s): Hull, K. E., Nelson, R. L. Source: Social Forces Year: 2000 Volume (Issue): 79(1) pp. 229-264

---

[*] *Editor's Note: This bibliography is not formatted properly according to the rules of the APA. Nevertheless, it has been included here for reference purposes.*

7. Hawkins, M. (2003). City Focus: Chicago - Cutting-Edge Hip to Blue Chip: From River North to West Loop, Chicago's lively scene keeps growing. *ARTnews. 102(4),* 74

S.Ryan, O. (2005). Chicago Makes a Contracts Killing - America's financial center of gravity shifts from Wall Street to the Loop. *Fortune International.* 752(9), 22.

9.Waxman, L. (2001). Chicago's West Loop Gate Galleries in Chicago are moving to the West loop, where real-estate ventures and new art lead the way. *New Art Examiner. 28,* 58-63.

10.ASSOCIATES IN THE TRENCHES - Recent law grad empowers Chicago high school students facing tough legal issues. (2007). *ABA Journal.* 93(4), 35.

11.Mullender, R. (2003). Tort, Human Rights, and Common Law Culture. *Oxford Journal of Legal Studies. 23(2),* 301-318.

12.Gonzales, A. R. (2006). Remarks at the University of Chicago Law School. *Chicago Journal of International Law.* 7(1), 289-302.

I3. Meltzer, B. D. (2003). CENTENNIAL TRIBUTE ESSAYS - The University of Chicago Law School: Ruminations and Reminiscences. *The University of Chicago Law Review.* 70(1), 233.

14. Fox, L. J. (2000). ARTICLES - Dan's World: A Free Enterprise Dream; An Ethics Nightmare - In the May 2000 issue of this Journal, Daniel R Fischel, Dean of the University of Chicago School of Law, argued in favor of allowing lawyers to engage in the practice of law while combining and sharing profits with non-lawyers, commonly known as multidisciplinary practice. This issue - Perhaps the most important facing the legal professional in the last century — Continues to be a subject of much debate in the American Bar Association, American law schools, and law firms across the country. Currently, Rule 5.4 of the Model Rules Professional Conduct, adopted by every state, prohibits lawyers from forming multi-disciplinary practice firms (MDPs). In this article responding to Dean Fischel's arguments, Lawrence J Fox sets out his opposition to MDPs. *The Business Lawyer : a Bulletin of the Section on Corporation, Banking, and Mercantile Law, American Bar Association.* 55(4), 1533.

15. Carrington, P. D. (1994). The Missionary Diocese of Chicago. *Journal of Legal Education. 44(4),* 467-518.

16. Keller, E. A. (1953). *Christianity and American capitalism.* Chicago: Published for the Council of Business and Professional Men of the Catholic Faith by the Heritage Foundation

17. T.Rose JS. (2002). Beauty and business: commerce, gender, and culture in modern America. [Review of: Scranton, P., ed. Beauty and business: commerce, gender, and culture in modern America. New York: Routledge, 2000]. *Business History Review. 76(2),* 393-5.

18. Schleef, D. (2000). "That's a Good Question!" Exploring Motivations for Law and Business School Choice. *Sociology of Education.* 73(3), 155-74.

19. Heyman, G. M. (2002). The Harvard Pigeon Lab, 1970-1998: Graduate students and matching law research. *Journal of the Experimental Analysis of Behavior.* 77(3), 380.

20. Oddi LF. (1988). Comparison of self-directed learning scores among graduate students in nursing, adult education, and law. *Journal of Continuing Education in Nursing. 19(4),* 178-81.

21. Heins M, Fahey SN, & Leiden LI. (1984). Perceived stress in medical, law, and graduate students. *Journal of Medical Education. 59(3),* 169-79.

22. Helmers KF, Danoff D, Steinert Y, Leyton M, & Young SN. (1997). Stress and depressed mood in medical students, law students, and graduate students at McGill University. *Academic Medicine : Journal of the Association of American Medical Colleges.* 72(8), 708-14.

23. Kellner R, Wiggins RJ, & Pathak D. (1986). Distress in medical and law students. *Comprehensive Psychiatry.* 27(3), 220-3.

24. Pritchard ME, & McIntosh DN. (2003). What predicts adjustment among law students? A longitudinal panel study. *The Journal of Social Psychology. 143(6),* 727-45.

25. Murphy, E. F. (1980). Mentoring Graduate Law Students in American Legal History: Some Work of Willard Hurst. *Wisconsin Law Review. 1980(6),* 1105-19.

26. Clancy J, Brodland G, & Fahr S. (1972). A psychiatric clerkship for law students. *The American Journal of Psychiatry.* 729(3), 322-6.

27. The Unsimple Life - Grad students blog about what it's really like to examine a breast, study law, or student teach. How useful are their musings? (2006). *U.S. News & World Report.* 740(13), 48.

28. Law Beat - Law students learn real life. (2000). *ABA Journal. 86, 22.*

29. Brennan, P. M. (2002). To Beginning Law Students. *First Things : a Monthly Journal of Religion and Public Life.* (128), 19-20.

30. Manderson, D., & Turner, S. (2006). Coffee House: Habitus and Performance Among Law Students. *Law & Social Inquiry.* 57(3), 649-676.

31. Religion, scholarship, & higher education: perspectives, models, and future prospects: essays from the Lilly Seminar on Religion and Higher Education By: Sterk, Andrea (Editor). Notre Dame, Ind. : University of Notre Dame Press, 2002. Publication Type: Book
http://search.ebscohost.com/login.aspx?direct=true&db=rfh&AN=ATLA0001335990&site=ehost-live

32. A research note on religiosity as opiate or prophetic stimulant among students in England and the United States. By: Perkins, H Wesley. Source: Review of Religious Research, 26 no 3 Mr 1985, p 269-280. Publication Type: Article PDF Full Text

33. Measuring religiosity by direct and indirect methods : a multiple replication. By: Nudelman, Arthur E.. Source: Review of Religious Research, 17 Wint 1976, p 102-106. Publication Type: Article PDF Full Text

34. Lindholm. J.A.. Goldberg. R.. & Calderone. S. (2006). The Spiritual Questing of Professional Career Aspirants. Seattle Journal for Social Justice, 4(2), pg. 509-560.

35. College Students' Perceptions of Spiritual People and Religious People. By: Cook, Stephen W.; Borman, Patricia P.; Moore, Martha A.; Kunkel, Mark A.. Source: Journal of Psychology & Theology, 28 no 2 Sum 2000. p 125-137. Publication Type: Article HTML Full Text PDF Full Text

36. Religiosity of college students : stability and change over years at university. By: Hunsberger, Bruce. Source: Journal for the Scientific Study of Religion, 17 no 2 Je 1978, p 159-164. Publication Type: Article
Full Text From ATLA: Click here for ATLA Serials electronic resource PDF Full Text

37. Religious experience amongst a group of post-graduate students : a qualitative study. By: Hay. David. Source: Journal for the Scientific Study of Religion, 18 Je 1979, p 164-182. Publication Type: Article

38. Religious behavior of graduate students. By: Greeley, Andrew M.. Source: Journal for the Scientific
Study of Religion, 5 Fall 1965. p 34-40. Publication Type: Article
Full Text From ATLA: Click here for ATLA Serials electronic resource

39. Research on Law Students: An Annotated Bibliography Kenneth H. Barry; Patricia A. Connelly American Bar Foundation Research Journal > Vol. 3, No. 4 (Autumn, 1978), pp. 751-804 Stable URL: http://links.istor.org/sici?sici=0361-9486%28197823%293%3A4%3C751%3AROLSAA%3E2.Q.CO%3B2-8

40. The Alienation of Law Students Paul D. Carrington; James J. Conley Michigan Law Review > Vol. 75, No. 5/6. Faculty Essays in Honor of the 75th Anniversary of the "Michigan Law Review" (Apr., 1977), pp. 887-899 Stable URL: http://links.jstor.org/sici?sici=0026-2234%28197704%2F05%2975%3A5%2F6%3C887%3 ATAOLS%3E2.0.CO%3B2-C

41. Anxiety and Depression among Law Students: Current Knowledge and Future Directions
Matthew M. Dammeyer; Narina Nunez Law and Human Behavior > Vol. 23, No. 1, The First 20 Years of Law and Human Behavior (Feb., 1999), pp. 55-73 Stable URL: http://links.istor.org/sici?sici=0147-7307%28199902%2923%3A1%3C55%3AAADALS%3E2.0.CO%3B2-V

42. Negative Attitudes of Law Students: A Replication of the Alienation and Dissatisfaction Factors
Paul D. Carrington; James J. Conley Michigan Law Review > Vol. 76. No. 6 (May, 1978), pp. 1036-1043
Stable URL: http://links.istor.org/sici?sici=0026-2234%28197805%2976%3A6%3C1036%3ANAOLSA%3E2.0.CO%3B2-K

Interview 1
Who: Post Grad Student studying for the bar
Date: July, 9th 2007
Location: Chicago Kent College of Law

Sean: Ok, um and what grad school did you go to?

Guy: I went to St. Thomas University in Miami, Florida.

Sean: And you said you are from here?

Guy: Yes, I am originally from the area.

Sean: Alright um, the first section is going to be about motivations. Like what was your motivation to pursue law?

Guy: Um I just felt like continuing my education would help further my career. I felt like undergraduate school wasn't enough really to get ahead. It's just status quo now.

Sean: Um were you satisfied with law school? Is it what you thought it would be?

Guy: Uh it's not what I thought it would be. Um it's a lot different from undergraduate; it is a completely different process of learning. Uh I learned a lot but um you know, I was happy with school I guess.

Sean: What are some of your main goals in your life? That's kind of a broad question.

Guy: [Laughing] I don't know. Uh normal stuff: have a family, good career, wife, kids, things like that.

Sean: Uh who has been a major influence in your life and why? Like family or some role model?

Guy: Um probably my grandfather. He was just always just a hard worker and he never really got to get an education but he always made sure his kids and grandkids knew the value of an education. And made a, strive to do whatever we could do, as far as we could go in education, so.

Sean: Um what is, like, being successful to you?

Guy: Um, you know I don't think it's money or anything like that. I think successful is actually waking up and not doing a job but having an occupation that you enjoy that makes you happy and then being able to also have time with your family.

Sean: Um, what is your living situation? Like do you commute?

Guy: Yeah, right now since I moved from Miami kind of abruptly, um I didn't have time to look for a place, so I am commuting from my parent's home actually right now.

Sean: So, you are looking for a job here in Chicago.

Guy: Yeah.

Sean: The next section would be, have you had any type of financial struggles to be here in law school?

Guy: I am sorry what, oh yeah. Uh I mean you know tuition and living expenses are supposed to be covered by students' loans but they really undervalue how much your living expenses are. So loans definitely aren't enough to like barely make it. So you have to do stuff to subsidize, you know, what you live off. So for me it was having to work through law school which isn't necessarily easy, trying to balance and studies and working. You can only work part time.

Sean: Alright um, have you had any struggles with leaving family and friends back at home like when you went off to school?

Guy: Yeah, you know I moved to Miami to go to school and that was the only reason why I went there and I didn't know anybody so I left all my family and friends behind. But I sort of did that on purpose because I knew law school was going to be hard for me because I am not a good reader. I am not like an English, and I was never good at that stuff. I was good at math so I knew I would have to focus and living in Miami, I didn't have any family commitments on the weekends or at night or I didn't have friends calling me. All my friends were in law school so we were on the same schedule. So I sort of intentionally left them behind. Although I miss them it was easier to focus that way.

Sean: Uh, do you feel like there are high expectations placed on you by family, friends, or society?

Guy: Uh yeah I guess now that I finished law school. I have to, you know, make something of myself. You know?

Sean: Um, do you feel there is a stereotype for lawyers? Like what would it be? And have you experienced that yourself?

Guy: Uh yeah I guess there is definitely a stereotype. And it's, I don't know, being a jerk, um being very, I don't know how to put it eloquently but, picky, like um very detail oriented. I mean, I don't know if I've so much experienced those stereotypes because right now all I do is hang around other people that are either in law school or attorneys. I guess when I would work part time dealing with clients, yeah they always think, you know, you're charging too much or, you know, they would always like free services. And so I guess you have a stereotype of being expensive and that you can just fix everything too for them.

Sean: Ok only a few more questions on the back, which are Christian related.

Guy: Alright.

Sean: Um, do you have any religious or spiritual beliefs or practices?

Guy: I am Catholic.

Sean: How do your religious beliefs interact with the things you learn in law school? Like your decision making. Do they mesh together or collide?

Guy: You know it's, I don't know, uh I really, you know, there is not really many cases on religion specifically. I mean the constitutional law, yes they touch on it a bit. Otherwise it's two separate issues. And I've never been interested in dealing with anything with morals as far as law goes. I would rather do business transactions.

Sean: What ways do your beliefs play out in your life? Like church involvement, prayer or reading the Bible. Is it like a routine?

Guy: Uh I mean, what it plays in my life. Yeah I go to church. Um I try and you know live like I am supposed to according to the Bible.

Sean: Has anybody like, well let's see I think that's about it. Have you ever believed in anything else? Or have you always been a Catholic?

Guy: I've always been Catholic.

Sean: Well that's it, man.

Interview 2
Who: 28 year old Post Grad Student Studying for the bar
Date: July, 10th 2007
Location: Chicago Kent College of Law

Sean: Ok, um first part will be about motivations. What was your motivation to pursue law?

Guy: Honestly, I wanted to be a lawyer since I was little. Uh I just always like to argue my side of the story and just kind of get in it with people.

Sean: Um, were you satisfied with law school? Is it what you thought it would be?

Guy: Yeah it was. As far as being satisfied goes, it could have been done in two years instead of three.

Sean: Um. What are some of your main goals for your life?

Guy: Uh well main goals for my life. I have kind of accomplished most of them. Um, that was getting through law school, which I have done. I guess now I got to pass the bar. I mean these are very near term. Uh you know I got a wife that I love, so now I'm just trying to go to work and figure out what the next step is.

Sean: Do you see yourself continuing doing your work here in Chicago?

Guy: Yeah I'll be working in Chicago for at least the next 4 or 5 years.

Sean: So who has been a major influence in your life and why?

Guy: Uh, well I guess I would have to say my parents, um, just because they raised me and they taught me everything about living life.

Sean: What is your living situation?

Guy: I live three miles north of the city. Most days I take the "L" downtown. Sometimes I drive.

Sean: Have you had any type of financial struggles while you were in law school?

Guy: Uh not too bad, I mean not more than most students. I'm kind of in a unique situation where I've run my own business as a computer consultant for the past 7 or 8 years. So yeah I did that through college and all through law school, so it kept me, uh it kept me a little bit better off than some.

Sean: Do you feel, like was any high expectations placed on you by family, friends, and society?

Guy: Yeah I would say so. I mean I was always kind of above average intellectually. So you know, I come from relatively blue collar background. So with my parents it was always, not just *my* parents, just everyone around me -- so I was expected that I would end up being in college and then going on and just doing more than just a 9 to 5 job kind of thing.

Sean: Do you feel there is a stereotype for lawyers, and what would it be? And have you had any experience with that?

Guy: Uh yeah, I mean a lot of people misunderstand exactly how differentiated the legal profession can be. So there is some people who just think, you know, everybody out there is a litigator or everybody is an ambulance chaser or something like that. So I think there are a lot of stereotypes from people outside the profession and even, I would say, inside the profession. There are some stereotypes in that lawyers tend to see one another in terms of, I don't know-- sometimes big law lawyers like all be sometimes look at each other as we are all a bunch of greedy F****.

Sean: Do you have any religious or spiritual beliefs or practices?

Guy: Yeah I am non-denominational Christian.

Sean: How do your religious beliefs interact with the things you have learned in law schools?

Guy: Well, you know, growing up and going to church you kind of see and hear only one side of a lot of stories. Being in law school, especially in a very liberal law school and a very liberal city, I am thrown in an environment where now you're hearing only the other side of the argument. And it's kind of, it's given me some perspective in the sense of now when I go back and I hear some of the one sidedness that you get from the church, kind of turned off by that and I am like why aren't we discussing that there is a whole other side of this issue. So I think it has broadened but I think it's also made my faith deeper because it's made me have to think about it a lot more and really figure out, ok how much of this is coming from what I know of God and Jesus versus um, you know, some conservative pastor who has his own political views and possibly his own agenda.

Sean: In what ways do your beliefs play out in your life like church involvement, prayer, reading the Bible?

Guy: Well being in law school you don't have a whole lot of free time but you, I've tried to find -- I had a real good church before I moved out here. I'm from OC, California and I was really plugged in all through college and then when I got out here, I haven't found a church I really like. But they still, I would say, factor in to my home life just in the way I, that I try to behave as a husband and try to run my house and interact with my wife. Things like that.

Sean: Um, well I think that's about it.

Guy: Cool.

Interview 3
Who: Current Grad Student Male
Date: July, 10th 2007
Location: Chicago Kent College of Law

Sean: Um what was your motivation to pursue law?

Guy: Um I'm an engineering undergrad. I came to law school to go to patent law. Basically I'm not hardcore, and I am not that in depth interested with engineering. So patent law is middle of the road.

Sean: Have you been satisfied with law school so far? And is it what you thought it was going to be?

Guy: Umm not really satisfied. Like grading is kind of ridiculous, kind of arbitrary. Um I don't know, you can know a lot about a class and just not do good on the final because the final doesn't really test knowledge. It is for test taking skills.

Sean: What are some of your main goals after graduating?

Guy: Um just a job in patent law and live here or the west coast.

Sean: Who has been a major influence in your life and why?

Guy: I would say most of my peers. I mean that's where I learned the most from probably. Uh my parents, but I was really independent from my parents.

Sean: So most of your friends?

Guy: Older peers maybe.

Sean: What does being successful mean to you?

Guy: Having close friends and being financially secure.

Sean: What is your living situation? How do you commute? Do you live downtown?

Guy: Yeah I commute. Um I'm about 25 minutes north of downtown.

Sean: Do you take the "L"?

Guy: No I take the bus.

Sean: Um, so how do you feel about going to school in the Loop?

Guy: It's alright. It's hard to get to the library sometimes. Um accessibility is always a problem, you know, busy place. The hustle of the city is kind of nice sometimes.

Sean: Have you had any type of financial struggles to be here in law school?

Guy: Yeah it's real expensive. I'm like 40 K in debt right now from one year.

Sean: Have you had any struggles leaving friends and family to go to school?

Guy: Not so much. I'm from the suburbs so. And I went to U of I downstate so I'm not that far from family or friends.

Sean: Do you feel like there are high expectations placed on you by family, friends, or society?

Guy: Yeah of course. I've always done well in school, so I guess my family and friends expect to continue that and I feel like that's kind of a burden on me.

Sean: Do you feel like there is a stereotype for lawyers?

Guy: Not as much as people say there is. I mean there is in general, but people -- like if you say you know a lawyer then, like, most of the time the person, they accept them and they approve of the way the person conducts themselves.

Sean: I have heard a lot of people say ambulance chasers.

Guy: Yeah that's like the perception. But when you ask individual people, they will say they know a couple of lawyers and they aren't bad people most of the time.

Sean: Do you have any religious or spiritual beliefs or practices?

Guy: I grew up Christian and I strayed from it. Um engineering and sciences and seeing how things work like physics and like all the stuff.

Sean: What denomination? Protestant? Baptist?

Guy: It was Protestant.

Sean: Do you say you're a Christian now?

Guy: No I'm not a Christian now.

Sean: Have you had a memorable experience with a Christian, good or bad?

Guy: Not really good or bad. It's kind of been the middle of the road. I guess one of my friends started dating a guy that was really into religion and stuff. She completely changed and kind of judgmental. I mean, like, she got extreme so fast but she kind of backed off that and became more accepting of other people.

Sean: Do you perceive Christians to have anything that you want in your life? If so what?

Guy: Always good family values. Yeah I mean the, just the values I guess.

Sean: Yeah well that's about it.

Interview 4
Who: Current Grad Student Female
Date: July, 11th 2007
Location: Chicago Kent College of Law

Sean: So what was your motivation to pursue law?

Girl: That's a really hard question. Ha ha, um well, I was a political science major in undergrad. So I studied government a lot, and I was pretty interested in maybe doing something with political office or politics and so I kind of always had that in the background. But then I did a year of Americorps service and I worked with children and youth and I worked in a pretty low income community and I decided what I wanted to do in law was to represent people who don't have the same access of representation.

Sean: Are you satisfied with law school so far?

Girl: I am. I guess it's as horrible as I thought it would be.

Sean: So when you graduate, what are some of the main goals you have?

Girl: I would like to work with legal aid.

Sean: So who has been a major influence in your life and why?

Girl: My entire life -- this semester sadly, no -- but in my life my parents are really supportive of me and everything I do.

Sean: What is your living situation?

Girl: I take the "L."

Sean: How do you feel, like, going to school in the Loop?

Girl: It's ok. It's not a great atmosphere because you're looking at buildings all day long and it's just not pretty or whatever.

Sean: Have you had any type of financial struggles to be in law school?

Girl: Yes, I have tons of loans and it's really daunting to think about what I'm going to do after law school, how I'm going to pay for that.

Sean: Do you feel like there are any high expectations placed on you by family, friends, or society in itself?

Girl: I guess. But nothing, I mean, my friends and family are proud of me no matter what I do.

Sean: Do you feel like there is a stereotype for lawyers? If so have you experienced that?

Girl: A little bit, but none that seems to be undeserving.

Sean: Some things I have heard were ambulance-chasers.

Girl: But I mean some lawyers are like that and so I guess people like us are trying to break those stereotypes.

Sean: Do you have any religious or spiritual beliefs or practices?

Girl: Not really right now.

Sean: Have you ever had a memorable experience with Christians, either good or bad?

Girl: Um I mean, I definitely have friends who are religious but no bad experiences.

Sean: Have you ever been to a Christian church?

Girl: Yes.

Sean: How was it?

Girl: Good. I grew up going to church.

Sean: Do you perceive Christians to have anything that you want in your life?

Girl: I guess I really don't know.

Interview 5
Who: Current Grad Student from DePaul
Date: July, 13th 2007
Location: DePaul Center Barnes and Noble Cafe

Felicia(F): Where did you go for undergrad?

Eryk: University of Michigan.

F: And you just finished your first year?

Eryk: Of law school, yeah.

F: When is your projected graduation date?

Eryk: 2009.

F: So what was your motivation to pursue law?

Eryk: Uh, I don't, there all trusty per se. Originally in high school I really didn't want to go to law school. It was like the last thing on my mind. And then in college I started out as an econ major and then the Michigan business is like really cut throat and I really hated it. So I switched majors to history. As a history major you're looking at future, past. There weren't too many opportunities available to me other than like teaching and stuff like that. And I was always interested in law so I said, why not go to law school. So it's more like a whim actually.

F: So far are you satisfied with law school?

Eryk: *Definitely it's tough you know. But in undergrad I was very lazy and pretty social, party guy. And in law school the work is harder. I actually enjoy it. It's uh not like boring, like you actually like reading what you're reading.*

F: Is it what you thought it would be?

Eryk: *Pretty much as I thought it would be. Yeah now everyone gives you the horror stories about how hard it's going to be and I thought it was a lot easier than from what other people painted a picture of. But it's pretty much what I expected.*

F: What are some main goals for your life?

Eryk: *I'm still young. Cliché such as being healthy and all that stuff is one of them. I know a buddy and I want to open up our own record company but yeah that's a little tough. I want to play Ticketmaster too. That's a big goal of mine. You ever buy tickets through Ticketmaster?*

F: No.

Eryk: *You buy like a ticket to a 30 dollar show and it's the only way you can get the ticket if you don't actually go to the venue. And they are going to charge you about 13 dollars in service charges so that's like, 33 percent of the price is in service charges. And then I, like, bought tickets to Rage Against the Machine -- they are playing in Wisconsin -- so the ticket was expensive, like 59 dollars. And I bought 3 of them, for my friends, and the final total came out to 230 dollars for 3 tickets. And I want to set up a service. There has to be anti-trust issues first of all because you can only get them through Ticketmaste, like only certain things. Once I get the service that only charges 10 percent of the ticket price as service charges. There has to be a way. They are making profit hand over foot probably.*

F: Where would you see yourself 5 years after graduating?

Eryk: Probably hopefully being a partner at a law firm, like an IP law firm, or playing poker. One or the other.

F: What kind of law are you interested in?

Eryk: Probably intellectual property or corporate law or corporate IP. The problem with intellectual property law is that I don't have a technical background. So I can't do patent law, because you need a technical background. But it's such a growing field you know. Like actual PI is fine but intellectual property law is one of the higher job markets too.

F: Who has been a major influence in your life and why?

Eryk: Everyone influences me in different ways, but major influences -- I am pretty much a, uh, I am not a loner. I am very outgoing but I am a loner in, like, I don't follow. I am a leader where I just go my own way. I mean your parents are a major influence in everybody's life whether good or bad. I am the first person in my family to go to college, let alone go to law school. So ah, I mean, they were great. They paid for my undergrad when they probably couldn't afford it. Michigan is the most expensive public university in the country. So ah they really tried hard to set a good path for me. I hope I could be like that someday. They used to be strict in high school, but after college they were really laid back.

F: What does being successful mean to you?

Eryk: It's not fortune or fame, although it is part of it. It has to be, not really. Just being respected I think, being honest in what you do and helping others whether you make a ton of money doing it or not. And that's material things and success isn't based on materials things. So uh, so basically help when you can, the cliché.

F: Are you trying to achieve that success?

Eryk: Right now I believe I'm on a path towards it. It's hard to see it. I would like to answer that question 10 years from now and look back. I do a lot of activities and I'm obviously in school so I do as much as I can -- I'm not going to say all that I can -- but as much as I can to be on that path.

F: Would you say you've somehow achieved success so far?

Eryk: Sure, I mean like I said, I am the only person in my family to attend college. s I used to volunteer with kids, basketball, coach, stuff like that. I mean, you know, success is relative and personally I don't think I am quote-endquote successful but I am also not unsuccessful, you know?

F: What is your living situation?

Eryk: Well I live with my parents still to save money. So I live out by O'Hare Airport so I have like an hour commute to school each day. It's kind of rough but. It is kind of weird because I really can't hang out with my law school friends as much during the year because a lot of them live around here.

F: How has it been going to the school in the Loop?

Eryk: I really don't see it that way. And I see it as going to school as a 9 to 5 almost and the location really does that. I really don't stand back and look around and say, "Wow I'm in the Loop." It's just another day in the office.

F: Have you had any type of financial struggles to be here in law school?

Eryk: I have a lot of loans right now. Until they come crawling out. Right now I try not to take out too much money. Right now there aren't any financial struggles but there will be probably.

F: I remember you saying you didn't work this past year. Do you plan on working?

Eryk: During law school?

F: Yeah.

Eryk: I was already offered a job with the admissions office for the school year, but if I can get a job with a law firm I'll take it.

F: Get more experience that way?

Eryk: Yeah more experience, in network, money, all the above.

F: Have you had any struggles with leaving family and friends back home?

Eryk: Well yeah, I did that for undergrad. I only called my parents once a week.

F: My parents usually if I don't call them once a week, they are calling me.

Eryk: I told my parents straight up, you know, "I am going away and if anything happens I'll call. If not I'll call once a week."

F: Do you feel like there is high expectation put upon you by friends, family, or society?

Eryk: Wow, family, friends. Growing up when I was younger I went to a gifted school. I had a high IQ and my parents thought, well whatever. But when I was in college, like I said, I partied a lot. A lot of the times I felt bad about it, you know. My parents sent me here even though I got good grades, but uh, like, all my friends from the neighborhood are blue collar type. Like I am a pretty laidback person, like I said, so I don't really look at expectations as laying down on me. In college I had a month period where I was like ah, you know, but now, like, I am -- whatever happens, happens.

F: So how does this affect your decision making, because of expectations from family or friends?

Eryk: You know, not much personally. Like sometimes instead of going out I'll stay home and study but that's not expectation from others. That's for my own personal benefit.

F: Do you feel like there is a stereotype for lawyers and what would that be?

Eryk: Yeah, there is. I mean everyone expects a stuffy person; it's like a stereotype with athletes as well in high school. I was a three sport athlete so I was one of the top students in the class. Everyone equates jocks with being dumb. In law school I would think you would have the nerdy type kids but that's far from the truth. I mean it's very diverse. You have people play in operas and people in rock and roll bands. I mean it's really interesting. So I had stereotypes about law school also. You got the guy with the glasses, chubby and bald – it's not like that.

F: Are they different since you have been in law school?

Eryk: Yeah for sure. Like a lot of lawyers are outgoing people. They are determined obviously but they're not just stuffy, like sit in front of a computer all day or reading a book all day. That kind of opened my eyes. I'm happy about that also.

F: Do you have any religious or spiritual beliefs or practices?

Eryk: I'm Catholic. I come from a Catholic family, used to live with my grandma, I used to go to church every week. I did the required religious classes. I'm not believing in God but I'm not deeply Catholic. I don't go to church every week anymore. I do pray once in a while just to a higher being but not the Catholic God.

F: How do your beliefs interact with law school?

Eryk: I would say very minimally if at all. So yeah, they don't.

F: Since DePaul is Catholic, did that play in your decision on going there?

Eryk: No not at all. A lot of the kids that go here that I sought out don't even know they go to a Catholic university. A lot of professors are not Catholic. If you want to pursue, like, spirituality within law school context, those avenues are open. But I honestly, it didn't affect me any way.

F: How have your beliefs changed since you have been in Law School?

Eryk: They probably haven't.

F: That's ok. There is no wrong answer. I think that's pretty much it.

Interview 6
Who: Post Grad Student studying for the bar
Date: July, 6th 2007
Location: In front of John Marshall Law School

S: What was your motivation to pursue law?

Guy: I was a finance major as an undergrad. It was kind of just always my plan, I think, to go on to law school to get a professional degree.

S: Were you satisfied with law school? Is it what you thought it would be?

Guy: Yeah it was a lot of work. I don't think I was able to anticipate the amount of time it would take, but uh -- day to day type of activities -- but yeah, it was a good experience.

S: What are some of the main goals in your life now since you have graduated, and have you achieved any of those?

Guy: Right now I just want to pass the bar. I need to find a full time job. Right now I'm clerking at an office and uh I am just looking for a house and stuff like that.

S: Who has been a major influence in your life and why?

Guy: Both of my parents, hardworking people, didn't come from much a background with school, or kind of professional lives, and built quite a bit for themselves.

S: What does being successful mean to you?

Guy: Success, you know I, it's such a broad question. For me personally, achieving a level of respect among your peers is an important thing.

S: What is your living situation? Like, do you commute?

Guy: Yeah I live in Lincoln Park. I have a roommate, a friend from college, and we just rent. I take the train.

S: When you went to school here in the Loop -- how was that experience?

Guy: I like it. Its, I mean, sometimes it kind of wears on you. The city life, it was good. Um I mean, you have to take in account every day you have a bit of a commute and it's kind of an adjustment but the Loop is great. I like it a lot.

S: Have you had any type of financial struggles to be here in law school?

Guy: It's a continual financial struggle. It's overwhelming -- the amount of debt you incur.

S: Do you feel like there are high expectations placed on you by family, friends, or society?

Guy: I think everyone has their own expectations -- what it is to be a lawyer, what kind of lawyer they think you should be. And how easily that's achieved is another story. What your idea is when you go into law school may change as you progress through, in what kind of law you want to practice, what your proclivities are.

S: Do you feel there is a stereotype for lawyers? What would it be? And have you experienced it?

Guy: Sure. I think some lawyers -- most of lawyers -- have a stereotype of being money hungry, you know, type of ambulance chasers. But I mean it's necessary, ah profession and society. They do a lot of good too.

S: Have you experienced that at all?

Guy: You know, only in jest. Nothing really, like, sincere.

S: Do you have any religious or spiritual beliefs or practices?

Guy: Yeah, I am raised Lutheran actually and went to private grade school.

S: How do your spiritual beliefs interact with law school?

Guy: Not really. I mean, law school, especially nowadays, ethics are a big part of law school. It's not much that would interfere with your religious beliefs. I can't think of a specific time at all that would interfere with your beliefs, aside from people like to party a lot, blow off steam, and I guess it depends what kind of background you come from in that respect.

S: In what way do your spiritual beliefs play out in your life such as prayer, church, or reading the Bible?

Guy: Church I don't go to as much. It's kind of tough. I mean, I don't have a church up here. I am not from here. I haven't looked into it. I think I have a pretty open dialogue through prayer.

S: So where are you from?

Guy: Peoria. Two and a half hours south of Chicago.

Sean: So you never believed anything else? You have always been a Christian?

Guy: Nope. I have always been a Christian.

Interview 7
Who: Post Grad Student Studying for the Bar
Date: July, 6th 2007
Location: Chicago Kent Law School

S: What law grad school did you go to?

Neal: Chicago Kent.

S: Are you going to pursue your career in Chicago?

Neal: No, actually I got a job out in D.C.

S: What was your motivation to pursue law?

Neal: I think more than again as a career choice. Like my background was a technical background but I didn't want to just do technical. So law was a good blend: I could do technical, also like reading, writing. It was a good combination of areas.

S: Were you satisfied with law school? Was it what you thought it would be?

Neal: I would say so for the most part. No surprises.

S: What are some of the main goals in life?

Neal: I think long term -- make an impact. I think you want to try to make a positive impact overall and feel like you did something positive in your life.

S: Where do you see yourself after graduating?

Neal: Washington D.C.

S: Who has been a major influence in your life and why?

Neal: For the most part, parents. They have been with me, set a good example. Just really hard working and honest people.

S: What does being successful mean to you?

Neal: I think basically it's what you do for others. So, like, how wide does your influence spread, how many people you are affecting is how successful you are.

S: Would you say you have achieved that success so far?

Neal: It's too early. I think it will be something long term. Even, I think, when you're working it's going to be hard. Once maybe when you're set, you can do what you really want to do, maybe do other things. But the beginning, when you come out of school, you're just trying to pay off debts and get settled.

S: What was your living situation?

Neal: First year lived in Lincoln Park. Then I commuted from home to save money. I took the "L."

S: How did you feel about going to school in the Loop?

Neal: I don't feel like it's a campus, because it's just this building.

S: Have you had any type of financial struggles to be here in law school?

Neal: Taking a lot of debt. It's just me. I haven't had any financial support from my parents or anyone else. I've taken out a lot of loans so I feel the burden on paying them now.

S: Do you feel there is a high expectation placed on you by friends, family or society?

Neal: Um, I would say not really society. Mostly family, not really friends. But really just family.

S: What expectations and how does it affect you?

Neal: In my culture you are suppose to support your parents. In a sense it affects me that I know whatever I do, I am not just providing for myself but also for my parents. So, it decides what career I choose money-wise because I know what I do, I have to support my parents also. Like I couldn't say I want to just try art out because I need to support my parents.

S: Do you feel there is a stereotype for lawyers?

Neal: I think there is: money greedy. I think law is like any other profession -- you have a variety of people. Some are very selfless and some are doing pro bono and really they are in the same debt as me and they aren't getting paid much, but they are doing it because they want to. Then there are those who do it for the money. There is a wide range.

S: Do you have any religious or spiritual beliefs or practices? If so what are they?

Neal: I don't go to temple every Sunday. I go to special holiday. And I am northern Indian, B.A.P.S.

S: Have you had any memorable experiences with Christians, whether good or bad?

Neal: I guess the most people I meet would be Christians but they aren't strongly practicing as Christians ones I do. I generally have a positive experience and they're usually open-minded, caring, positive things. I have had a little negative, like the ones who don't practice it but preach it and are close-minded.

S: Have you ever been to a Christian church?

Neal: I have been to a couple. It was nice. I liked it, welcoming.

S: Have you ever believed anything else other than Hinduism?

Neal: No, been like that since I was little.

S: Do you perceive Christians to have anything in their life that you would like?

Neal: I think there is a strong sense of community which I think is really good especially here in the city.

Interview 8
Who: Male Post Grad Student Studying for the Bar
Date: July, 6th 2007
Location: Chicago Kent College of Law

Sean: What was your motivation to pursue law?

Guy: I wanted to be in a profession that was [unclear] but at the same time willing to help people and make a change in society.

Sean: Were you satisfied with law school? Is it what you thought it would be?

Guy: Yeah it was kind of what I thought it would be. I learned a lot. It dragged on after a period of time -- probably could have been a 2 year program out of the three. But I was satisfied.

Sean: What are some of the main goals for your life now that you graduated?

Guy: I mean to be successful, to enjoy the profession, to help my clients.

Sean: Who has been a major influence in your life and why?

Guy: My father. Always been an attorney, really motivated me to go to law school. He is very ambitious, hard worker, you know, stays on top of things.

Sean: What does being successful mean to you?

Guy: Enjoying what you do.

Sean: What's your living situation? Do you commute?

Guy: No, I live real close to school.

Sean: How do you feel about going to school in the Loop?

Guy: It's perfect because I live 6 blocks away. So it's convenient. It's in a good area. It's close to all the law offices.

Sean: Have you had any type of financial struggles to be here in law school?

Guy: No, my family has been very supportive. I did take out loans and they helped by paying for supplies and for a place to live.

Sean: Have you had any struggles leaving your family and friends back at home?

Guy: Yeah at first when I moved out here because I am from Michigan. I did find it difficult at first because my friends and girlfriend at the time were in Michigan and my family was all there. So it was a little of an adjustment.

Sean: Do you feel like there are any high expectations placed upon you by family, friends, or society?

Guy: Sure, I feel like my parents place high expectations for me to be successful and that's probably why I went into a career that I found was going to be rewarding. And then now that I am an attorney, people will have expectations of me to know a little about the, well, when it's not necessarily the case.

Sean: Do you feel there is a stereotype for lawyers? What would it be? Have you experienced it?

Guy: Depends for what type of law you do. I feel like there a stereotype for trial lawyers just to go after money but that's not always the case. So it kind of depends what type of law you do. If you do pro bono and public interest law you're helping people.

Sean: Do you have any religious or spiritual beliefs or practices?

Guy: Related to law or no?

Sean: Just personal.

Guy: Well I am Jewish, Jewish heritage. I am a practicing Jew but not very religious.

Sean: Do your religious beliefs interact with what you studied in law school?

Guy: Not really. They have been pretty exclusive.

Sean: In what ways do your beliefs play out in your life such as church, reading the Bible, or prayer?

Guy: Um, it's definitely not church involvement, or reading the Bible either. My religious practices consist of prayer on the high holy days, which for the Jewish religion are the main days of worship.

Sean: You were brought up in Jewish heritage?

Guy: Yes.

Sean: Have your beliefs changed since you have been to law school?

Guy: No. No effect.

Sean: Have you had any memorable experiences with Christians, good or bad?

Guy: Yeah, on a daily interaction, that are not of Jewish faith, that are Christian or Catholic or Protestant, whatever it be. And the way I see it, I don't really think of it as a, regard as to someone who is Jewish or not Jewish or Catholic, and I just interact with on a regular basis and hear what they have to say, whether it's religious or not.

Sean: Do you perceive Christians to have anything that you would want in your life?

Guy: No, I don't see it as a difference of religion.

Interview 9
Who: Grad Student at DePaul
Date: July 12th, 2007
Location: DePaul College of Law

Felicia (F): First of all, what undergrad school did you go to?

Kim: Villanova University.

F: What was your motivation to pursue law?

Kim: I was a history and political science undergrad and I took a year off from college and worked for a party planner, which is completely different from law school. But basically I came to law school because I wanted to do immigration law because I know friends who aren't from this country and saw what they were going through and, you know, that seemed like the avenue to do that, to help that situation. So that was initially the reason why to go to law school.

F: So while you were in undergrad, was that something you were thinking about?

Kim: I kind of toyed with the idea but I didn't think I wanted to go and I knew I didn't want to go straight after college. I thought I needed at least a year to think about and really be committed to the decision. It's a big commitment so I wanted to be 100% sure that is what I wanted to do.

F: So are you doing the full time three year program?

Kim: Yeah.

F: So far are you satisfied with law school?

Kim: Yeah I am. I like the school part about it, and I really like the professors, and I like the material. And the only part I really don't like is the competition, and it's just part of it really. Doesn't matter really where you go to school -- it's built into the nature of it.

F: Do you think that because it's law school or grad school?

Kim: I think because it's law school. Because you're graded on a curve so you're graded against your classmates which I have never had in undergrad or anywhere else. So that was a big adjustment to make.

F: So is it what you thought it would be?

Kim: Yes and no. I guess the academic part of it is what I thought it would be like. It's as difficult and challenging as I thought it would be. But I didn't think I would meet, like, I have met a lot of really neat people in law school, you know, a lot of really good friends that I really didn't expect. I expected more like a job.

F: Did that play a role in your choice of coming to this school?

Kim: It reminded me a lot of Villanova which is very much like that -- where you know it's not just you come to school and go home and there is two distinct lives. Like they intertwine a lot and there is a lot of people that watch out for each other, and they are nice people. The professors and the students, pretty much the whole atmosphere.

F: So where do you live?

Kim: I live in Lincoln Park.

F: So you commute?

Kim: Have I just taken the "L."

F: What are some of your main goals for your life?

Kim: Um well I would like to be independent and self sufficient on my own before, like, because I would like to have a family and stuff and I would like to know I have established myself before that. Which is another thing I like about this because I feel like it's my own path to do whatever I do and then whatever grows from that would be great. But I would like to stay in Chicago, and I don't know if I want to stay a lawyer as long, my whole life. I might want to go into teaching.

F: So you want to stick around the Chicago area?

Kim: Yes, I picked it here.

F: So who has been a major influence in your life?

Kim: My mom, probably for the same reason. Because I see her as a very independent person, and she is really smart and hasn't let anything get in the way of that in what she wanted to do. And she has always told my sister and I," You need to do what you want to do and do what it takes to get there and don't let things get in the way just because you want something else." I kind of see her as the one who has it all: she has a great job and a great education and she has a family and she seems to *balance and I envy her.*

F: Is that what you're striving for?

Kim: Yeah, the balance part is difficult. I don't know how she does it.

F: It's a learned experience.

Kim: She went to grad school while we were all still really young. And I mean, I am not married and don't have kids so I can't imagine doing that on top of grad school.

F: Are there many students that are doing grad school on top of having a family?

Kim: There is a good amount that are, not sure how many are in the full time, but mostly in the night program. But in our full time there is a lot of married students, I know that much. Without kids, newly married mostly.

F: What does being successful mean to you?

Kim: I think being successful means being happy with what you're doing as well as also doing it well. I don't think it's money. You see these people going into public interest law -- you really make no money. You could be making so much more money doing something else. The workload is just as difficult and the job is just as competitive so it's not money that gets them there. It's the drive that gets them there, how they feel at the end of the day and they feel this is where they want to be and I am doing what I want to be doing and I am good at it. I think that's being successful at your job.

F: Are you trying to achieve that definition of success?

Kim: I think so. I am trying. It's the first years so I really don't know exactly what I want to do, just feeling it out. So I see those people and it's, wow, those people and they must really love what they do and they don't get all the glory. I wasn't really aware before I came to law school how many are in the public sector.

F: So how are you trying to achieve that success?

Kim: Well I am in the Public Interest Law Association. It's more of a group that gives you a heads up on what's going on around and they give volunteer opportunities. Like there is a certain organization that needs legal help that will let law students help them. And that's actually good to get out there and see what you can do with what you're learning in class and make it a reality, not just an abstract thing.

F: Would you say you have achieved success so far?

Kim: I think I am on the way. I don't think I have achieved it, only been here one year. It's a very humbling experience, so you are here and, wow, as far as I have come, there is so much more to be done.

F: How do you feel about going to school in the Loop?

Kim: I love it down here. I like it because where I live in Lincoln Park is a lot of undergrads. I live by the DePaul undergrad campus. It's nice to be down here because there is a lot of young professionals everywhere and you're right by stock exchange and just looking around it reminds you of how many opportunities are here in Chicago.

F: How does the campus being in downtown feel?

Kim: It's very different than from where I went to college. My undergrad was a traditional campus, so this has been different since it's all in one building. I don't, I guess I just got used to it. I like being down here in the hustle and bustle of things. I don't think I would have liked it as an undergrad but being older it's better.

F: Have you had any type of financial struggles to be here in law school?

Kim: Financial struggles yes. Well basically everyone here is living on student loans. It's a big adjustment at least to me. I didn't have loans in undergrad so this is something new and learning how to budget your money and put it off until you can afford certain things because Chicago is an expensive place to live.

F: So you don't have a job right now. You didn't work this first year?

Kim: Yes, I am working this summer but during the first year no. They kind of discourage that. I have had friends who tried that.

[At this point the recorder ran out of tape. So I did the rest of the interview without recording.]

F: Have you had any struggles leaving family and friends to come to college here?

Kim: Not really with my family. Most of my family lives around the Chicago area. So, I just have to organize my time to see them.

F: Do you feel like you have any high expectations placed on you by family, friends, or society? And how have you dealt with them?

Kim: My family is happy that I got here and they just want the best for me. There is the expectation for me to prove the stereotype wrong. Expectations help me focus.

F: Do you feel that there is a stereotype for lawyers?

Kim: Yes, that they're wealthy and their personal view takes a back seat to what they're doing. It's not true and it mostly comes from the movies. Lawyers are very passionate about what they do. People just look at the face of things and not the elements of them.

F: Do you have any religious or spiritual beliefs or practices?

Kim: I was raised Catholic and went to a Catholic undergraduate college. Religion is more about the community. Now I don't go to church that often except to spend time with family and friends. It's time that is set aside for the family to get together.

F: How do your religious beliefs interact with studying law?

Kim: It gives me more of a social awareness and a greater public interest.

F: Did you choose to go to DePaul because it is a Catholic school?

Kim: Well I recognized some of the same Catholic school traits that I liked at Villanova. If someone hadn't been to a Catholic school before they may not notice that DePaul was a Catholic school.

F: Have your beliefs changed since you've been in law school?

Kim: It's made me more aware of the different problems facing people that I could help with, but my core beliefs have stayed the same.

Interview 10
Who: Female Post Grad Student from DePaul, first Interview
Date: July, 5th 2007
Location: In front of DePaul School of Law

Sean: What was your motivation to pursue law?

Girl: To be honest my motivation was: I was a political science major and I didn't know what to do after college. There wasn't a great motivation.

Sean: So are you satisfied with law school so far?

Girl: Yeah, I graduated. Does that matter?

Sean: No, that's fine. Was it what you thought it would be?

Girl: Yeah it's pretty much what everyone says it is.

Sean: What are some of your main goals in life?

Girl: Well I am going to be doing liberal litigation, after I pass the bar. I am working at a mid-size law firm.

Sean: Who has been a major influence in your life and why?

Girl: I had one writing professor that helped me get my job and he, like, helped me write a lot better once I got to law school. So I think he was a big impact on it.

Sean: What does being successful mean to you?

Girl: I think being successful has to do with liking what you're doing. I don't think that money is a big factor, but it definitely helps. But I think as long as you don't wake up dreading going to work is success.

Sean: Would you say that you have achieved this success?

Girl: I don't know yet. I guess I will find out when I start working. But I have worked at my firm during school and I like it so I think it will be good.

Sean: So what is your living situation?

Girl: I don't live in the Loop, I live in Bucktown. It's just west of the city and I take the "L."

Sean: How do you feel about going to school in the Loop?

Girl: It's interesting because my undergrad was in a rural, no big city around. I like being in the city because there is a lot going on.

Sean: Have you had any type of financial struggles to be here in law school?

Girl: Yeah well, I pretty much had to put myself through law school. My parents didn't help me out at all, so I was working the entire time I was in law school and I took out federal loans the whole time. So I am in debt now, but it makes me prouder to know I did it myself. I made it through.

Sean: Have you had any struggles with leaving family and friends back at home?

Girl: Yeah at first it was nice to be away from my family, but now I have been here for 4 years and I miss them. But I am only an hour flight away so I try to go see them.

Sean: Do you feel like there is an expectation placed upon you by friends, family, or society?

Girl: Yeah I think so. I don't think I knew how much responsibility is put upon the profession but it's kind of cool because you feel exclusive group.

Sean: Do you feel like there is a stereotype for lawyers? What would it be? And have you experienced any of that?

Girl: I think a lot of people think they are overpaid, and they are liars, and certain ambulance chaser thing too. But I think there are lawyers like that, but I think the majority of them are hard working and honest people and it's sad that some people that ruin it. I think for the most part.

Sean: Do you have any religious or spiritual beliefs or practices?

Girl: Well not so much since I have been here. But I grew up in a really religious, like my family is really religious. And I always went to Christian or Catholic schools growing up other than college. Um really don't practice anymore. I don't get to church often. I believe.

Sean: How do your religious beliefs interact with things you have learned in law school?

Girl: I don't know. I have never really thought about that. It never really affected me.

Sean: In what ways do your beliefs play out in your life such as church involvement, prayer, reading the Bible?

Girl: It's definitely less now, which it is bad. That's the way it goes. I am busy. I know that's a bad excuse, but I try to get to church as much as I can, but not close to what it should be.

Sean: Have your beliefs changed since you have been in law school?

Girl: I don't think my beliefs have been changed but the practices have.

Sean: Have you ever had another belief?

Girl: No my beliefs are the same. I think just from being in the city you encounter more people with a lot of different beliefs, so I, like, have had more discussion about more religions.

**Interview 11
Who: DePaul Grad student
Date: July, 5th 2007
Location: In Barnes and Noble Cafe**

Sean: What was your motivation to pursue law?

Guy: Social action, protect civil rights and the idealistic aspirations. Just to have an avenue towards social change, to be able to affect issues that are important to me, and I think too as a career path.

Sean: Are you satisfied with law school so far?

Guy: I don't think so. I am going into my third year, my last year. I have a lot more interests outside of law school, but the problem with the first year you don't have much time to study anything else, engage yourself with anything else, just overwhelmed with legal studies. So it's not satisfying in that sense because all the other interests are suppressed.

Sean: Is it what you thought it would be?

Guy: Hard to say because my expectations were a little foggy. But it's pretty similar to what I expected. The atmosphere at least at DePaul that surprised me, that most of the people aren't engaged politically, just see it a means to an end, just as a high paying job. So there's a real sense of disinterest in the issues I thought would be important to law students.

Sean: What are some main goals for your life?

Guy: Working, practicing law for at least a couple years after graduation -- maybe employment discrimination law or civil rights law, or government agency or an N.G.O, a non government organization. Or more hopefully becoming a writer and doing stuff that's not practicing law.

Sean: Do you see yourself here in Chicago?

Guy: No. My family is here but I will probably move to New England, or New York.

Sean: Who has been a major influence in your life and why?

Guy: Personal influence in my life -- two friends from college: one is an aspiring novelist and actor and he is pursuing a career in Los Angles, having some success and he is inspiring because he is always energetic. In terms of people I don't know personally is -- the Dalai Lama has had a big effect. I am not religious, but I went to everywhere he is: positive thought, kind of reconciling perspectives on philosophy and religion.

Sean: What does being successful mean to you?

Guy: It means to me being proud of what you're doing and helping people in a way that you feel best, and being happy with your situation in life, with the people you spend time with, achieving career goals.

Sean: Would you say you have achieved any success?

Guy: Some of it, success that we are talking about is long term. Yes successful in the sense that JD is a worthwhile pursuit if you have the time and willing to spend the time.

Sean: What is your living situation?

Guy: I live in the city, Lincoln Park. I take the bus.

Sean: How do you feel about going to school in the Loop?

Guy: It is a city environment. It doesn't feel like a college environment, and there are homeless people in the neighborhood. You are right in the heart of Chicago, so you get the rush of the city life. Then you have the law school that is one building.

Sean: Have you had any type of financial struggles to be here in law school?

Guy: I have not.

Sean: Have you had any struggles leaving family and friends back at home?

Guy: Uh, no. Well not family because they live right outside the city. I have had struggles leaving friends because I have friends scattered around the country because I went to a school in the south and they all spread out.

Sean: What school did you go to?

Guy: Emory in Atlanta.

Sean: Do you feel like there are high expectations placed upon you by family, friends or society?

Guy: Absolutely, yes I do. Of course from family in my case because my family is in the legal profession and they see it as a secure stable root to success, maybe not the way I see success, so I think they are very concerned. In fact I have talked to a lot of people and I have realized that my father has been grooming me to go to law school. But in our generation I believe parents groom their kids in a direction but never explicitly say exactly what the direction is.

Sean: Do you feel there is a stereotype for lawyers?

Guy: Yes, lawyers have a horrible reputation but maybe for a good reason in terms of, you know, being extensively, that they are abusing the system, and they are getting away 12 million dollars of coffee spilling on my lap. People see lawyers as taking advantage of this, think of it as blood suckers of the professional world. But of course stereotypes are true in many cases and it depends on how they are painted and it's really fun to make lawyer jokes. Before I went to law school, I was pursuing a career in writing. I was a critic, and it was a totally different reaction when I would say I was doing this. It was kind of artistic in its element opposed to me saying I am in law school. To be a lawyer the reaction is totally different. They kind of automatically characterize you in a way.

Sean: Do you have any religious or spiritual beliefs or practices?

Guy: No.

Sean: Have you had any memorable experiences with Christians, good or bad?

Guy: Yes, a close friend of mine, it was good and bad. In college, for example, one of my best friends grew up in Texas in a Methodist community and he was affected by going to college and it changed his views on his religion and the girl he cared for a great deal. And in high school they were very close. While her views stayed the same, his views started to change, and she believed that people who didn't believe, that didn't believe that Jesus was their personal Savior, we are going to hell. His views started to change and it affected their relationship. And he shared these stories with me, and I told him my point of view. So it was good and bad, and I think my friend was seeing people a little less judgmentally and more receptive and while the girl he loved his whole life was not entering that framework and was still in her view where she saw him drifting in the wrong direction. You know it was kind of sad to see and hear his stories about it. It was good and bad. I believe he was becoming a better person and, for example, he didn't believe I wasn't going to hell which was good, but the fact that his friends and family still saw him this way and college affected him and caused a rift between the two.

Sean: Have you ever been to a Christian church?

Guy: Yes.

Sean: How was that?

Guy: Communal, friendly. I have been to a few. I was going out of mere curiosity, trying to understand the community and the people and their particular sect of Christianity, but never with the intent to go back -- observe but to understand as a people and how it affects them.

Sean: Have you ever believed anything else?

Guy: I believe in the importance of scientific inquiry but most importantly the goodness of human beings, that we have the potential to care for each other. Wherever it came from, whether it was created by some greater force or biologically evolutionary developed, I don't think at the end of the day it matters all that much. I think there is a universal appreciation, the ability of humans that makes us unique, that we are going to die. For that reason we should be good to others, and Golden Rules, do unto others as you do unto yourself. These beliefs are whether or not they believe that are important or whether they believe they are God-given or whatever the reason, at the end of the day we should find a common bond. So I believe that is more important.

Sean: Do you perceive Christians to have anything you want in your life?

Guy: Yes, the sense of community, the depth of inner connection. My friends that are Christians or religious, they have this sense of togetherness. But importunely I believe it's based on exclusivity, because if you don't believe the same kind of things, then you're kind of automatically an outcast to that community. I mean when you look at Northern Ireland Protestants and Catholics, I mean the conflicts are created. I mean people that believe the same kind of things, that strange type of conflict is not very much different from the sense of community I am talking about. The thing that Christians have that I would want is more a sense of being on the same page, being able to share with people, every week to go or whatever kind of rituals you're doing, be prayer or conversation, just a way to connect to other people.

Interview 12
Who: Post Grad Student studying for the bar
Date: July, 5th 2007
Location: In Front of DePaul School of Law

Sean: What were your motivations to pursue law?

Guy: To be a prosecutor.

Sean: Were you satisfied with law school?

Guy: I am done with it. I mean DePaul is good as some and better than others.

Sean: What are some main goals for your life?

Guy: I have a job so I am going to take it from there.

Sean: Who has been a major influence in your life?

Guy: Sh*t, my old man and a bunch of philosophers that I read about in undergrad.

Sean: What's your living situation?

Guy: I commute from the suburbs.

Sean: Have you had any type of financial struggles to be in law school?

Guy: No, ran a business beforehand -- after undergrad but before law school -- and I was able to make a decent amount of money doing that.

Sean: Have you had any struggles with leaving friends and family back home?

Guy: No everything has been pretty cool. I try to mix them up so it generally works.

Sean: Do you feel like there is any high expectation placed upon you by friends, family or society?

Guy: Uh, no. I think as a lawyer if you're a somewhat of a decent person and you're not money obsessed, most people are actually surprised, and lowers their expectations for you.

Sean: Do you feel like there is a stereotype for lawyers? If so what would it be and have you experienced this at all?

Guy: Yeah and it's probably well deserved. By about, I mean in my mind, a stereotype means more often than not. And it's more often than not true, which that means there is still a good 30 or 40 percent who fall inside that stereotype. But I would say more often than not, I'm the good guy and people usually don't have a problem putting away criminals.

Sean: Do you have any spiritual or religious beliefs or practices?

Guy: Nominally Catholic. I was raised Catholic, but I don't agree with anything the church says. But I still call myself a Catholic.

Sean: Have you had any memorable experiences with Christians, good or bad?

Guy: Yeah, the fire breathers that want to condemn everyone, but then I know the ones that spend their time giving to charity.

Email Interview 1
Name: Robert Cooper   **Graduate School: Chicago-Kent College of Law**
Date: 07/14/07   **Projected Graduation Year: 2009**

What was your motivation to pursue law?

A: Law is a versatile degree that plays to my strengths. I have always had particularly strong reading and writing skills so law seemed a logical choice.

Are you satisfied with law school so far? Is it what you thought it would be?

A: Yes and no. The law is almost a little too much like I thought it would be -- very rigid and inflexible. It isn't very exciting, and sometimes that can weigh you down.

What are some of your main goals for your life?

A: I hope to raise a family, take care of my parents in later life, and fight oppression (usually in the form of conservative minded politicians) at every possible opportunity.

Where do you see yourself after graduating?

A: In a midsize law firm.

Who has been a major influence in your life and why?

A: My grandmother and parents. They are the living incarnation of the moral virtues you often read about.

What does being successful mean to you?

A: Success to me is doing well enough to support myself and my family. It also involves fighting against those who try so hard to impose their beliefs on other people and attempting to improve the lives of the less fortunate.

Are you trying to achieve that definition of success? If so, how?

A: One step at a time. I've attained my undergraduate degree and my law degree is underway. Hopefully after graduation I will be completely self-sufficient.

Would you say that you have achieved success? How?

A: I will not be successful until I have attained complete self-sufficiency.

What is your living situation?

A: I have a studio apartment in the city which I pay for with loans.

How do you feel about going to school in the Loop?

A: It's fantastic to see the skyscrapers on the way to and from school.

Have you had any type of financial struggles to be here in law school? If so, what do those look like?

A: I'm 40 grand in debt and I had 25,000 in savings before I began. Law school is hellishly expensive.

Have you had any struggles with leaving family and friends back home and how have you handled those struggles?

A: No, I'm closer to family and friends from home now that I live in Chicago than I was while completing my undergraduate degree.

Do you feel like there are high expectations placed on you by family, friends, or society? What expectations? How does that make you feel? How does it affect your decision making?

A: My family and friends expect me to succeed, but this is no greater a burden than I place upon myself.

Do you feel that there is a stereotype for lawyers? What would it be? In your experience, how would you consider it true or false?

A: There is a negative stereotype that all lawyers are assholes. In my opinion, there is a solid foundation for this opinion. Though most of the assholes are Republican.

Do you have any religious or spiritual beliefs or practices? What are they?

A: I am agnostic. I believe it is entirely possible that a God of some kind exists in some form but I also believe that no one has any knowledge of such things and to claim to have such knowledge is both arrogant and pompous.

If so, how do your religious beliefs interact with the things you are learning in law school? How about the decisions you are making?

A: My religious beliefs play no part in my education.

How did you come to a decision about what you do/don't believe?

A: I have weighed the issue a thousand times, read multiple religious doctrines, considered the writings of several philosophers and drawn the most logical conclusions.

In what ways do your beliefs play out in your life?

A: *I consider the events around me in light of my beliefs and I weigh the possibility of things occurring as mere coincidence against the possibility of divine intervention. It is my belief that the world around us is defined by random events stemming from freedom of choice.*

Have your beliefs changed since you began attending law school?

A: *No.*

Have you had any memorable experiences with Christians, either good or bad? If so, can you describe the situation?

A: *I know a number of Christians who are very good, charitable people. I know even more who oppress those around them and force their beliefs upon others. It has been my experience that most Christians are narrow minded people -- brainwashed from early childhood onward who are incapable of thinking for themselves.*

Have you ever been to a Christian church? If so, how was your experience?

A: *My parents are Christian and I was raised as one before I took the time to evaluate things from myself. Church is a relatively pleasant experience, although it usually feels artificial.*

Email Interview 2
Name: George Lattas
Graduate School: DePaul University
Specification: JD/MBA
Projected Graduation Year: 2008
Date: July 14, 2007

What was your motivation to pursue law?

A genuine interest in the pursuit of social justice and the ability to maneuver the landscape of the American business and legal system. A law degree, in my eyes, best equips an individual to tackle whatever problems may arise in his life and simultaneously serves as a stepping stone to other endeavors in either business or politics.

Are you satisfied with law school so far? Is it what you thought it would be?

For the most part. Aside from the rigidity that comes with first year assessments and grading, law school has been what I expected. I am very satisfied with the rigors that accompany graduate school, particularly within the legal academy, and feel like these past two years have certainly been the most enriching in my academic life thus far.

What are some of your main goals for your life?

I intend on impacting the community that I live in as a successful attorney/entrepreneur. I hope to continue my education in either the formal university setting or continuing my education through my practice. I eventually intend on being involved in politics and being somebody that history remembers.

Where do you see yourself after graduating?

Making money in either corporate America or in private practice.

Who has been a major influence in your life and why?

My parents. As the son of Greek immigrants, the value of education was always something that was imbued in me from a very young age. My parents worked very hard to ensure that their children would be afforded every opportunity to succeed.

What does being successful mean to you?

Success means happiness in my life which includes my profession, my family, and within my community. I also measure success by how much money I earn within my productive life as a result of employing my education and work ethic.

Are you trying to achieve that definition of success? If so, how?

Certainly. I try to impact my community by serving as the President of the SBA [Student Bar Association] and creating opportunities for the College of Law to increase its presence in the legal community. Additionally, I work hard to earn money to support my life and lifestyle, working 6 days a week. *Finally, I give back to the community at large by contributing through community service, giving over 100 hours a year for the past 10 years.*

Would you say that you have achieved success? How?

Within the context of being a law school student, I believe that I have tried my hardest to be successful. I believe I have failed in the context of being in the top 10% of my class, but given that reality, I aggressively pursued all possibilities to distinguish myself from the universe of all other law school students, enrolling in the JD/MBA program and successfully running for President of the SBA.

What is your living situation?

I own a condo in the South Loop.

How do you feel about going to school in the Loop?

It's amazing. There is nothing better than attending a university in the heart of a metropolis. Chicago is my city and going to school in the city makes sense for anyone who intends on practicing here.

Have you had any type of financial struggles to be here in law school? If so, what do those look like?

Obviously. I had to take loans out to finance my degree. The amount that I pull out is extensive and something that I think about frequently.

Have you had any struggles with leaving family and friends back home and how have you handled those struggles?

No. I'm from here.

Do you feel like there are high expectations placed on you by family, friends, or society?

Certainly. The expectation from my family is that I complete school and find an occupation that will support me. Society's expectations on me are irrelevant; nevertheless, the general expectation that an attorney is an awful human being, etc, etc, is annoying.

What expectations? How does that make you feel? How does it affect your decision making?

The expectation that I become an ethical attorney is the only one that makes sense to me and affects my decision making by forcing me to be always cognizant that everything I do going forward can affect my ability to work as an attorney.

Do you feel that there is a stereotype for lawyers? What would it be? In your experience, how would you consider it true or false?

Yes, that we're all scum. It's annoying and stupid and false.

Do you have any religious or spiritual beliefs or practices? What are they?

I was raised Orthodox Christian but am uncertain of my religious beliefs at this point in my life.

If so, how do your religious beliefs interact with the things you are learning in law school? How about the decisions you are making?

To the extent that my religious identity molded me into the person that I am, sure, it affects my decision making process — i.e. my morals, ethics, etc. . . . It doesn't really interact with learning the law at all.

How did you come to a decision about what you do/don't believe?

Through my experiences, living and growing as a human being. Law school didn't affect my religious beliefs at all. I had concluded and am at peace with my beliefs for a few years now.

In what ways do your beliefs play out in your life?

I have no idea how to answer that question. ?

Have your beliefs changed since you began attending law school?

Sure. I'd like to think I have become a far more critical, logical and analytical person.

Have you had any memorable experiences with Christians, either good or bad? If so, can you describe the situation?

Yes. They're generally good aside from those Christians who believe that their interpretation of God is the only valid interpretation and that only through the Grace of the Blood of Christ can one attain salvation. Those presumptions are problematic, ignorant, and the anti-thesis of Christ's message in my opinion. Most such Christians who attempt to proselytize to me often find themselves questioning themselves after our conversations.

Have you ever been to a Christian church? If so, how was your experience?

Yes. It's fine. The Orthodox Church is beautiful and its services trace back to those of the Apostles.

Sean Watson's Reflections

The Loop was pretty cool and what I noticed about the law students that I interviewed was that most of them had religious beliefs of some kind—whether they were Christian, Hindu, Jewish or something else. They were very open and didn't mind stopping what they were doing for a few minutes to be interviewed. The majority of the people who had religious beliefs admitted that they were not very devout in their faith or consistent in spiritual practices. Most of them had a good vibe about them, made sure they got their point across, and gave an answer to every question. From what I understand, the majority of them go to law school because of the pressure from family members to be successful. Law students seem to always be on the move, but will take a little time to stop what they are doing to answer some questions. Most of them smoked and a lot of the time I would interview them while they were out on their smoke breaks. They always made sure the interview would be short and quick. Some seemed uncertain about their motivation for attending law school. They just thought it was a good next step. The Hindu man I spoke to was different in that his motivation was to help support his family. I believe that comes from his culture and upbringing. I didn't hear many people speak of money as the key to success—that was encouraging. In general, law students don't really stand out in the crowd. They look just like everybody else. So, in order to find law students, I had to stake out the front entrances of the law schools. Also, it was summer, so really the only students around were those studying for the bar exam or working in law firms. One of the students gave us the tip of going over to Chicago Kent

Law School to talk with students getting out of exam prep classes there. This proved to be a huge, God-given breakthrough for us as we were able to talk to several students there.

Words that come to mind when I think about the students I met:
- Fast
- Motivated
- Insecure
- On a mission
- Set in their beliefs
- Open to talk
- Smokers
- Nicely dressed

Chapter 13:
Connecting with Law Students in the Chicago Loop:
Considering the Missiological Implications of Student-led Organizations

Cody C. Lorance
Church Planting Leader / Pastor
Trinity International Baptist Mission
Carol Stream, IL

Introduction

"Chicago is critical because so many students find connections that then open up opportunities for them . . . and it's interesting that most of our students come from outside of Chicago, but 80% stay in Chicago. Why? Because they make connections here, they make friends here — it's a fantastic legal city" (Chicago-Kent College of Law, 2007).

Harold J. Krent
Dean and Professor of Law
Chicago-Kent College of Law

"Since [law students have] usually held jobs while in school, they have a terrific work ethic and don't expect any head starts or shortcuts. And their Chicago connections, aided by outstanding alumni opportunities, help them bring in clients" (John Marshall Law School, 2007).

Jill O'Brien
Hiring Partner
Laner, Muchin, Dombrow, Becker, Levin, & Tominberg Ltd.

As is suggested by the quotes above, I want to address the issue of law students and "connectedness" in this chapter. As I began to look over the data gathered by Felicia Schwake and Sean Watson this summer and as I heard first-hand accounts of their experiences, I noticed one idea that kept coming up. This idea is hinted at in the previous chapter where Sean described the students he encountered as "fast," "motivated" and "on a mission." The impression I began to get was that these particular students were just about as busy as college students get. These students were not the laidback art connoisseurs that Tony Romero found hanging out at an art gallery. The students at Kent, John Marshall, DePaul and other Loop-area law schools come across as driven and focused young men and women in school to get something accomplished, studying to get ahead, graduate and advance their career. Now, the missionary in me considered this fact and asked, "Well, then how will we ever manage to connect with students like this? How will we form redemptive relationships and effectively make disciples among such busy people?"

The answer, I think, has to do with connections.

Loop-Area Law Students in Perspective

But before we get into all that, it is important that we get to know what exactly we are dealing with here. The Loop, that skyscraper-studded heart of downtown Chicago (bounded by the Chicago River to the west and north, by Lake Michigan to the east and Roosevelt Road to the south), is now known as the largest college town in the state of Illinois, boasting more than 52,000 students (Fuechtmann, McLaughlin, Kelly, Hewings, & Morgenthaler, 2005, p. 2). Law students make up about 5% of that total if we count only the two law schools that are technically in the Loop. In the table below, I have listed the Loop-area law schools and some recent enrollment figures:

Table 1: *Loop-area Law School Information*

School	Location	Enrollment
DePaul University College of Law	Loop	1,100
John Marshall Law School	Loop	1,511
Chicago-Kent College of Law	West Loop (about a block west of the Loop)	974
Northwestern University School of Law	Near North Side (community immediately north of the Loop)	238
Loyola University Chicago School of Law	Near North Side	740

(Loyola University Chicago School of Law, 2007), (Chicago-Kent College of Law, 2007), (Northwestern University Law, 2007), (Fuechtmann, McLaughlin, Kelly, Hewings, & Morgenthaler, 2005, p. 9), (DePaul University College of Law, 2007)

A few thousand students may not sound like much, but the law student body may play a much more significant role in Chicagoland than you think. Let us consider a few facts. Earlier I quoted Harold Krent's statement that most Chicago-Kent students come from outside of Chicago but "80% stay in Chicago." He's not wrong. In fact, about a quarter of all Loop-area college students actually secure some kind of employment in the Loop before they graduate (Fuechtmann, McLaughlin, Kelly, Hewings, & Morgenthaler, 2005, p. 30), and the numbers may be considerably higher for law students in particular. In fact, the John Marshall Law School reports that nearly 90% of their graduates secure employment in the region (John Marshall Law School, 2007). The picture that is painted is of students who come to Chicago from all over the country and world to attend Loop-area law schools, make significant connections with Chicagoans, and then just stay here. To be sure, more information is needed in order to confirm that this is really happening, but at least for now, I'm intrigued by the idea. Could law students be among the most socially connected individuals in Chicagoland? If so, what are the missiological implications for those of us who are concerned with reaching them with the gospel?

Connections

Well then, let us go back to this idea of connections. As I have already mentioned, one of the greatest challenges in making disciples among Loop-area law students appears to be related to their busyness. The question is, "How will we ever get them to slow down long enough for us to connect with them and show them Jesus?" Again, I think the answer lies in the connectedness of law students.

Acting on a hunch (that I would like to think came from the Holy Spirit), I began to search the Loop-area law school websites. In particular, I was interested in the student-led organizations that were operating on the various campuses. My assumption was that these extracurricular groups would be few. After all, law students are so busy with their studies and jobs that they certainly would not have time to participate in a club. Nothing, however, could be further from the truth. At the John Marshall School of Law, I found that there were roughly 60 student organizations (John Marshall Law School, 2007). At DePaul the number was 27 (DePaul University College of Law, 2007). Thirty-six clubs were listed on the Chicago-Kent website (Chicago-Kent College of Law, 2007), 39 at Loyola's law school (Loyola University Chicago School of Law, 2007), and Northwestern, with the smallest enrollment of all, had 44 student clubs listed (Northwestern University Law, 2007).

It seemed clear that Loop-area law students were very much involved in activities beyond the classroom. To be honest, I was shocked! There I was, scratching my head, trying to figure out how to convince these extremely busy students to take time out for something beyond school and there they were, already engaged in all sorts of clubs, organizations, and activities. Perhaps law students are not so narrowly focused after all. There are things they will take time for.

What things? Now, that is the key question. If extremely busy law students are investing what precious little free time they have in causes and clubs and organizations, just what exactly are they doing? What do law students care enough about to spend extra time on? Is it possible for missionaries to develop outreach and discipleship strategies that could tap into those interests? My next task was to take a look at each of the 208 Loop-area law student organizations and try to understand what the main purpose of each was. I found that the organizations could each be placed in one of 16 categories. Of course, each single organization could be said to serve multiple purposes, but for the majority I was able to discern a single, primary organizational function. (There were 11 clubs which seemed to have two equally important functions; these I have placed in two categories each.) In the table below, I have listed these 16 categories and the number of organizations for which that category is the primary function.

Table 2: *Primary Functions of Loop-Area Law Student Organizations*[*]

Category	Total Organizations	Percent of All Organizations
Social Justice	52	25
Partisan/Political	12	5.7
Industry-Based	36	17.3
Primarily Networking	25	12
Ethnic / Culturally Specific	39	18.7
Animal Rights / Environmental	8	3.8
Gay, Lesbian, etc.	5	2.4
Religious	16	7.6
Military, National Security, etc.	4	1.9
Criminal Law Focused	4	1.9
Student Newsletter	1	0.4
Marital Help for Students	1	0.4
College Recruiting	1	0.4
Food & Drink Clubs	3	1.4
Performance / Competition	7	3.3
Academic / Learning / Research	5	2.4

---

[*] *Note: Percentages will not add up to 100% due to the fact that 11 student organizations have been placed in two categories. Total number of organizations, 208, with 11 Organizations listed twice = 219. Those listed twice are: National Lawyers Guild grouped under social justice and partisan; Decalogue grouped under religious and ethnic; and White Collar Criminal Law grouped under criminal law and industry-focused. Note also that each chapter of an organization is counted separately. Thus, if the Decalogue chapters are meeting at both Loyola and John Marshall, these are counted as two clubs even though they are both a part of the same national organization.*

The following graph provides a visual representation of the same information:

Chart 1: *Primary Functions of Loop-Area Law Student Organizations*

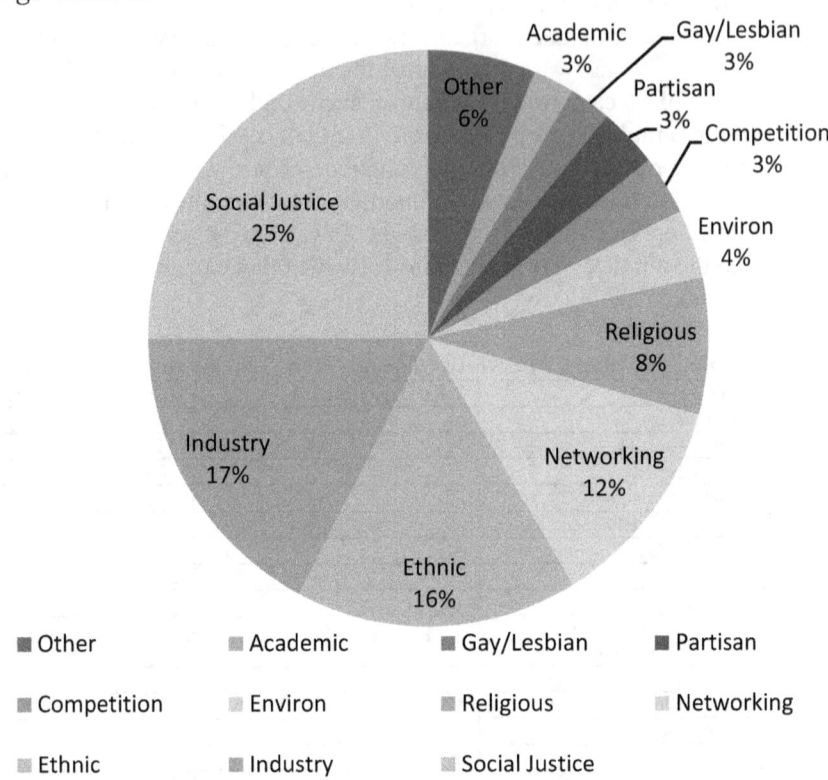

What does this information tell us? First, it indicates that in their free time, many law students are investing significant time and energy in activities that are specifically geared towards helping them in their future career. Twenty-nine percent of all the student organizations are focused on either a specific area of legal practice or general networking with other legal professionals. It seems that many law students want to use their extra time to build connections and relationships with potential future colleagues, clients, employers and the like. These are those "Chicago connections" that Jill O'Brien mentioned (John Marshall Law School, 2007) and it is surely what Krent was referring to when he said that Loop-area law students "make connections here, they make friends here — it's a fantastic legal city" (Chicago-Kent College of Law, 2007).

The second thing that stands out is the quarter-slice of pie in the chart above; social justice seems to be a huge focus for Loop-area law students. Far from the stereotypical "ambulance-chasers," many of these students are really interested in law because they want to do good and make the world a better place. Many of the student organizations are focused on promoting civil rights and volunteerism and on joining the fight against poverty, hunger and human trafficking.

Thirdly, there is a surprising number of student clubs that form on the basis of ethnicity alone. There are clubs for Asians, African-Americans, Greeks, Italians, Russians, Hispanics, and others. This seems a bit unusual to me. Could this be something quite peculiar to law students — the importance of networking with others from your same ethnic community in order to more easily secure future employment and clientele and to better serve that community? Moreover, does this point to racial and ethnic barriers in the law student community that are greater than among the general population?

Finally, we should note that fully 8% of all law student clubs are religious in nature. There are 16 religious organizations on a total of five college campuses. About a third of those are Christian-oriented clubs with a total of 4 Protestant groups. There are also 5 Jewish clubs, 4 clubs for Muslims, 2 for Roman Catholics, and 1 club for Mormon law students. It would seem that the problem is not that Loop-area law students are unspiritual or anti-religious. Religion and spirituality is clearly one of the major purposes for which students will engage in extracurricular activities. However, there does seem to be a dearth of Biblical witness on these campuses. One law school, DePaul, does not actually have any student-led Christian club yet has Muslim and Jewish clubs. This is particularly disturbing since DePaul is itself a private Christian (Catholic) university.

Conclusions

How do we reach Loop-area law students for Christ? How do we make disciples among them? Well, the research here is incomplete at best. An extensive survey, some participant observations of club meetings, and numerous additional interviews would undoubtedly provide a wealth of insights into the mind of Christ and will of God for these people. However, the information I have shared in this chapter helps us at least to begin to find an answer. Again, it all seems to hinge on this idea of connectedness. How do law students connect with each other, with the world, and with God? How do we connect with them? When we consider the time that these students spend on extracurricular activities related to career advancement, social justice, ethnicity, and religion, it becomes clear that there are genuine opportunities to make those redemptive connections.

Networking and Career Advancement

Since many law students seem willing to spend significant time on activities outside of class that could prove helpful to their career interests, it makes sense that a missional strategy designed to reach out to these men and women should seek to provide opportunities for such activities. Some possibilities could include recruiting Christian legal professionals to provide redemptive mentoring for law students. These same professionals could be tapped as speakers at free luncheons or other events designed to attract law students and give them networking opportunities. Missional strategies could also include efforts to put law students in touch with potential future clients. For instance, why not invite the Hispanic law student club to come as a group to a local Spanish-speaking church in order to do a legal question and answer session? The students could see this as an opportunity to connect with future clients and to serve their ethnic community. The church, on the other hand, has the opportunity to share Christ's love with the students.

Social Justice

To be honest, this one just seems too easy. As followers of Jesus Christ, we should be the world's leaders when it comes to fighting injustice globally. Jesus himself understood and described his mission in social justice terms such as "proclaiming liberty to the captives" and "preaching good news to the poor" (Luke 4:18). It is true that the ultimate goodness of the Good News lies in the eschatological hope it provides, but there is also wholeness in its message. Jesus fed the hungry, healed the sick, and freed the oppressed. When we stand against evil in any form we are participating in His mission. Proclaiming the gospel means sharing good news where it is needed most and fighting against sin wherever it has gripped individuals, communities, and nations.

In this commitment to social justice, we followers of Jesus find significant common ground with Loop-area law students. They too want to oppose the evil that is so prevalent in society and in that battle we have the opportunity to fight side by side. Can you imagine the opportunities for gospel witness that could result from working together with law students to combat racism, hunger, or human trafficking? How can missionaries incarnationally join these students in their endeavors for justice? How can we invite them to come alongside us in ours?

The Humanity of Law Students

Some final comments deserve to be made related to the humanity of Loop-area law students. Ethnographic research tends to lead us to discoveries of the peculiarities of the peoples we study. However, it would be a detriment to our missiological aims to overlook that which makes law students like everybody else. If I take a step back and consider the main themes that seem to be the focus of law student organizations, I see something that is almost surprisingly human. Most law student organizations are focused on career interests, social justice, ethnicity, or religion. What human longings do these themes point too? Are not the career-oriented organizations really a manifestation of that very human pursuit of physical security and financial success? Does not the abundance of social justice clubs simply point to the desire to live a life that is full of meaning and purpose — what Maslow referred to as "self-actualization" (Maslow, 1943, p. 10)? And what about ethnic clubs? Maslow might also explain this one in terms of "self-actualization," but anthropological insights are more helpful to us at this point. Paul Hiebert has written about the importance of the role of culture in the formation of one's personal sense of identity. He points out the tendency of people in cross-cultural, bicultural, or multicultural contexts to seek to periodically "reaffirm [their] sociocultural identities by participating in what they represent" (Hiebert, 1985, p. 239). Certainly this cultural reaffirmation process is happening to law students as they participate in ethnic-based clubs. Finally, participation in religious clubs is indicative of the fact that law students, like most of the rest of us, are asking those old and great existential and spiritual questions about reality, the universe, God, and the meaning of life.

So this "bird's eye view" of law student organizations presents us with a perspective on law students that shows them to be young men and women who desire to attain some level of physical security and material success, who want to understand and cling to who they are in the world, who are seeking to live for a purpose greater than themselves, and who long to know God. We must be careful not to miss this glaring humanity. Rebecca Pippert has asked would-be evangelists and missionaries to consider the meaning of Christ's declaration, "As the Father has sent me, even so I am sending you" (John 20:21). Writes Pippert:

> *How then did the Father send him? Essentially Jesus became one of us. The Word became flesh. God became human. The implications of the incarnation are vast, but one area that greatly affects evangelism is this: Jesus gives us permission to be human. . . . God didn't send a telegram or shower evangelistic books from heaven or drop a million bumper stickers form the sky saying, "Smile, Jesus loves you." He sent a man, his Son, to communicate the message. His strategy hasn't changed. He still sends men and women—before he sends tracts and techniques—to change the world. You may think his strategy is risky, but that is God's problem, not yours.* (Pippert, 1999, pp. 29-30)

Pippert described Christ's method as one of transparency and radical identification with the human condition and pointed to the "profound humanness" of Jesus as allowing people to really begin to perceive His divinity (Pippert, 1999, pp. 30-31). Perhaps one of the greatest potentialities for mission advance among Loop-area law students lies here—in the bounteous opportunities for followers of Christ to simply come alongside their fellow humans in openness, sincerity, and love and to share Christ in the context of authentic friendship.

Truly, there are many opportunities for followers of Jesus to impact the Loop-area law student community for Christ. It will take creativity, divine wisdom and fervent prayer. It will also require Christ-followers who are willing to share not just the plan of salvation but their very lives with law students (1 Thess. 2:8). Of course, we know that the harvest itself is not impossible. God's arm is surely not too short to save law students in the Chicago Loop. However, in order for us to see and participate in God's harvest among these people, we must begin to care more and more about what God cares about — namely, the students themselves.

References

Chicago-Kent College of Law. (2007). *Chicago-Kent College of Law: Student Organizations*. Retrieved 12 21, 2007, from Chicago-Kent College of Law: http://www.kentlaw.edu/students/organizations.html

Chicago-Kent College of Law. (2007). *Chicago-Kent Students: Student Body Profile*. Retrieved 12 20, 2007, from Chicago-Kent College of Law: http://www.kentlaw.edu/students/

Chicago-Kent College of Law. (2007). *Kent Law Virtual Tour*. Retrieved December 20, 2007, from Chicago-Kent College of Law: http://www.kentlaw.edu/virtualtour/broadband.html

DePaul University College of Law. (2007). *DePaul University College of Law 2007-2008 Admission Profile*. Retrieved 12 21, 2007, from DePaul University College of Law: http://www.law.depaul.edu/applicants/student_life/fact_sheet.asp

DePaul University College of Law. (2007). *Student Organizations and Journals*. Retrieved 12 21, 2007, from DePaul University College of Law: http://www.law.depaul.edu/students/organizations_journals/

Fuechtmann, T. G., McLaughlin, G. W., Kelly, J. S., Hewings, G., & Morgenthaler, S. (2005). *Higher Education in the Loop and South Loop: An Impact Study*. Chicago: Greater State Street Council and Central Michigan Avenue Association.

Hiebert, P. (1985). *Anthropological Insights for Missionaries*. Grand Rapids: Baker Book House.

John Marshall Law School. (2007). *JMLS Employment Statistics*. Retrieved 12 21, 2007, from John Marshall Law School: http://www.jmls.edu/careersvcs/employment_statistics.shtml

John Marshall Law School. (2007). *John Marshall Law School Career Services Office Recruiting Brochure*. Retrieved December 20, 2007, from John Marshall Law School: http://www.jmls.edu/careersvcs/pdf/2007%20Fall%20Recruiting%20Brochure.pdf

John Marshall Law School. (2007). *Student Organizations at the John Marshall Law School.* Retrieved 12 21, 2007, from John Marshall Law School: http://www.jmls.edu/students/organizations/index.shtml

Loyola University Chicago School of Law. (2007). *Admission Fact Sheet.* Retrieved December 20, 2007, from Loyola University Chicago: http://www.luc.edu/law/admission/jd/FACT_SHEET.html

Loyola University Chicago School of Law. (2007). *Student Organizations.* Retrieved 12 21, 2007, from Loyoly University Chicago School of Law: http://www.luc.edu/law/activities/organizations.html

Northwestern University Law. (2007). *Class Profile, Admissions, School of Law, Northwestern University.* Retrieved 12 21, 2007, from School of Law, Northwestern University: http://www.law.northwestern.edu/admissions/profile/

Maslow, A. (1943). A Theory of Human Motivation. *Psychological Review , 50*, 370-396.

Northwestern University Law. (2007). *Student Organizations.* Retrieved 12 21, 2007, from Northwestern Univeristy Law: http://www.law.northwestern.edu/studentorgs/

Pippert, R. M. (1999). *Out of the Saltshaker & Into the World: Evangelism as a Way of Life.* Downers Grove, Illinois: InterVarsity Press

[On the following pages is an example of survey content that could be used to further explore how law students spend their time. It was developed by Cody C. Lorance and Tony Romero.]

On an average week, how much time do you spend on extracurricular activities related to:

    1. Networking with people in your field

        ☐ 0 hrs.   ☐ 1-2 hrs.   ☐ 3-4 hrs.   ☐ 5-6 hrs.   ☐ 7+ hrs.

    2. Community service, social justice, etc.

        ☐ 0 hrs.   ☐ 1-2 hrs.   ☐ 3-4 hrs.   ☐ 5-6 hrs.   ☐ 7+ hrs.

    3. Religious and/or spiritual activities

        ☐ 0 hrs.   ☐ 1-2 hrs.   ☐ 3-4 hrs.   ☐ 5-6 hrs.   ☐ 7+ hrs.

    4. Your cultural or ethnic background

        ☐ 0 hrs.   ☐ 1-2 hrs.   ☐ 3-4 hrs.   ☐ 5-6 hrs.   ☐ 7+ hrs.

Please choose an option that best describes your feelings on the particular statements.

1. It is important that I work to secure my future job while I am still in school.

   ☐ Strongly Disagree ☐ Disagree ☐ Agree ☐ Strongly Agree

2. Networking now means I will have much better opportunities in the future.

   ☐ Strongly Disagree ☐ Disagree ☐ Agree ☐ Strongly Agree

3. Not enough is being done to eliminate social injustice.

   ☐ Strongly Disagree ☐ Disagree ☐ Agree ☐ Strongly Agree

4. Fighting for justice is a lawyer's most important duty.

   ☐ Strongly Disagree ☐ Disagree ☐ Agree ☐ Strongly Agree

5. Religious practices and/or spiritual beliefs impair a legal representative from performing his or her duties well. Religion causes biased views among legal representatives.

   ☐ Strongly Disagree ☐ Disagree ☐ Agree ☐ Strongly Agree

6. Religious practices and/or spiritual beliefs have an important role in my life.

   ☐ Strongly Disagree ☐ Disagree ☐ Agree ☐ Strongly Agree

7. It is important for me to be successful financially.

   ☐ Strongly Disagree ☐ Disagree ☐ Agree ☐ Strongly Agree

8. It is important to me that my time be spent on things that will benefit me financially.

   ☐ Strongly Disagree ☐ Disagree ☐ Agree ☐ Strongly Agree

9. It is important for me to associate with other lawyers from my own ethnic background.

   ☐ Strongly Disagree ☐ Disagree ☐ Agree ☐ Strongly Agree

10. It is important that I represent clients of my ethnicity and background before others.

    ☐ Strongly Disagree ☐ Disagree ☐ Agree ☐ Strongly Agree

Chapter 14:
Building God's Church in Postmodern and Cross-Cultural Contexts: *Discipleship Rituals in the Book of Ezra*

Cody C. Lorance
Church Planting Leader / Pastor
Trinity International Baptist Mission
Carol Stream, IL

Introduction

It was a crisp autumn night. My wife and I, church planters working among South Asians in the Chicago area, had just brought a very successful neighborhood outreach event to a close. Our Hindu and Muslim friends had slowly filtered out, each being sure to tell us how much fun they had and that they looked forward to seeing us again soon. As they left, a calm gradually fell over our house — the pleasant and contented sigh that always seems to follow things like that. It was accompanied by a deep, deep sense that God had come. He had been faithful.

With barely a word our half-dozen or so volunteers began washing dishes and putting away food. They were quite a sight—mostly young, postmodern, missional, zealous, earthy. And then there were our friends from Ethiopia—spiritually gigantic, holy, real. I watched the quiet activity of cleaning and straightening for a bit and then just knew that God was not finished with us yet. His Spirit seemed to hover over the room and press down on every soul, gently whispering, "I've got more for you tonight."

Taking my cue from the Spirit, I slipped out and went to the garage where I kept my "pulpit." Really it was just a humble configuration of spare particle boards which I had quite unskillfully nailed together in hopes of using it someday for preaching if we ever actually got to the point of having regular church services in our home. Taking it into the house I plopped it down in the middle of the living room and covered it with a table cloth. I then went to the refrigerator where I had some flat bread and cranberry juice. We had to do this. We needed this.

Moments later we were all gathered around that little makeshift pulpit-turned-Communion-table. Some words were said, some Scripture, some prayer. Then, as one body, postmodern and international, we ate and drank. It was a simple action but an immensely valuable one that had the effect of immersing us into the spiritual reality of who we were that day—not just volunteers at an outreach event but Israelites in Egypt, disciples in an upper room, a bride looking forward to a wedding feast. Our discipleship ritual that night gave way to spontaneous worship, prayer, and preaching. It seemed clear that God was building us, His Church.

...

As a somewhat young guy myself, I was discipled by a generation of believers who understood the idea of ritual as essentially negative. Rituals were "empty" and they inevitably led to scary things like works-righteousness and idolatry. Ritual, I was taught, had no place in the proper practice of Christian spirituality. As a result, my tendency was to think of evangelism and discipleship as largely a matter of communication. Doctrines and ethics were to be systematically presented to individuals who were then considered to be "disciples" once they had personally adopted the Christian system of beliefs and practices, an event often signaled by their completion of a fill-in-the-blank workbook.

This conception of discipleship, unconsciously ritualistic itself, not only falls flat among postmoderns and non-Western peoples but more importantly falls short of the commission Jesus Christ has given His followers. The Great Commission call to global disciple-making is not just a calling to communicate theology and ethics but a call to build God's Church—to take those who are "not a people" and, through the power of the Holy Spirit and the grace of God, to transform them into "God's people" (1 Pet. 2:10). Christian disciple-makers are called to do no less than to transfer people from an old reality into a new one.

In that sense, the Church's calling to global disciple-making is not unlike the mission of Zerubbabel, Haggai, Ezra and other leaders of the post-exilic period of Biblical history. These were persons charged by God with the task of constructing a covenant people out of a band of spiritually broken exiles. As a missionary and pastor working among postmoderns in a multicultural context, I came to the Biblical book of Ezra for answers because I saw in it a reflection of my own mission field. I needed to learn from the fact that leaders like Ezra did not merely present to individuals a set of doctrines and ethics to memorize but rather sought to disciple a whole community by immersing it in a new spiritual reality through the use of rituals, ceremonies, and symbols. In this chapter, I would like to examine four discipleship rituals in the book of Ezra in order to illustrate the power of ritual to disciple whole communities by transferring them from one spiritual reality to another.

Background and Structure of Ezra

The book of Ezra opens some fifty years after Nebuchadnezzar's Babylonian army destroyed Jerusalem in 586 B.C. and chronicles a period of roughly a century following the return of the first Jewish exiles from captivity. In terms of its content, the book features lists of those Jews returning from exile, a recounting of the temple's reconstruction in Jerusalem, preserved correspondence with Medo-Persian kings (often from groups opposing the Jewish efforts of reconstruction), and an account of the beginning of Ezra's work as a spiritual reformer.

The structure of the book of Ezra (see Table 1) is significant to understanding its message. Essentially, the book records two returns of the Jews from captivity. The first return, occurring around 536 B.C., directly followed the edict of King Cyrus which permitted the Jews to return to Jerusalem and rebuild the temple. This return was led, at least in part, by Zerubbabel[*] and is covered in the first six chapters of the book. The last four chapters of the book of Ezra record the return led by Ezra the priest in about 458 B.C. This return followed an edict by King Artaxerxes that Ezra was to go to Jerusalem in order to teach the Jews living there how to live by the "Law of the God of heaven" (Ezra 7:21).

Each of the two halves of the book of Ezra may be broken down further so that the book essentially has a four-part structure. The four sections speak of a process by which the exiles were gradually transformed into God's covenant people as they reinstituted the sacrificial system of worship (1:1-3:6), reinstalled the temple-based priesthood (3:7-6:22), reaffirmed their commitment to the Torah (7:1-8:36), and recommitted themselves to be God's holy and chosen people (9:1-10:44). Each of the sections is highlighted by a discipleship ritual that was designed to help this community to further enter into the reality of being God's covenant people.

In the following table, I have presented my view of the structure of Ezra:

---

[*] See Ezra 2:2, 3:8, 4:2, 5:2. Jeshua and Sheshbazzar are also mentioned variously as leaders of this return, Jeshua as a leading priest (Ezra 3:2) and Sheshbazzar as governor (5:14). There is some debate as to whether Zerubbabel and Sheshbazzar are the same or different persons. Zerubbabel is also referred to as governor (Hag. 1:1, 14; 2:2, 21). Nevertheless, throughout the first half of the book of Ezra, Zerubbabel appears as the most prominent leader of the Jewish people.

Table 1: *The Structure of the Book of Ezra*

I. First Return from Exile (1-6)

a) The Return of Sacrifice- 1:1-3:6
Discipleship ritual: The Feast of Booths
1. The Edict of Cyrus and the inventory of articles for the temple (1:1-11)
2. The list of returning exiles (2:1-70)
3. Observing the Festival of Booths upon beginning of burnt offerings (3:1-6)

b) The Return of a Holy Priesthood- 3:7-6:22
Discipleship ritual: The Passover
1. Work on the temple begins (3:7-13)
2. Opposition from neighboring peoples leads to a halting of the work (4:1-24)
3. Work resumes and is completed under prophetic leadership; the Passover is observed (5:1-6:22)

II. Second Return from Exile (7-10)

a) The Return of the Law- 7:1-8:36
Discipleship ritual: The Pilgrimage to Jerusalem
1. Synopsis of Ezra's return (7:1-10)
2. Letter of Artaxerxes and Ezra's doxology (7:11-28)
3. List of pilgrims (8:1-14)
4. The Pilgrimage to Jerusalem (8:15-36)

b) The Return of a Chosen People- 9:1-10:44
Discipleship ritual: The Sacred Assembly of Repentance
1. The news of intermarriage and Ezra's prayer of repentance (9:1-15)
2. Calling upon Ezra's leadership; proclaiming an assembly (10:1-8)
3. The Assembly of Repentance (10:9-17)
4. The list of the guilty (10:18-44)

Four Discipleship Rituals in Ezra

The Feast of Booths—Ezra 3:1-6

Soon after the first group of exiles returned from captivity, they gathered in Jerusalem to begin work on the temple. Their first order of business was to build the altar so that burnt offerings could be resumed as quickly as possible. In strict accordance with the Torah, morning and evening sacrifices, New Moon sacrifices, and the festival calendar were all reinstituted. The book of Ezra tells us that since it was in the seventh month (*Tishri*) when the altar was completed, the community celebrated the Feast of Booths (Ezra 3:4).

The Feast of Booths (also called Feast of Tabernacles) was a week-long annual ritual prescribed in the Torah as a commemoration of the years that the Israelites were led and cared for by God in the wilderness following their deliverance from slavery in Egypt. It is described in the book of Leviticus:

> *On the fifteenth day of the seventh month, when you have gathered in the produce of the land, you shall celebrate the feast of the LORD seven days. On the first day shall be a solemn rest, and on the eighth day shall be a solemn rest. And you shall take on the first day the fruit of splendid trees, branches of palm trees and boughs of leafy trees and willows of the brook, and you shall rejoice before the LORD your God seven days. You shall celebrate it as a feast to the LORD for seven days in the year. It is a statute forever throughout your generations; you shall celebrate it in the seventh month. You shall dwell in booths for seven days. All native Israelites shall dwell in booths, that your generations may know that I made the people of Israel dwell in booths when I brought them out of the land of Egypt: I am the LORD your God.* (Lev. 23:39-43)

For a generation of Jews who for the most part had been brought up in Babylon, the observance of the Feast of Booths must have had a powerful discipling effect. First, in merely constructing the altar they were identifying with the great altar-building patriarchs Abraham, Isaac, and Jacob (cf. Gen. 12:8, 26:25, 35:1). Moreover, their leaders were teaching them to put a priority on worship by making it the first item on the reconstruction agenda. But the observance of the feast itself had the powerful effect of connecting this post-exilic generation to the ancient generation that had wandered forty years in the wilderness prior to entering the Promised Land. This was not just a matter of learning a story about pillars of cloud and fire, manna, and quail but about entering into a new spiritual reality; in the ancient history of God and His people, a new community found their own identity as a people loved by God and cared for in an exilic wilderness of their own making. Now, in fulfillment of His promise, God was bringing them into the Promised Land just as He had done so many generations before.

The Passover—Ezra 6:13-22

In spite of determined opposition from the neighboring peoples in the region, the Jews completed the rebuilt temple in 516 B.C., exactly seventy years after it had been destroyed by the Babylonians. The people celebrated with a special ceremony of dedication in which they officially installed priests and Levites to serve in the temple (Ezra 6:18). The book of Ezra describes the observance of Passover and the Festival of Unleavened Bread following the construction of the temple. According to the text, it was a time of great joy for the Jews (6:22). It was also a time for discipleship.

The observance of Passover was significant for the discipleship of this Jewish community. The author of the book of Ezra seems to emphasize this ritual's connection to the reinstallation of the temple-based priesthood (cf. 6:18, 20). Indeed, this was a time in which the whole community was learning what it meant to be a "kingdom of priests" and a "holy nation" (Exod. 19:6). The priests and Levites were learning how to be ceremonially clean and the people were learning to be separated from unclean practices (Ezra 6:20-21). Furthermore, the Passover had an effect similar to that of the Feast of Booths in that it connected a new generation to the ancient history of God and His people. As the post-exilic community partook in the Passover meal and sacrificed Passover lambs, as they ate bitter herbs and bread made without yeast, they were finding in the story of the Exodus their own story of God's deliverance from captivity.

The Pilgrimage to Jerusalem—Ezra 8:15-36

The third discipleship ritual was not one prescribed by the Torah but rather was one birthed out of the circumstances and experiences of a new generation of God's people. Nearly a half-century after the work on the temple was completed, the priest Ezra led a group of exiled Jews on a four-month spiritual pilgrimage from the heart of Babylon to the house of

God in Jerusalem. The account of this return in the book of Ezra is chiefly concerned with issues related to the spiritual formation of the returning exiles (see Table 2).

The pilgrimage began with three days of spiritual preparation at an encampment in Babylon. During this time, Ezra called upon all the pilgrims to be engaged in prayer and fasting (8:21-23). Ezra also used this time to develop leaders by commissioning them to specific responsibilities. First he assigned several men the task of going to the city of Casiphia to recruit Levites to join them in their pilgrimage to Jerusalem. Then, before setting out from their encampment, Ezra appointed several others to the task of guarding the sacred articles and offerings for the temple. A major emphasis of the text here is that God blessed all the Jews participating in the pilgrimage in that the prayers of the community were answered (8:23, 31), the recruitment of Levites was very successful (8:18-20), and those charged with delivering articles and offerings for the temple faithfully fulfilled their duties (8:33-34). By the time the pilgrimage culminated in a great worship celebration at the temple, this group of Jewish pilgrims had been transferred from the spiritual impoverishment of Babylonian captivity to the new spiritual richness of being faithful servants of the God of Israel.

In the following table I have broken down the structure of this pilgrimage in detail.

Table 2: *The Pilgrimage to Jerusalem*

I. Recruitment of Levites and Temple Servants (8:15-20)

   A. Three days encampment at Ahava (15a)
   B. Ezra appoints leaders to recruit Levites and temple servants in Casiphia (15b-17)
   C. God grants success to the recruiting efforts "by the good hand of our God on us" (18-20)

II. Proclamation of Prayer and Fasting (8:21-23)

   A. Ezra decides not to ask for a military escort in order to demonstrate to the king the faithfulness of God whose "hand . . . is for good on all who seek him" (22)
   B. Ezra proclaims a time of fasting and prayer (21, 23)

III. Delegation of Responsibility to Leaders (8:24-30)

   A. Ezra consecrates twelve leaders for the task of guarding the sacred articles and various donations for the temple (24-27)
   B. Ezra verbally commissions the leaders (28-29)
   C. The leaders accept their commission (30)

IV. Journey to Jerusalem and Subsequent Period of Rest (8:31-32)

   A. Ezra's band of pilgrims set out from the Ahava Canal on the 12th of Nisan (31a)
   B. The group is protected from "the enemy" and "ambushes" by the "hand of our God" (31b)
   C. After four months, they arrive in Jerusalem and rest for three days (32)

V. Depositing Sacred Articles, Gold, and Silver at Temple (8:33-34)

   A. The leaders Ezra commissioned fulfill their sacred task by presenting the articles and donations to the priests at the temple (33-34)

VI. Worship at the Temple and Delivering the King's Orders (8:35-36)

   A. Ezra's pilgrimage reaches its climax in a great time of worship as the pilgrims present many burnt offerings to God (35)
   B. The pilgrims deliver the orders of Artaxerxes to local governing officials securing assistance for the people and temple (36)

Chapter 14: Building God's Church　　　　　　　　　　　　　　　　Lorance

The Sacred Assembly of Repentance—Ezra 9:1-10:44

The final discipleship ritual in the book of Ezra was also born out of the circumstances of the participating community. Some time after Ezra had settled into his new life in Jerusalem, he was alerted to a crisis that had developed. Numerous people, including priests and Levites, had begun to intermarry with the neighboring non-Jewish peoples, which resulted in a syncretization of Judaism with the "abominations" of the surrounding pagan cultures (9:1-2).

Ezra responded by modeling repentance publicly. He tore his clothes, pulled hair from his head and beard, sat in a state of silent disgust, and then prostrated himself before the Lord (9:3-5). Lifting up his hands, Ezra prayed a prayer of confession and repentance to God in the hearing of all those gathered around him (9:6-15). The impact of Ezra's example was profound. The people began weeping and confessing their sin. A sacred assembly was proclaimed and "all the men of Judah and Benjamin" gathered in Jerusalem before the temple, in the rain, to deal with their sin (Ezra 10:9). Over the course of the next three months, all those charged with intermarriage were put on trial and, if found guilty, pledged to divorce their wives and presented guilt offerings (10:19).

Modern Christian sensitivities are rightly grated upon by this putting away of foreign women and children.* However, it is important to note that this event is presented in the book of Ezra as the right solution to the crisis that arose in the community. By intermarrying with pagan peoples, the Israelites were disobeying God's command to be separate:

---

* A few considerations may help Christians to begin to reconcile this event with the command to "love your neighbor as yourself." The Jews had created a bad situation by blatantly disregarding God's clear commands. As a consequence of their sin there was a clear solution but not an easy one. Even after the Jews acknowledged that the intermarriage was sinful, the threat of syncretism remained as long as unconverted pagan women were included in the community. Our hearts break at the image of a woman and her small children being thrust out into the cruel wilderness to fend for themselves, but this is the reality of the brokenness created by sin—the sin of God's people refusing to obey him and the sin of unbelievers who refuse to turn in faith to God and so find refuge under His wings (cf. Ruth 2:11-12). Without a doubt, dealing with sin is messy and painful and it would not do for a holy God to simply accept our apology and overlook the problem. One might say that after sin has entered the scene, the picture is not supposed to be pretty anymore. What, after all, do we think of the cross of Christ if not the bloody solution for humanity's sin?

> *You shall not intermarry with them, giving your daughters to their sons or taking their daughters for your sons, for they would turn away your sons from following me, to serve other gods. Then the anger of the LORD would be kindled against you, and he would destroy you quickly.* (Deut. 7:3-4)

Disregarding this command had indeed led to syncretism with pagan practices throughout Israel's history, and it was beginning to happen again in Ezra's day (Ezra 9:1). God had a reason for commanding Israel to be separate from the pagan nations, a reason His people had chronically neglected:

> *For you are a people holy to the LORD your God. The LORD your God has chosen you to be a people for his treasured possession, out of all the peoples who are on the face of the earth.* (Deut. 7:6)

The sacred assembly of repentance became then not only a time to confess sin and deal with the problem of syncretism but, more importantly, it became a time for a community of people to affirm their identity as God's treasured possession—to enter into the reality of being the chosen people.

"Prescribed" and "Proclaimed" Rituals in Ezra

When all four of these discipleship rituals are considered together, an interesting balance can be identified between those rituals prescribed by the Torah (the Feast of Booths and Passover) and those "proclaimed" rituals that arose from the circumstances of the participating community (the Pilgrimage and the Sacred Assembly). It is important to note that while all four had the effect of discipling a community by helping them to enter into a new spiritual reality, the rituals did so in different ways.

The Feast of Booths and the Passover both had the effect of connecting a new generation of God's people historically to the Lord and His people Israel. These rituals were commemorations of historical events from Israel's past in which God worked on behalf of His covenant people. In these particular instances, participation in the ritual meant that Israel's deliverance from captivity and entrance into the Promised Land would cease to be merely stories from the ancient past and would become the spiritual reality in which a new generation could find its own identity as God's covenant people. A participant from this new generation would understand, "It was not just my ancestors who were delivered and brought into the Promised Land; it was my generation and me as well."

The "proclaimed" discipleship rituals had a different effect in that they connected the God of Israel with the intimate and vital realities of the current generation. The emphasis in Ezra's pilgrimage and in the sacred assembly of repentance was not on some event in Israel's past but on what God was doing in the present circumstances of His people. The power of this kind of ritual is that it brings vitality to the participating community. The Lord goes from being the God who "did" and "was" to the God who "does" and "is."

Certainly there is a lesson to be learned from the balance between "prescribed" and "proclaimed" discipleship rituals. Where the prescribed ritual provides continuity with the historic faith, keeping new generations grounded in terms of their theology and identity as God's covenant people, the proclaimed ritual provides vitality to a community of faith who is thus enabled to see God concerned with and at work in their own lives and circumstances.

Conclusion

As I said from the outset, Christian disciple-makers are called to do no less than to transfer people from an old reality to a new one. The New Testament imagery, which echoes the imagery of the book of Ezra, is one of transforming rubble — "living stones" — into a temple in which God lives by His Spirit (Eph. 2:19-22, 1 Pet. 2:4-10). Though largely neglected by Western evangelical Christians, discipleship rituals provide a way for this kind of transformation to take place. Today's pastors, missionaries, and other Christian leaders must combine deep sensitivity to the Holy Spirit, thorough cultural understanding, and a firm commitment to the empowerment of indigenous leaders in order to develop timely and meaningful discipleship rituals that will effectively build God's Church. Such reflection is especially importance for cross-cultural ministry and ministry that is focused on the "next generation."

www.ingramcontent.com/pod-product-compliance
Lightning Source LLC
Chambersburg PA
CBHW061342300426
44116CB00011B/1948